Abodrites

Bremen
Verden
SAXONY

Munster
HESSE
Paderborn
THURINGIA
Cologne
Fulda

Frankfurt
Ingelheim
Mainz
Worms Lorsch
AUSTRASIA
Strassburg

Wiltzi

Sorabians

Bohemians

Regensburg
DANUBE R.
BAVARIA

Salzburg

The Alps

Milan

LOMBARDY

Genoa
Ravenna

SEA

CORSICA

in 768 A.D.

Charles's Kingdom
Carloman's Kingdom
Conquests of
Charlemagne to 814 A.D.
Satellite Lands
Byzantine Territory

Avars

DRAVE R.

SAVE R.

ADRIATIC SEA

TERRITORY CLAIMED BY THE POPE
DUCHY OF SPOLETO
ROME
DUCHY OF BENEVENTO

MacDonald

Charlemagne

Charlemagne

from the Hammer
to the Cross

by RICHARD WINSTON

THE BOBBS-MERRILL COMPANY · INC.

PUBLISHERS

INDIANAPOLIS · NEW YORK

First Edition

A Prefatory Note on Sources

A COLOSSUS astride the watershed of history, with one foot in the ancient world, the other in the medieval; a conqueror who ranks with Alexander and Caesar; a saint unofficially canonized; founder of the Holy Roman Empire—Charlemagne appears to us in many guises. His story has been encrusted with the rubies and emeralds of legend like the ornate crucifixes of his age. But gems do not hide the stark form of the cross, and we may, if we will, know the true Charlemagne who never went on a voyage to Jerusalem or dreamed that he was fighting for *dolce France*.

For the life of Charlemagne is far better documented than is commonly supposed. We need only turn to the contemporary sources. There we meet not the majestic, remote, white-bearded patriarch in glittering brocades of the medieval epics and the sixteenth-century Flemish painters, but a beardless, mustachioed, restlessly energetic and essentially "popular" king who pointedly dressed in the simple linens his subjects wore. Largely because he himself so nobly encouraged arts and letters and reanimated a torpid culture, we are able to follow the intricacies of his diplomatic and military activities, to study the development of his thought, his legislation and religious views, to piece together the social and economic life of the lands he governed, and to see the man himself in the midst of his numerous family and his entourage of warriors, poets and thinkers.

The contemporary sources on which I have drawn for this biography fall into a number of categories: biographical, annalistic, historical, hagiographical, documentary, epistolary, literary and legendary.

Among the contemporary biographies, the *Life of Charles the Great* (*Vita Caroli Magni*) by Einhard takes first place. Not nearly so detailed as we should like to have it, sometimes erroneous and sometimes obscuring the truth rather than clarifying it, this *Life* nevertheless gives a more honest and intimate portrait of Charlemagne than any other single source. It has the inestimable merit of having been written by one who lived at the court of Charlemagne, who served the king and loved him. And it is the only biography of Charlemagne that is strictly contemporary. The other so-called life of Charlemagne by the Monk of St. Gall was written seventy years after his death, is full of droll and occasionally significant anecdotes, but can hardly be considered a reliable source.

Two biographies of Charlemagne's son, Louis the Pious, one by Thegan and the other by an anonymous writer usually referred to as "the Astronomer," show us the great Charles in his relationship to the one legitimate son who survived him. In addition, there are lives of his cousins, Adalhard and Wala; the lives of Popes Stephen II, Hadrian I and Leo III; and the many lives of saints, bishops and abbots (Boniface, Sturm, Willehad, Liudger, Leoba, Leafwine, Willibrord and others).

A year-by-year chronicle of events in the Frankish realm can be found in the annals, the most important of which are the officially inspired Royal Annals (Annales regni Francorum), which were revised and expanded at various times by personages at Charlemagne's court. Dry, terse and slanted though these annals so often are, they are on the whole trustworthy guides. They must, of course, be checked against the "lesser annals" kept by various monasteries, and supplemented by information drawn from the records of synods and national assemblies, and from other sources.

Deeds and charters, inventories of royal estates, the estate roll of the Abbey of St. Germain des Prés—from such documents as these we can deduce a great deal about commerce, industry and the life of the common people under Charlemagne. De ordine palatii by Hincmar, Archbishop of Reims, describes in detail how Charlemagne administered his kingdom and conducted his national assemblies. The capitularies, as Charlemagne's edicts are called, embody the king's conception of his government and his ultimate aims. These capitularies cover a multitude of subjects both ecclesiastical and secular. They provide a running record of Charlemagne's efforts to civilize his countrymen, to reform Church and State, to promote prosperity and to protect the weak against the tyranny of the strong. Sometimes, also, they show the great King of the Franks and Emperor of the Romans resorting to a policy of blood and iron.

Relationships between the Frankish Empire and the Papal See are mirrored in the letters of the popes to Charlemagne, which by order of the king himself were collected in the Codex Carolinus.

But Charlemagne was not only a political figure; he was also a profound theologian and one of the foremost intellectuals of his age.

Alcuin, in *De Rhetorica*, addresses him as "the father of the world" whom God has "illuminated with the light of all knowledge." In the *Caroline Books*, of which Charlemagne was ostensibly and perhaps actually the author (the question is discussed later), we find Charlemagne taking a reasonable middle position between the two extremisms of his age: image smashing and image worship.

For insight into the complex personality of a man who could be now kind, generous and paternal, now vindictive, unscrupulous and savage, we turn to the volumes of the *Epistolae karolini aevi*. There are only twenty-three of Charlemagne's own letters. But there is a rich hoard of more than three hundred letters of Charlemagne's intimate friend, teacher and "minister of education," Alcuin. Alcuin wrote indefatigably to highly placed persons everywhere on the Continent and in Britain, and to Charlemagne himself. Alcuin's inquisitive and active mind, his role as mentor of the king, and the deep affection which linked him with his master combine to make these letters precious historical documents and mines of information on the psychology and private life of Charlemagne.

Charlemagne hunting, Charlemagne surrounded by his beautiful daughters, playing host to a pope or exchanging jests, riddles and anagrams with his friends—these homelier aspects of the ruler are vividly portrayed in the eulogies, lyrics and epic fragments written by his witty and gifted courtiers such as Angilbert, Dungal, Theodulf and Alcuin. Considered purely as poetry, Carolingian verse does not quite belong to the ages; but it is invaluable to the biographer and social historian.

This lengthy list by no means exhausts the source material on which this biography is based. Other sources are referred to in the text. In conclusion, I should like to acknowledge my indebtedness to the French and German scholars whose works are cited in the bibliography. Their painstaking editing, criticism and analysis of sources have enormously simplified the task of all who follow after them.

The reader should note that in this book all phrases and sentences set off by quotation marks are cited from the primary sources. The few exceptions to this rule are clearly noted where they occur. Translations, unless otherwise indicated, are my own. I have sometimes translated from standard French or German translations without checking these against the original Latin.

RICHARD WINSTON

Contents

Charlemagne

CHAPTER ONE

New Kings for Old

IT WAS SO common for their rulers to be born bastards that the tough and practical-minded Franks ignored the slurs cast on their new king's birth during the great coronation ceremony which took place at Noviomum in Northern Francia (the modern Noyons) on an October day in the year 768 A.D. The new king's name was auspicious, for he was the namesake as well as the grandson of Charles the Hammer, the hero of Christendom, who had stopped the onrush of the Saracens when they threatened to overrun all Gaul. The fame of the Battle of Tours, thirty-six years before, still lingered in men's minds. Among the nobles of the Frankish realm who heaved young King Charles upon their shields at Noyons there were doubtless men who had crossed swords with the heathen on that day and who had experienced the joyful surprise of finding the Saracen camp abandoned the next morning—the enemy having fled, leaving all his booty behind.

The times were also auspicious, for the realm was at peace. Before his death, Charles's father, Pepin the Short, had crushed his most troublesome foes and added the great Duchy of Aquitaine to the patrimony of his sons. The borders of Frankland were intact, and for the present the pagan Saxons of the north were not burning churches and martyring missionaries. True, an envoy from Pope Stephen III had just arrived from Rome with wild tales of confusion, conspiracies and bloodshed over the succession to the throne of St. Peter. But Italy was far away and most of the Franks hoped that their new king would return to his grandfather's policy and avoid entanglements with the ancient imperial capital.

There was every reason but one to look forward to a reign of peace and prosperity. But that one reason weighed on the minds of nobles and commoners alike as they roared their "May the king live forever!"

in the vulgar Latin of the Neustrian Franks or in the old German spoken by the Austrasian Franks. The difficulty was that there were two separate coronation ceremonies taking place this same day. In the near-by town of Soissons sixteen-year-old Carloman, second son of Pepin the Short, was also being raised upon a shield. At Soissons, as at Noyons, spears rang upon spears when the traditional salute to a new king was given. For Pepin had followed the disastrous custom of German monarchs and had divided his kingdom between his two sons as if it were a private estate. By the wholly visionary theory of the partition, the two kings each held the title of "King of the Franks, Patrician of the Romans, Illustrious Man," and they were expected to rule Frankland as one realm. Even had the brothers loved each other as royal brothers rarely have, and even more rarely in the history of the Franks, such a scheme was unlikely to work out for long.

In fact there was little love lost between Charles and Carloman. Animosity between an elder and a younger brother is common enough. In addition to the ordinary causes for such hostility, Carloman might with some justice feel entitled to his father's entire inheritance. He was undeniably legitimate, while his brother Charles had been born before their father's and mother's marriage was sanctified in a religious ceremony. Powerful supporters of Carloman such as Duke Otker, whose sister was wedded to the famous Roland of song and legend, could make much of such a stain on Charles's birth.

But their whispers made little impression on the majority of the Franks. Even churchmen, who presumably would be sensitive to matters of legitimacy, paid little attention to the charge of bastardy. In the middle of the eighth century the Church was just beginning to assert rights over the ceremony and character of marriage. Although the Franks had been Catholic since the sixth century, their Merovingian rulers had continued to practice polygamy. According to Boniface, the saintly English missionary who converted the pagans of the German forests, many bishops and deacons in Frankland kept four or five concubines. If the clergy took such liberties, no one could complain about the behavior of kings.

The disadvantage of birth did not, therefore, seriously threaten the position of young Charles when he ascended the throne. His father Pepin had merely not bothered to have his marriage to Queen Bertrada sanctified, and Pepin might have thought no more of the matter if Bishop Boniface had not been so frequent a visitor to his court.

The zealous missionary had been appalled by the conditions he found in Frankland—ignorance and vice among the clergy, superstition and immorality among the laity. "The Franks are little better than the heathen," he wrote to Pope Zacharias—and no doubt he repeatedly urged Pepin to repair the irregularity of his marriage.

But it was not until shortly before Carloman was born that Pepin invited the blessings of the Church upon a marriage already valid by Germanic custom because a son had been born to it. He did so at this time because he needed the Church, and Boniface, to legitimize his rule over the kingdom of the Franks. For although Pepin had all the powers of a king, he governed officially as major-domo—or, to use the term which has the sanction of tradition, as mayor of the palace.

The Merovingian dynasty which reigned over the Franks had been founded at the end of the fifth century by Clovis, who had started his bloodthirsty career as a mere chief of a small tribe of Germans living in the region of the lower Rhine. Clovis conquered and divided among his sons the greater part of what is now France and Western Germany. But the vital strength of his line diminished from generation to generation, and the real power was seized by the chief officer of the court, the mayor of the palace. In the words of Einhard, Charlemagne's biographer:

"There was nothing left for the king to do but to be content with his name of king, his flowing hair and long beard. . . . He had nothing that he could call his own beyond this vain title of king, and the precarious support allowed by the mayor of the palace. . . . When he had to go abroad, he used to ride in a cart drawn by a yoke of oxen driven, peasant fashion, by a plowman; he rode in this way to the palace and general assembly of the people. . . . The mayor of the palace took charge of the government."

It should be noted in passing that it was no disgrace for the king to ride in an oxcart. The cart, like his flowing hair, belonged to an ancient Germanic tradition of priest-kingship. By keeping on the throne the do-nothing kings of the fading Merovingian line, the mayors of the palace were satisfying the prejudices of the people. It would no more have suited their purpose to make a mockery of the king than it would today suit the Prime Minister of Great Britain to reduce the British royal family to beggary. And although the fiction was then as

well understood as the fiction of the king's rule in any modern constitutional monarchy, it served its symbolic purpose.

The mayorship of the palace became hereditary, and for over a
hundred years the chief stewards of the king's household ruled in the
name of phantom kings. Sometimes there were gaps in the line of
puppet-rulers, and during the intrigues of a wild and bloody era there
might be several puppets reigning simultaneously in different parts
of the Frankish kingdom. By the time of Charles Martel (Charles
the Hammer), however, Merovingians were growing scarce, and in the
last four years of his "reign" Charles Martel ruled as mayor of the
palace in the name of a nonexistent master. We have documents
from the last years of his administration which are dated, with an
oddly humorless effort to preserve the fiction: "In the first [or second or third] year after the death of King Theodoric, Charles being
major-domo. . . ."

But after the brief interregna, some new scion of the royal family
always was fetched out of obscurity, and this is what Pepin and his
brother Carloman* did when they became joint mayors of the palace
after their father's death in 742. The two new mayors evidently felt
the need for some binding symbol of authority to steady their untried
and divided power. Although no chronicler considered the ascension
of the new king sufficiently important to be worth mentioning, from
743 onward documents begin to be dated in the glorious reign of
Childeric III. All that we know about Childeric is that eight years
afterward he was, in Einhard's words, "deposed, shaven and thrust
into the cloister by command of the Roman pontiff."

Einhard was after all an apologist for the new dynasty of Carolin-
gians, and he therefore makes light of a revolutionary and illegal step.
In reality the act was not so simple. By deposing Childeric and taking
the crown for himself, Pepin was substituting a fact for a fiction—but
he was also violating a centuries-old tradition. Since his act shaped
the whole subsequent history of Europe, and since it laid the foundation for the career of his son, we must linger over it for a moment.
Charles is the only ruler in history with whose name the epithet "the
Great" has become completely merged—so that he is known to us as
Charlemagne, the French form of Carolus Magnus—and his greatness
has overshadowed that of his less colorful father. But in a sense Pepin

---

* To distinguish him from his nephew this Carloman will be referred to as
Carloman the Elder.

began almost all the work that Charles completed, and in raising himself from mayor to king Pepin was preparing the way for Charles to raise himself from king to emperor.

At the time of his father's coronation Charles was nine years old—old enough to enjoy the pomp which accompanied the new ceremony, if not quite mature enough to understand the political background of what was happening. It must have pleased him to see his mother, to whom at this age he would naturally be closer than to his warrior father, sharing in the ceremony, being crowned and anointed as had been no other queen before her in the history of the Franks. Later on, the new status his mother thereby acquired was to be a source of disquiet to him.

The deposition of Childeric took place only a few years after Pepin had become sole ruler of the Franks. For in the year 747 Pepin's brother, the elder Carloman, had renounced the world, been tonsured by the hands of Pope Zacharias himself and had entered the famous monastery of Monte Cassino. The act was not altogether unheard of in those times; several Anglo-Saxon kings had done the same. And only the year before Hunald, duke of the virtually independent Aquitaine, had surrendered his duchy to his son and gone to spend the rest of his days as a monk. Hunald's retirement was an act of penance; he had treacherously put out the eyes of his own brother.

Carloman the Elder, too, apparently felt the need to do penance for an act of treachery. More conservative, less flexible and sterner than his brother, he had allowed himself to be carried away by passion when it became necessary to crush a rebellion among the Alemannians who inhabited the southeastern frontier of the kingdom. Ever since their conquest by Clovis the Alemannians had been in revolt against Frankish overlordship. Rebellion, token submission when the Frankish army entered their province, and a new armed uprising as soon as the Franks left—this had been their consistent pattern. In a burst of impatience Carloman the Elder had resolved to give them a terrible lesson.

In 746 the Alemannians had submitted once more, were ostensibly again part of the Frankish kingdom and as such subject to call to the national assembly. Carloman convoked such an assembly at Cannstadt. When the Alemannian nobles arrived, his armed Franks surrounded them and slaughtered thousands of them. The example of this act was to exert a fearful fascination on the mind of his nephew

Charles; it foreshadowed a similar horror forty years later. Carloman himself was almost immediately stricken with remorse, and that same year he informed his brother that he wished to retire to a monastery.

Thus, without lifting a hand, Pepin found his position immensely strengthened. He became sole ruler over a state embracing all of modern Belgium and the Netherlands, the northern halves of what are today France and Western Germany exclusive of Saxony, and he held a nominal overlordship over Bavaria and southern Gaul. For several centuries forces of disintegration had been at work, splitting the old Roman Empire of the West into fragments. Now the forces of cohesion had gained ascendancy once more, and the Europe of 750 A.D. was beginning to resemble the Europe of 1950 A.D. in one respect: it was a political structure in which a few large powers controlled the destinies of the Continent.

As sole ruler, Pepin was now strong enough to do away with the fiction of the mayoralty and become king in name as well as in fact. Yet the prestige of a line of kings who had ruled the Franks for two hundred and fifty years was very great among the people. The Merovingians were so venerated that every member of the royal family was considered to be equally a king. Their long hair and flowing beards, which Einhard makes fun of, were symbols going back far into the heathen past of the Franks. All the descendants of Merowig were held to be a race of mortals superior by birth to ordinary men.

Since the Merovingian tradition was heathen, Pepin decided to oppose to it the moral weight of Christianity. In this resolve he was ardently supported, guided and counseled by his saintly mentor, Boniface.

At this time Boniface was over seventy and nearing the end of a colorful career that was unique in accomplishment and yet characteristic of the times. A contemporary of the famous Anglo-Saxon scholar, the Venerable Bede, he was the foremost among that distinguished group of Benedictine monks who carried the culture and piety of Anglo-Saxon England to the continent of Europe. The significant place names in his life have a familiar ring to us. He was born in Devonshire, studied at Exeter and acquired a reputation for great learning as head of the school at the monastery of Notshalling. From his youth he mingled easily with the great, was early employed on an important mission from King Ine of the West Saxons to the Archbishop of Canterbury. He quickly made a name for himself in the

Church and among the secular dignitaries of the time. But the religious passion which had made him wish to enter a monastery in earliest childhood drove him restlessly across the sea to undertake the thankless task of converting the Frisians.

This mission in Frisia was scarcely successful, but it provided Boniface with valuable training for his later work. After a brief return to Britain, where he refused the opportunity to become abbot of his monastery, he set out for Rome to meet Pope Gregory II. The pope sent him into the marshes and forests of Thuringia and Hesse, where he was to spend the greater part of his life converting the German and Slavonic tribesmen, educating the local clergy and founding monasteries—among them the great monastery of Fulda, which became for Germany such a center of culture as Jarrow was in England. Out of Fulda there later came the future biographer of Charlemagne, little Einhard.

On one of his expeditions into Hesse, Boniface succeeded in dramatizing the power of Christianity in a way that kindled the imagination of his contemporaries. He terrified the pagan Germans and struck at the heart of their religion by killing the visible manifestation of their god. A generation later Charlemagne, when he sought to Christianize the pagan Saxons by force of arms, was to imitate the example of Boniface.

The paganism of the Germanic tribes was not some local and peculiar tribal religion casually practiced by bands of savages. These heathen were still loyal to rites and a body of belief of ancient and honorable ancestry, with a complex mythology extending far back into the preliterary past of the "Aryan" race. Many of the gods in the Greek pantheon had their Germanic counterparts, and although in various localities different gods might take first place—as Catholic communities lay stress on different saints—there was an essential unity about paganism as it confronted Christianity. Prophecy, magic spells, worship at trees and springs, taking auguries by the flight of birds and in other ways, making sacrifices—these practices were as common among the Germans as among the Romans and Greeks. Thor the Thunderer was not identical with Zeus-Jupiter, the Father of Lightning; but there were strong resemblances between them.

The chief symbol of Thor was the oak tree, which was sacred also to Jupiter and was worshiped by the Celtic Druids of Gaul, England and Ireland. The wood of the oak was of great hardness, and useful for many purposes. In the primeval forests the tree might grow to tremendous girth. Above all, it was host to the mysterious mistletoe which lived as a parasite among its branches, remained green throughout the winter when the leaves of the tree itself had browned, and which was valued as an antidote to all poisons, a cure for epilepsy, a charm against fires and a warder-off of lightning. Reason enough for the oak to be held sacred by peoples who practiced agriculture reluctantly and lived in the heart of the great forest which in these times spread over all of central and northern Europe.

Into this forest came Boniface and his hardy band of monks, carrying an instrument that the Germans knew more as a weapon of war than as a homely tool: the ax. He made his way to a famous sacred grove near Geismar, in Hesse, and with his own hands, before the eyes of the pagans "who cursed him inwardly," proceeded to cut down the huge holy oak that stood there. No thunderbolts struck him down; Thor's hammer did not crush him. Instead, after only a few strokes, the mighty mass of the tree plunged to the ground and "as if obeying a higher power burst at once into four parts." Why had the pagans stood by and watched the work of destruction? Perhaps they had reposed too much confidence in their god's ability to defend himself, or perhaps they were overawed by soldiers lent to Boniface by the Hammer of the Franks. But when the mighty oak yielded so readily to the ax the pagans were, we are told, "transformed, laid aside their former wickedness, praised God and believed." Boniface hewed the fallen tree into timber with which he erected a chapel and dedicated it to St. Peter. As so often, the Christian missionaries incorporated into their own the religion they overthrew.

We cannot be certain that Boniface had any soldiers with him on these expeditions, for such a fact would naturally be ignored by the monkish chroniclers. Yet it is quite likely, for Boniface was a frequent visitor to the court of Charles Martel, Charlemagne's grandfather. He was deeply concerned about the state of the Church in the Frankish kingdom, where no synod had been held in more than seventy years, where bishops were so thoroughly secularized that they engaged in private wars to expand their territory, and where the mayor of the palace made a practice of rewarding his landless warriors by handing over to them Church offices and estates. Although Boniface got little satisfaction from Charles Martel in matters that touched the Frankish leader's purse or political aims, Charles was quite willing to help the conversion of the Germans of Hesse and Thuringia. Missionary work there was valuable for securing his eastern borders.

As missionary, bishop and papal legate, Boniface's relations with Charles Martel were not unfriendly, but they left something to be desired. Charles Martel did not respond when the pope, through Boniface, appealed to him for aid against the Lombards, who were threatening the independence of the papacy. But with the accession to the mayoralty of Carloman and Pepin, the Anglo-Saxon came into his own. Carloman and Pepin's wife Bertrada were far more pious than Charles Martel had been; and Pepin recognized that the Church could be a powerful instrument of policy in holding together the disparate elements making up the Frankish kingdom. Almost immediately after the death of Charles Martel, Boniface was allowed to convoke the first church synod in East Frankland, and henceforth such gatherings of church dignitaries became a feature of the assemblies of the Franks. Perhaps the influence of Boniface also played a part in Carloman's decision to retire from the world after the massacre at Cannstadt.

Throughout his career Boniface had been an ardent upholder of the power of the papacy. He had received his mandates for missionary work directly from the pope, and in his negotiations at the courts of the Frankish mayors of the palace he had sought to tie the largely independent Frankish Church more closely to the Holy See. Now that Pepin had determined to take the title of king for himself, Boniface saw an opportunity for a momentous political and religious step—one which was to lead directly to the great conflicts between the spiritual and the temporal powers in the later Middle Ages. Boniface would repay Pepin for his services to the Church by giving his new office the awesome sanction of the Vicar of Christ. At the same time, the prestige and power of the Church would be enormously magnified. For if the pope had the right to confer a crown, he stood by implication above all temporal rulers.

The momentous step was not undertaken without preliminary negotiations in which Boniface combined the roles of papal legate and representative of the Frankish Church. When all was ready, messengers were sent to Pope Zacharias to put the fateful question. One of these messengers was Fulrad, Abbot of St. Denis, who was at that time also acting as tutor to young Charles and as Pepin's chaplain and virtual prime minister. Fulrad asked the pope "his opinion in the

matter of the kings of the Franks, who were hindered by their feebleness of mind from exercising sovereignty." (He might have added
that they were also hindered by the mayors of the palace.) The pope
replied as expected that "it is better to give the name of king to him
who has the wisdom and the power, rather than to him who has only
the name of king without the authority." The stage was then set for
a coronation unique in the annals of the Franks.

The place chosen for the making of the new king was Soissons on
the Aisne, the city from which Clovis had started his conquest of his
neighbors, so that Pepin was asserting his claim to be the true heir
of the Merovingian dynasty. There, in the open space between the
city and the even then ancient abbey of St. Medard, the temporal and
spiritual lords of the nation gathered to heave their new king upon
the shield, "according to the custom of the Franks."

There would be ladies present also, although the Franks no longer
permitted women to take part in their councils as their ancestors had
done in the days of Tacitus. The women wore over their under tunic,
with its close-fitting sleeves, long and voluminous dresses of wool,
linen or imported silk. Embroidered cloth for dresses was bought
from the Frisians, who were famous for their colorful textiles. The
dominant feature of the dress of both men and women was the wide,
richly adorned girdle made of leather or strong embroidered cloth.
Bright disks of gold, silver or bronze were pressed or sewn into these
belts, and a great deal of artistry was lavished on the ornamental
buckles with which they were held together. To confine their blond
and red-gold braids, the noble ladies wore diadems or circlets woven
with gold threads and studded with Syrian garnets, rare topazes and
turquoises. Or if they were not so wealthy, they contented themselves with polished bits of violet or azure glass, or mother-of-pearl
or ivory. Nor did they shrink from adding to all this display rings
and bracelets of gold, pearl necklaces, and hairpins with heads shaped
like birds or fantastic beasts.

The men wore the traditional linen shirts and close-fitting, knee-
length tunics. They too loved color, and their tunics were sea-green
or azure, their shoes scarlet leather embroidered in gold and with in-
steps set with emeralds and pearls. Their legs were cross-gartered with
scarlet bands, and above these they wore scarlet hose. Their fur mantles, clasped over the right shoulder, were cut so that they fell to the
knees on the sides, but almost to the ground in front and back. They

let their hair grow long, and (like the women) held it at the crown with a circlet. Although they were beardless, they affected a drooping mustache.

But the principal items of a man's dress were his shield and *spatha*, his sword, for the splendor of the sword was the sign of a man's station in life. Swords had names and personalities of their own, and the poets have sung the praises of Siegfried's Balmung, Roland's Durendal, Charlemagne's Joyeuse. Hilts and scabbards were ornamented with gold and jewels, and relics of a saint might be enclosed within the hollow hilt. But even the simplest type of unadorned sword was highly valued and high-priced; a sword without a scabbard was worth the equivalent of three cows.

The shield, which no Frankish warrior might lose without being called a coward, was made of wood and covered with leather which was often painted or gilded. These shields were used not only for the elevation of kings, but also to carry the dead away from the battlefields. The *Nibelungenlied* says:

> *Dô die herren sâhen, daz der helt was tôt,*
> *Si leiten in ûf einen schilt, der was von golde rôt*
> (When the lords saw that the hero was dead,
> They laid him on a shield which was red with gold.)

The Franks still spoke of themselves as barbarians, in contrast to the Romans. And in some respects they were still barbarians in our contemporary sense of the word, given to savagery in warfare, hard drinking, gambling and a violent lust for treasure in the form of gold or silver—treasure which they hoarded like Siegfried's Fafnir and Beowulf's Grendel. But by the time of Pepin's coronation they had been in contact with Roman civilization for at least eight hundred years, and a cultural interchange that flowed both ways had taken place between Romans and Germans. This is a fact too often forgotten. They were no longer simple tribesmen like the Germans Tacitus described. Within less than thirty years, as we shall see, the burgeoning of intellectual life which has been called the Carolingian Renaissance was to take place among the Franks. Although Charlemagne himself initiated and fostered this cultural rebirth, he did not create a culture out of nothing. In mind as well as dress the eighth-century Franks combined sophistication with a crude love of display.

For that matter, the character of Charlemagne himself showed that same fusion of opposites. It is, after all, a highly civilized duality.

Primitiveness and sophistication met again in the ceremony that took place at Soissons. As colorful as the dress of the crowd was the contrast between the stocky mayor of the palace, in the prime of life, and the tall, gaunt figure of the bishop who officiated. It was Boniface himself who performed the new part of the ceremony—new to the Franks, at any rate, although it had been used by the Anglo-Saxons and Visigoths and dated back, perhaps, to the crownings of the kings of Israel.

What was new—and Christian—was the anointment of the king with holy oil, and the administering of an oath. The holy oil symbolized the benediction of the Church—and Pepin thereby became the first European monarch to refer to himself as king "by the grace of God." Like the Merovingians, he became sacred, but his sacredness was Christian, not heathen. Henceforth no earthly power could legitimately remove him. Yet being king by God's grace and being anointed by the saintliest man in Europe carried with it obligations. There were limitations on the king's power which were expressly stated in Pepin's oath. He swore to keep peace with the Church of God, to suppress injustice, to mingle mercy with equity in all his judgments; and in advance he implored God to pardon his mistakes.

The implications of this ceremony for the later history of Europe could not, of course, be foreseen. Pepin had enormously strengthened the claim of the Church to temporal as well as spiritual sovereignty. Strong popes would build on this new base until the Church was one of the dominant factors in the political structure of Europe. A straight line leads from Pepin's coronation to Henry the Fourth's humiliation at Canossa three hundred years later.

But for the present the struggle between Church and State had not yet begun, and all was still harmony. The King of the Franks had the legal sanction he wanted, and the papacy had obtained a Defender of the Faith, which it sorely needed. Pepin was promptly asked to reverse the hands-off policy of his father and come to the rescue of the hard-pressed papal state which Pope Gregory the Great had created virtually singlehanded a hundred and fifty years before. After some hesitation Pepin consented to act in behalf of Rome.

In the middle of the eighth century Italy was still ostensibly a part of the Roman Empire, but the seat of Roman power was now at

Constantinople, not Rome. Here in the ancient city of Byzantium, where Constantine had founded his New Rome, there still persisted the tradition of an empire that had ruled most of the known world. But this Eastern Empire was Greek in language, Asiatic in its absolutism, ceremoniousness and luxury, and Roman only because governmental fictions persisted with remarkable tenacity in men's minds. Its connection with the mother-city of Rome had been growing increasingly tenuous ever since Diocletian's division of the Empire into eastern and western halves at the end of the third century. The western half was shattered by barbarian invasions which the Eastern Empire withstood; and the Empire proved unable to hold Italy firmly within its orbit. Rome and the whole Italian peninsula became an inferior outer province, administered by imperial governors known as exarchs. The capital of the Exarchate was the fortress-city of Ravenna, on the eastern coast of Italy, and the domain over which the exarchs ruled shrank or expanded accordingly as the Roman emperors at Constantinople had or had not military forces to spare for the defense of Italy.

Rome and the surrounding lands, which had come to be known as the Duchy of Rome, fell almost by default into the control of the popes. Nominally the popes were subjects of the emperor, who still exercised the right to confirm their election. In practice they were virtually independent. To the north and south of the Duchy of Rome and the Exarchate of Ravenna lay the German Kingdom of the Lombards, and the popes struggled to preserve their independence by keeping a delicate balance of power between the Empire and the Lombard kingdom. But the Lombards were pushing steadily southward, swallowing up the lands of the Exarchate and threatening to take Rome itself. Only the prestige of the pope as the titular head of all Catholic Christians had so far restrained them from devouring the whole Duchy of Rome.

In the same year that Pepin was crowned and anointed King of the Franks (751 A.D.), the Lombard king, Aistulf, succeeded in capturing Ravenna, the capital of the Exarchate. He promptly demanded that Rome submit to him, and threatened—according to the papal writers who make the Lombards out as ferocious monsters—that he would kill all the inhabitants of Rome with a single sword. Pope Stephen, who had succeeded Zacharias, alternately pleaded, exhorted and threatened excommunication. He led a procession to the basilica of Our Lady on the Esquiline and hung on the crucifix the forty-year treaty of peace which the King of the Lombards had signed with

him—and had broken within four months. He sent panicky letters
to the heretical emperor of Eastern Rome, Constantine Copronymus
(so called by his enemies, who alleged that as an infant he had soiled
the baptismal font), requesting the emperor to deliver Rome from
the sons of iniquity. Finally, in despair, he resolved to lay his case
personally before King Pepin.

After an exchange of letters, Pepin sent Chrodegang, the Bishop of
Metz, and Duke Otker to conduct the pope to Frankland. In the
fall of the year 753 the pope left behind him the weeping people of
Rome, who pleaded with him to stay with them, and set out on his
long journey. He traveled with a large party which included the
Frankish emissaries and a representative of the Roman emperor—that
is, Constantine. They went first to Pavia to argue once more with
King Aistulf. Aistulf was obdurate; he refused to restore to the pope
any of the "lost sheep"—the cities he had already captured, which in
fact belonged to the emperor rather than to the pope—and he did his
best to keep Stephen from going on to see Pepin. But the Lombard
king was not yet prepared to go to war with the Franks. When Otker
and Chrodegang summarily demanded that he let the pope continue
his journey, Aistulf reluctantly consented. The pope left hastily, before Aistulf could change his mind. Perhaps he was also urged to
speed by the Frankish envoys. They may have seen that he was
wavering, for crossing the Alps in November was no mean enterprise
for an old man. It was, in fact, so trying that he paused to rest at
the abbey of St. Maurice in Switzerland, and there he was met by the
ubiquitous Abbot Fulrad of St. Denis, Pepin's intimate counselor.

Where Fulrad was, his pupil would not be far behind him. As a
mark of honor to the vicar of St. Peter, and perhaps with a conscious
desire to introduce his eldest son to the duties of public life, Pepin
sent young Charles to meet the pope on the road and accompany
him to Ponthion, where the king, his family and a large retinue were
staying.

So the young man who was to become one of the greatest of rulers
steps upon the stage of history. This meeting with the pope is the
first mention of Charles in the contemporary annals, and we would
be happy to know more about it. But unfortunately only the bare
fact is stated, without commentary, and we are given no indication of
what the heir to the Frankish throne thought of Pope Stephen or
what impression the eleven-year-old boy made on the pope and his

attendants. That Charles must have been a precocious child is implied, for Pepin would not have sent him if he had not expected him to conduct himself with dignity. It is probable also that Charles already spoke Latin fairly well—if not the Latin of Rome, then the Latin of Paris—so that he could greet the pope in his own language. For Charles had been well instructed by his tutor and his mother, Queen Bertrada.

We may picture him, then, as an eager, flaxen-haired boy, already tall—in manhood he would be some six feet four inches—excited by the honor that was being conferred on him. No pope had ever before set foot on Frankish soil; indeed, popes had seldom left the city of Rome except when they went unwillingly to Constantinople on orders from their sovereigns, the emperors. Even though Stephen was coming to Frankland as a suppliant, his visit was a unique mark of favor, and the eleven-year-old boy must have been as keenly aware of this as his elders.

It is highly symbolic that in our first glimpse of Charles we see him advancing to meet the supreme head of the Church. In a sense this meeting foreshadows the dramatic ceremony which took place in Rome nearly fifty years later, when another pope placed on Charles's white head the imperial crown and hailed him as Emperor of the Romans. It foreshadows also his lifelong intimate relationship with the Holy See, which colored all his political and intellectual attitudes. Embryonic in this meeting is his deep affection for a later pope, Hadrian, whose death he was to lament as the loss of a dear friend.

Nor is it assuming too much to imagine that the meeting with Pope Stephen itself partly determined Charles's theological bent, his keen interest in Church affairs and the missionary fervor he manifested throughout his reign. The boy's heart must have pounded as he went forward to kneel before Stephen and receive his blessing. For Charles had been reared in a deeply religious atmosphere. His mother was noted for her piety; his uncle had given up a kingdom to become a monk; his tutor was abbot of one of the greatest monasteries in the country; and he had seen and been spoken to by Boniface, who even in his lifetime was recognized by all who knew him as a saint. Now this boy, who had been surrounded throughout his childhood by an atmosphere of devoutness, was kneeling before the living representative of St. Peter himself—an imposing presence in his full vestments, with dalmatic, stole and shoes all made of cloth of gold, and with orphreyed chasuble of soft blue silk. How could Charles help remembering this meeting for the rest of his life?

And if Charles had any doubts of how much reverence was due to His Holiness, his father's action dispelled them. For when the pope was within three miles of the royal residence at Ponthion, Pepin and a great throng of Frankish nobles and courtiers came out to meet him. The king bowed down to the ground before the pope and thought it no disgrace to lead Stephen's horse by the bridle as though he were an equerry. It was the sixth of January, the Feast of Epiphany, and the people paid homage to the Holy Father as the three kings had paid homage to the babe in the manger.

The pope had come to Frankland partly on his own business, partly on the business of the Roman emperor at Constantinople, who wanted the Exarchate of Ravenna wrested from the Lombards and had not the power to do it himself. The emperor was willing enough to use Pepin and the pope as pawns, if he could; in any case, he had nothing to lose. Stephen also wanted the Lombards thrown out of Ravenna, but he was none too eager to see the exarch regain possession. He was not prepared to renounce his allegiance to the legitimate Roman emperor, but it would be convenient if the Holy See controlled Ravenna and the rest of the Exarchate. For the present, Stephen's hopes were modest; he wanted to expand the Duchy of Rome so that the Church would hold a solid block of territory in the center of Italy, separating the Lombards of the north from the Lombard duchies of Spoleto and Benevento in the south. But even at this time there must have dangled before him the alluring dream of an Italy controlled entirely by the Church, of the establishment of a great Roman theocracy to replace the defunct Western Empire.

At Ponthion, Stephen extracted from Pepin a promise to recover the cities of the Exarchate. For whom exactly they were to be recovered was for the time being left open; it was a question which need not be settled definitely until the King of the Franks was in a position to carry out his promise. But first, war with the Lombards would have to be formally decided on by the national assembly of the Franks on the first of March. The Marchfield was the traditional survival of the ancient Germanic constitutional monarchy.

To that Marchfield came an unexpected and unwelcome guest on a mission which plunged the royal household into the midst of a family quarrel. Upon young Charles the bitter disputes among his elders made a lasting impression and set a pattern which he himself was to follow later in his relationship with his younger brother, Carloman, after the two boys succeeded to their father's throne.

The guest was Carloman the Elder, Charles's uncle and his father's brother, who seven years before had turned all his powers over to Pepin and had become a monk. He attended the Marchfield on orders from his abbot at Monte Cassino, who instructed Carloman to oppose the pope and to defend the Lombard king's right to the lands he had seized. It was an odd situation for a monk, whose vows of obedience should certainly have included unquestioning submission to the head of the entire Church; but Monte Cassino was in the territory of King Aistulf, and the abbot gave his order to Carloman at the request of his Lombard master. Carloman undoubtedly had private motives for carrying out those orders.

Carloman had a clear advantage over the pope when, as he probably did, he addressed the assembled nobles at the Marchfield, which was held at Berny, near Soissons. He could speak to them in their own German language; he had the prestige of one who had formerly ruled over them; and he was advocating the traditional Frankish policy of friendship with Lombardy. He must have made the point that the Lombards had marched alongside the Franks when his father, Charles the Hammer, drove back the Saracens. His father, too, he would recall, had refused the request of an earlier pope to intervene in the affairs of Italy. Carloman need not have said so, but it would be clear to his listeners that he was defending a policy of conservatism against the radical and innovator, King Pepin, who had brought in a foreign power to give him his crown and was now preparing to drag his people into a war for the sake of that foreign power.

Carloman's arguments carried weight with the Frankish notables, and a large number of them vowed they would withdraw their forces from the army if the king insisted on making war against the Lombards. But the decisive voice in the assembly was Pepin's. Aided by the religious enthusiasm which the pope's physical presence had stimulated, he carried the day, and the Marchfield voted for war. The dissenting nobles were not yet so independent of the king as the barons of the later Middle Ages were to become, and they did not dare to commit the crime of *herisliz*, or desertion in time of war. They did not carry out their threat to withdraw forces, although later in the year we hear of their grumbling over the difficult crossing of the Alpine passes.

Pepin did not take kindly to interference, and his subsequent treatment of Carloman the Elder was hardly marked by that brotherly love which the Church enjoined. The contemporary chroniclers do not tell us whether Carloman had begun to regret his renunciation of the world and was hoping to regain his half of the kingdom. But even if he had no such intention, his coming to the Marchfield had divided the people into two factions, one for and one against the proposed Lombard war, and it was inevitable that the pro-Lombard faction should look to him as its leader. Pepin evidently thought there was danger of civil war. He promptly had Carloman arrested and took into custody also the monks who had accompanied his brother from Monte Cassino.

Pepin was by nature disposed to be trustful. He was also a classically German paterfamilias, much concerned about the future of his family. Unlike his father before him and his son after him, he was reasonably monogamous. At one time he had considered divorcing his strong-willed wife Bertrada, but his intention could not have been too earnest, for a word of admonition from the pope had restrained him. He had only two sons, and he was determined that they would succeed him as kings of the Franks.

Now he felt that the succession was threatened by Carloman the Elder's action. After his own death the pro-Carloman, pro-Lombard faction among the Franks might attempt to set up one of Carloman's sons as king. For Carloman had several sons whom he had "commended" to his brother when he renounced the world. These sons must have been educated at the Palace School along with young Charles, must have grown up with him and been his playmates. Now Pepin felt that they, too, were dangerous, and he chose the means which were conventionally used to dispose of potential pretenders to a throne: he had them tonsured and sent to a monastery. To young Charles this unexpected punishment of his innocent cousins must have been something of a shock.

The tonsuring of Carloman's sons was accompanied by another coronation, as Pepin's first coronation had followed on the shearing of King Childeric. Pepin was about to go to war, and a king was as mortal as other men—particularly in those times, when a strong king led the charge against the enemy. He determined to have his two sons crowned immediately, so that there would be no trouble over the succession. Apparently he did not think of trouble between the two brothers, although from his own experience and his knowledge of Frankish history he should have foreseen this possibility.

During all that summer preparations for the Lombard campaign went forward. Meanwhile Pepin took his family and the royal household to his beloved monastery of St. Denis, where Abbot Fulrad was playing host and nurse to Pope Stephen. The pope, worn out from the hardships of travel, had fallen ill. In a letter written the following year to Pepin he complained that he had sorely tried soul and body by coming into that vast and remote land of Gaul, where one was afflicted by intense heat and cold, floods and "most atrocious mountains," as well as "divers other perils."

According to legend, the pope was sick unto death and recovered only at the miraculous intercession of St. Denis himself. At any rate, when Pepin arrived expecting to find the pope's dead body, he found Stephen well enough to perform the rite the king desired of him. On July 28, 754, with Stephen officiating in the part that Boniface had taken three years earlier, Pepin and his queen were once more anointed as rulers of the Franks. In addition—and this, of course, was the point of the ceremony—Pepin's two sons, Carloman and Charles, shared in the unction and were duly proclaimed kings along with their father. For some years afterward the pope, whenever he wrote to Pepin any one of his official letters, used the salutation: "To the three kings of the Franks."

At this same ceremony Stephen conferred on all three the high-sounding title of Patrician of the Romans. The exact meaning of this title, and the pope's right to give it, have been endlessly debated. Strictly speaking, only the Roman emperor had the right to make patricians, and Stephen may have been acting on instructions from Constantine. Then again, Stephen may have been exceeding his authority. Whichever was the case, the practical effect was to make Pepin and his sons protectors of Rome. And by accepting the title Pepin was once more defying the partisans of Carloman and turning his back on the policy of his father, who had been offered a consulship by Pope Gregory and had refused it.

After this second coronation within three years, Pepin set out with Pope Stephen, his household and his army on the military expedition. He stopped off for a time at the ancient city of Vienne on the Rhone, the former capital of the Kingdom of Burgundy, where he could see the columns of the Roman temple of Livia and Augustus which still stand there. Here he left his wife and probably his younger son.

Here also, in one of the numerous abbeys of the city, he placed his brother. It was no longer necessary to guard Carloman so closely; his life was clearly ebbing away. Grief-stricken at the failure of his mission and the lifelong semi-imprisonment he had unwittingly inflicted on his sons, Carloman had fallen ill. He lingered on into the following year, perhaps tended by Bertrada. Then he died "in peace," the chronicles emphatically state, shortly after Pepin returned from his Italian expedition. There is no hint of foul play in any of the sources, and although the murder of brothers was far from unknown in the Middle Ages, such an act would have been wholly incompatible with Pepin's character; had not Pepin time and again forgiven his half brother Grifo, who repeatedly rose in open rebellion against him? Pepin provided a rich coffin and sent Carloman's remains back to Monte Cassino, where the king turned monk soon became the subject of many legends.

Pepin may have taken young Charles with him on this first Italian expedition. At twelve Charles could not very well take an active part in the fighting, but he was not at all too young to practice with weapons in maneuvers, to learn how an army behaved on the march and to absorb lessons in strategy from his father and his uncle Jerome, one of Charles Martel's illegitimate sons.

The Frankish army that set off across the Alpine passes was not composed of professional soldiers, although all the men could fight, and fight well. Most of them were freeholders, owners of one or two small manors, who were subject to the *Heerbann*, or national levy, and who had to provide their own equipment. Each man was required to bring to the point of assembly a shield and lance, a bow with an extra string, and twelve arrows. He also had to provide himself with food for three months. These supplies, covered by leather aprons, were carried in vast numbers of ox-drawn wagons which formed the cumbersome baggage train of the army.

Most of the soldiers were infantrymen. But since the days when Charles Martel mounted some of his men in order to combat the Saracens with their swift Arabian horses, a body of cavalry had become a regular part of the Frankish army. Since horses were expensive, only the greater lords could afford them, and these lords were generally surrounded by a body of mounted retainers. The rich wore coats of mail formed of interlocking steel rings. Less wealthy men had to be content with leather vests covered with overlapping plates of steel. The neck, the upper part of the arms and the thighs were also protected. A few of the Franks had steel helmets, but most of them fought bareheaded. All the men of the upper classes would never be parted from their swords; some of the more powerful mounted men also carried the terrible mace, a long club with a head made of a steel ball filled with lead for weight.

It was not without reason that the Franks were famous for their *furor teutonicus*, not by chance that they had subjected the Burgundians, Alemannians and Bavarians. They were fierce soldiers, and with the subject nationalities fighting beside them they usually had the advantage of numbers in battle. It was a considerable host that marched to the pass of Mount Cenis. The malcontents who had resisted the idea of going to war complained of the hardships of crossing the Alps, and the Romanized Franks from the plains of Neustria were frightened by the snow-clad peaks that towered over them and the wild rocky gorges beneath them. But Pepin had his men well in hand and pushed steadily on toward Italy.

He had sent an advance guard ahead of him to Susa to secure the pass, and as it turned out the main body of his army was scarcely needed. For although King Aistulf was fully prepared, his soldiers evidently had little heart for war against the dreaded Frank. A battle was fought at the entrance to the pass, and the tiny advance guard totally routed the entire army of the Lombards. They succeeded, we are told, because they put their faith not in their own strength but in the aid of God and St. Peter. In after times Pope Stephen took great delight in referring to this victory of a small force over a great host as if it were a miracle which he himself had produced by his direct intercession with St. Peter.

King Aistulf escaped capture only by sliding down a rocky slope, and the Lombard army fled, leaving behind their dead and "much treasure, gold and silver and numerous ornaments." When King Pepin arrived he found the campaign virtually finished, the decisive battle of the war already fought. He marched on to besiege the Lombard capital of Pavia, but this was scarcely more than a perfunctory gesture, for Aistulf no longer had any means of resistance and sued for peace.

The significant line in the tale as it is told by the chroniclers is that Aistulf pleaded with the Frankish *sacerdotes et optimates*, the priests and the nobles, to intercede for him. Carloman's mission had not been without some effects; the Lombard king still had many well-wishers in the Frankish camp. Having dragged them unwillingly into the campaign, Pepin thought it politic not to offend them further by needless bloodshed. His own temperament, too, prompted him to be merciful, and he granted Aistulf lenient terms.

In the treaty of peace Aistulf acknowledged Pepin as his overlord, promised to right the wrongs he had done to the Holy See, to give up Ravenna and the other cities he had seized, and to pay reparations—a large sum of money which in those days was simply and honestly called tribute and which helped the victor to pay the expenses of the war. The money was delivered on the spot; fulfillment of the other conditions of the treaty was left to the future. Winter was coming and Pepin did not want to linger in Italy; his army was not geared for a protracted campaign. As soon as the treaty was signed he set out for home, leaving behind Abbot Fulrad and Jerome to conduct the pope back to Rome.

Historians have expressed amazement that Pepin should have so easily trusted Aistulf to keep his promises, that he should have marched away content with his treasure, as if he had been on a simple plundering raid, without taking any guarantees to insure that the political ends of the war would be attained. Yet there is nothing surprising about his confidence. He had administered a thorough defeat to Aistulf. He had no reason to imagine that the Lombard king would be so reckless as to offend him again in the near future. He had immensely weakened the whole Lombard army and stripped the kingdom of much of its portable wealth. Aistulf was now in a far less favorable position to oppose Pepin's will than he had been before the campaign began.

The miscalculation which forced Pepin to repeat his Lombard campaign in 756 was not Pepin's but Aistulf's. Before the Frankish army departed, Aistulf gave rich gifts to many of the Frankish chiefs, and he must have formed a view colored by wishful thinking of the opposition to Pepin within the Frankish camp. He had no doubt talked with the supporters of Carloman, and he gravely overestimated their strength and underestimated Pepin's hold over his own people. There would be no second invasion of Lombardy, Aistulf thought; next time the Franks themselves would revolt against Pepin's policy of foreign entanglements. And so the moment the Frankish army crossed the Alps into Frankland, Aistulf resumed his harrying of the Papal See. He felt quite safe from the Franks, and he was determined to punish the pope for the part Stephen had played in the disastrous defeat.

During the whole of the following year Pope Stephen bombarded the Frankish court with letters that ranged in tone from pleas to imperious demands. He launched a campaign of atrocity stories worthy of the best modern propagandists. In violation of their promise the Lombards had surrendered none of the stolen cities, he wrote; they were burning churches, raping nuns, smashing images, stealing vestments and digging up the bones of saints. (This they might well have done; everyone in this period considered any means of getting hold of saints' relics quite justified.) They were ravaging the countryside and besieging the city of St. Peter itself.

In the end a reluctant Pepin went through the same performance once more. He marched into Italy again, forced Aistulf to submit, deprived him of more treasure and made him swear the most solemn oath that he would never again rebel against his Frankish masters. This oath, as it happened, Aistulf never had the opportunity to break. That winter, while he was hunting in the royal woods near Pavia, his horse dashed him against a tree and he was killed. The pope, of course, was delighted; he wrote to Pepin that the tyrant, the devil-inspired destroyer of the Church of God, had been struck by divine wrath and hurled into the infernal regions.

This second campaign in Italy would be no more than one of the many fruitless wars of history, painful to the participants and meaningless to posterity, had Pepin not attempted at this time to rid himself and his successors of the vexatious problems of Italy and turn back to the affairs of his own dominions. He was getting more than a little impatient with the pope's long-winded letters of complaint and admonition, and there were important matters at home which needed settling. He wanted to finish his father's work of driving the Saracens out of Septimania, the extreme southern part of Gaul, and he wanted to settle accounts with Waifar, the Duke of Aquitaine.

This time, therefore, Pepin made sure that the Lombards formally surrendered Ravenna and the other cities they had taken. He then disposed of these cities by deeding them to the pope and his successors forever. Representatives of the Roman emperor protested that the cities were not his to give, since they belonged to the Exarchate; but Pepin ignored these objections. Perhaps he told the emperor that he was not depriving the Empire of these lands, since the pope was as much the emperor's subject as the exarch had been. In any case, there was nothing the emperor could do about it; he continued to maintain friendly diplomatic relations with Pepin.

This deed, the famous Donation of Pepin, created the States of the Church which made the papacy a powerful temporal force in European affairs for over a thousand years and which kept Italy divided until 1870. It led to innumerable struggles between popes and emperors, popes and kings. But the more immediate results concern us here, and these were the opposite of what Pepin intended. He himself, it is true, refused for the rest of his reign to be bothered again about the affairs of Italy. He was determined that he would not a third time cross the formidable barrier of the Alps. But his son Charles would not be able to escape the obligations that had been incurred by Pepin's championship of the pope's cause and by Pepin's gift to the Holy See.

In fact, it is doubtful whether Charles ever wished to escape from those obligations. His visits to Italy with his father's army during those impressionable years of boyhood seem to have strengthened in him that love for the warm south which has always been a trait of the German character. Charlemagne visited Rome four times and would certainly have gone there more often had he been less occupied with the affairs of a far-flung realm.

CHAPTER TWO

The Brothers

THROUGHOUT the remaining twelve years of his father's reign Charles was busy fighting with his father's army in another southern land, where many survivals of ancient Roman culture could still be found. This was the great Duchy of Aquitaine, which comprised at that time almost all the land south of the Loire and east of the Rhone—almost a fourth of the present area of France. Aquitaine was a rich land of prosperous farms and many great cities: Bourges, Poitiers, Clermont, Toulouse, Limoges, Bordeaux, Saintes. Its subjugation was vital to King Pepin both strategically and economically.

The Aquitanians had been conquered successively by the Vandals, the Goths, the Saracens and the Franks; yet they still thought of themselves and called themselves Romans. Roman amphitheaters, Roman baths, Roman aqueducts were still in use in cities like Bordeaux and Saintes. The Germanic peoples who had settled in the land had intermarried with the conquered population and become assimilated, as later the Northmen were to be assimilated in Normandy. Here in Aquitaine the tremendous power of survival of Roman civilization was exemplified almost more strongly than in Rome itself; and during the prolonged war which was to last until the end of Pepin's life Charles learned more than the art of conquest. Much of his later devotion to the art, the architecture, the language and the grand political conception of the Romans must have been the outcome of his experiences in Aquitaine.

Unhappily, we know nothing definite about those vital years of Charles's life when he was growing from boyhood to manhood. The chroniclers tell us of nothing but the interminable Aquitanian war, and in connection with it they mention casually that he went to this war with his father in the year 761. Undoubtedly he had fought on

the battlefield earlier, and this special mention probably means that
at the age of nineteen he was given some kind of command over
troops. There must have been from the first something inspiring in
the quality of his leadership to give rise to those oral traditions of a
mighty warrior which were later woven into the great poetic romances
about Charlemagne and his paladins.

Less than a hundred years after this time the legends had already
begun, and that gossipy old fabulist, the Monk of St. Gall, was to
picture Charles in his young manhood as a man of iron, possessing
the strength of four men, able to bend bars of iron with his two hands.
In his highly imaginary yet significant account of Charles's advance
to the walls of Pavia, the Monk writes: "Soon Charles was seen, a
giant of iron; on his head a helmet of iron; gauntlets of iron on his
hands; his breast and shoulders clothed in an iron cuirass. His left
hand brandished a lance of iron, while his right hand clasped the iron
of his invincible sword. Even his horse had the color and the strength
of iron." Clearly, Charles made upon his contemporaries a lasting
impression of a man of commanding stature, powerful beyond the
average, immune to fatigue and possessing a restless energy. His biographer Einhard adds a few details: his nose was rather long, his eyes
large and lively, his voice surprisingly high in pitch for a man his
size. We can discount Einhard's remark that he was somewhat stout,
though so well proportioned that this did not seem to be a defect.
Einhard knew him in later life; in his twenties Charles was no doubt
a typically lean young Frankish warrior.

Hunting and swimming—his favorite sports all through his life—
hardened and toughened his strong frame. Charles had the same
fierce passion for the chase that animated all the men of the Middle
Ages, and he often outdistanced his companions in pursuit of the
stag or the wild boar. Riding, too, was as natural to him as breath-
ing. For his father's court never stayed long in one place. Pepin
followed the custom of Frankish kings, moving about continually
with his family and his household retainers—both in order to see to
affairs in different parts of the kingdom and in order to distribute
among the various royal estates the expenses of maintaining his court.
By the time Charles had reached manhood he had seen and lived in
most of the dominions he was to rule; and this traveling, too, must
be accounted an important part of his education.

Of the education of his mind we must judge from what we know about the standards of the time and Charles's later accomplishments. His mother and Abbot Fulrad gave him that thorough instruction in the principles of the Catholic faith which were to make him in manhood a "most Christian king" and something more than an amateur in the intricacies of theological doctrine. In a letter to Charles a Bishop Cathwulf testifies to Bertrada's influence: "O king, if Almighty God has raised you above your contemporaries and all your predecessors in honor and glory, you owe this above all to the virtues of your mother." From Fulrad Charles undoubtedly had lessons in statecraft as well as religion; the good abbot of St. Denis was one of King Pepin's most trusted counselors and envoys.

At the palace school the seven liberal arts of ancient Rome were still being taught, as they were to be taught for another thousand years to come. The curriculum was divided into the trivium of grammar, logic and rhetoric, and the quadrivium of arithmetic, music, astronomy and geometry (although the terms *trivium* and *quadrivium* may not have been used until after Alcuin's arrival in Frankland). The last two subjects were probably somewhat neglected in Charles's early training. But in arithmetic he was certainly well grounded, and we find him later on struggling to pound the elements of accounting into the slow or unwilling minds of the stewards who ran the royal estates. His regular revenues, like those of all Frankish kings, came largely from the income of these estates, and the wealth which as king later enabled him to launch vast civic projects and maintain a large body of household troops was due as much to superior management of his inherited lands as to the acquisition of new royal domains.

There is circumstantial evidence that Charles was highly musical. There was no pure music in his day. Secular music was the handmaiden of poetry, and Charles was fond of listening to the heroic epics and ballads that recalled the real or legendary history of his people. He had a collection of Frankish songs made, and it is the sorrow of every student of German literature and philology that his collection has not come down to us. The *Heldenlieder* that sprang up around his great forerunner, Theoderic the Goth, were already being sung, and his compilation probably contained early versions of the *Nibelungenlied*, the great German epic of the Middle Ages which was refashioned by Richard Wagner into the *Ring* cycle.

When Charles was fifteen an organ arrived at Pepin's court. It was a gift to Pepin from the Roman emperor; in spite of Pepin's donation

to the pope, the emperor evidently still wished to keep on good terms
with the Frankish king. This organ is mentioned in many of the annals; it was the first ever seen in Frankland. The sonorous accompani-
ment it gave to the high, pure voices of the boys' choirs as they sang
their Gregorian chants excited wonder and delight among the people.
We do not know that Charles tried to learn how to play it himself.
We do know that he took a lifelong interest in chanting, in the training of choirs and the proper singing of the psalms.

Grammar, too, was one of his favorite subjects, and for most of his
life he remained something of a pedant about it. The language of
the people had already drifted so far from classical Latin, which still
remained the model for the written language, that even the clergy
had the greatest difficulty writing and speaking "correct" Latin. An
amusing example of this is to be found in the correspondence between Boniface and Pope Zacharias. Boniface questioned the pope
on the validity of baptisms by a priest who "in consequence of his
ignorance of Latin, breaking the language, so to speak, said: '*Baptizo
te in nomine patria et filia et spiritus sancti.*' " (The pope decided that
the baptisms were nevertheless valid.) The vulgar tongue which was
to be French was already emerging, but this was not so evident to the
speakers as it was to the philologists of a later era. One of Charles's
first acts when he ascended the throne was to order better instruction
for the clergy, so that they would be able to conduct services in correct Latin—which the common people could scarcely understand. It
was only in the last year of his reign that he recognized the vulgar
tongue, rescinded the previous order and commanded that services be
conducted in the language of the people—the *lingua romana rustica.*
In rhetoric also he excelled—not, perhaps, so much in the theory
(until his later years when Alcuin wrote a book on the subject for
him) as in the practice of it. Throughout his life he was able to find
fitting expression for his thoughts, to speak easily and freely and per-
suasively to foreign ambassadors and to the national assemblies of the
people. This does not seem so remarkable to us today, but in his time
the king's fluency was wondered at and commented on. The refined
oratory of the Romans—product of city life and republican institutions—had remained alien to the German character and German
habit, and Charles's eloquence was recognized as exceptional.

Some time during Charles's young manhood he was married. But
our sources, meager enough for this whole phase of his career, totally

fail us when we look to them for more than the mere fact. His wife was named Himiltrude; she was "a noble Frankish lady"; she bore him a son and a daughter who were named Pepin the Hunchback and Rothaid; and she was given to Charles by his father—that is to say, King Pepin arranged the marriage. That is all we really know; everything else is conjecture.

Charles's brother Carloman had two children of his own by the time he was eighteen, and Charles himself was probably equally young when his father provided him with a wife. Still a boy, with a boy's intransigeance toward fate, it must have been a terrible blow to him to discover that his first-born son was deformed. The child was fair of face and well proportioned; but the lump on his back debarred him forever from being Charles's heir. Charles kept the boy at court and even gave him precedence over his younger brothers later on. But in the early days of his marriage the sorrow Charles felt over this son must have turned into coldness toward his wife. For when, as we shall see, he wished to make a political marriage he did not hesitate to divorce Himiltrude.

Immediately after his coronation as king of half of Frankland, however, Charles could devote little time to his personal affairs. He had to feel his way into the problems of kingship, to accustom himself to making decisions and sitting in judgment without the aid and authority of his father. He had to settle the numerous questions that arose from the division of the realm. Among the thorniest of these was one which resulted from the comparatively new system of distributing land by king's gift, or *benefice*, in return for military or other services. Charles's grandfather had in this way given away vast areas of land—much of it church land rather than his own—in return for obligatory services. Something very like feudal allegiance was already beginning to develop, although true feudalism was still in the future. But even now lords who held lands in both parts of the former kingdom owed allegiance and services to both Charles and Carloman. Given friendly relations between the brothers, such divided allegiance would not have caused trouble. But their relations were far from friendly.

Charles would have been happy, at this early stage of his reign, to take over his father's administrative staff intact. Men who could read and write and do ordinary clerical labors were scarce enough in Frankland; capable administrators were even scarcer. But unfortunately the administrative officials had been divided along with the land of the kingdom. Between Charles and his brother Carloman there almost

immediately began a tug of war over Charles's old tutor, Abbot Fulrad of St. Denis, who was undoubtedly one of the most important
men in the two kingdoms. He had been King Pepin's right hand, and
we have seen that he was chosen to conduct Pope Stephen into Frankland. Now he became one of Carloman's chief advisers, presumably
because St. Denis (as part of Burgundy) fell into Carloman's part of
the kingdom. Both kings courted the abbot, Carloman by confirming
the abbey of St. Denis in all its former rights and immunities, and
Charles by presenting St. Denis with lands. Charles's gift had more
substance.

The case of Abbot Fulrad seems to have been symptomatic. There
were undoubtedly other contests between the two young kings for the
services of talented men. But such maneuvering was only a prelude
to the more serious trouble that had to follow, given the bad blood
between the brothers and the splitting in two of a kingdom that most
of the subjects still felt to be one. The past history of the Frankish kingdom had been an endless succession of fratricidal wars; even
Charles's father, Pepin, had been forced to fight his half brother
Grifo.

The trouble, when it came, was precipitated by an external event.
Within a few months after the dual coronations the gallant Aquitanians made one last attempt to regain their freedom. Old Duke
Hunald, the father of Waifar, threw off his monk's cowl and came
out of his retirement on the island of Rhé (in the Bay of Biscay) to
lead the revolt.*

The armed rebellion in Aquitaine could not have been entirely unexpected. The government of Frankland had changed hands, and
there was always the chance that the new kings would not be so strong
as the old. So, at least, a subjugated people would reason. Charles
had spent the winter of 768 in and around Aachen, in the heart of his
family's ancestral territory; but toward spring he began moving his
court and household troops westward. By Easter he was in Rouen,
closer to Aquitaine. When the revolt came he was ready for it and
acted with a promptness and effectiveness designed to impress his
people. He marched toward Aquitaine at once, with what forces he
had, without going through the tedious process of calling up the national levy. After all, he could count on aid from his brother. Or
could he?

* It is possible that the Hunald in question was a namesake of the old duke,
but not the same person.

By Pepin's will Aquitaine had been divided between the two brothers, so that each would have an equal interest in keeping the territory under control. And in fact Carloman also took action when the news of the revolt reached him. He moved westward with an army, while Charles marched southwest. The two brothers met at a place called Duasdives, near the northern border of Aquitaine, to discuss joint operations. But it was a case of the king of France's marching up the hill and then marching down again. Charles and Carloman could never agree about anything. We do not know what the brothers said to each other at that meeting, but from the result we can deduce the anger, the insults, the recriminations. Carloman sulkily refused to cooperate; he turned around and went home, washing his hands of the whole Aquitanian affair.

Carloman's behavior was not altogether unwelcome to Charles. It gave him an opportunity to try his mettle, and it placed on his brother the onus of desertion in time of war. If he defeated the Aquitanians without help, his own army would gain in self-confidence and he could count on future support from many of his brother's nobles who would consider Carloman's action shameful. That was important to Charles, for even this early in his reign he was certainly thinking of himself as the natural ruler of the entire kingdom. He was not prepared—not yet, anyway—to go to war with his brother, but from the first he tried to undermine Carloman's authority. There are hints of this scattered all through our sources. Although we know how he disliked his brother, it is possible for us to conceive of his acting in this way quite honestly, without rancor, out of the sincere conviction that unity of the Frankish kingdom was inevitable and absolutely necessary. He could not help seeing his brother's weakness. Carloman had not the personal strength to unify Frankland, and Charles did have it. To recognize the truth of this was for Charles not vanity but objectivity.

With a fine unconcern, then, for the smallness of his forces, Charles marched boldly on into Aquitaine. His brother, his mother and his older advisers may have thought him reckless, but Charles knew what he was about. He had fought in Aquitaine only the year before; he had seen that the duchy was exhausted by years of warfare; and he knew that he would have the powerful support of the Church against Hunald, a monk who had broken his vows. He would have had the support of the Church anyhow, for was he not the champion of Christendom, to whom the pope looked for protection against all his enemies? The lower clergy would persuade the people to welcome the Franks as saviors; the bishops who controlled vast ecclesiastical estates would withhold their support from the Aquitanian rebel. Already at the beginning of his career Charles was making use of an institution that was ultimately to become one of his strongest weapons. It is no paradox that he could make use of the Church and at the same time believe with sincerity and fervor in its divine mission.

As he had expected, the rebellion collapsed as soon as he made a show of force. Hunald fled before him without offering resistance; the war turned into the pursuit of a fugitive. Charles took the opportunity to make a little geopolitical capital. He marched to the Dordogne, near to where that river flows into the Garonne and also near Bordeaux, which was even then a great city, the seat of an archepiscopate and a busy port. The Garonne formed the border between Aquitaine and Vasconia (Gascony). Here, since his soldiers had had no fighting to occupy them, Charles put them to work building the fort of Frontiacum, whose purpose was less to secure Aquitaine than to intimidate the Duke of Vasconia. Again, in this first campaign, Charles was establishing a principle he was to follow for the remainder of his reign—to fortify his borders and use the forts and their garrisons either for security or as jumping-off points for future conquests. Almost instinctively he made use of the old Roman imperial idea. He was an empire builder from the first.

Hunald had taken refuge with Duke Lupus of Vasconia. Charles forced the duke to surrender the fugitive and perhaps to accept some kind of vague subject status. Hunald's further fate we do not know, although it became the subject of much speculation and many romantic legends. According to one such legend, he fled to the court of King Desiderius at Pavia. In all probability his real fate was confinement in a monastery—which would mean only a resumption of the life he had led until the year before. Commitment to a monastery for life was Charles's usual way of disposing of defeated rulers. Frankish mores had come a long way since the days when a Clovis split the skulls of his enemies with one quick blow of his ax.

Within two short months Charles had smashed all possibility of further resistance in Aquitaine, and henceforth that rich province was to be an integral part of the Frankish kingdom. He now turned north again toward "home"—that is, toward Aachen which in future years he was to make his capital. No doubt he paused on his way to pray at the tomb of St. Martin in Tours; he is likely to have sought the intercession of this most famous saint of Frankland to help him with the weighty decisions he now had to make. His personal situation and the broader political relationships of his realm constituted one problem in his thoughts, and in actuality. The core of that problem was his wife Himiltrude.

Charles was sufficiently religious to regard with some awe the church doctrine that marriage was an inviolable sacrament, even though that doctrine was as yet by no means firmly established. But he was unwilling to apply it to himself. His natural heartiness rebelled against asceticism in any form. All his life he was unable to keep the regular church fasts, and was liberal in granting dispensations from them to those who suffered a similar weakness. To the very last he persisted in eating roast meats against the advice of his doctors. He was equally unwilling to discipline his other appetites. Continence was repugnant to him; although he admired it in others, he himself never remained unmarried for more than a few months at a time. And, as we shall see, he later treated the sexual adventures of his daughters with remarkable leniency. He might pray for forgiveness for his sinful nature, but he never let scruples stand in the way of his frank enjoyment of the things of the flesh.

Now his marriage no longer gave him pleasure. He could not love the mother of a deformed son. And for all her noble birth, Himiltrude was not a princess. Charles was approaching the age of thirty and beginning to think along dynastic lines.

There was, as a matter of fact, a princess in the offing, and Charles's mother Bertrada had been talking to him about her. These days, when Bertrada talked, Charles listened. Since her husband's death Queen Mother Bertrada had occupied a unique position in the Frankish world. A strong-willed woman—so much so that King Pepin had sometimes chafed at her energy—she was now the sole tangible representative of the formerly united Frankish kingdom. The Franks had been ruled by queens in the past, and it is scarcely surprising that they still tended to look to this woman for guidance of their affairs, rather than to her untried sons.

Charles's first biographer, Einhard, makes quite a point of Charles's filial respect for his mother; he says that only on one occasion—which we shall soon come to—was there ever disagreement between them. We need not take Einhard at his word; possibly he protests too much and was answering contemporary gossip which pictured the relationship between mother and son as often strained. But there can be no doubt that for the first two years of his reign Charles was inclined to defer to his mother. Those were years when the pope in the salutation of his letters to the rulers of the Franks addressed Bertrada, his *religiosa filia*, first and the two kings second. They were years that a modern French historian (Joseph Calmette) has called *l'heure de Berthe*. Bertrada's hour was brief and it ended with a thunderclap that shook Europe and infuriated a not-yet-old woman who was trying to do her best for her sons. It was not her fault if her well-conceived policy was better adapted to the last years of King Pepin's reign than to the first years of Charles's. She wanted to hold what Pepin had won by making peace with all neighbors. Charles was not yet old enough to be conservative.

Bertrada's plan, as she presented it to Charles, fell in with his desires. She had a princess in mind for him. If he consented to a royal marriage, he could divorce Himiltrude for reasons of state. Personal motives need never be mentioned. The marriage Bertrada wished to arrange had such obvious advantages that no one could possibly protest, least of all Himiltrude. It was, in fact, a dynastic marriage of the sort that in later centuries enabled the Hapsburgs to acquire enormous power without fighting for it.

The princess in question was a daughter of Desiderius, now king of the Lombards. She is nameless; in the one source where she is called Desiderata, which would be our modern Désirée, the word is most probably not meant as a name. And she is also characterless; the sources tell us nothing at all about her. But who she was is less important than what she was—a *Lombard* princess. It was quite clear to Charles, as soon as his mother proposed this match to him, that it involved a virtual alliance between Lombardy and his half of Frankland. That might be interpreted as a return to the pro-Lombard policy of his late uncle, Carloman the Elder, and as such a step backward. But it was also a thrust at his brother Carloman, since Carloman's lands bordered directly on the Lombard kingdom of Italy, while Charles's territory nowhere touched Italy.

More important for Charles than these considerations was the relationship that such a marriage would establish with a cousin of his, Duke Tassilo of Bavaria. Here we have the beginning of the great drama that was to be played out over the next quarter of a century

between Charles and Tassilo—a drama replete with frame-ups, show
trials, public confessions and promises of repentance that have a peculiarly twentieth-century air.

Tassilo was the same age as Charles. His father was Odilo, Duke of
Bavaria, long an enemy and ultimately a subjugated vassal of Charles's
father. His mother, Hiltrud, was a daughter of Charles Martel and a
sister of King Pepin. From the first Pepin had taken a kindly interest
in his sister's son. After the death of Odilo he set the six-year-old boy
on the threatened ducal throne and supported his claim by force of
arms. He gave the duchy to Tassilo as a benefice; that is to say, Tassilo "held" Bavaria for him as one of his great vassals. This was a
significant event—one of the earliest examples in history of the essentially feudal relation of vassalship, which was to dominate the
medieval period. Benefices, or fiefs, existed as a mode of landholding;
it had become customary for kings to pay their officials by grants of
land which they held in return for their services and which were carefully distinguished from alodial or freehold land. Now this system
of landholding was being transferred from the private to the public
sphere.

Tassilo's mother held the reins of government during his childhood. But by the time he was fifteen he was already ruling independently in Bavaria, and Pepin thought it wise to impress on the boy his
vassal status. Tassilo was ordered to come to the Frankish national
assembly at Compiègne, and there he "commended" himself to his
lord by laying his hands in Pepin's. "He swore countless oaths," say
the annals, "touching the relics of the martyrs with his hand and
promising King Pepin *and his sons Charles and Carloman* that he
would be faithfully subject to them like a vassal to his lord. . . . He
swore by the bones of St. Denis, St. Germain and St. Martin that
he would keep these oaths all the days of his life." The Bavarian
chiefs who came with him took similar oaths.

Young Tassilo's pride was probably stung at having to swear homage to a boy his own age and to an even younger cousin. As he grew
older he became increasingly independent and awaited only the opportunity provided by Pepin's involvement in Aquitaine to free himself completely from his uncle's overlordship. Only six years after
those solemn oaths he made the final break by refusing to provide
troops for Pepin's Aquitanian campaign. Thereafter he dated his decrees by the years of his own reign and signed himself "prince." Pepin,

on his deathbed, tacitly acknowledged the independence of Bavaria by making no provision for dividing it between Charles and Carloman.

Duke Tassilo's Bavaria was a wedge of Christianity thrusting out to the north, east and south into the territories of pagan tribal groups. To the north lay the unconverted Bohemians, to the east the great Pannonian plain which was occupied by the cousins and successors of the Huns, the Mongol Avars. On the south Bavaria extended into present-day Austria, and throughout the eighth century Bavarian missionaries went south and east to convert the Slavic Carantani, the inhabitants of what is now known as Carinthia. The center from which these missionaries worked was Salzburg, where St. Boniface had established a diocese in 739 A.D. Here at Salzburg Bishop Vergil, known as Vergil the Geometer for his eminence in science, lived, worked and founded a cathedral. Vergil was active in politics as well as religion and was one of Duke Tassilo's most trusted advisers.

Even as a boy Tassilo had been praised by the bishops of his duchy for being "though of tender age" superior to his predecessors "in understanding of the Holy Scriptures." His religious bent was as pronounced as that of Charles, and he made use of eminent members of the clergy in much the same way that Charles did, and for much the same reasons—because they were literate, intelligent, capable and honest, and because he was a firm believer in the unity of Church and State. Throughout his reign as ostensible duke and actual king of Bavaria he made large gifts to the Church, founded monasteries and fostered missionary activities. In fact, his attitudes and conduct strongly resembled those of his cousin Charles. Whether this was due to the Carolingian family nature, the outlook of youth or the needs of the age, we cannot at this distance say. Tassilo has been charged with indecisiveness, which was certainly never one of Charles's faults. But perhaps the Bavarian duke's hesitations, backtrackings and spasmodic efforts to defend his independence against Charles can be accounted for less by his character than by his situation. The fact was that Tassilo had far fewer resources at his disposal than Charles. His country was small and less wealthy in men and materials than the Frankish kingdom. Shrewd diplomacy, false promises and powerful allies were his best weapons.

Bavaria's natural ally, geographically, was Lombardy. Tassilo's need for a firm alliance with Lombardy became acute in 763, after his outright break with King Pepin. Before Pepin extricated himself from the interminable Aquitanian war, Tassilo made sure of Lombardy by marrying a daughter of Desiderius, the Lombard king. Her name was Liutperga, and like Desiderius' other daughters she seems to have been a high-spirited, intelligent and forceful person, rather resembling Queen Bertrada.

Tassilo's marriage was one excellent reason for Charles to consent when his mother proposed that he marry Liutperga's sister. At one stroke, then, his brother Carloman would be surrounded by a happy family from which he was excluded: Charles on his west and north, Tassilo on his east and Desiderius on his southern border. Hemmed in by these allies unfriendly to him, Carloman would be helpless if the day came when Charles should decide to take all of Frankland for himself.

But marriage to a Lombard princess would not only make an ally of Tassilo. It was also a stroke aimed against Tassilo, and to Charles this was probably the more important aspect of the matter. That Bertrada was as aware of this as Charles is indicated by her ingenious proposal to make the tie with Lombardy doubly strong by arranging a double marriage. Charles would marry a daughter of Desiderius and Charles's only sister, Gisla, would be married to Adelchis, Desiderius' son and coruler.

All the negotiations were carried out by Bertrada herself. She set out on a pilgrimage to Rome and visited en route all the important personages in the drama that was shaping up: Carloman, Tassilo, Desiderius and Pope Stephen.* From Carloman she extracted a promise of reconciliation with Charles. She persuaded Tassilo that the projected marriages were not dangerous to him. She then went on to Rome and made the rounds of the churches like any pious pilgrim. With the pope she discussed ecclesiastical problems but carefully concealed her plans for a Franco-Lombard alliance. The pope complained to her—as he was always complaining to any Frankish emissary who would listen—that the Lombards were still threatening him and had defaulted on their promises to restore a number of Italian cities.

Bertrada listened sympathetically but without the slightest intention of doing anything to help. Intermittent warfare between the papacy and the Lombards had been going on for years, with the Lombards encroaching on the pope's rights and the pope crying woe and

---

* This is Stephen III. Stephen II, the pope who visited Frankland, died in 757 A.D.

damnation. The truth was that the popes themselves were partly to blame for their own predicament. They committed the folly of borrowing money from the Lombards, who were already entering the profession of moneylending with which they were to become identified in the later Middle Ages. When the popes were unable to pay back the loans, the Lombard king would seize one or another of the cities claimed by the papacy. Then—as Bertrada for all her piety viewed the situation—the Franks were expected to come with an army and save the popes from the consequences of their own folly.

Bearing the blessings and good wishes of the unsuspecting pope, Bertrada left Rome and returned to the court of Desiderius at Pavia. When she recrossed the Alps into Frankland, she brought back with her the Lombard princess. She had driven a hard bargain and got something for Pope Stephen after all. In return for the alliance with Frankland, which he badly wanted, Desiderius returned to the papacy some of the cities he had seized. This would, Bertrada thought, placate the pope when he found out what had happened.

Stephen was kept in the dark for so long that when he finally heard the first vague rumors of the Franco-Lombard *rapprochement* he did not even know whether the bride was intended for Carloman or Charles. But he was terrified; he felt that he had been betrayed by his only supporters and was being left to the mercy of Desiderius. At once he dashed off a letter to both kings of the Franks so savage and immoderate in its language that the recipients must have been stunned. The pope wrote at great length, peppering his text with quotations from the Scriptures:

"It has come to our knowledge that Desiderius, the king of the Lombards, wishes to marry his daughter to one of you. This would not be a marriage but disgraceful concubinage. . . . Would it not be the height of madness if the glorious race of the Franks and your own noble royal dynasty were to be contaminated by a union with the perfidious and stinking Lombards, who cannot even be called a nation and who have brought leprosy into the world? 'For what fellowship have righteousness and iniquity or what communion hath light with darkness?' By the will of God and your father's choice you already are united in lawful marriage with beautiful wives of your own Frankish race, and to these wives you ought to cleave in love. . . . How can you make common cause with those treacherous Lombards who are always in arms against the Church of God and who have invaded our province of Rome? Do you recall your father's reply to the Emperor, Constantine Copronymus, who asked that your noble sister, Gisla, be given in marriage to his son? Your father declared that your family did not marry foreigners and would do nothing against the will of the apostolic see. . . ."

The letter ended in a burst of grandiloquence and thunderous threats:

"Wherefore Saint Peter himself, prince of the apostles, guardian of the keys to the Kingdom of Heaven . . . by all that is lawful, by the living and true God, by the ineffable divine omnipotence, by the tremendous day of judgment, by all the divine mysteries . . . adjures you not to wed the daughter of Desiderius or to give your noble sister Gisla in wedlock to his son. . . .

"Should either of you do what is unpleasing to God and have the temerity to ignore our remonstrances, let him be warned that by the authority of Saint Peter he is then under the ban of the most fearful anathema, an alien from the kingdom of God and doomed with the devil and his most wicked ministers and all impious men to the eternal flames. But he who shall obey and observe this exhortation shall be worthy of divine illumination, with all heavenly blessings, and of exaltation to everlasting glory with all the saints and elect of God."

This letter, insolent in tone though it was, considering the true power-relationships between the Frankish kings and the Holy See, reveals nevertheless a shrewd insight on the part of the pope into the emotions and family feelings of the Frankish royal house. Pope Stephen twice refers to Gisla, as if aware that Charles's thirteen-year-old sister was the darling of the entire family. Unusually well educated for a girl, bright and of independent mind, she was the particular favorite of Charles. And even though thirteen was not an unusual age for marriage (as the pope's letter itself indicates, a betrothal in infancy would have been quite in order), the thought of sending this charming child off to a foreign country and an unknown husband was abhorrent to Charles. Just as in later years he was unwilling to give up his daughters, he was now reluctant to let his sister marry abroad.

In his letter Stephen deliberately played on the racial theme, and his references to Gisla by implication stressed the dangers to her of a foreign marriage. Those dangers were only too well known to Charles, who was as well instructed in history as any man of his age. Without a following of her own to protect her, a princess was subject to the whims of her husband and might well suffer the fate of that Queen Galsuenda of Spain whom her Frankish husband, King Chilperic, had strangled in her bed at the instigation of his mistress. Charles would remember, too, the story of the daughter of Theoderic, the Gothic king of Italy. She had married the son of Gaiseric, the king of the Vandals. Gaiseric suspected her of trying to poison his son and sent her back to her father with her nose and ears cut off!

It was, moreover, far easier for the mother to marry off the daughter than for the brother to see his sister leave. The pope's warning fell in with Charles's own reluctance, and he decided at once to fulfill only half the bargain, in spite of the solemn oaths that his mother and the Frankish noblemen with her had sworn at the court of Desiderius. Charles refused to send Gisla off to Lombardy to marry Adelchis.* However, he went ahead with his own new marriage. What the fate of Himiltrude was we do not know. Her son, Pepin the Hunchback, remained at court, and we shall find later that he was not without bitter feelings toward his father.

The Lombard princess, Charles's new wife, is unfortunately a complete cipher. All that the sources tell us about her is that she remained queen of Frankland for a year and then was sent packing. Charles divorced her and returned her to her father as if she were an unwanted bolt of silk. We can only guess at the reasons. Undoubtedly political developments now obscure to us played a part, and undoubtedly these were only a pretext. For if Charles had liked her he would have kept her, as in later years he kept Fastrada, whom everybody at his court seems to have disliked and of whom even his official biographer speaks disrespectfully.

All his life Charles remained singularly domestic and even uxorious.

* Because Gisla entered a convent in her girlhood, most historians have assumed that she felt a religious vocation and was unwilling to marry. In view of her age and the customs of the time, this is improbable. The decision was obviously Charles's. Gisla later became Abbess of Chelles, but this was a post of honor at which she could work or not as she pleased. Her piety and religious duties did not keep her from being a frequent guest at Charles's secular court, where she was a great favorite. Charles provided her with so much wealth in worldly goods that we later find her making grants of land to the monastery of St. Denis.

He was deeply attached to his wives, but he chose them for himself.
The only two wives he divorced—and he was to have many more—
were those who had been picked for him by his parents: Himiltrude
and the Lombard princess. In his private as in his public life he was
unwilling to be bound by the past. This is not to say that his temper
was revolutionary—far from it. He felt toward the past and the traditions of his people the same sort of piety that he showed all his life
toward his mother. That is (in this sense we must interpret Einhard's
remark on their good relations), he respected both so long as they did
not interfere with what he believed to be his mission. More and more
as he matured he was becoming conscious of what that mission was:
to bring light into darkness. In the history of the Franks and of all
Western Europe since the collapse of Roman power, darkness had
been gaining the ascendancy. Charles meant to check and turn history as if it were an aurochs, and he approached his task like the practiced hunter he was—fearlessly and with zest, making no unnecessary
innovations but taking advantage of the lie of the land and the nature
of the beast.

The repudiation of the Lombard princess was a decisive act that
sent history hastily retreating in another direction. It involved the
reversal of the entire peace policy which had been the subject of so
many delicate and involved negotiations during the past two years. It
was a direct affront to Desiderius and to the conservative, pro-Lombard faction at the Frankish court which had given so much trouble
to Charles's father Pepin in years past. It abruptly ended the influence of Queen Mother Bertrada on public policy and announced
to all that Charles intended to rule the kingdom in his own name.
Henceforth Bertrada would remain the honored widow, a welcome
member of the family circle but entirely without power.

Bertrada did not take this demotion without protest, and many
Frankish nobles sided with her. Instead of placating them, Charles
further scandalized the court by remarrying immediately. His new
bride was a child no older than his sister Gisla, a Swabian girl of
noble birth who was either twelve or thirteen years old at the time
of the marriage.

Divorce and remarriage involved the honor of other persons as well
as Charles himself, and Charles was by no means surrounded by
sycophants. His twenty-year-old cousin Adalhard, the son of Pepin's
brother Bernhard, was one of the Frankish chiefs who had taken the

usual oaths at the court of Desiderius—that the princess would not be repudiated and that the terms of the alliance would be faithfully observed. In a fury, Adalhard came before Charles and told him he refused to serve the new queen whose relationship with Charles was, as far as he was concerned, adulterous. After this outburst Adalhard left the court and retired to a monastery. His father, Uncle Bernhard, took a less idealistic view of marital ties. Bernhard stayed with Charles, and we find him two years later leading an army corps for Charles against the Lombards.

In spite of all this opposition the choice of Hildigard—this was the child bride's name—was a good one for Charles. The years of his marriage with her were clearly the happiest of his life. All contemporaries praise her beauty, mildness and charitableness. In her short life she gave Charles five daughters and four sons. It was she who surrounded him with that bustling family atmosphere that he loved, that provided the proper counterpoint to the necessarily grim business of ruling an expanding domain. Charles's love for Hildigard, as well as his tendency toward uxoriousness, are documented by all the details that have come down to us about his private life. It was the subject of much gossip at his court, as an amusing story by the Monk of St. Gall implies.

Charles had promised a vacant bishopric to a certain young man. He then ordered the young man to hide behind the curtain close to his throne. There he would hear, the king remarked ironically, how many others would be willing to help him achieve that high office.

"Now when the courtiers who were always on the watch for death or accidents heard of the bishop's death . . . they began to plead for the bishopric through the king's intimates. But Charles clung to his intention and rejected all of them; he would not break his word to his young friend, he said. At last Queen Hildigard . . . came in person to ask for the bishopric for one of her own clerks. The king said he would not and could not deny her anything, but he still wanted to keep his word to the little clerk. But the queen, as is the way with women, thought a woman's opinion and wish was of more importance than the decisions of men. She hid her rising anger, lowered her strong voice almost to a whisper, and with caressing gestures tried to soften the king's firm mind. 'My lord and king,' she said, 'why do you want to give the bishopric to such a boy, who will only ruin it? I beg you, my sweet sire, my glory and my refuge, give it to your faithful servant, my own clerk.' Then the young man, who had been listening close to the king's chair, embraced the king through the curtain, exclaiming, 'My lord and king, stand fast and do not let anyone take away from you the power that God has given you.' "

In this case Charles resisted Hildigard's plea. But in how many others?

Some historians have thought that Carloman also objected to Charles's divorce, since at this time the brief reconciliation between the brothers disintegrated. But it seems more likely that Carloman felt in a stronger position vis-à-vis Charles now that Charles had recklessly thrown away the friendship of both his allies, Tassilo and Desiderius. At any rate, throughout the year 771 there were ugly rumors of an impending war between the two brothers, although we are never told which of the brothers was threatening aggression.

The only person who could have been pleased by the repudiation of Desiderius' daughter was the pope, who, however, had other things to think about. He was involved in the aftereffects of a conspiracy which he had exploited to play off Desiderius and Carloman against each other. The details of the affair make dreary reading today; but the upshot of it was that the pope sacrificed his two chief advisers, Christophorus and Sergius, and so offended Carloman that the young king was on the point of marching to Rome to punish him. Carloman's threats against Stephen seem to have sharpened the latent conflict between Charles and Carloman. By the end of the year everyone was expecting a civil war between the two brothers—one more in the long, ghastly series of fraternal wars with which the whole history of the Franks was tainted because there existed no settled principle of hereditary succession.

Then, on December 4, 771, Carloman suddenly died.

Luck is as essential to greatness as will or intelligence. If a great man fails to have luck we never know it, because his greatness remains only potential. In Charles's case the death of Carloman was sheer bounty handed to him by fortune. He probably would have become ruler of all Frankland anyway; but his subsequent greatness would have had a different quality if he had won his kingdom in a bloody civil war that ended with the killing or tonsuring of a brother. This fact was clearly perceived by a contemporary, Bishop Cathwulf, who in a letter to Charles congratulates him for having been raised to power over the whole kingdom *"sine sanguinis effusione"*—without the spilling of blood.

Charles knew how to make the most of his luck. He must have had some warning that Carloman was seriously ill, for just a few days before his death Carloman had presented the monastery of St. Denis with two villas in order—so the deed reads—"to prepare himself to appear before the Supreme Judge." Since Carloman had two sons who might be considered his heirs, Charles acted with the greatest possible speed. He immediately entered Carloman's kingdom and called a formal assembly of the great nobles to ratify his taking over his brother's domain. Presumably he had already been in touch with Abbot Fulrad, Carloman's chief adviser, and Fulrad came forward at once—along with a number of other lords lay and ecclesiastical—to swear fealty to Charles. The transfer of power was effected smoothly, without any haggling over the rights of the matter. Most of the lords must have recognized that it would be best for the kingdom to be reunited.

Carloman's wife, Gerberga, fled the country with her two sons. Accompanied by a number of nobles, she made her way to Lombardy, where she was welcomed by King Desiderius, for whom by now, after the shameful divorce of his daughter, any enemy of Charles was a good friend. Presumably the nobles who accompanied her were those "bad advisers" of Carloman who are repeatedly accused in the chronicles of having fomented trouble between the brothers. One of them is mentioned by name; he is the same Duke Otker who eighteen years before had guided Pope Stephen II into Frankland on that memorable occasion when Stephen crowned and anointed Pepin, Charles and Carloman.

When Charles heard of Gerberga's flight he exclaimed angrily that it was foolish, that she had nothing at all to fear from him. No doubt he meant this, in the sense that he certainly would not have behaved as had some of his predecessors among the kings of the Franks—notably Clothar and Childebert, who stabbed to death their own brother's sons, boys of ten and seven. But he would have sent Gerberga's sons to monasteries for the rest of their lives, whereas if they grew to manhood in some foreign country there was always the chance that they might someday recover their heritage.

Overnight, Charles had become the strongest ruler in Western Europe. The caution, hesitancy and slowness to move that had marked the first three years of his rule now came to an abrupt end. As soon as he had control over both halves of the kingdom he swung promptly into action, carrying out a plan that was perhaps formed partly by events but of which he was certainly conscious in its broad outlines. He turned his attention first to the east, then to the south and then to the west. To the north of his realm lay the open ocean, and there was no need for him to be concerned with that quarter until nearly the end of his reign. By then he would have accomplished within his own borders the great civilizing work on which his fame chiefly rests.

CHAPTER THREE

Lombards and Saxons

AS SOON as the assembly which had conferred a second crown on him was over and the funeral services for his brother duly completed, Charles went to the ancient royal palace of the Merovingians at Attigny on the Aisne to spend his Christmas. This palace, like the other royal villas, was no huge and drafty pile of stone like the fortress-castles of the later Middle Ages. It was built on an adaptation of the Roman plan, with a forecourt like a Roman atrium which led into the large reception hall. There was a great round throne room where the king sat in judgment and held his assemblies and councils. There was a huge dining room, its vast span of roof supported by two rows of columns which divided it into three parts: one for the king and his family, one for the officers of his household, and the third for guests.

Nor was the palace without civilized comforts. Hot and cold water pipes regulated the temperature of the rooms. There were bathrooms, laundries, a gymnasium. Like all the barbarian conquerors, the Franks had swiftly learned to appreciate the material benefits of Gallo-Roman culture. The dwellings of the slaves and serfs outside the high walls of the palace might still be simple huts with thatched roofs, but the nobles lived well and lavishly. Charles, in fact, was not nearly so fond of luxury and comfort as some of the members of his court.

Here at Attigny, while he feasted the many guests who came to congratulate him and to take the oath of loyalty, and while he rested in his own active fashion by leading his guests and household on great hunts in the royal forest of the Ardennes, he had time to dwell on the general picture and to consider the internal strengths and weaknesses of his kingdom.

Charles alone now bore the title *rex francorum*, King of the Franks, but he ruled also over many other nations and tribes who for the time being looked on the Franks as their natural leaders or their natural oppressors. Their roster, at the beginning of his reign as sole king, sounds echoes of that strange period in the history of Western Europe when the barbarian tribes of *Germania* were overcome by a restiveness that lasted for centuries—the period that German scholars call the *Völkerwanderung*, the migration of the peoples. Visigoths, Ostrogoths, Burgundians, Suevi, Franks, Lombards and other Germanic tribes had marched up and down over the ruins of the Roman Empire, carving out kingdoms for themselves. By the time of Charles's grandfather the Visigothic kingdom of Spain and southern Gaul had been smashed by the Arab invasion; but many Goths still lived in Aquitaine and Septimania, and Gothic customs and laws prevailed in these provinces. The Franks themselves had absorbed the Burgundian kingdom of southeast Gaul, but here too Burgundians still lived by their own law. Like all the Germanic conquerors, the Franks permitted every subject to be judged by his own law—the Roman law or the law of some "barbarian" tribe. (Only the Jews were excepted from this provision; they were subject to local law, whether Roman or German, unless they enjoyed the special protection of the king.)

Two large Germanic nations still remained outside Charles's orbit (since, as we have seen, the Bavarians were technically his subjects, although in practice independent). The more important of the two appeared to be the Lombards, who in the sixth century—when the migrations were coming to an end—had moved down into Italy proper. In the days of Tacitus (first century A.D.) their home had been in northern Germany, between the Elbe and the Vistula. There they had been neighbors of the Saxons and apparently good friends with them. From their earliest days they had shown a talent for conquest of smaller neighboring tribes and for intermarriage with their more powerful neighbors. The historian of the Lombards, Paul the Deacon, who was later to be a close friend of Charles and a member of his intimate court circle, tells us of the Lombard king Wacho who married off two of his daughters to kings of the Franks. And the antipathy of the Frankish kings to Lombard princesses appears also to have been an old story, for one of them disliked his Lombard wife so much that he gave her away to a Bavarian prince.

From their original home the Lombards moved southeast into Pannonia, that great province of the Roman Empire (comprising most of present-day Hungary) which was swept over in turn by almost all the barbarian invaders. They entered into an alliance with the Empire, which at this time was experiencing a rejuvenation under Justinian, and helped the imperial general Narses conquer the Goths. Throughout their stay in Pannonia they remained loyal to the Empire and were no doubt partly supported by an imperial subsidy, for the resources of the once prosperous province of Pannonia had long since been exhausted.

The Lombard soldiers who had fought in Italy under Narses had seen something of the wealth and beauty of the peninsula, and when Narses invited them "to leave their miserable fields in Pannonia and take possession of Italy," as Paul the Deacon puts it, they were delighted to obey the summons. Led by King Albuin, who is remembered also for making his wife drink out of a cup made from her father's skull, they marched into Italy. They were accompanied by an army of their old friends, the Saxons, whom Albuin asked to share the fighting and the spoils with them, and by a motley assemblage of other tribesmen—Gepids, Bulgarians, Sarmatians, Pannonians, Swabians, Bavarians and others. The Lombards themselves were apparently not too numerous.

The Lombards occupied the whole of northern Italy and most of the country south of Rome; only parts of the heel and toe of the Italian boot, and an hourglass-shaped strip of territory in central Italy, remained in the hands of the exarchs, the imperial governors at Ravenna. Upon this territory, as we have seen, the Lombards steadily whittled away for two hundred years—from the north, which was the Kingdom of Lombardy proper, and from the south where they had set up two great and sometimes virtually independent duchies, the Duchy of Spoleto and the Duchy of Benevento.

Immediately after the conquest of Italy the Lombards murdered many wealthy Romans and seized their property; they taxed the rest of the Roman subjects one third of the produce of their lands, as was the general custom of the barbarian conquerors. But once the bloodletting and plundering of the invasion period passed, they proved themselves good and on the whole wise rulers. The Lombard historian records with astonishment that violence ceased, people were no longer ambushed, plundered or enslaved, thefts and robberies no longer occurred and everyone could live as he liked without fear or care. The Lombards trimmed their ragged beards, adopted the dress and culture of their Roman subjects and eventually, in the seventh century, were converted from the Arian form of Christianity to Catholicism. This conversion to the religion of the subject population was a fundamental factor in stabilizing their rule. Their Catholicism saved them from the fate of the Arian Goths, who had preceded them as conquerors of Italy and whose dominion had foundered on the religious antagonism between themselves and the Catholic Romans. Although the Lombards repeatedly came into conflict with the pope for political reasons and were never quite so pious as the Franks, they had an essential religious unity with the Romans that enabled them to merge into the population of Italy as easily as the Northmen merged with the French population of Normandy.

The other great Germanic nation that bordered Charles's Frankish kingdom was that of the Saxons. Like the Lombards they were warlike; unlike the Lombards they were far from the influence of Roman culture and had retained their tribal organization as well as their ancient paganism. Moreover, they were still in their original homeland, descendants of those who had remained behind when Angles and Saxons went forth in wave after wave during the sixth century to conquer the island of Britain and either enslave the original inhabitants or drive them across the Channel to what thereafter became known as Brittany. While the Saxons in England were becoming Christianized and civilized, developing in the seventh and eighth centuries one of the highest cultures of the early Middle Ages, the Old Saxons—as the English called them—remained a numerous but disorganized people of pagan "barbarians." They were adventurous—as we have seen, they were willing to join the Lombard army as freebooters—and they possessed a fierce spirit of independence. They could co-operate in war but not in peace. After the conquest of Lombardy the twenty thousand Saxons refused to live under the rule of Lombard kings, although they had brought their families with them, intending to settle in Italy. They fought or bought (with counterfeit coins) their way back across Gaul to their old homes, only to find that the Frankish kings had meanwhile settled other tribes on their abandoned lands. Saxon intransigeance is well depicted in the almost contemporary narrative by Gregory of Tours which describes this incident.

The Suevi who had settled in the Saxon land, says Gregory, "offered the Saxons a third of their land, saying, 'We can live together without interfering with one another.'" Gregory continues:

"But the Saxons were angry at them because they had themselves held this land before, and they were by no means willing to be pacified. Then the Suevi made them a second offer of a half and then of two-thirds, leaving one-third for themselves. And when the Saxons refused this, they offered all their flocks and herds with the land, provided only they would refrain from attacking them. But the Saxons would not agree even to this and demanded battle. And before the battle, thinking that they had the Suevi already as good as slain, they discussed among themselves how they should divide their wives and what each should receive after their defeat. But God's mercy which does justice turned the issue another way. For when they fought there were 26,000 Saxons, of whom 20,000 fell, and of the Suevi 6,000, of whom 480 only were laid low; and the remainder won the victory. The Saxons who were left took oath that they would cut neither beard nor hair until they had taken vengeance on their adversaries. But when they fought again they were defeated with greater loss, and so the war ended."

The story as a whole sounds somewhat improbable, but no more improbable than many of the miracles that Gregory was so fond of relating. Even if Gregory has exaggerated the actual outcome of the battle, or the numbers of men involved, he has painted in true colors the temperament of the Saxons. They exhibited a similar obstinacy in their repeated refusals to submit to the domination of Charles's predecessors. Again and again they had come into conflict with the Franks, and in the sixth century had been compelled to pay an annual tribute of five hundred cows to the Frankish king. But the weak Merovingian kings of the Franks had been unable to hold them to this tribute, and both Charles's grandfather and father had warred with them. Recently, Pepin had launched a punitive expedition across the Rhine and had imposed an annual tribute of three hundred horses on the Westphalian Saxons. Incidentally, this change in the nature of the tribute—from cows to horses—was a sign of the growing importance of cavalry to the Frankish army.

A part of this same spirit of intransigeance was the prevalence among the Saxons of feuding (the feuds of Kentucky mountaineers are offshoots of an ancient tradition). The obligation of a man's kinsmen to avenge him if he were killed was a necessary social protection in a primitive society, and the blood-feud existed among all the early Germanic tribes. It could, however, easily become an instrument of social dissolution, and with Christianization and the rise of kingships, attempts to suppress feuding were inevitable. *Wergeld*, or blood-money (literally "man-money"), was one solution to the problem. Later wergeld was replaced by the concept that murder was a violation of the king's law rather than an offense against the kinsfolk of the murdered man.

The idea underlying wergeld has been much misunderstood. The modern mind recoils from the thought that a man's death can be made good by a payment of money to the relations, as if life could be evaluated in terms of coinage. But to the early and medieval German the compensation in money offered an alternative to the duty of revenge for homicide—a duty which otherwise could involve families in endless feuds. Kinsmen were not bound to accept a money compensation, but there would naturally be strong pressure on them to do so, since neighbors, chiefs and kings were interested in the preservation of general peace. Only Christianity and the growth of strong kings ultimately wiped out the blood-feud, and with it wergeld. Nevertheless, even among the English Saxons it persisted until after the Norman Conquest. In the eighth century it was still very much part of the order of life among the Continental Saxons. Where the institution of wergeld flourished, we can be certain that the society was organized, but not centralized. Wergeld was barbarian but not barbarous, and it passed with the growth of centralization.

Saxon society is indirectly described for us in one of the most remarkable literary documents of the Middle Ages: *Heliand*. The *Heliand* (which means Saviour) is a long poetic narrative of the Gospel story which was written by order of Charles's son, Louis the Pious, around 830 A.D., some twenty-five years after the final conquest and conversion of the Saxons. The poem was frankly intended as a propaganda tract; its purpose was to strengthen the new religion among the Saxons by presenting the Scriptures to them in their own language and in the alliterative verse form familiar to them from their lays and their versified catalogues of kings and heroes. The poet, who was one of the most famous minstrels of his people, had the genius to adapt not only the form but the content to the psychology, the traditions and the social system of the Saxons.

The essential framework of the Passion of Christ could not be changed, of course. But within that framework the poet followed the practice of the medieval artist who clothed saints and apostles in contemporary dress, thereby inadvertently telling us a great deal about his own time. In the *Heliand* Jesus and his apostles are a Saxon liege lord surrounded by his loyal thanes who live by his bounty and are sworn to defend him unto death. The relationship is that of the leader and his band of followers, the *comitatus*, which was described by Tacitus and was still a viable social institution eight centuries later. The greatest of crimes among Anglo-Saxons and Old Saxons was violation of the oath to the leader, betrayal of the lord; and one of the most moving and effective passages in the *Heliand* springs from the poet's deep feeling for this theme of loyalty. After narrating Peter's threefold denial of his Lord, the author of the *Heliand* adds to the Gospel story a passage that is strictly Saxon in spirit:

> Then felt
> Simon Peter sorest sorrow;
> Grief in his heart was grimly graved.
> With woe he remembered the Master's words
> That so short a while since, the Christ had spoken,
> Saying to him: in the sable night
> Ere the cock once crows you will cravenly
> Deny me thrice. Then the thane
> Was stricken by sorrow and silently slunk
> From the midst of men, mournful and sad,
> Regretting his boast and grieving the grave
> Sin on his soul, till a torrent of tears
> Burst from his breast. For this bitter
> Betrayal could not be atoned.

Earlier, when Peter behaves as a proper thane should and strikes off the ear of Malchus, the Saxon poet describes the scene with great gusto:

> Then wrathful and raging
> The fearless fighter stepped to the front,
> Near to his prince, his noble lord.
> His heart beat high; undaunted he drew
> His sword from his side and struck with full might
> At the foremost foe, so that Malchus was maimed
> By the sharp-edged blade. He struck off his ear,
> Slashing the head, slitting the cheek.
> Bright from the gash bubbled the blood,
> Welling from the wound.

Such reveling in battle and bloodshed was not precisely in the spirit of Christ's message, any more than Christ's reproof to Peter was quite in character. The poet makes Christ say of the angels he might call down from heaven that they would be "so skilled in battle that no man could withstand the might of their arms." A far cry, this, from the policy of Bishop Wulfilas, the apostle of the Goths, who in his Gothic translation of the Bible omitted the more warlike books because his people were in any case too fond of fighting. The author of the *Heliand* apparently felt that he could not make his countrymen understand a tame and meek Christ. For this reason he repeatedly insists that Christ's submission to abuse and suffering was necessary, an indispensable part of the sacrifice for the redemption of man. To hammer the point home he resorts to an ingenious variation on the Gospel story: when the soul of Judas Iscariot, who has hanged himself, goes down to hell, Satan learns of the impending crucifixion of Christ. In great alarm he tries to prevent it, for if Christ dies on the cross hell will lose its tenants. He therefore appears to Pilate's wife (wearing a thoroughly Germanic *Tarnhelm* which renders him invisible) and makes her see visions. Disturbed by these hallucinations "in broad daylight," she sends a message to her husband urging him to spare Jesus.

In his desire to present a Christ whom his people could respect, the Saxon poet also ignores Christ's lowly origins. Saxon society was a class society, with a hereditary nobility from whom the chiefs were drawn, and the proud Saxon nobles could not be expected to swear fealty to a heavenly prince who was the son of a churl (the Saxon equivalent of peasant). Therefore the poet emphasizes Christ's descent from the royal house of David. Both Joseph and Mary are "of noble race"; the apostles, too, are noble thanes, *ethilinge*. The two other classes of Saxon society, the free churls and the slaves, are not mentioned.

Geographically, too, Galilee and Palestine were conceived of in native terms. There were no towns of any size in Saxony, and in the *Heliand* the cities are called *burgs*—Rome-burg, Nazareth-burg, and so on. A burg was a wooden building with a great hall, surrounded by a cluster of smaller buildings in which the noblemen, his men and his servants or slaves lived. The whole complex of buildings was protected by a stockade. These stockades were so characteristic of Saxony that two of the three main branches of the Saxons—Westphalians and Eastphalians—took their name from the *falo,* or wooden posts, of which the stockades were built.

A good deal of feasting and heavy drinking went on in the great hall of the burg. Christian writers complain often and bitterly about the Saxon and Anglo-Saxon passion for drink. When drunk, men would revive old quarrels and fall to fighting. To avert general brawls, among the Anglo-Saxons heavy fines were imposed for fighting in the king's hall, and we may assume that similar laws were passed by the Saxon chiefs. (The Saxons had no king; their only political organization was a loose confederation of tribes.) We may also assume that such laws were not very effective.

Quaffing their beer in the great hall of a winter's night, listening to the minstrel—or possibly to the chief himself, for it was no disgrace for a nobleman to be skilled in music—singing songs with blood-stirring alliterative beat about the heroes of old, the Saxons' martial spirit was aroused. They would boast outrageously of their feats on the field of battle and be challenged by their fellows to prove these boasts. Drunken boasts were an obligation, and they would lay reckless plans for the future. And one day the following spring a band of savage fighters would swoop down on a Frankish settlement, burn the church, seize what goods they could carry, and lead the inhabitants away into slavery. Such raids were more or less frequent as the Frankish power waxed or waned.

The raids had been going on intermittently for a long time and would not, in themselves, have been sufficient cause for Charles to lead an army into Saxony. But between Christmas and Easter Charles must have had many long consultations with Abbot Fulrad, who was especially familiar with the half of the kingdom that Charles had recently acquired. It was obvious to both men that a good deal of disaffection existed among the former subjects of Carloman. A campaign against an external enemy would serve admirably to unite the nation and to establish Charles in the eyes of these new subjects as a strong and capable leader. But the campaign must be an easy one, providing booty without too much fighting, and it must be one which the whole country could agree was justified.

The only two potential enemies were the Lombards and the Saxons. Relations with Lombardy had been growing increasingly tense since Charles's divorce of the Lombard princess and Gerberga's flight to Desiderius. Desiderius had engineered a *coup d'état* in the papal court; the papal chancellor, Paul Afiarta, was now his creature. Immediately after the death of Pope Stephen and the election of Hadrian, a Roman aristocrat, as pope (February 1, 772), Desiderius demanded that the new pope crown and anoint the sons of Carloman as kings of the Franks. Charles, he argued, was a usurper who had unjustly robbed his brother's children of their rightful heritage. The petition was accompanied by open threats.

Hadrian was younger, tougher and braver than Pope Stephen, who had allowed control of his own officials to slip out of his hands and who not long ago had hypocritically written to Bertrada and Charles that his "son Desiderius" had saved his life from plotters. Hadrian refused even to negotiate with the Lombard king until Desiderius had fulfilled his obligation to the Holy See—namely, return of the disputed cities of the Exarchate. And when Paul Afiarta insolently threatened to "hog-tie" the Holy Father and bring him to Pavia unless he agreed to talk with Desiderius, Hadrian acted with decision. He expelled the pro-Lombard party from the seats of power in the Vatican, arrested Paul himself and sent him to Archbishop Leo of Ravenna, ordering Leo to exile the former papal chancellor to Constantinople. Leo disobeyed his instructions and had Paul put to death. Hadrian protested his innocence, but he was of course blamed for this execution. Archbishop Leo seems to have wanted to make trouble for Hadrian, and he succeeded.

The execution of Paul Afiarta outraged Desiderius. Accompanied by Gerberga and her sons, and by Otker and the other Frankish nobles who had fled with Gerberga, he led an army against Rome. Hadrian, making a hopeless show of defiance, fortified Rome. Meanwhile he sent messengers to Charles by sea, since the Lombards blocked all land routes. But the Lombards would reach Rome long before the Franks could have sent help, even if they intended to, and Hadrian had to rely in the end on his spiritual authority. Surprisingly, it proved a sufficient defense. Perhaps Desiderius himself would have braved the pope's threats of eternal damnation. But his followers did not dare, and Desiderius had to turn back from Rome. He continued to hold the cities of Faenza, Ferrara and Commacchio, which he had seized earlier.

This incident apparently prompted the members of the pro-Frankish faction among the Lombards to come out into the open. For there was such a faction, just as there was a pro-Lombard faction among the Franks. Augino, Raidolf, Ansahel, Gotefrid and other powerful Lombard nobles fled from Lombardy, abandoning all of their considerable property, and made their way to Charles. The exact date of their break with Desiderius is not given, but we do know that their property was confiscated by Desiderius in November 772. Perhaps some of them came before Charles as early as Easter, while he was at Heristal, to offer him their allegiance and their aid in overthrowing Desiderius.

Charles could only welcome such signs of shakiness in the whole structure of the Lombard kingdom. It was a great temptation to him to take up the Lombards' offer at once. War with Lombardy seemed inevitable anyhow. The time appeared ripe, and Charles was young, self-confident and temperamentally inclined to go straight to the point. But wiser counsels prevailed, and it is a good guess that Charles leaned heavily on the wisest counselor in his entourage, his old tutor and good friend, Abbot Fulrad. Fulrad had been avidly collecting land for his monastery of St. Denis for many years; we have already had occasion to refer more than once to some of the many grants of property to St. Denis from Pepin, Carloman and Charles. Such eagerness to add to the wealth of his monastery was quite in harmony with his worldly outlook on political life. Where politics and piety conflicted, piety yielded. Perhaps, too, Fulrad the ecclesiastic was less worried than Charles about the perils of the Bishop of Rome. A certain independence from Rome on the part of the Frankish Church was, after all, desirable. In this opinion Fulrad was ably supported by Charles's chancellor, Itherius, who had served Pepin in the same post. After all, these ecclesiastical advisers could point out, Pope Stephen had taken an offensive and authoritarian position on Charles's marriage to the Lombard princess the year before. It might well be the prudent course to let this new pope cool his heels. Hadrian must be given to understand that the Frankish king was his master, not his bodyguard. If Charles was at first a little shocked by such cynical advice, he quickly came to appreciate its wisdom.

Charles hardly needed the recommendations of Uncle Bernhard and his other "generals" in regard to the military arguments against invading Italy at once. He understood the difficulties of crossing the Alps with an army. He knew quite well that his army might be a little rusty, as well as faction-ridden, and that a war with Lombardy would not be the brief and easy campaign he needed. To declare war on the Lombards immediately, so soon after his brother's death, might well encourage revolts and treachery among Carloman's former subjects. He must first incorporate those subjects into his army. There were hundreds of counts, thousands of men, who had never fought under him.

The military and political arguments for staying close to home happened to coincide with his personal wishes, for at the moment he did not care for a long separation from Hildigard, who was already pregnant.

Charles therefore chose the statesmanlike course that Fulrad and Itherius advised. He delayed coming to any decision on Italy. Meanwhile, he issued order for the annual assembly of the Franks to be held at Worms, just south of Saxony. Here, in the ancient Celtic and Roman city, the former capital of the Burgundian kingdom, where the heroic and bloody lays of the Nibelungs were even then being sung, Charles reported to his army the latest news from Saxony. He told his men the story of the Anglo-Saxon missionary with the beautiful English name of Leafwine (Liafwin) who had ventured into the heart of Saxon territory while the Saxons were holding their own annual assembly and their pagan religious rites. Saxon worship of Thunar, Woden and Saxnot took place in a sacred grove and centered around the Irminsul, a great column or possibly an ancient tree trunk representing Yggdrasil, the tree that supported the universe. Around the Irminsul stood a group of buildings which housed the priests and the treasures of gold and silver that had been offered as tributes to the gods.

Leafwine, arrayed in resplendent ecclesiastical vestments, came to the sacred grove, interrupted the Saxons' worship and harangued them, urging them to abandon their idols and accept baptism. The outraged Saxons nearly killed him, but there were some who were close enough to Christianity or sufficiently scrupulous about the Germanic code of hospitality to speak up for him. One elderly Saxon named Buto reportedly said: "Ambassadors from the Northmen, the Slavs and the Frisians have often come among us. We received them in peace, heard what they had to say, and gave them presents in parting. Do you want to kill this man, who is an ambassador from a great god?"

The Saxons had great respect for Buto, and Leafwine was allowed to leave unharmed, in spite of his blunt threats that a great king was

coming to punish them for their hidebound heathenism. But shortly
afterward the Saxons revenged the insult to their idol. They ravaged
the Frisian territory around Deventer, which had been the center of
Leafwine's missionary work, and burned the church there.

Charles could easily make a good atrocity story out of this raid,
which in fact did not differ at all from the hundreds of others that
had taken place in the past. The story of the unfriendly reception
given Leafwine and the subsequent Saxon raid enabled Charles to
present his training campaign as a holy war.* The sword must prepare the way for the Word of Christ. There was no hypocrisy here.
Charles believed that heathens ought to be converted for their own
good. The thought that men could live in pagan darkness, outside the
embrace of the Church, filled him with genuine horror. Yet he never
insisted on conversion when pagans submitted without protest to his
political rule. Thus he permitted the Slavs who became his tributaries
to remain unconverted.

Leafwine not only provided a *cause célèbre* for the campaign; he
also turned Charles's thoughts toward the Irminsul. Charles remembered the tales he had heard about Boniface, the missionary who had
once dropped holy oil upon Charles's own head.** Perhaps on that
occasion, if Charles had dared to speak to the old man whose greatness and saintliness were well recognized even during his lifetime, he
had asked Boniface to tell him the story of the Oak of Geismar.
Now, at any rate, he resolved to imitate the saint's example.

The Franks assembled at Worms voted for war against the Saxons,
and Charles promptly led his army to the Saxon fortress of Eresburg,
near Paderborn. He took the fortress without too much difficulty.
From there he marched straight to the Irminsul, near the headwaters
of the Lippe. He moved so quickly that the Saxons had no time to
defend the sacred grove or to remove its treasures, which Charles was

---

* Actually the general situation on the border was the cause of a war which
could have been started at any time. This is indicated by Einhard's statement:
"There were causes which could disturb the peace any day, for our borders and
theirs meet almost everywhere in the open plain, except for a few places where
either large forests or mountain ranges separate both territories by a distinct frontier. Consequently, *on both sides* killings, robbery and burning went on incessantly. The Franks were therefore so irritated that they decided to abandon
retaliation and begin an open war against them [the Saxons]." (*Vita Karoli*,
ch. 7.)

** See page 24.

able to distribute among his men. Right at the start the first prerequisite for a successful campaign had been established: he had obtained booty.

The Irminsul itself and the buildings around it must have been structures of considerable solidity, for Charles spent three days leveling everything to the ground. During this work a miracle took place which convinced everyone in the army that the war was indeed favored by God. It was midsummer, very hot, and there was no water available. The men's thirst was intensified by exertion and by the dust rising from the wreckage. "One day," the annals tell us, "when everyone was taking the usual noonday rest, by God's will a tremendous volume of water suddenly gushed forth into the bed of a stream on the hill near the camp, so that there was enough for the whole army." An intermittent spring or geyser in the vicinity is presumably the explanation for this auspicious event.

After the destruction of the Irminsul, Charles advanced through Saxony to the River Weser, ravaging the countryside as he went. The campaign in fact turned out to be nothing more than a retaliatory raid against the Saxons. Neither side wanted a pitched battle; Charles was saving the strength of his army for next year, and the Saxons felt that they were no match for him. When Charles reached the Weser the Saxons entered negotiations, accepted his conditions (we are not told what they were) and gave him twelve hostages as evidence of good faith. Probably Charles exacted no more than a promise that the raids on Frankish territory would cease. He felt that he had accomplished the purpose of his campaign in laying waste the countryside. No more could be done without serious fighting, and Charles did not want to risk his gains at this point. He quickly returned to Frankland and was back with Hildigard in Heristal by the middle of October.

He had reason to hasten, for it was probably at this time that Hildigard bore him a son—his first child whom he could look upon as a legitimate heir.* The boy was named Charles—after the great-grandfather, Charles Martel, of course; but the affection Charles felt for his child bride was also expressed in his giving his own name to their son. Young Charles remained always Charles's favorite; he seems to have taken after his father and great-grandfather in character, and to have

---

* The exact date of this son's birth cannot be ascertained. There is, however, indirect evidence that young Charles was born in October 772.

inherited from his mother the quality of precocious maturity, for we find him in his thirteenth year entrusted by Charles with the command of an army.

In the light of the deadly determination with which Charles later pursued the conquest of Saxony, this first campaign seems to have been almost flippant, a preliminary skirmish or a phony war preceding the bloodier clash. It was serious enough, of course, for the Saxons whose farms were devastated; but the horrors to come were to be on so vast a scale that a few burned buildings and trampled grain fields would not signify. The great battles, the mass executions and mass deportations were still in the future.

Charles may have been satisfied with what he had accomplished. But he could feel only chagrin when he learned that Cousin Tassilo of Bavaria had been far more successful in a similar enterprise. While Charles was busy punishing a few Saxon farmers, Tassilo had at one blow, by a combination of force and political stratagem, conquered the heathen Slavs of Carinthia. Tassilo had found in Bishop Vergil of Salzburg a man of Boniface's stature to be apostle to the Slavs; and under Vergil's leadership the Christianization of Carinthia was going forward with remarkable speed. Charles might well ask himself whether Slavs were more susceptible than Saxons to the divine truths, or whether Tassilo was more efficient than himself.

And as if to claim his reward for this signal achievement, Tassilo promptly sent his son Theodo to Rome to be baptized by the pope in person. This was a rather singular act on the part of Desiderius' son-in-law at a time when Desiderius was virtually at war with the pope. Evidently Tassilo meant to keep on good terms with both sides and perhaps gain some advantage by mediation. For the present, Charles could only fume, and perhaps content himself with the thought that someday he himself might be able to profit by whatever power and territory Tassilo acquired now.

Charles had moved his family and court to the royal estate at Thionville on the Moselle when Peter, the envoy from Pope Hadrian, arrived from Marseilles. Almost at the same time Lombard envoys from Desiderius came before Charles to present their master's case against the pope. Sitting as if in judgment upon the two parties, Charles could taste for the first time the vast new power that had come to him with the acquisition of Carloman's kingdom. He grandly informed the envoys that he would reserve his decision, and sent them back home in suspense. Then he called a council of his chiefs to place the matter before them. The consultations gave him the opportunity to sound out the extent of pro-Lombard sentiment among his nobles, and he must have been dismayed to discover how strong it still was. Evidently he would have to placate this faction and demonstrate clearly that war was being forced on him.

The question of Frankish honor was involved, he could point out. His father Pepin had made an unequivocal promise to the late Pope Stephen that the cities of the Exarchate of Ravenna would be handed over to the Church. The Lombard rulers had nullified that promise and were now busy depriving the Church of its remaining cities in Italy and even threatening to take Rome itself. But since there was still some question as to the rightful ownership of the disputed cities and the lands around them, and since these cities were by now well integrated into the Lombard kingdom, he would nevertheless attempt negotiation. He proposed to offer Desiderius fourteen thousand gold solidi in compensation, if the Lombard king would surrender the disputed lands to the pope.

It was a large sum, but a war would undoubtedly be costlier. The nobles, who would have to help foot the bill, agreed. The offer was made.

Desiderius might have remembered that a similar offer had been made to his predecessor, Aistulf, by Charles's father Pepin twenty years before. And he might also have remembered the Lombard defeat and humiliation that followed on Aistulf's rejection of the offer. But whether because he was blinded by hatred, or considered Charles weaker than his father had been, or counted too heavily on internal opposition to Charles within Frankland, Desiderius behaved with the same foolish self-confidence as his predecessor. Very likely he was misled by Duke Otker and Carloman's widow Gerberga; exiles have a way of overestimating the strength of their own party back home. Whatever the reason, Desiderius refused the offer, as Charles no doubt had hoped he would. Charles promptly called the national assembly to meet at Geneva, near the Lombard border and in the heart of what had recently been Carloman's kingdom.

We possess a contemporary account of these national assemblies written by Charles's cousin Adalhard, who had probably around this time recovered from his fit of idealistic petulance over Charles's mor-

als and returned to the court to become one of Charles's first counselors and closest associates. Adalhard later wrote an account of the
Frankish administrative system which has been passed down to us in
a copy made by Archbishop Hincmar of Reims.

There were actually two assemblies annually, one in the spring and
one in the fall. The fall session was attended only by men of the
highest rank, who thus formed a kind of executive committee of the
general assembly. These men were called *seniores*, the word from
which the later *seigneur* was derived. Adalhard says of them:

"They discussed the affairs of the following year, so far as this was
necessary and possible, or matters of the current year which it was
essential to take care of at once. . . . Once the seniores had conferred
upon future ways and means and come to decisions, they kept these
decisions secret from all until the next general assembly, so that one
might think nothing had been discussed and decided. Thus, if the
matter was something concerning the internal or external affairs of
the kingdom which might have been hindered or prevented by the
knowledge of certain persons, or made more difficult by cunning rancor, secrecy averted such a mishap. If the situation at the next general
assembly required, in order for example to satisfy the other seniores
or to reassure the people or evoke the people's enthusiastic approval,
such matters would be brought up as though they had never been
discussed previously."

At the general assembly—still known as the Marchfield, although
since King Pepin's time it was usually held in May to make it easier
for foreign ambassadors to attend—the king laid his proposals in writing before the chiefs. The chiefs took these *capitula* which the king
had drawn up "under the inspiration of God," or else which had been
specially recommended to him in the time between assemblies. They
deliberated one or more days on these capitularies, according to their
importance. During their deliberations, palace messengers took their
questions to the king and carried back the answers. "No one not belonging to their council was allowed to come near their meeting place
until each point had been submitted to the ears and eyes of the glorious prince and all had concurred in what he with his God-given wisdom had determined. Thus one, two or more capitularies were dealt
with until by God's grace all necessary matters were settled."

"While the seniores were thus conducting their debates in the absence of the king, he himself mingled with the rest of the assembly,

receiving their presents, greeting prominent men, chatting with those he seldom saw, showing a sympathetic interest toward elderly men, relaxing with the younger men and devoting similar attentions to the clergy. But if the chiefs sitting in council desired his presence, he would go in to them and stay with them as long as they wished. They felt perfectly free to tell him their opinion on everything and inform him of their conclusions as well as their friendly differences."

Secular and ecclesiastical lords met separately, but could meet together if the nature of their business called for it.

"The king also considered it his task to ask each whether anything ought to be reported from his particular district. It was not only a right, but a duty of all to make inquiries, during the interval between assemblies, into matters that had taken place inside the kingdom and abroad. They were bound to seek information from fellow subjects and foreigners, friends as well as enemies, though they need not examine too closely the source of their information. The king wanted to know whether in any province or corner of the kingdom any unrest prevailed, what the reason for such unrest was, whether the people were complaining and whether there had been any disturbances which the general assembly ought to attend to, and so on. . . . In all cases where danger threatened the kingdom, he wished to know the causes and motives."

The procedures outlined by Adalhard give us a picture of an enlightened monarchy. Consultation was important, and the king made use of the national assemblies to persuade as well as command, but the final decision rested with him alone. While the description quoted above probably refers to the later portion of Charles's reign, when his administrative system was fully worked out, the basic elements had already existed under the rule of Charles's father and were certainly in operation by the beginning of the Lombard war. We can therefore take it for granted that the real decisions had been made by the "Senate" the previous fall, after the conclusion of the Saxon campaign, but had been kept secret until the general assembly in the spring. Now, at Geneva, "mingling with the rest of the assembly," Charles presented the problems of the papacy and Lombardy to his secular and ecclesiastical lords "as though they had never been discussed previously."

The assembly consented, though with reluctance, to a declaration of war, and the plan of campaign was laid out. Charles insisted on preparations for wintering the army in Italy—an unusual and expensive step which must have met with considerable grumbling, for summer campaigns were the rule. But Charles did not mean to underestimate his enemy.

The army was divided into two corps, one of which was placed under the command of Uncle Bernhard and sent over the Great St. Bernard (possibly this Alpine pass received its name from the expedition, since in Charles's time it was known as Mount Jupiter). Charles himself led the other corps through the pass of Mount Cenis. Desiderius had drawn up an army to defend the exit from the pass, and Charles, before attacking, made one more concession to the pro-Lombard party among his nobles. He repeated his offer of a money compensation in return for the surrender of the cities. It was again refused; Desiderius relied on the strength of the fortifications he had built, and apparently interpreted the offer as a sign of weakness.

A frontal attack where only a small part of their forces could be employed would undoubtedly have shaken the Franks severely. But while the Frankish army went into camp and negotiations were in progress, Charles outflanked the enemy by precisely the same device that his father had successfully used during the last Frankish invasion of Italy. He sent a picked body of troops over the winding, little-known mountain paths. At the same time the army of Bernhard was coming up behind the fortifications that Desiderius had built on the very spot where Pepin had once destroyed Aistulf's defense works. Desiderius, unsure of his hold over his troops, did not dare to risk a battle under such unfavorable conditions. He retreated and Charles, "by the aid of the Lord and the intercession of the holy apostle Peter," as the annals put it, marched unopposed into Italy.

As with so many of Charles's military feats, legend quickly surrounded this apparently miraculous triumph. It was said that a Lombard minstrel entered Charles's camp singing an offer to guide Charles into Italy over ways "where no spear would be hurled, nor shield raised against him." As a reward he asked for all the land roundabout as far as the blast of his horn could be heard. After carrying out his part of the bargain, he ascended a mountain peak, blew with all his might on his horn, and then went down into the valleys, asking everyone he met, "Have you heard the sound of a horn?" When anyone said yes, the minstrel gave him a box on the ear and cried out, "Then you belong to me."

The implication of Lombard treason underlying this story is un-

doubtedly its kernel of historical truth. Treason continued to plague
Desiderius on his retreat. Several divisions of his army simply disbanded and went home, and it was with greatly shrunken forces that
the Lombard king reached the safety of Pavia's almost impregnable
walls. His son, Adelchis, whom Bertrada three years before had tried
to betroth to Charles's sister Gisla, retreated with a portion of the
army to Verona, which was reputed to be fortified even more strongly
than Pavia. With Adelchis went Gerberga and her sons, and Duke
Otker, the Frank whose position and personality are a tantalizing
mystery—for he was considered important enough to be mentioned
repeatedly, though with exasperating brevity, in all the annals of the
time.

Charles closely pursued the withdrawing Lombards. Nowhere, until he reached the walls of Pavia, did he encounter any opposition.
The rapidity and ease with which towns and districts capitulated to
him gave him much food for thought. It was evidently a matter of
indifference to the Italians, who formed the bulk of the population,
whether they were ruled by Lombards or Franks. And the Lombard
chiefs also did not seem to care whether their overlord was Desiderius
or Charles, so long as they were left substantially in control of their
local affairs. Italy was already suffering from those intense local jeal-
ousies which were to keep the country divided for almost exactly the
next thousand years.

Up to this point in his career Charles had not questioned the wisdom of his father's policies. In all his activities he had been complet-
ing or repeating his father's work: finishing the conquest of Aquitaine,
taking up the taming of the Saxons where Pepin had left off. This
present invasion of Lombardy was, down even to the details, a repetition of Pepin's invasions of 754 and 756.

But now Charles began to see Pepin's treatment of the Lombards
as a combination of timorousness and sentimentality. Timorousness
in the face of the pro-Lombard party among the Franks; sentimentality in that Pepin himself shared some of the feelings of that party.
Perhaps Pepin had never forgotten the time during his boyhood when
he was sent to the Lombard court and formally "adopted as a son" by
the Lombard king Liutprand—a ceremony intended to stress the abid-
ing ties between Lombardy and Frankland. At any rate, Pepin had
twice held Lombardy in the palm of his hand, and twice he had accepted a ransom and returned across the Alps.

Charles had no such sentimental feelings about the Lombards. If anything, his experience with the Lombard princess had embittered him toward them. Why should he not seize his opportunity? Lombardy, perhaps all of Italy, was his for the taking. If he did not take it now, three Frankish campaigns would have been wasted.

When he reached Pavia with his army he made one attempt to capture the city by assault, saw at once that it was too strong, and settled down for a siege. A veritable Frankish town arose outside the walls of Pavia that winter. To protect his camp and at the same time to seal off the city from any possible supplies, Charles had ramparts thrown up parallel to the city walls. He had a chapel built, and sent home for Hildigard. She, although in an advanced stage of pregnancy, made the difficult journey across the Alps to Pavia and there, some time during the winter, gave birth to a girl who was baptized Adalhaid.

CHAPTER FOUR

Rome

AKING and general with a shade less of greatness might have remained before the walls of Pavia, conducting the siege operations. That is what Charles's father would have done. But in military, though not always in administrative matters, Charles knew how to delegate authority, and as yet he had not been disappointed in his underlings. His uncle and his other commanders were perfectly competent to hold the blockade around Pavia until the fortress-city was starved into submission. Meanwhile Charles did not want to waste time in inactivity, for he was always eager to keep moving and get things done. In a later year, when for once no campaign was being waged, we find the annals recording that "in order not to give the appearance that he was spending his time idly the king took ship up the Main to his palace at Salz in Germany and then returned by the same river to Worms." His was the restlessness of a man who all his life was confronted by a multitude of tasks simultaneously.

Winter in northern Italy was not too cold for military operations, as it would have been in northern Germany. With a boldness that sprang both from self-assurance and a shrewd sense of how divided and unstable the Lombard kingdom really was, Charles left the major part of his army at Pavia and marched eastward across Italy, down the valley of the Po. On the way he captured or received the surrender of a number of Lombard towns, but his destination was Verona. He was bent on capturing Adelchis, Gerberga and Otker, who were the focal points of Lombard resistance.

The stoutly walled city of Verona promptly surrendered to Charles; there is no mention of any battle. Perhaps the very smallness of Charles's force convinced the Lombards that it was hopeless to con-

79

tinue the struggle. If he could parade through enemy territory with only a fraction of his army, the whole of northern Italy must already have capitulated to him. Perhaps Pavia had already fallen. There was no way for Adelchis to communicate with his father Desiderius at Pavia, and probably he could not trust his own Lombard nobles. Verona was doomed to fall sooner or later. If Adelchis wanted to avoid the tonsure—which by seldom-violated custom would have made him forever ineligible to wear the crown—he would have to escape before the Franks circled the city.

Duke Otker and Gerberga, with Carloman's sons, created some diversion by coming out of the city and throwing themselves upon the mercy of Charles. Meanwhile, Adelchis slipped out of Verona. He made his way to Constantinople, hoping that time and the Eastern emperor would provide him with the means to regain his kingdom. He was well received. The emperor, Constantine V, conferred on him the title of patrician—significantly enough, the same title already borne by Charles. With the Frankish power now extended into Italy, Constantine was willing to forget past enmities with the Lombards. Adelchis might be useful to him as a counterpoise to Charles.

The fate of Gerberga, of her sons and of Duke Otker is not known. There is some reason to believe that Otker may have been taken back into Charles's favor, for legend makes him one of Roland's companions.

Desiderius now remained the only formidable enemy of Charles in northern Italy, and Desiderius was shut up within the walls of Pavia. With the rest of Lombardy in Frankish hands, the Lombard king could expect no relief from outside. The siege could take care of itself; it still did not require Charles's presence. And Charles, maturing rapidly in statesmanship, was eager to settle his peace aims before the war came to an end. The ultimate fate of Lombardy, and the disposition of the imperial territory which had formerly constituted the Exarchate of Ravenna, could be decided only in consultation with the pope. Pope Hadrian, moreover, was showing more independence than Charles liked—a posture that was to become quite habitual throughout his long relationship with Charles. Hadrian had already taken advantage of the confusion of war in Lombardy to make territorial acquisitions. He had persuaded the inhabitants of the Duchy of Spoleto, which lay to the east of the Roman Duchy, to desert Desiderius, place themselves under papal protection and swear allegiance to himself personally. Then, with the consent of the Spoletans, he had appointed a nobleman named Hildebrand as their duke.

As conqueror of Lombardy, Charles already felt that the Duchy of Spoleto was rightfully his. It would be wise, he thought, to negotiate with the pope while the fate of Lombardy still apparently hung in the balance, since until the fall of Pavia he could avoid making any definite commitments. He therefore decided to go to Rome while the siege of Pavia was still in progress.

Others in his entourage were as eager to go to Rome as Charles himself. Rome with its great basilicas, with its relics of innumerable saints and martyrs, where were to be found the tomb of St. Peter himself and a stone bearing the imprint of the Lord's foot, was now above all a great center of worship, to which streamed pilgrims from as far away as the land of the Angles. The many bishops and ordinary priests who had accompanied Charles's army into Italy longed to celebrate Easter in the mother-city of the Church.

Charles, too, was certainly stirred by the prospect of receiving Communion in the basilica of St. Peter itself; he was after all a man who dutifully attended Mass every morning. But for him Rome was also far more than the hallowed heart of Christendom. Charles, whose domains included a thoroughly Romanized Gaul, was not so unsophisticated as the Anglo-Saxon invaders of Britain who had been awed by the stone remains of Roman buildings, so that they spoke of them as "the wondrous works of giants." But even he had never seen such a massing of mighty monuments and stone buildings as still remained in Rome. The city had fallen on evil times since the days of Caesar; its population had shrunk and the great edifices of antiquity were falling into decay, already being used as a tempting source of marble and lime for the lesser structures of medieval builders or repairers. But as yet the Roman buildings were not being systematically quarried, as they were to be during the Renaissance. What Charles saw was still Rome the imperial, the mighty shadow of the greatest city in the world; the city whose language he spoke as easily and naturally as he spoke his native German, whose laws, customs, architecture and traditions had defined the greater part of the kingdom he ruled. The great empire whose capital was now Constantinople and whose language was Greek still called itself the Roman Empire, and so great was Roman prestige still that its inhabitants were infuriated when they were addressed as Greeks, not Romans. In Rome the Colosseum still stood, was still in use, and "while the Colosseum stands, Rome shall stand," the tradition held.

All who could be spared from Pavia were eager to make the pilgrimage to Rome. Bishops and abbots, dukes and counts formed the large and brilliant retinue that accompanied Charles, Hildigard and their two young children to the Eternal City at the end of the March of 774. There was a sizable guard of soldiery, of course, but no trouble was encountered on the road south.

Charles had not bothered to inform Hadrian in advance of his impending visit—a subtle hint that he was not accountable to the pope for his actions. "When Pope Hadrian heard that the King of the Franks was coming," the *Life of Hadrian* tells us, "he was almost overwhelmed by amazement." Very likely Hadrian felt considerable chagrin also, for Charles was behaving like a ruler come to inspect one of his cities, not like one head of state paying a formal visit to another. Nevertheless, Hadrian made the best of a bad situation. He prepared a welcome designed to impress Charles both with his cordiality and with his dual power as spiritual head of the Church and temporal lord of the Roman duchy.

The entire officialdom of Rome was sent ahead to Nova, thirty miles from the city, to greet Charles with waving banners. And when the Franks came within one mile of the city they found the militia lined up to salute them, and the school children waving branches of palm and olive and singing hymns of praise in honor of the King of the Franks. Priests advanced bearing the cross before them, as was traditionally done only on the reception of an exarch or a patrician of the Romans—the latter of which Charles was.

When he saw the cross Charles dismounted, and his nobles followed his example. On foot, as his father had come out to greet Pope Stephen twenty years before, Charles made his way to the steps of St. Peter's basilica. At the top of the steps Pope Hadrian awaited him. And Charles, overcome perhaps by the same feelings of awe and piety that had moved him as an eleven-year-old boy when he went to meet Pope Stephen, profoundly affected by the solemnity of his reception and the sight of this church which was the goal of all devout pilgrims, fell to his knees and kissed each step as he ascended. But then, as if to demonstrate to the throng that this act of abasement was in honor of St. Peter himself and not of his earthly representative, Charles seized the pope's right hand as soon as he reached the top

and unceremoniously pulled Hadrian along into the basilica—as if to
say, "Come, show your lord and master around his property."

With the pope at his side, Charles entered through one of the
three bronze doors, crossed the vast atrium and went into the basilica
proper. As they appeared the assembled clergy shouted, "Blessed be
he who comes in the name of the Lord!" Hadrian made an effort to
recover the mastery of the situation. He led Charles and his followers
down to the holy of holies, the tomb of St. Peter, and there all fell to
their knees and prayed. And for the moment Charles was sufficiently
overcome to ask the pope's permission to enter Rome (St. Peter's was
outside the walls of Rome), there to worship at the various churches.
So at least Hadrian's official biographer tells the story; perhaps the
request was in fact put somewhat less humbly.

Next day was Easter Sunday, and the pope again sent all his officials
to conduct the king and his retinue, with the greatest ceremony, to
Mass in the church now known as Santa Maria Maggiore. Here
Charles was shown the Holy Crib, even as it is shown to pilgrims
today. The ancient basilica has since been much rebuilt, but the
nave with its Greek marble columns and the mosaics on the architrave
can still be seen as Charles saw them that Easter of 774 A.D.

Mass was followed by a banquet at the Lateran at which, no doubt,
matters of a secular nature were touched on. But the following day
the round of religious ceremonies was resumed. Hadrian was shrewd-
ly bent on using to the full the power of his religious influence over
the Franks. The papal biographer, who is our chief source of information, does not tell us how Charles spent the intervening time. But
he must have gone sight-seeing as would any other visitor to Rome.
He would certainly see the great tomb of another Hadrian—the Roman emperor. He would be shown the towering obelisk in Nero's
Circus (actually built by Caligula) where St. Peter was crucified. Perhaps he went to watch a bullfight in the Colosseum.

Amid the ceremony and the sight-seeing, the feasting and the en-
tertainment, a good deal of serious discussion of political and religious questions went forward. Charles kept Chancellor Itherius close
by his side; he knew he needed the older man's prudence to check-
rein his own enthusiasm. For Charles was falling under the spell
of Hadrian's personality as well as the spell of Rome. Hadrian, ele-
gant and personable in appearance, came from a long line of the
highest aristocracy of Rome. His uncle, who was responsible for his

upbringing after the early deaths of his father and mother, had held the high offices of consul—even in the eighth century there were still consuls at Rome—and *dux*. Hadrian himself had risen rapidly in the Church, distinguishing himself by his charity and asceticism, and had been elected pope with singular unanimity. At once adroit and forceful, friendly in his relations with people and severe in defense of church doctrine or ecclesiastical rights, he had come to the papacy at an unusually early age—probably about fifty—and was determined to make his pontificate a triumphant one for the Church.

Charles was conscious that he was engaged in a subtle political duel with Hadrian, but at the same time he felt a strong personal liking for this Roman nobleman. In fact, on this visit to Rome there sprang up a friendship between the two men that was destined to last more than twenty years and to survive a number of spells of strained relations between the papacy and the Frankish court.

The duel with Hadrian concerned the exact limits of the "patrimony of St. Peter" and the role of the Frankish and papal powers in Italy. Hadrian's aim was to obtain sufficient territory from Charles to form a substantial state, a Roman duchy capable of defending itself. As long as the Lombards had ruled Italy, Hadrian and his predecessors had been able to appeal to the Franks for aid. But to whom, he asked with disarming bluntness, could he now appeal against Charles himself? Even if Charles had only the friendliest feelings toward the Papal See, what guarantee was there that Charles's successors would be equally co-operative? St. Peter must be given the wherewithal to stand alone in a hostile world.

Charles was not at all inclined to further these ambitions. He seriously doubted whether temporal power ought to be linked so intimately with spiritual power—except where the temporal power was his. His conception of the relationship between the papacy and the Frankish kingship differed widely from Hadrian's, for he was beginning to see the papacy as the spiritual arm of the Frankish state. The thought was not yet fully matured in his mind; only many years later was he to formulate it precisely in a letter to Hadrian's successor: "It is my duty, by the grace of God, to defend the Church of Christ against the assaults of pagans or the ravages of infidels which may threaten her from without. . . . It is your duty, most holy father, like Moses to lift up your hands in prayer to God for the success of my arms. . . ." As yet Charles would not have ventured to lecture a pope on his duty, or to suggest that the Church was an adjunct to the Frankish monarchy. But he was much disturbed by Hadrian's claims and particularly by Hadrian's assumption of power in the Duchy of Spoleto.

Yet Charles wanted to be generous. The warmth of his reception in Rome, the intellectual kinship he felt with Hadrian, and his natural piety, combined to produce the grand and dramatic scene that took place on the Wednesday following Easter Sunday. On that day, in a solemn ceremony in St. Peter's basilica, Charles presented Hadrian with a new donation as confirmation of his father's earlier gift to Peter's earthly representative.

The text of this document has been lost. But its phrases must have been highly ambiguous, for Charles and Hadrian subsequently interpreted it in widely differing senses. According to the papal biographer, Charles granted the pope the entire Exarchate of Ravenna, the provinces of Venetia and Istria, the Duchies of Spoleto and Benevento, and the island of Corsica—that is to say, virtually all of Italy except Lombardy proper. The biographer exaggerated, of course, for Hadrian himself, in his many letters to Charles, never laid claim to so vast a patrimony. But Hadrian was undoubtedly deceived. Perhaps, seeing Charles's rapt expression as he knelt before the altar and as he devoutly lifted the copies of the Gospels lying on the body of St. Peter in order to deposit beneath them the writ of donation, Hadrian could not suspect that Charles meant to deceive him. At least, Hadrian thought, his possession of the Duchy of Spoleto was being confirmed, and the cities of the Exarchate which the Lombards had taken would now be restored to him. Surely his bitter enemy, Archbishop Leo of Ravenna, who was ruling the capital of the former Exarchate like an independent sovereign, would now be confounded. Surely his most excellent son Charles would be as generous in deed as he was in word.

But Charles could not keep his word. Hitherto he had been a military leader, but the hot, refined, forcing atmosphere of Rome rapidly developed the latent statesman and diplomat in Charles. Although he could not yet have grasped fully the ramifications of Italian policy, he sensed that he must not let the pope become a great power in Italy. To offset Lombardy, it had been logical for Frankland to strengthen the papacy. But now Charles himself would be Lombardy, and his interests became those of his newly acquired territory. This was no time for sentiment. Even as he made his promises to the pope, Charles could see what his next steps must be. He would gently detach, by negotiation, the entire Duchy of Spoleto from the possession of the pope. Hildebrand, the new Duke of Spoleto, had already had his hair cut Roman fashion, as a sign of his submission to the pope. But once Pavia fell and Charles held all the northern part of the Lombard kingdom, Hildebrand would understand where the true power lay. As for Ravenna, the pope's rival there, Archbishop Leo, could also be useful. By playing off Leo against Hadrian, Charles could see to it that neither acquired too much territory or influence.

In the ensuing months Charles successfully carried out this policy. Each successive stage of the pope's disappointment can be read in his increasingly anxious letters to Charles during the next two years. Finally Hadrian complains that the subjection of the Lombards has done him no good at all; none of the promises has been fulfilled and he has even lost some of Pepin's gifts to St. Peter. The Archbishop of Ravenna has seized many cities of the Exarchate and claims that he has received authority from Charles to do so. "It is being said that the king no longer loves the Holy Father," Hadrian writes piteously.

For the present, however, all was harmony. Charles was quite willing to promote those closer ties between the Frankish Church and Rome which Boniface had advocated; and to assist the king in this mutually advantageous task the pope presented him with a copy of the collected canons of the Roman Church. This was more than a gesture; its importance must not be underestimated. Church law as embodied in these canons expressed the spirit of Roman jurisprudence. Henceforth the principles of Roman law, which was far more suited to the needs of empire than tribal Germanic law, would be able to spread, through the Church, into parts of Frankland and Germany that had never been touched by Roman civilization. In accepting the canons from Hadrian and introducing them into Frankland, Charles was fulfilling his historic mission to fuse the disparate traditions of Roman and Teuton into a European culture. In his own person he represented at once the raw metals and the end product of the alloy.

Charles had already determined to annex Lombardy to his Frankish kingdom. It was probably Hadrian who suggested to him the novel method of annexation which he adopted. It was a method without precedent in Frankish history, but one peculiarly suited to the problem of governing two countries separated by the imposing barrier of the Alps: the device of a personal union under one ruler such as, in modern times, has successfully united the scattered dominions of the British Empire.

With Hadrian's blessings, Charles returned to the siege of Pavia. That city, wasted by plague and famine, held out a little more than another month and then capitulated. Desiderius emerged from the walls that had sheltered him and held him prisoner for more than half a year, and promptly disappeared within the walls of a Frankish monastery, where he spent the remainder of his life. His wife Ansa was sent to Frankland with him, and they were accompanied by one of their daughters. Whether she was Charles's former wife, as seems likely, we have no way of knowing. The contemporary annals are tantalizingly uninformative about these personal dramas. Charles's troubles with the family of Desiderius were, however, by no means over. For years afterward the Lombard king's other two daughters incited their husbands, Duke Tassilo of Bavaria and Duke Arichis of Benevento, to conspire against Charles.

When Pavia threw open its gates and Charles marched into the city at the head of his Franks, two hundred years of independent Lombard rule in Italy came to an end. But the kingdom of the Lombards itself did not die, for Charles now took the step suggested by Hadrian and had himself proclaimed king. Henceforth he styled himself *Rex Francorum et Langobardorum*, King of the Franks and of the Lombards. It was as the successor to Desiderius that he accepted the homage of the Lombard dukes and counts who came hastening to Pavia to take the oath of fealty. For the present he left the structure of the kingdom intact, although he might have learned from his experience in Aquitaine that at least a sprinkling of Frankish counts among the native rulers was indispensable.

Taking the crown of Lombardy was an enormously profitable venture for Charles. Instead of contenting himself with a part of the Lombard treasure, with a ransom in gold and silver, as his father had done, Charles had seized all of Desiderius' hoard—and it must have been considerable, since the annals make special mention of it. Moreover, he automatically succeeded to all the royal domains that Desiderius had owned. Italy had a long tradition of taxation, and Charles could collect the revenues of cities whose commerce with the Eastern

Empire still brought them a prosperity that few towns in Frankland enjoyed. This access of wealth strengthened Charles's hand when he dealt with the greater nobles of his own kingdom. It enabled him to check the feudalistic tendency toward independence on the part of "the barons" which soon after his own day was almost to destroy the power of national kings. It also enabled him to keep an army in the field far longer than was customary, and to do so without stripping the Church of its lands as his grandfather had been compelled to do.

Only one of the Lombard dukes refused to pay homage to Charles as King of the Lombards. This was Arichis of Benevento, whose duchy occupied almost the entire southern part of Italy. As the brother-in-law of Adelchis, Arichis could be expected to help in any attempt that the son of Desiderius might make to regain his inheritance. An independent Lombard duchy the size of Benevento endangered Charles's whole position in Italy, and Charles would probably have marched promptly south with his well-rested army—even though it had been under arms for such an unusual length of time— if he had not received a series of sad tidings from Frankland.

Part of the bad news was personal. He had sent his infant daughter, Adalhaid, back to Frankland, perhaps because he was afraid to expose her to the plagues that were sweeping through Pavia and to the dangerous Italian climate in summer. This decision proved unfortunate, for the baby did not survive the journey. Although in those times infant mortality was common, Charles was deeply affected. He ordered that the baby daughter be buried in the chapel of his ancestor, St. Arnulf, at Metz, and nine years later he requested his friend Paul the Deacon to compose a suitable epitaph in verse for her gravestone.

The other news was of a sort that Charles was to receive frequently in years to come. A king could not remain far from home without inviting trouble—rebellion of lately conquered subjects, or foreign invasion. The latest difficulty was a combination of rebellion and invasion. Word had trickled across the fluid borders to Saxony that Charles was far away across the Alps with the bulk of the Frankish army. The Saxons, eager to avenge their humiliation of two years before, had poured south into the land of the Hessians, killing and burning. The inhabitants fled into the fortified places, abandoning their lands and houses to pillage. The church at Fritzlar, which had been consecrated by Boniface himself, was robbed of its relics and its silver cross, and the Saxons attempted to set fire to it. They failed because, so the annals tell us, "two youths in white garments appeared and protected the church against fire."

When word of this Saxon uprising reached Charles he decided at once to let Italian affairs rest for the time being. He had already spent nine months in Italy and was eager to return home. And an invasion of Frankish territory could not be countenanced.

It was midsummer now, and crossing the Alps with an army was therefore no great problem. Charles himself did not hurry, but he sent four columns ahead to fall on the Saxons before they realized that the Frankish army was back. His men moved so fast that they took the Saxons completely by surprise. As Charles had expected, they encountered no organized army, only bands of raiders. His columns fought a number of sharp skirmishes with a numerically inferior enemy and advanced into Saxony, where they burned and plundered and then retired into Frankland before the end of the year. It was the old pattern of raids and counterraids that had marked the history of Franks and Saxons for hundreds of years.

But Charles was not so content as his father and grandfather had been with the repetition of this old pattern. No peaceful construction in the potentially fertile and prosperous region of the northern Rhineland was possible so long as the interminable Saxon raids continued. Charles fretted over the destruction of property, the burning of crops and buildings, the damage to churches, the waste of time, energy and money on punitive expeditions that accomplished nothing of permanent value. He could not, of course, foresee the vast waste and destruction that would result from his attempt to put an end to the situation. Peaceful penetration of Saxony by Christian missionaries was beginning to show results, but Charles was unwilling to wait for the effect of a slow process of conversion. As he saw it, Christianization of the Saxons was essential to permanent pacification of the country. And the Saxons were a stubborn people who would not submit to Christianity unless they had first been subdued by force.

CHAPTER FIVE

Frankland

CHARLES pondered the problem of the Saxons during the fall and winter of 774-775. Meanwhile he moved about Austrasia, Francia and Neustria, the three principal provinces that formed the heartland of the old Frankish kingdom, gathering into his hands the reins that had slackened somewhat during his absence in Italy. He stayed for a considerable time at Quierzy, near Paris, where his father had made the grant of the Exarchate of Ravenna to Pope Stephen.

At this period of his reign Charles had no fixed capital; twenty years were to pass before he settled permanently in Aachen. He had palaces on many of his estates, and the royal progress around his domains was both a necessity and a pleasure. He could hunt in different royal forests; he kept in touch with his subjects and dispensed justice among them; and by moving he was also effecting economies, for the heavy expense of maintaining the court was thus distributed among the various royal estates. In a country of poor roads, where the best highways were still those built by the Romans, it was easier to bring people to the source of supplies than to bring supplies to the people. And traveling around as he did, Charles became aware of the state of the roads. One of his earliest and most important reforms was to launch a road-building program. Moreover, he enforced the traditional law that the people bordering a road were responsible for its upkeep.

Bridges were needed everywhere, he discovered, and he promoted their construction by a system of private enterprise. Builders of new bridges were given the right to charge tolls for the use of them, and on the other hand skilled bridge workmen were exempted from such tolls. At the same time Charles forbade the abuses that were already creeping into the system of toll bridges. No one must be made to cross a bridge solely in order for the owner of the toll right to collect his toll. If a stream could be forded, it was the privilege of the traveler to decide whether or not he wished to use the bridge.

By the time Charles set up his permanent capital at Aachen the roads had been so far improved that it was possible to provide supplies for both the court and the "civil service" that Charles had meanwhile developed.

The royal estates called "vills" were complex agricultural settlements dominated by a manor house or palace. Such palaces were located at Attigny, Compiègne, Düren, Frankfurt, Heristal, Ingelheim, Liége, Thionville, Worms and many other places besides Aachen. Charles was precise to the point of pedantry about the details of estate management. He insisted on an annual inventory, and one such inventory by his *missi*, or royal commissioners, has fortunately survived. It gives us a remarkable picture of life on a royal estate and of the quality of country life in general in the eighth century.

The imperial estate of Asnapium contained a three-room house built of stone in the best manner. The entire house was surrounded by balconies and had eleven "apartments for women." This phrase does not mean that the women were confined to their rooms like oriental wives; there is ample evidence that in Charles's day the women mingled with the men in the three great halls. Rather, the women's apartments were workrooms where domestic labor by female serfs was done under the supervision of the lady of the house. These rooms were well heated.

"There were seventeen other houses, of wood, with a similar number of rooms and other fixtures, all well constructed. One stable, one kitchen, one mill, one granary, three barns.

"The yard was protected by a fence with a stone gateway. . . . There was also an inner yard surrounded by a hedge, well arranged and planted with a variety of trees.

"Vestments: coverings for 1 bed; 1 tablecloth; 1 towel." The scarcity of linen suggests that the members of the royal household brought their own when they visited this estate. That was a nuisance, and Charles later ordered that "in each of our estates the chambers shall be provided with counterpanes, cushions, pillows, bedclothes, coverings for the tables and benches . . ."

"Utensils: 2 brass kettles; 2 drinking cups; 2 brass caldrons; 1 iron caldron; 1 frying pan; 1 pair of andirons . . . 1 chisel; 2 augers; 1 ax; 1 knife; 1 large plane; 1 small plane; 2 scythes; 2 sickles; 2 spades edged

with iron. Enough wooden utensils." The high value of metal implements, even those so simple as a knife, is indicated by this last
clause. Wooden utensils were too common and of too small value
to be worth listing.

The catalogue goes on to mention all the farm produce found on
the estate. The grains and legumes included spelt (German wheat),
wheat, rye, oats, barley, beans and peas. Fifteen times as much barley
was planted as rye or wheat; oats were the next most common grain.
The estate also produced beer (as might be deduced from the amount
of barley), butter, lard, cheese, possibly salt (at any rate it had a
large stock of salt). It raised 51 head of old beef or draft cattle,
5 three-year-olds, 7 two-year-olds; 7 yearlings; a considerable assort-
ment of horses; 50 milk cows; 20 young bulls, 38 yearling calves, 3
bulls, 260 hogs, 100 young pigs, 5 boars, 150 sheep with lamb, 200
lambs, 120 rams, 30 goats with kid, 3 bucks, 30 geese, 80 chickens
and 22 peacocks. Peacocks were highly esteemed for food as well as
for their beauty.

As was customary, a number of subsidiary manor houses were attached to the royal "manse," and these were also carefully inventoried.
It is specially mentioned that the investigators found no craftsmen
such as goldsmiths, silversmiths or blacksmiths, a defect that Charles
in his ordinances attempted to remedy.

The principal ordinance of Charles dealing with administration of
the crown lands was the *Capitulare de villis,* or Decree Concerning
the Estates, a document which has been subjected to exhaustive investigation by economic historians. It is a comprehensive, if singularly ill-organized, set of directions to the stewards of the royal estates
that tells as much about the mind of Charles as it does about agricultural conditions in the eighth century. While this capitulary dates
from the middle period of Charles's reign, rather than from his early
years, it is evidently a summary and reiteration of older decrees. From
the first Charles was interested in and often distressed by the conditions he found on many of his vills, and he set about remedying
defects with his usual energy and attention to minute detail. He
jealously guarded the upkeep of the royal forests attached to his estates and sternly suppressed poaching and unauthorized clearing of
land, while at the same time directing that suitable forest land not
set aside for hunting should be cleared. He warned that the forest

must not be allowed to encroach on existing cleared land. He ordered a determined campaign to exterminate wolves.

We can see him, as we read this capitulary, riding about his estates with his stewards, watching the manner in which lard, smoked meat, sausage, salted meat, wine, mustard, cheese, butter, malt, beer, mead, honey, wax and flour were being prepared, and insisting that all be done "with the greatest cleanliness." The same concern for hygiene that made him so fond of swimming and hot baths prompted him to forbid the time-honored custom of treading out grapes with bare feet. He visited the cowbarns, pigsties, sheepfolds and goat stables and commented on the state of disrepair in which he often found such buildings. "Necessary repairs must be made in good time, not postponed so long that new buildings must be constructed," he ordered. He paid particular attention to the stud, for he loved fine horses and raised such noble thoroughbreds that Pope Hadrian, when presented with one (he had been given a pair, but one died on the way to Rome), greedily asked for more. "These noble animals, when all look upon them with applause, proclaim the fame and glory of your name," Hadrian wrote to him.

Beekeeping, fruit raising, animal husbandry, the selection of seed to produce better stock, the textiles, dyes and implements needed for the "women's work"—Charles had as deep a knowledge of the details of these far from simple matters as any of the men who were directly in charge of the farms. And he had, moreover, a better conception than the practical stewards of an over-all plan and long-range improvements. He saw to it that if fish were sold from his ponds, the ponds were to be restocked. He specified no less than seventy-four types of plants which he wished cultivated on his estates—including almost all of our common garden vegetables (except those originating in the Americas) and the usual wide variety of herbs that characterized medieval gardens: mint, parsley, rue, sage, savory, juniper, tansy, coriander, among the familiar ones, and a great many others that are no longer cultivated. As far as possible he sought to make each estate an autarchic community able to provide entirely for its own needs. To this end he ordered that each steward should have in his district good artisans, "blacksmiths, goldsmith, silversmith, shoemakers, turners, carpenters, swordmakers, fishermen, fowlers, brewers of beer, cider, perry and other beverages."

The stewards in charge of royal estates were paid, like other officials of the crown, by benefices, grants of land for their own use. Unfortunately they were sometimes inclined to treat the king's estates as if these were also benefices. Charles attempted to deal with such abuses by reminding his stewards that "our vills have been established for our own use and must provide for our needs alone, not for those of others." He is not, he reassures his stewards, trying to oppress them by all his demands. But he warns them also not to oppress those beneath them. The peasants and artisans on his estates must not be reduced to poverty or employed by the stewards for forced labor on the stewards' own land. The stewards must not require these men to cut wood or perform any other service that is not for the benefit of the crown.

The estates were military as well as agricultural units. They provided wagonloads of supplies as well as men for the army, and between campaigns were storehouses for arms. The wagons were roofed with leather, and Charles ordered that they be made watertight, so that in fording streams the contents would not get wet. "In no wagon must shields, lances, bows and arrows be lacking." Stewards were responsible for all the gear of war and must see to it that all articles were returned to the weapons chamber at the end of a campaign.

But all was not grim necessity and efficiency on these farms. The vineyards and the orchards of apple, plum, peach, medlar, filbert, mulberry, fig, walnut, cherry and many other trees were certainly useful, but they were also laid out to delight the eye and mind. Flowers were planted so that the altars in the churches could be decorated and so that the king and queen might take pleasure in their gardens. Charles ordered each steward to keep "swans, peacocks, pheasants, ducks, pigeons, partridges and turtledoves for the sake of ornament."

The peasant whose labor was the foundation of all this production might be free, half free or slave, but whatever his status his life was essentially the same. He owned his own wooden house and a small amount of tillable land, meadow, perhaps a vineyard and a wood lot, and he usually had the right to fatten his pigs on the acorns in the domain woodlands. His cropland consisted of long strips in among strips owned by other peasants and by the "big house," so that good and bad soil was fairly evenly distributed and the work of plowing, cultivating and harvesting was usually done communally. In return for these possessions the peasant owed about half his week's labor time to the steward—that is, some three days a week. Charles repeatedly issued decrees forbidding work on Sundays and church holidays—an indication that the hard-pressed peasant usually found a seven-day week necessary if he were to finish up the work on his own holdings.

The peasant also owed various dues, chief among them his contribution to the army (when he himself, if a freeman, was not called up) and his tithe to the Church. At certain times of the year he was required to bring traditional "gifts" of eggs, wine or suckling pigs to the steward, and if he wanted justice in some legal affair he would also be well advised to have a gift or two for the judges, in spite of Charles's order forbidding judges to accept bribes. In ordinary legal affairs his judge was the steward himself; but theoretically every peasant had the right to appeal a case to the king. Many succeeded, for Charles comments on the labor time lost by such proceedings.

These peasants were a superstitious lot who clung to many an ancient magic rite, in spite of the warnings of their priests and stewards. They were filled with awe of the earth. "They considered the field a living creature which had to be tamed, before cultivation was begun, by magic spells. . . . At the first plowing an egg was laid before the plow; if it broke, the earth was willing to accept the sacrifice. . . . Taboos were observed to guard the health of the earth. Women who had just given birth and people with lung sicknesses were not permitted to approach the field. When bodies were taken to the grave, the procession must not cross any cultivated field."*

Every peasant village had its magician who saw to it that the spells were properly observed. These magicians provided potions and spells for healing sick cows, oxen, chickens and children, and were always obliging about concocting philters to help lovelorn peasant girls win their peasant Tristans. Pagan beliefs died hard; as has often been observed, the Church had to confer on innumerable saints the powers of heathen spirits before the simpler folk could be weaned entirely away from their ancient religion.

Among the more expensive of magic rites was the custom of burying deep in the ground a part of the seed for sowing, as a sacrificial offering to Erda, the goddess of earth, who might otherwise be of-

---

* H. E. Jacob, *Six Thousand Years of Bread*, New York, 1944.

fended when the peasant rudely drove his plow into her body. Charles vainly called on his stewards to stamp out this practice for the eminently sensible reason that it was wasteful: less seed was sown and the harvest was diminished.

Like labor on the land the world over, the peasant's life was necessarily one of hard, almost unremitting toil—all the harder since he could work only part of his time for himself. But he had his pleasures also, and among the chief of these was dancing in the churchyard at night (sometimes in defiance of an outraged priest, sometimes with the rustic priest or sexton joining in the dancing and the singing of bawdy songs) and going to the market fairs. For the peasant the fair was the one great occasion of the year when he could step out of the narrowly circumscribed life of the village and catch a glimpse of the great world. At the famous fair of St. Denis, for example, which had been founded in the seventh century by the Merovingian king Dagobert—*"le bon roi Dagobert"*—he could rub elbows with Venetian, Syrian and Jewish merchants, with Gascons, Lombards, Frisians, Saxons and Anglo-Saxons, and even occasionally with Mongolian Avars from the plains of Hungary. He could listen to glittering tales of faraway places that he could never hope to see. And the goods on display in the booths afforded visible proof that at least some of these tales were true. For only strange and wonderful people could have fabricated "robes made of pheasant-skins and silk, or of the necks, backs and tails of peacocks in their first plumage." Imported spices, pearls, perfumes and intricately wrought articles of gold, silver and iron were expensive because transportation was slow and difficult. But commerce by no means came to an utter standstill at any time during the misnamed "Dark Ages."

Nor were the fairs solely occasions for the display of goods. Like any modern country fair, they had their midways. Jugglers exhibited trained bears, monkeys and other animals, performed feats of strength and agility, practiced sleight of hand, and sang. Juggling was an old and honorable profession until the later Middle Ages. The minstrel Taillefer who led the Normans into the Battle of Hastings, "singing of Charlemagne and of Roland, and of Oliver and the vassals all who died at Roncesvalles," was also a juggler who exuberantly tossed his sword high in the air and caught it as he sang.

Naturally the peasants could not buy any of the expensive foreign wares offered at the market fairs, but the Frankish nobles could and did. Immediately after the establishment of a personal union between the kingdoms of Frankland and Lombardy, Italian merchants were able to pour across the border with Eastern finery, of which the Franks were excessively fond. Charles himself objected to their wasting money on frills. The Monk of St. Gall tells an amusing story of how Charles gave his courtiers an object lesson by leading them on a hunt while they were wearing their silks and pheasant skins and ermine wraps. "They scoured the thickets; they were torn by branches of trees, thorns and briers; they were drenched with rain, smeared with the blood of wild beasts. . . . When they returned and began to take off their dresses of skins and slender belts, the creased and shrunken garments could be heard . . . crackling like dry, broken sticks." Charles's own sheepskin needed only a brushing to be once more clean and white. "Charles took it in his hand and showed it to all present, and said, 'Oh most foolish of all men, which of these furs is more valuable and more useful, this one of mine which I bought for a single shilling [solidus] or yours which you bought for many pounds?'"

Nevertheless, the nobles continued to spend on finery the wealth they had acquired in Lombardy as the spoils of war, and fairs such as that of St. Denis did a vigorous trade. The tolls from this fair were a rich plum to the Abbey of St. Denis, and officials of the surrounding districts were constantly attempting to claim a share in them. Among the judicial decisions that Charles was required to make during the winter at Quierzy was the settlement of a suit between St. Denis and the officials of Paris. Abbot Fulrad protested encroachments on the tolls of the St. Denis fair, and Charles, deciding in his favor, forbade the Paris district to take any of these tolls.

This judgment has a significance that goes beyond the confirmation of St. Denis' privileged position among the landowners of Frankland. It was typical of innumerable similar cases that have come down to us in the documents of abbeys and churches. Historians have made much of the vast landholdings of the Church during the Middle Ages; it has been estimated that at various periods the Church owned as much as one third of the land of Western Europe. This is not surprising; almost every landowner gave gifts to some church or monastery during his lifetime, so that his soul would receive the benefit of prayers after his death. But the lands so acquired were by no means permanently and inviolably held. What counts and kings gave with one hand they took away with the other, through greed or need. Thus

Charles's grandfather, Charles the Hammer, had stripped the Church of much land in order to reward his secular lords for their services in his many wars. Pepin restored some of this property, and Charles more, but even these great defenders of the Church sometimes rescinded their gifts or misappropriated church lands. In 767, for example, the year before Charles became king, more than half of the domains of the Abbey of St. Wandrille was still in the hands of "beneficiaries." The Church could never be certain of its possessions. As each new king came to the throne, bishops and abbots thronged to him seeking new grants to confirm the old ones given them by former rulers.

Private persons, too, felt that the lands of the Church were fair prey, if they could get away with it. Since the possessions of a single monastery might be scattered all the way from the English Channel to the Rhine, or even the Po, and since records were not kept any too well and were frequently destroyed by fire, it was often quite easy for a local nobleman to seize an estate belonging to a distant community of monks. It was all the easier if he were an heir of the donor and had some tenuous legal claim to the property. Local sentiment would be on his side, and he could easily find many witnesses to testify that the property had always belonged to his family. The monks could produce their deeds of gift—but members of the clergy had been known to forge documents.

When ecclesiastics disputed among themselves over the possession of land, both parties were certain to produce valid-looking deeds. Thus Charles had to decide between two powerful members of his clergy, the near neighbors Bishop Herchenrad of Paris and Abbot Fulrad of St. Denis. Both laid claim to the monastery of Plaisir, near St. Germain-en-Laye. Both produced documents. Bishop Herchenrad had a deed given him by a certain Aderaldus; a man named Hagadeus had presented the same property to St. Denis. Who had owned the property originally and therefore had a right to give it away? There was insufficient evidence, and Charles therefore ordered the matter to be settled by the "ordeal of the cross."

This time-honored procedure of appealing to the judgment of God was not especially favored by some ecclesiastics, who were more aware than Charles of its pagan origins. But Charles believed in it and insisted that all his subjects "believe in the judgment of God without any doubt." He was overburdened with legal judgments and could not afford the time to give every case the careful, almost pedantic attention that he devoted to Church, State, road building, bridge construction and the number of beehives on his farms. The use of the ordeal enabled him to silence his conscience in such matters. And in the particular case at hand it offered a convenient way to avoid offending two good friends and powerful lords of the Church.

Fulrad and Herchenrad attended the ordeal but did not submit to it themselves—that would have been beneath their dignity, and they were in any case both old men. Each provided a champion who was required to stand in the royal chapel with arms outstretched in the form of a cross. Fulrad won; Herchenrad's champion dropped his arms first, and the bishop thereupon publicly withdrew his claim.

CHAPTER SIX

Saxons and Lombards

C HARLES was now, in the early months of 775, thirty-three years old. In little more than six years he had far more than doubled the kingdom he had inherited. Almost immediately after his accession to the throne he had solidified his possession of the Duchy of Aquitaine. Then he had incorporated the whole of his brother Carloman's kingdom into his own, had brought the Saxons nominally under his jurisdiction and had added to his crown the entire kingdom of Lombardy, comprising most of northern Italy. In those six years he had so well established his right to rule that the Merovingian dynasty was as good as forgotten. Who could remember that the first king of the new Carolingian line had been crowned only twenty-four years ago?

In his personal life also Charles had reason for satisfaction. He had a beautiful young wife who was now no longer a child, and a healthy heir who bore his name, resembled him and was growing rapidly; he had also several daughters by Hildigard and a son and daughter by Himiltrude. His sense of beauty and his awareness of the cultural treasures of the Roman past had been stimulated by his prolonged stay in Italy and his visit to Rome. He was eager to return to Rome and was definitely planning to go to Italy again in October. His mind was in a ferment, filled with imperial, religious and intellectual aspirations. Very likely around this time he began the practice of listening, at table, to readings from Augustine's *City of God*, the book which was to be his favorite throughout his life. And he also began, under the tutelage of the grammarian Peter of Pisa, those academic studies which were to culminate, when he had more time, in the famous Palace School.

Undoubtedly the pressure of the military campaigns had kept him from devoting his full attention to administrative reform and legislation. Of the more than one hundred capitularies issued during his reign, only one dates from before 779, and even the date of this one is disputable. Partly, of course, this disproportion results from the accidents of survival; the royal archives were not established on a satisfactory basis until later in Charles's reign. But there can be no doubt that during the first ten years of his kingship Charles was too young, energetic and busy with conquests to draw up those infinitely detailed and careful guides to the conduct of his realm known as the capitularies. He was building and consolidating an empire now. Later he would make its laws.

Consolidation, it became apparent during the winter in Quierzy, was far more difficult than initial conquest. He pondered the long history of Saxon raids and Saxon revolts, and as the result of his pondering he first applied to the Continental Saxons that adjective which in after years was to become the label of their cousins in Albion— "perfidious." That winter, say the annals, he decided "to wage war upon the perfidious and oath-breaking Saxon people until they were conquered and converted to the Christian religion, or totally annihilated." The words sound like direct quotation, and we are justified in assuming that Charles used these very phrases when he addressed the general assembly at Düren in July. For the "March" or "May" Field was held in late summer; after two years of campaigning his army had to be given some rest for a few months at least. And, as we shall see later, there were other reasons for advancing the date of the general assembly to the midsummer months.

What had led Charles to so grim a decision, to vow what today would be called genocide? Toward the conquered Lombards he was on the whole tolerant and merciful. In later years, when he overcame Slavs, Avars and Saracens, he did not insist on involuntary conversion of the conquered peoples to Christianity. There were still a good many heathens among his Frisian subjects, but he was content to let their conversion take place naturally, so to speak, through the slow, patient missionary work of the school at Utrecht. The Danes were his near neighbors and pagan also; yet he did not attempt their conversion or conquest. Why this intolerance toward the Saxons?

Part of the reason is to be found in the peculiar horror that Saxon religious practices must necessarily arouse in a Christian. The Saxons were occasional cannibals and practiced human sacrifice. In the law he later issued concerning Saxon territory Charles expressly states:

"If anyone deceived by the devil shall have believed, after the manner of the pagans, that a man or a woman is a wizard or witch and eats men, and on this account burns that person and gives the person's flesh to others to eat, or eats it himself, let him be punished with the loss of his head and life. . . . If anyone shall have sacrificed a man to the devil and after the manner of pagans offered him as a victim to the demons, let him be punished by death."

No wonder that Charles was impatient with the slow progress of the missionaries and determined to precipitate the Christianizing of Saxony.

He had other reasons for impatience and concern. The Saxons were a numerous people; their emigrations to Britain, the number of Saxon freebooters who had joined the Lombard invasion of Italy, their many raids on Frankish territory and their expansion to the west, south and east of their original small holdings near Holstein are all evidence for considerable pressure of population. Paul the Deacon was so impressed by the "great hordes of people who are born in the north" that he believed the northern climate was healthier and more favorable to the increase of nations than lands lying "closer to the glow of the sun." He speaks also of "populous Germany."

The Saxons were not only numerous but as fierce in battle as the Franks, and they possessed the natural advantage that barbarians always have over a civilized state: they had less to lose in warfare. They had no cities to be burned or plundered; their property, consisting largely of cattle and horses, was highly mobile and easily hidden. Consequently their raids were always more damaging to their opponents than retaliatory raids could be to them.

Along with this advantage, of course, went the natural disadvantage of the barbarian as against the organized state: disunion. So long as they remained disunited they could be defeated piecemeal by the Franks. By exploiting divisions among the German tribes the Roman Empire had been able to hold the barrier of the Rhine for centuries. But when the Empire weakened, and when at the same time a number of German tribes combined to form the nation that became known as the Franks, the Roman lines crumbled and the barbarian invaders poured into Gaul. Charles was a descendant of those same barbarians and one who knew well the history of his own people— far better than we can know it today, for not only did he have access to manuscripts long since lost but he could also draw upon the traditional songs that preserved so much unwritten history. He could therefore easily foresee the dangers to his growing Frankish Empire if the Saxons should unite as the Franks had once done.

The political organization of the Saxons was at present loose, but it contained significant potentials for unity. The three great Saxon provinces of Westphalia, Angria and Eastphalia (proceeding from west to east) were divided into hundreds of districts—*gaue*. "The old Saxons did not have a king," states Hucbald, the biographer of St. Leafwine, "but satraps [*i.e.*, chiefs] over the various districts. It was their custom to hold a general assembly once a year in middle Saxony, near the river Weser, at a place called Marklo. Here all the district chiefs would meet and also twelve elected representatives of the nobles and an equal number of representatives of the freemen and the serfs. There they renewed the laws, settled the most important judicial cases, and decided in common what would be done in the course of the next year in matters of war as well as peace."

If Hucbald's account is correct, the Saxons possessed one of the oldest parliamentary democracies in the world. They jealously preserved this democracy by seeing to it that in time of war a temporary duke was chosen *by lot* to lead the army. Thus no military leader could raise himself above the other nobles and become king.

Now, however, there were signs that the Saxons, too, were being caught up in the trend of the times, which was a trend toward larger amalgamations of power. (A law of alternation was at work here; the forces of feudal disunity, which were beginning to operate, were producing by reaction stronger national states just as they did in the later Middle Ages, after feudal factionalism had for a long time reduced the national states to virtual impotence.) A Saxon chief named Widukind, one of the richest among the Saxon nobles and allied by marriage to the King of the Danes, had emerged as a popular leader of the freemen and serfs. He was beginning to rally the Saxons together with alarming success. Fearless, sensitive and intelligent, Widukind might very well found a kingdom in Saxony. The British Saxons had, after all, shown themselves quite amenable to the institution of kingship.

As King of Frankland and Italy, Charles now stood toward the Germans on his border in a position resembling that in which the Roman Empire had once been placed. And he feared with good reason the

possibility of a united kingdom of Saxony confronting his realm on
that open plain of North Germany where the borders were so fluid.
He could understand and sympathize with the Saxons and their
aspirations; they were, after all, doing what the Franks had done before them—uniting under pressure to fight a vigorous state power in
the west. They were Germans like himself and his Franks; their language was very similar to his. And for that very reason they were all
the more menacing. Charles could judge their potentialities by those
of his own people. They were cousins, and he could feel toward them
the ambivalent hatred reserved for kinsfolk, the same hatred he sometimes felt for his dangerous cousin Tassilo, the Duke of Bavaria.
Moreover, the possibility that the Saxons might someday join forces
with Tassilo's Bavarians was a nightmare. If they did so, Alemannia,
Austrasia and Thuringia—the entire western part of his kingdom—
would almost surely be lost.

The threat to annihilate the enemy, then, sprang from fear. The
alternative that Charles offered the Saxons—conversion to Christianity—was partly the outcome of his theocratic bent, which had been
greatly stimulated by his recent visit to Italy and the meeting with
Pope Hadrian. But it was also a shrewd political measure, the simplest and most effective way Charles knew to consolidate conquered
territory. The Church followed the flag. Those Saxons who became
Christians were cut off from the community of their fellow pagans
and thrown into a natural alliance with the Christian Franks. There
is record of a number of Saxons who were forced to abandon their
homes and flee from Saxony after their conversion. The Saxons themselves considered a sincere acceptance of Christianity as treason. If
Charles could provide these converted Saxons with military protection until they were numerous enough to defend themselves, he would
be able to hold Saxony with the assistance of Saxons. In the long
run, he knew, conquest rested on the consent of the conquered.

Charles understood quite well the difference between a religion imposed by force and a religion arrived at by persuasion. But with the
Saxons, force seemed to be the only choice, since they killed or drove
away all the missionaries who attempted to preach to them. If by
force he could bring about a nominal acceptance of Christianity, so
that churches could be built in Saxon territory and priests could conduct services there, he could then trust the missionaries to convert
an intimidated congregation into devout believers. The very fact of

Frankish oppression would speed the conversion, for was not Christ the consolation of the oppressed?

Immediately after the national assembly at Düren, Charles began his invasion of Saxony. He crossed the Saxon border into Westphalia, which his army had not entered in the first campaign three years earlier. Quite likely his coming was unexpected, for he was not opposed and met with singular success, taking at his first assault the strong fortress of Sigiburg. This fortress was a huge stockade enclosing some thirty acres and protected by a bluff at its rear and by stout walls on the more accessible slopes. Like most of the Saxon burgs, it was meant to be big enough to serve as a place of refuge to which the population of the surrounding countryside could flee in case of danger. But unless manned by a good part of that population, it was too big to be defended by its small permanent garrison. The speed with which Charles advanced explains his easy triumph; the population had no time to seek shelter in the fort.

The fall of the Sigiburg opened the way into the heart of the Ruhr—then a peaceful countryside of farms and forest without a single city or town. Leaving a Frankish garrison at Sigiburg, Charles marched, apparently again unopposed, to the fort of Eresburg, which he had captured in the campaign of 772 and which the Saxons had recaptured and destroyed last year. These two forts, he thought, were the keys to Saxony, and accordingly he rebuilt the fortifications and again left a garrison behind. Then he proceeded deep into Saxony. He was met at the Weser River by an army of Angrians and defeated them in battle. They surrendered to him, and Charles then crossed the river, leaving a large force behind to guard the crossing. The Eastphalians resolved to submit rather than to fight the Franks alone. They came to Charles, took an oath of homage to him and gave hostages.

The Westphalians had meanwhile rallied from their surprise and shock. Widukind gathered together at least part of an army and again demonstrated that cunning in which he excelled. The Frankish detachment that Charles had left behind at the Weser was taking it easy; its guard was relaxed and the soldiers were in the habit of taking afternoon naps. One afternoon a sizable body of Westphalian Saxons mingled with Frankish troops who had been sent out as foragers. The Saxons' language and appearance were close enough to those of the Franks for them to carry off such a deception in broad daylight. Returning to the camp with the foragers "as if they were their comrades," the Westphalians fell upon the sleeping troops and slaughtered many before they were driven off.

When Charles returned and learned what had happened he must have been as furious with his own men as with the Saxons. He knew how dangerous such laxness could be, although he could not, of course, foresee the frightful penalty his men would have to pay for laxness three years hence, in the pass at Roncesvalles. He was all the angrier because of the blow to his prestige. For a good part of his success in Saxony was due to the fear his mere presence was beginning to inspire among the Saxons. A legend of invincibility was growing up around him, and it was a useful legend. To restore it he immediately pursued the Westphalian army, caught up with it and overwhelmed it by his superior numbers. The Westphalians, too, capitulated and gave hostages.

This blitz campaign had taken a scant two months. But the Franks had done more than merely march and fight two battles. They set villages and farmhouses on fire, trampled the grain, slaughtered livestock; in a word, they pursued a deliberate policy of devastation. The Saxon population suffered frightfully. Charles had no need to issue orders that such terror be practiced; only a policy of mildness would have required special orders. But he did not wish to prevent the ravaging. It would take him many years to learn that terrorism only stiffened the Saxons' resistance. Like many leaders of men, Charles was given to outbursts of fury when crossed. Convinced that what he was doing was for the good of all, he resented being hampered by inferior men and took cruel reprisals for opposition. When things went wrong he was inclined to feel that his own bent toward mercifulness was at fault, and he went to the opposite extreme. Again and again in times of stress and in the face of opposition his normal good nature vanished and he fell into ungovernable rages.

Charles had good reason to be touchy at this time. He had taken serious losses in the Saxon campaign, and now the news from Lombardy was also bad. Charles received from Pope Hadrian a letter that described an ominous situation:

"We have often called your attention to the incessant evil plans that are being forged against you by Dukes Hildebrand of Spoleto,

Arichis of Benevento and Hrodgaud of Friuli. . . . In accordance with your wish, we sent our faithful treasurer Stephan to Spoleto to confer with the duke and to receive hostages from him. But Hildebrand behaved toward him with great arrogance, for envoys from Dukes Arichis of Benevento, Hrodgaud of Friuli and Reginbald of Chiusi had come to him and arranged for them to join with the Greeks and Adelchis, the son of Desiderius, this coming March. They would attack us by land and water, conquer the city of Rome and lead ourselves into captivity. Then they would place Adelchis once more upon the Lombard throne and break with you. Therefore we implore you by the living God and the Prince of Apostles to hasten to our aid immediately, lest we be destroyed."

Charles suspected that the pope was exaggerating the extent of the conspiracy in order to involve his own enemies, Arichis and Hildebrand. These two dukes, Charles thought, would probably keep their peace, for the time being at least. However, Charles had his own sources of information: two of his ambassadors were in Italy at the moment, and he knew that there was something to the story, at least as far as Hrodgaud of Friuli was concerned. A revolt was brewing, if not already in progress, and there was no reason for him to discount the possibility that Adelchis might return from Constantinople at the head of a "Greek," that is, an imperial, army. There was no way as yet for Charles to know of the death of the Emperor Constantine V, which would probably interfere with any such plans on the part of Adelchis.

Saxony was obviously far from pacified, and Charles had postponed his planned October journey to Italy. Now he was reluctant to take any sizable army into Italy for fear of new Saxon reprisals. But suppression of Hrodgaud's impending revolt was also essential, and Charles accordingly set out across the Alps immediately after Christmas with a small body of picked troops, "the bravest of his men," say the annals. Of the hardships of this forced march in the dead of winter there is no mention, but they must have been formidable.

By the time Charles reached Italy the revolt had already taken place: Treviso, Friuli and a number of other cities had risen. The rest of Lombardy remained loyal, however, and Charles had little difficulty suppressing the rebellion. Hrodgaud was killed in battle, the city of Treviso taken after a short siege. By Easter the uprising was over. Charles promptly confiscated the property of the rebels, took a number of them back to Frankland as prisoners and placed Frankish counts with Frankish garrisons in the insurgent cities.

As Charles soon learned, there had been reasons for the revolt that went beyond the mere personal ambitions of Hrodgaud and his fellow conspirators. The war of conquest of two years before and the prolonged stay in the country of a Frankish army of occupation had disrupted the economic life of Lombardy. Untilled fields, followed perhaps by a year of unfavorable weather, had resulted in a terrible famine in Lombardy. Men were selling all their goods for food, and even selling themselves and their wives and children into slavery. Charles heard ugly stories that the Romans were selling Christian Lombards to Saracens as slaves.

Charles did what he could to alleviate the sufferings of the Lombards. He issued a decree rescinding any legal transactions in which from pressure of necessity men had sold goods or property for less than the true value. After the fall of Treviso he remained in Italy until midsummer, moving from city to city and personally regulating affairs that he had hitherto left to his envoys and to local Lombard dukes. But in spite of Pope Hadrian's pressing invitations he did not go to Rome.

He may well have pretended to the pope that he did not wish to travel too far from Frankland for fear of trouble on the Saxon borders. But the real reason for his avoidance of the pope lay in his unwillingness to meet the pope's demands. Far from suppressing the "insolence" of the archbishop of Ravenna, as Hadrian demanded, and far from enlarging the papal dominions, Charles was now supporting Archbishop Leo and pursuing a policy toward the Papal See as unbending as that of the Lombards had been. He did not threaten the pope, of course—he had no need to—but also he did not grant the pope's requests. In effect he was making it clear to Hadrian that he was the true ruler of Rome and the arbiter of Italy. He was taking quite seriously his title of "patrician of the Romans"; in that capacity he would if he chose (and later he did so choose) even sit in judgment on a pope.

Hadrian resented Charles's betrayal of his proffered friendship. In his letters to Charles he was alternately bewildered, hurt, nagging and even mildly threatening. And in the sphere of diplomatic negotiations he attempted wherever possible to act independently. But the other powerful personages of Italy fully understood the situation; the

Duke of Spoleto and the Archbishop of Ravenna, confident that they and not Hadrian had the king's ear, ignored the pope's proposals. Hadrian pressed for another interview with Charles; he would have left Rome and come to Pavia or Treviso if Charles had invited him. But Charles did not want to be lured again into promising more than he would willingly fulfill. Before there was any chance for the pope to pay a surprise visit to him, as he had descended upon the pope two years before, Charles set out again for Frankland. It was in any case time for the national assembly, which he had once more arranged to hold in midsummer this year.

Before he reached Worms, where the "May" Field was to convene, he was met by messengers bearing news that must have filled him with a deep sense of frustration. The Saxons had risen once more, attacked and taken the fortress of Eresburg which Charles had rebuilt only the year before. There were rumors of treachery; at any rate the powerful fort seemed to have surrendered far too readily to a small force of Saxons. Fortunately the Frankish garrison of Sigiburg had resisted the Saxon attack, then sallied out and driven the enemy off in confusion. But the Saxons were now busy fortifying their borders.

Which groups of Saxons were involved in this uprising the sources do not say. Probably they were Westphalians only, under the leadership of Widukind. And a deep cleavage already existed between Widukind and the other Saxon nobles, who were far readier than Widukind and his yeomen to accept Frankish overlordship and Christianity. The outcome is evidence for this: when Charles, moving with great rapidity, promptly led his army into Saxony no battles were fought. The majority of the nobles readily surrendered. Widukind was more dangerous to them than Charles. He was fomenting unrest among the common people and took little trouble to disguise his monarchical ambitions. Since he had not been elected to the office of army leader by the customary drawing of lots, the other Saxon nobles had a good pretext for refusing to follow him. They saw it as plain common sense to come with their dependents to the new fort that Charles had built, which was named in his honor Karlesburg, and there to pledge all their property as warranty of their fidelity to the Franks. They listened attentively to the eloquent preaching of Abbot Sturm of Fulda, whom Charles had placed in charge of the conversion of the Saxons, and submitted to baptism in the waters of the Lippe.

By now Charles thought that he understood the situation in Saxony. The majority of the chiefs were on his side, and he felt confident that the small minority of malcontents headed by Widukind would soon succumb to the attractive force of law, order and Christianity. As an impressive demonstration that he now considered at least part of Saxony Frankish territory he decided that the next general assembly, of 777, would be held at Paderborn, in southern Saxony.

The Saxon chiefs and their followings were required to appear at the assembly in Paderborn. Large numbers of them attended, repeated their oaths and pledges, accepted baptism if they had not already done so, and swore fidelity to Charles's sons as well as to Charles himself. For Hildigard, the "mother of kings," had already borne Charles a second son who was given the name of Carloman. To celebrate both the conversion of the Saxons and the birth of another heir, Charles ordered the building of a church at Paderborn.

The absence of Widukind was noted, of course. "Conscious of his crimes," the annals record, "he was afraid to present himself before the king and therefore fled to Sigifrid, the King of the Danes." Wiliness, a readiness to abandon the field so that he might someday return to fight again, were characteristic of the Saxon leader. But Charles took his flight as a good omen. Evidently Widukind no longer had sufficient support to remain safely in Saxony. In exile he was not likely to cause much trouble; he would probably settle down contentedly with his father-in-law as Adelchis seemed to be doing in his Constantinople exile.

Charles underestimated the popularity of Widukind and the pressures of a discontented peasantry who, in rising against their own masters, would continue to oppose the foreign enemy with whom those masters had allied themselves. Charles also mistook mass baptisms for evidence of sincere conversion to Christianity, and hence to the *Frankish* Church. He assumed that the further civilizing of the country could be left to the missionaries, and with considerable relief he turned his thoughts to other parts of his realm and to other adventures. As if fate were signaling, there appeared before the assembly at Paderborn a group of strange ambassadors, bearing a proposal to which Charles listened with growing interest and approval.

CHAPTER SEVEN

Fiasco

IN THE middle years of the eighth century the three great powers of the western world—the Frankish kingdom, the Byzantine Empire* and the Moslem Empire—underwent great upheavals almost simultaneously. In Frankland the Merovingian dynasty was formally deposed and, as we have seen, in 751 A.D. Pepin was crowned by Boniface as first king of the Carolingian line. In Constantinople the much maligned Emperor Constantine resumed, in 754 A.D., the image-smashing policy of his father, and the Empire was racked until his death by the frightful struggle between orthodox Catholics and the iconoclasts. In the Moslem world the Umayyad dynasty was overthrown, to be replaced by the descendants of Abbas, Mohammed's uncle, who represented the wider interests of the Mohammedan Empire as against the more narrowly Arabian policies of the Umayyads. The capital of Islam was transferred from Damascus to Bagdad, and the new Abbassid dynasty set about hunting down and murdering all members of the former ruling house.

The events in the East had their effect on the fortunes of the Franks. The iconoclastic controversy fostered that lasting hostility between the popes at Rome and the Byzantine emperors which led the popes to look to Frankland for support. The Abbassid uprising transformed Spain, the one point at which the Saracens were in contact with the Franks, into a powerful but isolated Moslem emirate. For one member of the Umayyad dynasty survived the slaughter of his family by the new Abbassid rulers. His name was Abdur Rahman; he made his way to Spain, the western outpost of the Arab world, and succeeded in establishing himself as emir of the peninsula. So bitter was the opposition of the followers of the Abbassids to Abdur Rahman

---

* The name is convenient, but it must be remembered that this "Greek" or Byzantine Empire was in tradition and fact the remnant of the Roman Empire.

that they preferred a pact with the infidel to submission to the last of the Umayyads. The governor of Barcelona, for example—his name was Suleiman—placed himself under the protection of King Pepin.

Under the Umayyad dynasty the Saracens had penetrated deep into Gaul. They had been stopped in the great battle of Tours, and Charles Martel had devoted many of the remaining years of his reign to fighting them. Pepin had continued his father's policy and ultimately succeeded in expelling them entirely from Gaul. It was only natural, therefore, that he should consider the Umayyads his enemies. It was natural, too, that he should look upon the Abbassids with favor. As he would see it, the Abbassids had done precisely what he had done—overthrown an outworn dynasty and established a new, progressive regime. He therefore entered into diplomatic negotiations with the Caliphate of Bagdad, negotiations which perhaps looked toward common action against the Umayyad ruler in Spain. His ambassadors returned, accompanied by Saracen emissaries whom Pepin had received with friendliness. Before anything more came of this interchange, King Pepin died.

Charles naturally took his views of Franco-Arab relations from those of his father. But for the first nine years of his reign he had been too busy in Lombardy or Saxony to deal with the affairs of Spain. The diplomatic relations between Frankland and Bagdad lapsed. Concerted action by Franks and Abbassids against the Umayyads was in any case hard to arrange when negotiations were so time-consuming: it had taken three years for Pepin's mission to go to Bagdad and return to report.

But now, as we have just seen, Charles felt that he had settled his most pressing problems in Lombardy and Saxony. He could afford to turn south and west, and there was certainly need for him to attend to the affairs of Aquitaine. It was many years since he had shown himself in that once troublesome province where, undoubtedly, he never felt quite so much at home as he did among the German nations to the east of his original kingdom.

Charles's father could scarcely have intervened in Spain, even had he wished to, since he did not succeed in pacifying Aquitaine until shortly before his death. But Charles had no such problem, and he therefore assented to a proposal that had probably been made once before to his father. For the embassy that came so opportunely to Paderborn was headed by that same Suleiman who had previously negotiated with King Pepin. If Charles would lead an army into Spain now, Suleiman told him, the usurper Abdur Rahman would be easily overthrown. Bagdad was preparing to send an army of Berbers against Abdur Rahman, and the people of Spain themselves would rise against the hated Umayyad. Charles could be certain of acquiring a number of cities in Spain; Suleiman would throw open to him the gates of the cities under his command. Penetration of Spain, moreover, would make it easier for Charles to control the unsubdued Basques or Vasconians on both sides of the Pyrenees.

Suleiman could play on Frankish fears of Saracen aggression, and Charles would be gullible about this. All Franks had vivid memories of the terrible Moslem onrush half a century before, which had been stopped only by the great union of "Romans" and Germans at the Battle of Tours. Charles, at any rate, wrote to Pope Hadrian that the Saracens were planning an attack on his territory, and it is doubtful that he would give this reason for invading Spain solely for the sake of propaganda.

It has been assumed that Charles relied too implicitly on the promises of Suleiman and was trapped into an adventure which he was unable to pursue to a successful conclusion. There is no good evidence for this view. Certainly he counted on profiting by the divisions among the Arabs, and also he expected to be welcomed by the Christian population of Spain, who were allegedly "groaning under the Saracen yoke" but who in fact were quite content with the tolerant rule of Abdur Rahman. Nevertheless, Charles prepared more carefully for the Spanish expedition than for any of his previous campaigns. Fully conscious that he would be opposed by a nation of famous fighters, he gathered together the largest army he could muster. Lombards, Burgundians, Goths and Romans from Septimania and the Provence, Franks from Neustria and Austrasia, and even Bavarians were drawn into a truly international army.

We can only speculate about the presence of the Bavarians. Why, after fifteen years of independence, should Duke Tassilo have consented to send a contingent of his men to join Charles's great levy? Possibly he was enticed by the hope of booty from the rich cities of Spain. Possibly also Charles or the pope had appealed to his well-known piety, had admonished him on his Christian duty to help against the Saracens, and had reminded him of the significant part played by Bavarians fighting under Charles Martel at the Battle of

Tours. But the most likely explanation—a guess warranted by the events that took place three years later—is that Charles was already beginning to apply strong diplomatic pressure to bring Bavaria back into the Frankish orbit. Secret negotiations of this sort could easily escape the notice of the annalists, who were generally none too well informed. And with the establishment of his rule in Saxony and Lombardy, Charles was now in a favorable position to bring Tassilo to terms.

Another indication that Charles regarded the Spanish expedition as a grave and difficult enterprise was his care to insist on an early start. To avoid the heat of the Spanish summer, to save time, and perhaps also to evade possible discussion of war aims which might prove embarrassing, Charles omitted the usual annual assembly. Instead, he moved early in the year into Aquitaine and celebrated Easter at Chasseneuil, in Poitou. Here Hildigard, who had accompanied him this far, remained behind in the royal vill to await her fifth confinement.

From Chasseneuil Charles led one half of his grand army directly across Vasconia into the western Pyrenees—without, so far as we know, even asking the Duke of Vasconia for the right of passage. The other half of the army took the eastern route across the Pyrenees.

A number of things went wrong from the start. Instead of welcoming the Franks as fellow Christians, the people of the Christian kingdom of Asturias in northwest Spain resisted him—in defense of their own independence and, possibly also, because they were in alliance with the Moslems. Charles had to fight his way into the Christian city of Pampelona. Meanwhile the uprising against the Umayyad Abdur Rahman fizzled away into nothing. Suleiman and his allies from North Africa quarreled among themselves, and when Charles arrived at Saragossa he found the city prepared to resist him. Suleiman had succeeded in taking Saragossa, but the populace would not allow him to turn their city over to the infidel Franks. Charles found himself facing the walls of a powerful fortress and lacking the siege machinery to assault it. He had received the formal surrender of Barcelona, Gerona, Huesca and perhaps a few other cities in Spain; he had reached the Ebro; but he could go no farther without taking Saragossa. And Abdur Rahman was undoubtedly gathering forces to attack him.

It is curious that we know so little about the campaign which was to become, in legend and song, the most famous war of the Middle Ages. We know, really, only that Charles began to retreat without having accomplished any significant conquest. The reasons for his retreat are veiled by the discretion of the annalists. Whether a disastrous battle was fought, whether his supplies were running out (the army carried only three months' provisions), whether Abdur Rahman had gathered an overwhelming host against him, we do not know. The legends speak of vast and bloody battles involving hundreds of thousands of men, and it seems scarcely likely that Charles would have retreated without even an attempt to take Saragossa by storm— even if he had already heard of the trouble at the other end of his kingdom, and the annals expressly indicate that he had not.

Whatever the reason, Charles was unable to consolidate his gains. He began his retreat, leading both the eastern and western contingents of his army back through Navarre, the way he had come. At Pampelona he halted long enough to raze the walls of the city—proof that he did not intend to leave a garrison behind and that he wished to punish the inhabitants for their resistance. Then the great army continued on its way across the Pyrenees and back into Frankland through the narrow pass of Roncesvalles.

There, at Roncesvalles, took place one of the most famous defeats in the world's history, a fitting climax to a campaign that had been but a series of miscalculations and disappointments. Circumstantially, but alas far too circumspectly, Einhard tells the "official" version of what happened. Charles, he says, returned from the Spanish expedition "safe and sound except for a reverse which he experienced through the treason of the Gascons on his way back through the passes of the Pyrenees. For while his army was marching in a long line, suiting their formation to the character of the ground and the defiles, the Gascons lay in ambush on the top of the mountain—where the thickness and extent of the woods in the vicinity made it highly suitable for such a purpose—and then rushing down into the valley beneath threw into disorder the last part of the baggage train and also the rear guard. . . . In the battle which followed the Gascons killed their opponents to the last man. Then they seized the baggage and under cover of night scattered with the greatest speed in different directions. The Gascons were aided by the lightness of their armor and the nature of the terrain where the encounter took place. In this battle Eggihard, the royal seneschal; Anselm, count of the palace; and

Hruodland, warden of the Breton frontier, were killed along with very many others."

What really happened must be read between the lines; what never happened, but could have, should have and poetically did happen may be read in the *Chanson de Roland*. For that Hruodland, warden of the Breton frontier, whom Einhard only mentions, was none other than the hero of the great French medieval epic, the mighty Count Roland who with his sword has conquered the known world for Charlemagne.

> *Jo l'en conquis ed Anjou e Bretaigne,*
> *Si l'en conquis e Peitou e lo Maine;*
> *Jo l'en conquis Normendie le franche,*
> *Si l'en conquis Provence ed Equitaigne*
> *E Lombardie e trestote Romanie.*
> *Jo l'en conquis Baiviere e tote Flandre . . .*

boasts Roland in the great death scene in which he pays tribute to his sword Durendal. Historically the only authentic traces of Count Roland are the mention in Einhard and a worn coin bearing the name *Carlus* on one side and *Rodlan* on the other. And yet through the distortions and loving embellishments of the poets some glimmering of the true history can be grasped. Not that the true history matters overmuch in this case, for the historical Roland, magnified and glorified by legend, has been swallowed up by the Roland of the Song. Hruodland was certainly one of Charles's great lords, since he had the right to strike his own coinage; but for all our insight into his character and accomplishments we must turn to the *Chanson de Roland*.

Between the lines of Einhard's account it is easy to see that what happened at Roncesvalles was the result of a blunder, of overconfidence and carelessness similar to that which caused the defeat at Lidbach, when the Saxons slipped into the camp and slaughtered the sleeping Franks. A rear guard led by some of Charles's foremost counts failed to take the elementary precaution of scouting the heights above the pass, walked into an ambush and was wiped out by a band of undisciplined shepherds who did not even have armor. There was something seriously wrong with the training of Charles's army. Had he been relying too heavily on sheer weight of numbers—and was that perhaps the trouble with the entire Spanish campaign?

The *Chanson* itself, in its characterization of Roland, gives us another indication of what went wrong. When the attack is about to begin, Roland refuses to blow his horn to summon the aid of Charles. The poet represents him as quick to anger and too proud for his own good or the good of his men. He considers it shameful to appeal for help and would rather die than be put to shame:

> *Mielz voeill morir que hontages me vaignet.*

Only after the battle is lost and his twenty thousand men lie dead upon the field does he see his error and raise the oliphant to blow the *feeble* signal that brings Charles hastening back through the pass.

There may well be a historical reminiscence in the poetic conception of Roland's pride, for we know of others among Charles's generals who behaved with similar foolhardiness. Four years after Roncesvalles the Saxons destroyed a Frankish army at Süntel because Charles's chamberlain Adalgis and his marshal Geilo were tempted into seeking personal glory. The circumstances were appallingly similar, and Charles, as we shall see, then took a frightful vengeance. At Roncesvalles he was cheated of his revenge, for the Basque mountaineers disappeared "so completely that they left behind them not even a rumor of their whereabouts."

Certainly there is historical reminiscence in the *Chanson de Roland's* description of Charles's terrible grief. The "twelve peers" or paladins of Charlemagne rest on no more historical basis than King Arthur's Round Table; but there is ample evidence of Charles's capacity for deep attachments. The men who fought by his side, who hawked, hunted and feasted with him, and governed his provinces, were his friends. His was a personal government, and he elevated to high positions men whom he loved for their personal qualities. Even the dry and laconic annals record that he was wounded to the heart by the death of these friends. The *Chanson de Roland* sings, in the incomparable music of the old French, of a sorrow almost beyond bearing:

> *En Rencesvals en est Charles entrez,*
> *Des morz qu'il trouvet commencet at plorer. . . .*
> *Sur l'erbe verte veit gesir son nevot;*
> *Nen est merveille se Charles at iror,*
> *Descent a piét, alez i est plein cors,*

Si prent lo conte entre ses mains ansdous,
    Sor lui se pasmet, tant par est angoissos. . . .

"*Amis Rodlanz, Deus metet t'anme en flors,*
En paredis entre les glorios!
Com en Espaigne venis a mal seignor!
Jamais n'iert jorz de tei n'aie dolor."

In Roncesvalles Charles now has set his feet,
And for the dead he finds begins to weep. . . .
He sees his nephew lying on green grass.
No wonder, then, that Charles is full of wrath.
Dismounts and goes to him; his heart is sad.
He holds the count between his own two hands
And on the body faints, so sharp's the pang. . . .

"My friend Roland, God lay your soul on flowers,
In Paradise with all the glorious host.
You came to Spain with a cruel overlord.*
No day shall pass henceforth that I'll not mourn."

The lament goes on, *laisse* after *laisse*. Charles cries that all his
strength is now gone, that he no longer has a single friend left under
heaven. He pictures himself at home in his hall, bitterly telling
strangers that he has left his count behind, dead in Spain. Forever
afterward he will reign in sorrow; every day henceforth he will weep
and complain for Roland. Again and again Charles faints, and then
in his anguish he begins to tear out his hair and wishes that he himself may die, so great is his sorrow.

Si grant dol ai que ne voldreie vivre.

But the poet reminds us that there is work still before him. The
dead must be buried, and new armies are coming up that will challenge him again.

So it must have been on that hot August 15, 778 A.D. ("*Clers fut li
jorz e belle fu li soleilz*"—"Fair was the day and brightly shone the

---

* Not, as often translated: "Cruel was the day you came to Spain, my lord."

sun") when Charles returned through the pass of Roncesvalles and found his friends and followers among a welter of plundered, overturned wagons. Stripped of their precious armor and weapons, their bones crushed by the rocks that had been hurled down upon them from above—so he must have found them, dead to a man. No enemy was in sight; there was nothing to do but bury his dead and turn with a heavy heart back toward Frankland. With a heavy heart, and sick from the frustration of his need for revenge.

The contrast of death and life presented itself all the more vividly to him when he reached Chasseneuil, his starting point, and found that Hildigard had meanwhile given birth to twin sons—one who was given the name Lothar and who was to die in infancy, and the other, baptized Louis, who was destined to succeed Charles upon the throne.

So deep an impress on the minds of the people was made by the disaster at Roncesvalles that the biographer of this Louis, writing sixty years later, declared that he need not mention the names of the men of the rear guard who were killed in the mountains, since they were so well known. There can be no doubt that from the first the imagination of the people seized on the peculiar circumstances of the battle: the wild mountain pass, the mysterious appearance and disappearance of the enemy, the helplessness of a great army to combat a guerrilla ambuscade, the prominence of the victims and the drama of a desperate fight to the last man. Songs relating episodes of the defeat must have sprung up almost immediately. Soon, when the Gascons had become an integral part of the French nation, the Saracens would be blamed for the ambush. Perhaps there was even some historical truth in this; the Basques may have been acting in concert with Abdur Rahman. But in any case the "paynim" enemy was better suited to the spirit of the Crusades.

Ultimately the scattered songs coalesced into the wonderful *Chanson de Roland*. We shall never know for certain whether the monk Turoldus, who tells us at the end of four thousand lines that he is "declining,"* was author, compiler or only a mere copyist. But whatever his role, there can be no doubt that many anonymous minstrels contributed to the composition. The *Song of Roland* was in a sense

---

* *Que Turoldus declinet*. This phrase has been variously interpreted, but the evidence favors "declining health."

the production of a whole people, and certainly it was loved by a whole people. As Henry Adams has said:

"No modern opera or play ever approached the popularity of the 'Chanson.' None has ever expressed with anything like the same completeness the society that produced it. Chanted by every minstrel,—known by heart, from beginning to end, by every man, woman and child, lay or clerical—translated into every tongue,—more intensely felt, if possible, in Italy and Spain than in Normandy and England, [it was] perhaps most effective, as a work of art, when sung by the Templars in their great castles in the Holy Land."*

* *Mont-Saint-Michel and Chartres*, Chapter II.

CHAPTER EIGHT

The Subkingdoms

IN THE *Chanson de Roland* thirty-six-year-old King Charles had become the aged emperor, with many years of rule and conquest behind him, who sighs over the laboriousness of his life:

"Deus!" dist li reis, "si penose est ma vide!"

For no sooner is he finished with one onerous task than he finds himself confronted by another.

The picture is true of the life of the historical Charles. Charles returned from Roncesvalles more conscious of human mortality than he had been for many years. He now had four sons by Hildigard, four legitimate heirs: young Charles, Carloman, and the newborn twins, Louis and Lothar. And he had been made forcibly aware that he too could be the victim of a surprise attack such as had cost the lives of Roland, Anselm, Eggihard and so many others. As soon as possible he would have to settle the succession to his throne, so that if he should die suddenly his sons would not be deprived of their birthright. And since the Franks had no law of primogeniture, he would have to make arrangements to prevent that bickering among his successors which had caused so much warfare and murder in the past history of his country.

The plan Charles decided on was in keeping with his father's tradition, for Pepin had had Charles and his brother crowned along with himself when he first deposed the Merovingian monarch. As usual, however, Charles improved on his father's solution: he would set up subkingdoms and make each of his sons king of a part of the Frankish realm. Full execution of this plan, however, would have to wait until he had time to visit Rome, as he had been intending to do before the Spanish expedition.

121

Aquitaine would obviously be one of the subkingdoms, and as a preparatory step Charles reorganized the administration of that province. Evidently Aquitaine, with its long history of hostility to the Franks, had not behaved well during the Spanish campaign. Perhaps there had been rumblings of revolt there; perhaps Charles simply decided that the native Aquitanian counts were too independent. In any case, he now made a clean sweep of all the positions of power in the country. He saw to it that the bishops were made aware of their dependence on him, and he replaced a great many native counts, abbots and vassals of the crown by Frankish officials "whose prudence and fortitude were such that it would be unwise for anyone to attempt craft or violence against them." In particular he saw to it that Franks were put in charge of border areas and of the royal domains. The practiced husbandman had observed that a good part of the wealth of his Aquitanian estates had not been flowing in the right direction. (In spite of the reforms these revenues continued for some time to go astray.)

But evidence of mismanagement was not the worst of the difficulties that made his life so laborious. When he reached Auxerre, south of Paris, where he began disbanding his army, word came to him that the Saxons had risen again. A Saxon army—of Westphalians under the leadership of Widukind, it seemed—had launched one of the most savage raids since the beginning of the Saxon war. In spite of the dramatic scenes at Paderborn the year before, Saxony was far from pacified. This time, too, the Saxons had not even attempted to take booty. The raid was clearly one of revenge for the humiliation and ravaging of Saxony in previous years. It was an attempt to spread terror among the Franks to counter Charles's terror among the Saxon population. "The bitterness of the enemy recognized no distinction of age or sex," say the annals. The raiders came close to the famous monastery of Fulda, and while Abbot Sturm, bent with age though he was, courageously went forward to meet the marauders, his terrified monks bundled up the bones of St. Boniface, their most precious possession, and fled into the woods.

Charles could not keep so great an army in the field for the rest of the year, especially after the losses of the disheartening Spanish campaign. Although the Saxons had penetrated as far as the Rhine—that is, deep into Frankish territory—a new campaign starting so late in the year was hardly practicable. He therefore permitted the greater part of the army to continue disbanding, and sent against the Saxons only some detachments of Austrasians (that is, Eastern Franks) and Alemannians who would anyway be traveling toward the Rhine to reach home. The Saxons were already retiring, and these troops succeeded in driving them back across the border.

But it had been a sorry year.

The winter was further saddened by the death of one of his twin sons, Lothar, who lived only a few months. And by early spring there were signs that the Spanish expedition was destined to cost the lives of civilians as well as soldiers. So large had been the levy that not enough men had been left at home to tend the crops. The precarious agrarian economy—always, in the Middle Ages, sensitive to warfare and to weather—had broken down, and a frightful famine afflicted the entire country. With the slow transportation of the times, food could not be shipped from the few areas of abundance to the areas of scarcity. There were many deaths from starvation.

After ten years of unbroken successes, Charles was for the first time facing the consequences of failure and personal tragedies. He turned for consolation and reassurance to his religion and asked himself privately (as, late in his life, he was to ask publicly) wherein he had failed in his duties toward his Church. For in March, shortly after the death of his infant son, he called a council of his bishops, abbots and counts, and the result of their deliberations was a decree dealing with a variety of religious matters. There were many abuses to be corrected. Bishops had been appointed to office but had not yet been consecrated; this was to be done at once. Abbesses were sternly ordered to remain in their convents and not to go traipsing abroad. (They were still gadding about six hundred years later; see Chaucer's *Canterbury Tales*.) Bishops were reminded to pay more attention to the morals of the clerics in their dioceses.

Charles attempted also to make some restitution to the Church for the properties it had lost since the days of Charles Martel by the assignment of ecclesiastical estates to laymen. Holders of such property were ordered to pay their rents. In cases where the *precarious letters* (grants of the right of tenancy on church property) had been forgotten or deliberately destroyed, new ones were to be made out, thus confirming the Church's legal claim to the property.

But for all his desire to support and strengthen the Church, Charles

was in the same predicament in regard to church property as his father
and grandfather had been. He had to have the right to dispose of it as
he saw fit, in order to pay the expenses of his wars. The decree or
capitulary of 779 therefore makes a careful distinction between tenancy agreements entered into voluntarily by bishops or abbots and
those conferred by the king's command—*precariae de verbo nostro*.
These latter remained in the possession of the grantees on the terms
set by the king and until revoked by the king himself. In effect, then,
church property was state property, just as the Church itself was in
essence an additional arm of the state administrative apparatus.

The most striking innovation in this capitulary—and therefore the
most significant demonstration of Charles's pious penitence, as well
as his sense that strengthening the Church meant strengthening the
state—was his insistence on payment of the tithe to the Church.
Moreover, he doubled this tax—henceforth not only a tithe but a
ninth as well must be contributed. This twenty-per-cent tax must
have been a considerable burden on a people who had in the past
ten years been compelled to support many costly wars. The tithe and
the ninth were, in effect, hidden state taxes; paid to the Church by
the people, they ultimately enabled the ecclesiastical estates to provide their due of men and arms to the army.

The very form of the capitulary indicates how the problems of
Church and State were becoming one in Charles's mind. For in addition to religious matters, the decree dealt with such secular affairs as
the punishments for robbery and perjury, the formation of armed
bands, the taking of guild oaths and the regulation of tolls. This
mingling of religious and secular matters was to be characteristic of
almost all his later legislation.

Penalties were savage, in accordance with the ideas of the age. A
robber would lose an eye for a first crime, his nose for a second, and
would be punished by death if convicted a third time. A perjurer was
condemned to the loss of a hand. However, denunciation was more
dangerous than it is nowadays, for if the alleged perjurer cleared himself, his accuser was subject to the same penalty.

The prohibition against the *trustes* or armed bands was directed
primarily against banditry and against groups of dismissed soldiers
who took to looting the countryside on their way to their homes, in
spite of the regulation providing that they were under army discipline
for forty days after disbanding. But the ban against trustes was also

aimed at suppressing private war, that hangover of earlier Merovingian times which was to become again so striking a feature of the later Middle Ages. Moreover, Charles was aware of how much prestige he had lost in the Spanish debacle, and he tended to be suspicious of his subjects. Greater centralization was his answer to possible sedition, and so he began at this time to extend the institution of *missi*, or royal commissioners, who traveled about the country dispensing justice and checking abuses.

Another sign of his wariness was the new law against the formation of guilds that required their members to take an oath. This law, incidentally, marks the first historical mention of the word *guild* and suggests, since guilds are a phenomenon of the towns, that commerce was recovering from the chaos of the earlier part of the eighth century and that with reviving commerce the towns were growing. Charles's decree against excessive tolls was a further aid to commerce. But trade had its disadvantages also, and he simultaneously found it necessary to forbid the export of "strategic materials"—armor and harness, that is.

After the legislative session Charles set out, with the assurance that he had strengthened the home front to the best of his ability, on another Saxon campaign. Its aim was primarily to punish the Westphalians for their last year's raids, and the Westphalians were the only Saxons who opposed him. In a single battle a Saxon force was routed, and the Franks marched where they pleased throughout Westphalia, ravaging the countryside as Hesse had been ravaged by Saxons the year before.

Although the military campaigns in Saxony were desultory and confined only to the summers, the religious campaign to convert the Saxons to Christianity was continuous. It had been directed all along by Charles's brave old friend, Abbot Sturm of Fulda, who had set up a missionary headquarters in the fortress of Eresburg. On his return march through Saxony Charles paused at Eresburg and was saddened to find the old abbot ill, feeble and obviously on the point of death. How many faithful friends Charles had lost in the past year! As a token of his concern, and in the hope that Sturm's life might still be saved, Charles ordered his personal physician, Winthari, to accompany the old man back to Fulda.

The effect of Winthari's ministrations suggests the state of medicine at the time and indicates that there was some justification for Charles's well-known hatred of doctors and his refusal to obey their orders. Sturm's biographer, at any rate, puts the blame for the abbot's immediate death directly on the doctor. "The physician, by giving the abbot a brew, of what sort I do not know, so increased the weakness which he intended to diminish that the severe illness was augmented." Sturm began to complain that the doctor had made him sicker, and ordered his monks to hurry to the church and begin ringing all the bells. Then he had them assemble at his bedside and addressed them for the last time. Eigil, the biographer, was present at the scene and recorded Sturm's moving last words:

"You, my brothers, know my endeavors—that I have labored up to this very day for your good and your peace, that I have taken great care to provide that this monastery may continue to fulfill the will of Christ after my passing and that all of you here will be able to serve the Lord faithfully. My sons, abide by your present intentions all the days of your life. Pray for me to the all-highest God, and if ever out of human frailty I have done ill to any of you or have unjustly harmed anyone, forgive me as I from the depths of my heart forgive all who ever committed any offenses against me—especially Lul, who always opposed me."

This last flare of resentment against Lul, the Bishop of Mainz, lays bare the wonderful obstinacy of the old man. The conflict between Lul and Sturm dated back a quarter of a century to their quarrel over the body of Boniface. Lul had wanted to keep the bones of the martyr at Mainz. Sturm insisted stubbornly that Boniface had asked to be buried in Fulda. He finally won his point when a deacon of the church had a convenient vision in which Boniface demanded that his body be removed to Fulda—where it promptly proved its saintly efficacy in its proper resting place by working many miracles.

Bishop Lul never forgave Sturm for this defeat, and for many years he intrigued against the independence of the monastery of Fulda, which he wanted to make subject to his episcopal authority. A monastery responsible only to Rome and the king was always a thorn in the side of the local bishop. In this case the normal bitterness was intensified by the personal enmity between Sturm and Lul, an enmity so deep that on his deathbed Sturm could not refrain from recollecting old wrongs, even as he declared his formal forgiveness of Lul.

The death of Sturm enabled Lul to win the promotion he had long aspired to. Very likely the great influence of Sturm, who did not hesitate to charge his old enemy with heresy and with having been improperly ordained, had retarded Lul's advancement. Now at last Lul received from Pope Hadrian the archbishop's pallium.

Four years had passed since Charles's last visit to his Italian kingdom—years during which Pope Hadrian had insistently requested him to hurry to Italy. The "unspeakable" Duke Arichis of Benevento was plotting incessantly against him, Hadrian maintained, and was in league with the imperial patrician of Sicily. The Neopolitans and Greeks, at the instigation of Arichis, had taken Terracina (on the coast of Italy, between Rome and Naples) from him. Duke Arichis and the patrician of Sicily were still conspiring with Adelchis, Desiderius' son, and were expecting him to come to Italy with an army.

By now Charles knew that Pope Hadrian's alarums were generally premature and somewhat exaggerated. The pope had after all got himself into a predicament by raising an army of his own, while Charles was busy with the Spanish expedition, and seizing the disputed city of Terracina. Now that it had been taken from him again, he was crying for help and alleging all sorts of dangers to Frankish rule in Italy. Nevertheless, Charles felt that Italy required his presence periodically. He did not deceive himself into thinking that his swift suppression of the abortive revolt of 776 had consolidated his power in the former Lombard kingdom beyond possibility of challenge.

A complex of other reasons called Charles to Italy. Rome also beckoned him. Perhaps he would find there, in making the pilgrim's round of the basilicas, spiritual refreshment after the sorrows and setbacks of the past two years. There was also the plan for his sons' future which he had conceived after the fiasco in Spain. And he was contemplating more vigorous pressure against Cousin Tassilo, for his attention was once more turning toward the East. The failing health of Leo IV, the Roman Emperor at Constantinople, was common knowledge; and Leo had only a minor son to succeed him. If the Empire were weakened by internal dissension—which seemed likely enough if a young boy succeeded to the throne—Charles might well be able to extend his power to the northern and even the eastern shores of the Adriatic. But to do so he needed to regain the control of Bavaria which his father had lost.

The unreliability of the Saxons alone made Charles hesitate to depart for Italy. He resolved on one more demonstration of strength in Saxony, to ensure that this time there would be no uprising there while he was busy in Italy. As early in the spring as the weather permitted he gathered a large army and marched northeastward, unopposed, clear across Saxony to the Elbe River. Here, apparently, he settled the frontier between the Saxons and the Slavic tribes living to the east of the Elbe. Again mass conversions took place. Large numbers of Saxons—"with their usual hypocrisy," say the annals—submitted to baptism.

It must have been with a sense of relief that Charles turned from the inhospitable heaths and forests of the "perfidious Saxons" toward the warmth, the sunlight and the monuments of Italy. Like a true German he was drawn by the Roman sun and Roman culture; and also like a true German he was wary of the lightheartedness, the color, the gaiety and the laxness of Italian life. The luxuries and beauties of Italy were potentially corrupting, and Charles's attitude toward them always remained ambivalent. Thus he would bring Italian mosaics and marbles to adorn his palaces in the north, but he persistently refused to wear Italian dress. Only twice in his life—and each time at the special request of a pope—did he consent to wear the Roman long tunic and cloak.

His love for Rome, then, was compounded with fear, a fear which explains why he visited the city only four times in his long life. And he kept his sons from visiting it as well.

On the present occasion Charles took Hildigard and his entire family with him on what was, for them, an exciting and pleasant vacation as well as a solemn pilgrimage. But the two oldest sons, Charles and Pepin, were left behind in stoutly Germanic Worms. Perhaps he explained to them that some responsible representatives of the royal family must remain in Frankland; but his real reason was an unwillingness to expose two impressionable boys to the seductions of Italy. Young Charles in particular, who was now ten and, according to all testimony, the image of his father, was being reared in the stern and old-fashioned Frankish tradition of his grandfather and great-grandfather. He was receiving early and thorough training in warfare and statecraft; in three more years he would be leading an army into battle.

Pepin, the son of Charles's first wife, Himiltrude, was already adolescent and would perhaps be even more subject to temptation in

Italy. But Charles had another reason for leaving the unlucky hunch-backed boy behind. For Pepin was about to be formally disinherited and to lose even the right to sole use of his name. Charles was planning to have the pope himself baptize Hildigard's second son, Carloman, and to rechristen this son with the name of Pepin.

It is impossible not to see behind this decision Queen Hildigard's gentle insistence. The presence of Charles's eldest son at court must always have disturbed her. She could not help seeing that in spite of his deformity he had ambitions to share the succession. These ambitions were nourished by Charles's kindness toward him—for he was always treated as a loved member of the household and given the precedence his age entitled him to—and by the glorious name he bore, the name of Charles's father and first king of the new line. His handsome face and personable manner had won him many friends at court. Malcontents, who would never dare to oppose Charles openly, lavished sympathy on the son whose mother Charles had wronged when he discarded her for the Lombard princess.

Busy as he always was with his plans, judgments, administrative affairs and, of late, linguistic and philosophical studies, Charles was inevitably less sensitive to the rumors and undercurrents of the Frankish court than was his wife. Hildigard could sense in the favored position of young Pepin a grave future danger to her own sons. For the past century Frankish rule had passed from a Pepin to a Charles to a Pepin to a Charles. How easily and dangerously could simple folk assume that Pepin was the destined heir. And, Hildigard could further urge on Charles, how ill-omened was the name of Carloman for her own son. The first Carloman had ended his life as a monk; the second, Charles's brother, had died young. In the nine years that had elapsed since Carloman's death Charles had attempted to heal the breach between the two parts of the original kingdom by rarely, if ever, referring to the three years of his brother's rule. Naming his own son after Carloman had been an ill-considered lapse from this policy, Hildigard could point out.

Charles could not escape the force of these arguments. Since he intended to make this three-year-old son King of Italy, it would be wise to support his tender years with a more regal name than that of Carloman. Though he must have felt great reluctance to offend his eldest son—even as Hildigard would not relish the role of cruel stepmother—the decision was taken.

Toward the end of the year 780 the royal household, with a large retinue, set out across the Alpine passes for the third time in seven years. They went to Pavia, the capital of Charles's Lombard kingdom, and there Charles spent the winter regulating the affairs of Lombardy.

So many appeals awaited him there, so many law cases had been held pending his judgment, that he was forced to issue an order—as he had done the year before in Frankland—restricting the right of appeal to the king's court. He instructed plaintiffs to attend the regular county courts; only after three trials before the count were they allowed to appeal to the king. Charles had to be jealous of his time; he wanted more hours of the day for the intellectual pursuits that were beginning to exert upon him an irresistible allure.

During the winter there came news from Byzantium that Emperor Leo IV had died, and rumors that his wife Irene had poisoned him. Leo had been a fanatical persecutor of image worship. According to one story, he had discovered two icons in Irene's apartment and had flown into such a rage that he threatened his wife with the severest punishments. When almost immediately after this incident he died of a sudden fever, suspicion was naturally directed against his wife—all the more so since the beautiful young woman who boasted of her Athenian origins was thought to be capable of any crime.

Leo was succeeded by his ten-year-old son Constantine, and Irene assumed the regency and actual direction of the government of the Roman Empire of the East. A woman whose resolution and courage was equaled only by her cruelty, Irene promptly set about reversing the iconoclasm which had been the dominant policy of the Empire for a generation. She moved cautiously, so as not to offend the powerful minority party of image smashers. Internally she ordered that there be no reprisals against the iconoclasts; externally she sought to strengthen her position by restoring good relations with the papacy—a natural step, since she was leading her empire back to orthodox Catholicism—and by making an alliance with the foremost power in the Christian world, the Kingdom of the Franks and Lombards.

Pope Hadrian was the natural mediator in such diplomatic negotiations, which at this juncture had advantages for all three parties concerned. Hadrian could hope for a middleman's pay in the form of the territories he had long been claiming as part of the "patrimony of St. Peter." A settlement between Irene and Charles would presumably also include a bettering of the strained relations between the papacy and Benevento on the one hand, between the papacy and the imperial provinces of Naples and Sicily on the other.

For Charles an alliance with Constantinople would give him time to consolidate Frankish rule in Lombardy. All these past six years since the conquest of Lombardy there had lurked in the background the constant threat that Adelchis, the son of the deposed Lombard king Desiderius, might land on the shores of Italy at the head of an army provided by the Eastern emperor. Again and again the pope had warned that such a landing was imminent; and although nothing of the kind had yet happened, Charles preferred to avert the possibility rather than have to fight for Lombardy all over again. Adalperga, the wife of Duke Arichis of Benevento, was obviously in constant communication with her brother Adelchis in Constantinople and with her sister Liutperga, Duchess of Bavaria. All three children of Desiderius had every reason to hate Charles and to urge their husbands to act in concert against him. Charles needed time to handle separately each of these potential enemies. An agreement with Irene, who was in the similar position of needing time to consolidate, was therefore desirable at almost any cost.

As it turned out, the cost was low indeed, since the request for the alliance came from the other side. When Charles arrived in Rome at Easter he was visited by two emissaries from Irene who proposed a marriage between Charles's eight-year-old daughter Rotrud and the ten-year-old Emperor Constantine. The marriage contract would include, of course, agreements on political questions. Irene, for her part, would guarantee to withdraw her support from Adelchis and Arichis and to recognize *de jure* the *de facto* Frankish rule in the former Exarchate of Ravenna. Charles for the time being guaranteed Byzantine rule over Venetia and Istria and promised not to attack Neopolitan territory.

Agreement was reached on all outstanding problems, including the ambiguous position of the pope, who up to this time had been in the Empire's view a subject of the Empire, in his own mind an independent prince, and in fact a vassal of Charles. Irene withdrew all claim to sovereignty over the papal states, and Charles contented himself with an actual but not formal overlordship in the patrimony of St. Peter. From this time on Pope Hadrian, as a sign of his independence, began dating documents from the years of his own papacy instead of by the regnal years of the Eastern emperor.

If there were mental reservations on both sides, they did not show

up in the marriage contract that was solemnly signed and sealed,
probably at the Lateran. Charles was bent on providing for his children at this time—the visit to Rome, in fact, centered around his
children—and was justified in feeling that he was doing well for his
eldest daughter in betrothing her to the Eastern emperor. Yet he was
always reluctant to part with his daughters, just as, ten years earlier,
he had been unwilling to send his sister Gisla to Lombardy to marry
Adelchis. Since, however, both parties were so young, the question
would not come up for some time. Meanwhile the situation might
change, and Charles could freely fortify his position.

Besides this betrothal, the great ceremony which had been planned
beforehand took place this Easter in the basilica of the Lateran. Pope
Hadrian baptized Charles's four-year-old son Carloman and renamed
him Pepin.* The pope also became the new Pepin's godfather. He
was proud of this relationship and insisted on it; in all his letters to
Charles thereafter he addresses Charles as *compater*, cofather.

The two children, Pepin and Louis, were then solemnly anointed
by Hadrian and pronounced respectively King of Italy and King of
Aquitaine. These titles served a dual purpose for Charles. They established the succession, for by the time the children were grown
men they would be accustomed to think of Aquitaine and Italy as
their own kingdoms and would be less likely to dispute with their
brothers over lands they had never expected to hold. And at the same
time the national pride of those two great provinces of the Frankish
empire would be satisfied. Italy and Aquitaine, both independent
nations less than ten years before, would be able to enjoy the illusion
of independence. In fact, Charles was binding them closer than ever
to Frankland. All actual power remained in the hands of the Frankish
advisers whom he appointed as guardians to his sons. Charles continued to use the title of King of the Lombards for himself. And, as
we shall see, he made sure, as his sons grew up, that they did not fall
too much under what he considered "foreign" influences. The two
royal sons stayed with him frequently, and he exercised the closest
supervision over their education.

For the present, however, he was parting with his sons, hard as
this would be on Hildigard and on himself. But Hildigard, that most
fruitful of wives, had a new baby girl named Gisla to occupy her

---

* Hereafter he will be referred to as Pepin, and Charles's son by Himiltrude as
Pepin the Hunchback.

mind; and Charles felt it essential actually to install the two boys in
their kingdoms. Presumably the ceremony in Pavia, with Pepin, was
similar to the rather comic formal entrance of Louis into Aquitaine—
which has been recorded by Louis' biographer. Accompanied by his
baiulus Arnold, whose office was that of guardian and administrator,
and by a retinue of nurses and soldiers, Louis was carried as far as
Orléans in a cradle. There he was dressed in armor made specially
to fit him, placed on a horse whose reins he clutched with his chubby
baby hands, and so rode into his kingdom—a man on horseback.

For his services, Pope Hadrian claimed his reward. The pope felt
that a good many promises made in previous donations of territory—
by King Pepin and by Charles himself in 774—still remained unfulfilled. It was probably at this time that, to back his claims, the pope
presented to Charles one of the most remarkable of historical for-
geries: the "Donation of Constantine."* This document purported
to be a gift by the Roman Emperor Constantine, the founder of Constantinople and the first Christian emperor, to Pope Sylvester and all
his successors of "the city of Rome and all the provinces, districts and
cities of Italy or the western regions." Constantine declared that he
had been stricken by leprosy which none of his many physicians could
cure. He was then advised by his pagan priests "that a font should
be set up on the Capitol and that I should fill this with the blood of
innocent infants; and that if I bathed in this blood while it was still
warm, I might be purified of the leprosy. Then, a multitude of innocent infants having been gathered, the pagan priests prepared to
slaughter them and fill the font with their blood. But seeing the tears
of the mothers, I was filled with abhorrence, pitied them and ordered
their sons to be given back to them."

After this act of mercy the priests of St. Peter and Paul came to
Constantine and congratulated him on having refrained from spilling
innocent blood. "Since you have thus put a limit to your vices," they
said, "we have been sent by our Lord Christ to tell you how to regain
your health. Listen, therefore, to our admonishment and do what we

---

* Estimates of the date of the Donation of Constantine vary widely. In a
letter of Pope Hadrian's to Charles written in 778, however, the pope expressly
refers to Constantine's generosity toward the Church and urges Charles to imitate
it. For the argument in favor of dating the document about this time, compare
Hollnsteiner, *Das Abendland*.

tell you. Sylvester, the bishop of the city of Rome, has fled to Mount Serapte to escape your persecutions. There he lives in the darkness of caves with his clergy. Send for him, and he will show you a pool and dip you into it. When he has dipped you for the third time, the leprosy will go out of you. When this has been done, reward your Saviour by ordering that the churches throughout the world be restored. Purify yourself by abandoning all idols and adoring and cherishing the living and true God. . . ."

Constantine took their advice and went to Sylvester, who first proceeded to instruct the emperor in the articles of the Christian faith. Then, after proper penance, Constantine was baptized. "Being placed at the bottom of the font, I myself saw a hand from Heaven touching me, and I rose clean, the filth of leprosy wiped away."

In gratitude for this cure, and in order that the supreme pontificate may "be adorned with power and glory even more than any earthly rulers," Constantine decides to turn Italy over to the rule of the pope and to transfer his capital to the East, where he will build a New Rome in the province of Byzantium. "For where the priests and the head of the Christian religion have been established as supreme by the Ruler of Heaven, it is not fitting that an earthly ruler should have power."

This wonderful donation was then placed in a familiar spot—upon the body of St. Peter himself; and presumably Pope Hadrian now removed it from beneath the donations of Pepin and Charles to have a copy made, so that he might show it to Charles. Whether Charles suspected the forgery (which was not proved to be such until the Renaissance) is doubtful; but the document did not have the effect on Charles that Hadrian had hoped for. Far from making him more receptive to the papal claims, he became suspicious. Hadrian was really going too far and asking for too much. Did he expect Charles, like Constantine, to turn all of Italy over to him? Did he expect Charles to recognize him as supreme ruler of all Christendom, above all earthly sovereigns?

Charles had no intention of doing anything of the sort, and the reward he fixed on for the pope was more in the nature of a consolation prize. He granted to St. Peter the territory of Sabina, that mountainous region northeast of Rome whence, in the mythical past, the Latins had carried off the Sabine women. But even this grant was made only on condition that the pope prove by specific documents his claims to ownership, and that the exact borders of Sabina be defined. Hadrian's old antagonist, Itherius, now Abbot of St. Martin's in Tours, and Chancellor Maginarius, were appointed to look into the rights of the matter. And Itherius proved again, as he had six years earlier, that he was a genius at procrastination when it came to surrendering any territory to the pope. He found fault with the documents, did not agree with Hadrian's definition of the Sabine borders, and so strongly contested every point that the pope fell into a rage of frustration. He protested that the royal commissioners were being misled by "perverse and wicked men," that he was not asking for the property of others but only for what was rightfully his, and that he had secured as witnesses "men more than a hundred years old" to testify that the *estates* in question had been, of old, part of the patrimony of St. Peter.

Hadrian was certainly not getting the best of his bargains with Charles. Charles had flatly refused the pope's request to attack Naples and retake the pope's "possessions" in Neopolitan territory. Hadrian's claims to rule in entire territories were already dwindling to efforts to recover isolated estates belonging to the Church. Charles, on the other hand, was getting everything he wanted out of Hadrian.

For in another matter of the greatest importance Pope Hadrian proved amenable to Charles's plans. With his eastern flank secured by the alliance with Constantinople, Charles was at last able to strike at the independence of Bavaria. Cousin Tassilo and his Lombard wife had ruled almost untroubled by Frankish demands for nearly twenty years. Through all this time Tassilo had maintained the best of relations with the papacy. Like Charles, he had richly endowed monasteries, had built churches and had energetically pursued the conversion of his pagan neighbors. Hadrian approved of Tassilo as a dutiful son of the Church and somewhat feared him also as the brother-in-law of the Beneventan duke. But the pope could do no more than urge Charles to be moderate; in all political matters he was of necessity completely subservient to Charles.

Hadrian could, at any rate, ease his conscience with regard to Tassilo by recalling that a religious issue was involved. For at Compiègne a quarter of a century before Tassilo had "commended himself" to King Pepin as his vassal and had sworn solemn oaths of allegiance—allegiance to his cousin Charles as well as to his uncle. As supreme bishop of the Church, Hadrian was justified in reminding Tassilo that

oaths were inviolable, especially when they had been sworn upon the
bones of so many and such powerful saints.

Two emissaries from Pope Hadrian were therefore sent to Tassilo
to remind him of the oath of Compiègne. They were accompanied
by envoys from Charles bearing a pointed invitation to Tassilo to
present himself in August at the annual assembly of the Franks, to be
held in Worms, and there renew his oath of allegiance. Charles himself then left Italy for Worms, stopping at Milan to have Archbishop
Thomas of that city baptize the new baby of the family, Gisla (named
after Charles's sister). No doubt the ceremony took place in the
Basilica of St. Ambrose, the church in which, according to legend,
Bishop Ambrose had baptized Charles's favorite writer, St. Augustine.

Tassilo might have replied that oaths taken under duress were not
binding. But he was still under duress. The combined pressure from
Charles and the pope was too much for him. Submission seemed to
Cousin Tassilo his only choice, but he was also suspicious and unwilling to put his head into the lion's mouth. He would come to
Worms, he said, but only on condition that Charles give hostages as
a guarantee of his personal safety. Ties of kinship were all very well,
but Tassilo had no desire to be shorn and made an involuntary monk
for the rest of his life.

Charles resented the implication that a safe-conduct was necessary
for his beloved cousin—all the more so since he had in fact been considering the possibility of arresting Tassilo, deposing him and forcing
the Bavarian nobles to accept a *fait accompli*. Nevertheless, he badly
wanted Tassilo to come to Worms. A token submission, even if he
should not be able to hold Tassilo to it, would give him a legal pretext for future action against his cousin. Moreover, he wanted the
opportunity to speak with the powerful Bavarian nobles who would
accompany Tassilo to the assembly. Perhaps they could be bribed.
Charles would be forty in six months, and he was beginning to look
for easier ways than brute force to accomplish his ends. Were not any
means justified against a perjurer and deserter like Cousin Tassilo?
And were not any means justified that helped him create the great
Frankish state which would be the City of God?

So Charles was beginning to think. It is curious that the next decade of his life—the decade between forty and fifty, which was marked
by a great intellectual burgeoning, by that interest in education, theology, philosophy, astronomy, music, rhetoric, poetry and all other cul-

tural pursuits which was to stimulate the Carolingian Renaissance—
was also distinguished, in Charles's political activities, by deviousness
and sometimes by cruelty.

Since it was important to have Tassilo obey the summons, no matter what conditions he imposed, Charles gave the hostages—and Tassilo came to Worms. He was received in a fashion that must have
surprised him. He had come laden with gifts to soften his cousin's
hostility. But there were no signs at all of hostility. Instead, Charles
returned his gifts manyfold. All that was asked of Tassilo in return
was the renewal of his old oath of loyalty and obedience, and the
whole matter was put to Tassilo as if the meeting had been called
solely so that Charles's sons might be included in Tassilo's allegiance.
As a guarantee of the oath, Charles asked only for twelve hostages, to
be delivered later, and then Tassilo was permitted to depart—"with
honor," say the annals.

Perhaps at the sight of his cousin, so much like himself in age and
intellectual interests, Charles was swayed by that impulse toward
friendliness which was so strong in his nature. Certainly at this time
he did not wish to push Tassilo to the point of ultimate surrender.
But there was a fundamental difference of ambitions between the
two men that sooner or later had to culminate in bitter antagonism.
The difference was symbolized in their choice of wives. Tassilo, the
enlightened, pious and intellectual ruler, was happy in his marriage
with one of the intellectual daughters of Desiderius. Charles, also
briefly married to another of Desiderius' daughters, had been unable
to abide her. After a year he had divorced her and married a child,
a submissive, maternal young woman who could influence him only
by cajoling, never by convincing him. In short, Charles, also an enlightened, pious and intellectual ruler, had that additional streak of
tyrannical ambition, of stubborn unwillingness to brook interference,
which made him the natural victor, his cousin the natural victim.

But for the present his intellectual rather than his tyrannical traits
were uppermost. He awaited eagerly the new guests whom he had
invited to his court.

CHAPTER NINE

The World of Culture

RECENT French historian has disdainfully dismissed the Carolingian revival of learning in a few words: "What possible point can there be in trying to rehabilitate this gloomy age, to glorify this abortive renaissance? Neither Charlemagne nor his companions were responsible for its failure. They were too close to their barbaric past, and were not ripe for civilization."*

Monsieur Sedillot has fallen into the trap that awaits historical tourists who pay only the briefest of visits to a past civilization and then flit on to the next point of interest. Like the American in Europe who sees only the inadequacy of local plumbing, he has judged and found wanting a culture that does not meet the standards of urban industrialism. Is it not obvious that our contemporary concern with schools of existentialism, say, or with the distinctions among capitalism, communism and socialism, will seem a thousand years hence as incomprehensible to historians of his temper as the eighth century's concern with adoptianism, iconoclasm or the *filioque* controversy? The human mind has always worked with the materials it had at hand. It is risky to judge and condemn the intellectual achievements of one age by the standards of another. Aristotle was not a fool because he thought the universe consisted of fifty-five concentric hollow spheres—any more than Niels Bohr was a fool when he framed his "solar system" model of the atom. Both men were working with the information available to them, and both men were adding to man's understanding of the universe. Physical science has moved so rapidly in modern times that Bohr's brilliant theory had to be abandoned within ten years after it was conceived (and Bohr himself was

* René Sedillot, *An Outline of French History*, New York, Alfred A. Knopf, 1953.

foremost in abandoning it), whereas a variant of Aristotle's conception continued to be accepted for well over a millennium and a half. The slower pace of scientific development in the past does not mean that every thinker from Aristotle to Copernicus was an intellectual dwarf. The modern schoolboy is not greater than Euclid because he knows far more about mathematics.

Charles, King of the Franks and Lombards, was the Alexander rather than the Aristotle of his time. Yet his mind, which had hitherto expressed itself principally in political action, in conquest and consolidation, was now beginning to range wide in less practical realms. He had begun studying grammar with the aging Peter of Pisa, and grammar included "literature," the examination and interpretation of literary and above all scriptural texts. He was seeking someone to teach him astronomy, to give him lessons in music and versification, to help him with Biblical and patristic criticism, to answer his questions about the origins of things, to discuss ethical and theological problems with him. He was a great talker, so much so that the members of his court thought him a bit loquacious. Now he wanted people around him with spry and subtle minds who could hold up their end of a conversation on subjects other than hawking and hunting—although he, in common with all noble Franks of his day, dearly loved to speak of his falcons and hounds, his successes or failures on the great hunts which all his life were to take up much of his leisure time.

To satisfy his longing for intellectual stimulus he began gathering around himself both reputable scholars and bright young men. The Monk of St. Gall, who as always embroiders the facts of Charles's life with charming fantasies and yet so often hits on essential traits of Charles's character, has constructed a fine legend out of this activity. The Monk writes:

"Now it happened, when Charles had begun to reign alone in the western parts of the world, and the pursuit of learning had been almost forgotten throughout all his realm . . . that two Scots came from Ireland* to the coast of Gaul along with certain traders of Britain. These Scots were unrivaled for their skill in sacred and secular learning; and day by day, when the crowd gathered around them for business, they exhibited no wares for sale, but cried out, 'Ho, everyone that desires wisdom, let him draw near and take it at our hands; for

* The Irish were universally called Scots at this time.

it is wisdom we have for sale.' Now they declared that they had wisdom for sale because they said that people cared not for what was freely given, but only for what was sold. . . . For so long did they make their proclamation that in the end . . . the matter was brought to the ears of King Charles, who always loved and sought after wisdom. Wherefore he ordered them to come with all speed into his presence and asked them whether it were true that they had brought wisdom with them. They answered, 'We both possess and are ready to give it, in the name of God, to those who seek it worthily.' Again he asked them what price they required for it, and they answered: 'We seek no price, O king. We ask only a fit place for teaching and quick minds to teach, and besides these food and clothing. . . .'

"This answer filled the king with great joy, and first he kept both of them with him for a short time. But soon, when he had to go to war, he made one of them named Clement reside in Gaul, and to him he sent many boys both of noble, middle and humble birth, and he ordered as much food to be given them as they required, and he set aside for them buildings suitable for study."

Although the two "Scots" probably never attempted to cry wisdom in the market place, the Monk conveys a true picture of Charles's pleasure in finding men of learning, of his zeal in setting up schools for boys of all classes and of his generosity toward good teachers. His own thirst for learning made him value education highly. Moreover, he recognized that only by raising educational standards could he recruit the corps of administrators he needed for his rapidly expanding kingdom. Under the Merovingian kings of Frankland enough of the Roman schools had survived to supply educated laymen for the offices of government. But that system had broken down during the disorders of civil wars and Saracen invasions in the early part of the eighth century, and even the ecclesiastical schools were in a bad way.

The most important secular school in the Frankish realm was, of course, the Palace School, in which Charles's own boys and the sons of his chief nobles were being or were to be educated. For this school Charles wanted to find the best available teacher.

The Monk goes on to tell us: "When Albinus [Alcuin], an Englishman, heard that the most religious Emperor* Charles gladly entertained wise men, he entered into a ship and came to him. Now

---

* A characteristic slip on the part of the Monk. Charles was at this time only king.

Albinus was skilled in all learning beyond all others of our times, for he was the disciple of that most learned priest Bede, who next to Saint Gregory was the most skillful interpreter of the Scriptures."

The association had not begun in quite this fashion. It was due partly to a lucky accident. On his recent visit to Italy Charles had stopped for a short time at the city of Parma. There, by good fortune, he had met the famous Anglo-Saxon scholar who was returning from a mission to Rome.

Alcuin was about ten years older than Charles himself. Born around the time that the Venerable Bede died at Jarrow, he had been raised in the Cathedral School at York in the tradition of Archbishop Egbert, one of Bede's disciples. It was a great tradition, for in the early part of the eighth century, while on the Continent Boniface was bemoaning the ignorance and license he found even among the clergy, England was a center of learning.

The emphasis in the studies at the Cathedral School was on the history and doctrines of the Church, of course; but the "seven liberal arts"—grammar, rhetoric, dialectic, arithmetic, music, geometry and astronomy—were not neglected. In the library at York, of which Alcuin soon became the head as he became also director of the Cathedral School, the ardent young disciple of Egbert was able to study the works of Pliny, Cicero, Vergil, Ovid and possibly also Horace and Terence. Most of the Roman classics, however, were known to him only at second hand, through the sixth-century writings of Boethius and Cassiodorus, or through the encyclopedic compilations of the seventh-century Spanish bishop Isidore. But the greatest influence on Alcuin would naturally be the Venerable Bede, whose simple, clear and classical Latin style Alcuin imitated to advantage.

Latin required intensive study in England, for in the Anglo-Saxon kingdoms there was no tradition of Latin speech as there was on the Continent in Spain, Gaul and Italy. Precisely because the classical language was unaffected by a related "vulgar" tongue, a "purer" Latinity flourished among the English scholars than was to be found anywhere on the Continent. Bede's great gifts as a stylist enabled him to make the best possible use of this classical tradition in his *Ecclesiastical History*, which is not only the best and almost the only source on the early history of England, but which is a book that still makes lively reading. It might well have served Alcuin's contemporaries as a model of intelligence and coherence.

Yet it was to Bede's theological books, with their emphasis on allegorical interpretation of the Scriptures, that Alcuin's bright but essentially conventional and highly orthodox mind was most attracted. He was excited by these lessons which, as he wrote, "opened out the mysteries of Holy Scripture and gave us to look into the abyss of law ancient and unfulfilled."* Through Alcuin's popularization of Bede's method, allegorical exegesis (a method whose roots go back to Origen and Augustine) became the characteristic medieval approach to the Scriptures. The historical significance of the Bible was almost entirely neglected.

Essentially Alcuin was a schoolmaster, content to cull from the writings of the past and put together textbooks whose contents were adapted to the needs of students. That he was one of the great teachers of the age is evident from the devotion of his many talented pupils, to whom he gave such thorough preparation that they fitted easily into high ecclesiastical posts all over Europe. Nor did he lose touch with his pupils once they had gone out into the world of the Church. With all of them he kept up a warm correspondence in which a somewhat pedantic didacticism is always mingled with his genuine friendliness. Sometimes his letters were in verse, most of it mediocre.

In the year that Charles embarked on his disastrous Spanish expedition (778) Alcuin was given complete charge of the school and library of the York Cathedral, which he had unofficially headed for some time. Here, with his placid and retiring temperament, he might have remained, quietly teaching for the rest of his life. But a new archbishop, Eanbald, was installed at York in 780 and, following the custom, sent to Rome for his pallium—that woolen band ornamented with crosses which was originally conferred by the pope as a sign of favor but which by the late eighth century had become a necessary symbol of the archbishop's authority and of his submission to the pope as head of the Church. The honor of fetching the pallium from Rome went to Alcuin.

The journey was one Alcuin undertook with pleasure, not only because he was eager to visit Rome and speak with the pope but because it gave him the opportunity to visit many friends and former pupils

---

* Cited by Eleanor Duckett, *Alcuin, Friend of Charlemagne*, New York, The Macmillan Company, 1951. In the discussion of Alcuin I have leaned heavily on Miss Duckett's excellent biography, and used some of her translations. She is, however, in no way responsible for my conclusions.

on the way. Travel was not too difficult; there was constant intercourse by sea between Frisia and England, and many Frisian traders were settled in the Anglo-Saxon kingdoms. The Frisians—the ancestors of the Dutch—were already noted for trade and their thriving dairies; we find Alcuin in a poem greeting Bishop Alberic of Utrecht as "lord of many cows." From Utrecht Alcuin apparently made his way down the Rhine and the Moselle to what is now Southern France, and thence into Italy.

In the course of his return trip from Rome, bearing the pallium for his archbishop, Alcuin and Charles met at Parma. The delight Charles took in this cultivated Englishman can be surmised from the warm friendship that so rapidly developed between them. Charles promptly invited Alcuin to come to his court and be director of the Palace School. He indicated that Alcuin would be also in general charge of educational affairs in the Frankish kingdom. There was much work to be done in Frankland, he urged. He often received letters from monasteries stating that the brethren were offering pious prayers on his behalf, but most of these letters were characterized by "correct thoughts and uncouth expressions." As he himself wrote, "What pious devotion dictated faithfully to the mind, the tongue, unskilled for want of study, was not able to express in the letter without error." He needed an inspiring teacher whose authority in the field of knowledge was unchallenged. To such a teacher he would give all the support needed to carry out an ambitious program. Would Alcuin consent to "sow the seeds of learning in Frankland" as he had already done in his native England?

The worldly rewards that Charles offered were tempting, even though Alcuin had inherited wealth of his own back home. But more appealing than these to a man of Alcuin's caliber was the opportunity for a wider sphere of activity than he could ever find as head of a school in the small kingdom of Northumbria, which in recent years had been racked by political disturbances. A lover of stability and legitimacy, Alcuin was deeply troubled by the bloody uprisings which had driven two kings into exile within six years. In Northumbria no one was free from fear; the earth, as he was to write later, "was stained with the blood of rulers and kings." Charles, on the other hand, was the secure ruler of a great and growing state which stood in the closest relations with Alcuin's beloved Church.

Alcuin was also favorably impressed by this candid and outspoken giant of a man, with his rather large nose and high-pitched voice, who showed a schoolboy's eagerness to learn. For the great king plied Alcuin with respectful questions on the Scriptures and the stars, humbly addressed him as "Father"—though he was a mere deacon—and assured him that if he accepted and came to Frankland he would find a king and all his courtiers among his pupils. Alcuin knew how rare it was to find love of learning combined with political power. Then too the king's ability to understand and speak Greek was a formidable accomplishment to Alcuin, and a further recommendation. For Alcuin himself had no facility or easy familiarity with Greek; the tags of Greek in his writings are borrowed from his predecessors. The prospect of being at a court where he could learn as well as teach was a further enticement; for, the king informed him, there would be a Greek teacher at court. In the arrangements for the betrothal of Rotrud to young Constantine it had been agreed that a Byzantine official named Elissaeus would reside at Charles's court (or, rather, travel about with it) in order to instruct the princess in the Greek language and in the customs of the Empire of the Romans.

Alcuin agreed to the king's proposal, provided that Archbishop Eanbald and his own king gave their consent. Then he returned to England with the pallium for Eanbald.

Alcuin and Eanbald had long been engaged in directing the rebuilding of York Cathedral, which had burned down in Alcuin's boyhood, the year before Charles was born. But the work was now done, and the archbishop had no reason to hold Alcuin back from a greater destiny than he could offer him. King Elfwald of Northumbria also was not averse to having one of his subjects at the court of Charles. Good relations with the King of the Franks might provide him with sufficient prestige to maintain his shaky position, in spite of his turbulent nobles and the claims of his great neighbor, King Offa of Mercia, who styled himself king of all the English.

The way, then, was clear, and Alcuin, with many a backward glance at York (he wrote at this time a versified history of the city), crossed to the Continent and made his way to the royal vill at Quierzy, near Paris, where King Charles was spending the winter.

With Alcuin's arrival at Charles's court there began that many-sided intellectual activity which was to be the ornament of Charles's reign and to influence significantly the next thousand years. Alcuin had come primarily as a schoolmaster, and it is as teacher and minister of education that his activities were most important in the earlier years. His active role in doctrinal controversies belongs to the latter part of his life and of Charles's reign; his function as Charles's friend, riddle maker, question answerer and general mentor was incidental to his main work. Because he did that work so well, Charles would have kept him at his post even if there had not existed between the two men such strong mutual respect and affection.

The foremost task Alcuin faced was the improvement of literacy, which was at a woefully low level even in the monasteries. There were not enough schools, and the textbooks used were faulty. These faulty texts were further corrupted because they were copied by half-literate boys. Attempts were made to remedy this situation in a number of decrees issued by Charles but no doubt written by Alcuin. Every abbey was required to have a school where boys* might learn reading, the Psalms, musical notation, singing, arithmetic and grammar. If copies of the Gospel, Psalter or Missal were needed, these were to be made by mature men.

Alcuin and Charles insisted also on the instruction of upper-class children—which may seem strange until we recall that the Frankish nobles were primarily fighters, not scholars. One of the stories of the Monk of St. Gall tells how Charles, visiting a school, found the work of the lower-class children immensely superior to that of the young scions of the nobility:

"Then the most wise Charles, imitating the judgment of the eternal Judge, gathered together those who had done well upon his right hand and addressed them in these words: 'My children, you have found much favor with me because you have tried with all your might to carry out my orders. . . . Now study to attain perfection and I will give you bishoprics and splendid monasteries and will always honor you.' Then he turned severely to those who were gathered on his left . . . and flung at them in scorn these terrible words, which seemed thunder rather than human speech: 'You nobles, you sons of my chiefs, you superfine dandies, you have trusted to your wealth and have set at naught my orders which were for your own good; you have

---

* No provision was made officially for the education of women. Nevertheless, women obtained education somehow, for there were a good many highly cultivated ladies at the time—in particular Charles's own daughters and sister, and the wives of his rivals, Tassilo and Arichis.

neglected learning and gone in for luxury and sport, idleness and profitless pastimes. . . . By the King of Heaven, I take no account of your noble birth and your fine looks, though others may admire you for them. Know this for certain, that unless you make up for your laziness by vigorous study, you will never get any favors from Charles.' "

The point was, of course, that Charles needed educated young noblemen for administrators in his expanding realm. But it is unfair to put too utilitarian an interpretation on his policy. We must recognize that he believed in widespread education for its own sake.

At the beginning of Alcuin's activity the prime necessity was to teach teachers and to halt that progressive corruption of texts which, in an age when all books had to be reproduced by hand, resulted from the ignorance of copyists. So successful was Alcuin in his teacher-training program that after fifteen years, when he retired to the Monastery of Tours and his work was taken over by Bishop Theodulf of Orléans, it was possible to propose *universal free education.* "The priests are to have schools in the towns and villages," Theodulf ordered, "and if any of the faithful wish to recommend their children for the learning of letters, the priests must receive and teach these children. . . . And they are to charge no fee for their teaching and to receive nothing except what the parents may offer of their own free will and out of affection." The tremendous importance of this step can scarcely be exaggerated. Although the Carolingian school system suffered severely in the disorders that followed the reign of Charles, the aim and the ideal had been set for all time.

In addition to organizing education and overseeing the two monasteries of which Charles had promptly appointed him abbot, Alcuin obtained from England books which were not available in Frankland and began building up a library for Charles. Since elementary textbooks were sadly wanting, he also wrote a number of his own. These are cast in dialogue form, which Alcuin judged best suited for beginners and which also expressed the direct and personal relationship he liked to establish with his pupils. These textbooks were scarcely specimens of brilliant organization or logical treatment. Alcuin, for example, divides grammar into twenty-six "varieties": words, letters, syllables, clauses, dictions, speeches, definitions, feet, accents, punctuations, diacritical marks, spellings, analogies, etymologies, glosses, differences, barbarisms, solecisms, faults, metaplasms, schemata, tropes, prose, meters, fables and histories. Classification was certainly not Alcuin's strong point. But his writings on grammar, rhetoric, orthography and arithmetic were highly esteemed in their day—and long afterward—and they served their purpose. In Alcuin's schools the teachers were superior to their textbooks.

One of Alcuin's texts—the *Disputation between the Royal and Most Noble Youth Pepin with Albinus the Schoolmaster*—affords a remarkable insight into the medieval mind, with its obliqueness, fancifulness and love of epigrammatic formulations. Some of the questions are simple; some are the basic human questions with which philosophers and scientists have wrestled throughout the ages. But what strikes us about all the answers that Alcuin gives is the indirectness, the total absence of the natural-scientific point of view. Everything is reduced to a symbol. Egon Friedell* has remarked, in a striking exaggeration, that the medieval mind was really interested in only two things: God and the soul. Certainly Friedell has gone too far, but the dialogue between Pepin and Alcuin suggests how much truth there is in his statement. For example:

PEPIN	ALBINUS
What is writing?	The guardian of history.
What is speech?	The revealer of the soul.
What produces speech?	The tongue.
What is the tongue?	The lash of the air.
What is air?	The guardian of life.
What is life?	The joy of the good, the sorrow of the wicked, the waiting for death.
What is man?	The bondsman of death, a passing wayfarer, a guest upon earth.
What is man like?	An apple [a play on words: *homo, pomo*].
What is sleep?	The image of death.
What is faith?	Certain belief in an unknown and wondrous thing.

Questions on the parts of the body also lend themselves to succinct replies that to the modern mind are hardly informative, to the medieval mind were satisfactory and above all stimulating. For instance:

* In *Kulturgeschichte der Neuzeit.*

What is the beard?	The distinguisher of sex, the honor of age.
What are the lips?	The doors of the mouth.
What is the mouth?	The nourisher of the body.
What is the stomach?	The cook of food.
What are the feet?	A movable foundation.

More revealing still of the radical difference between the medieval and the modern approach are the answers to questions on natural science:

What is the sun?	The splendor of the universe, the beauty of the sky, the glory of the day, the divider of the hours.
What is the moon?	The eye of night, the giver of dew, the foreteller of storms.
What are the stars?	Pictures on the roof of the heavens, guides of sailors, the ornament of night.
What is winter?	The exile of summer.
What is spring?	The painter of the earth.
What is summer?	The reclother of the earth, the ripener of fruits.
What is autumn?	The barn of the year.

Evidently Alcuin and his contemporaries preferred to define things in terms of their effects; the modern mind makes an effort to include causes in a definition. There is no reason for us to smile at these answers as childish. Even had Alcuin known that the moon was a planetary body about one fourth the diameter of the earth, revolving around the earth at a mean distance of 240,000 miles, he would not have been interested. What mattered about the moon or any other heavenly body was their effect on human beings, their value as symbols of the divine order and their usefulness for calculating the date of Easter. Ptolemy and Aristotle, with their comprehensive and mathematically logical, if erroneous, astronomical systems, were forgotten in the time of Alcuin and Charles—forgotten because no one really wanted that kind of knowledge.

It must be remembered also that these texts of Alcuin's served to teach a foreign language to the German-speaking Frankish boys. As language lessons they were certainly superior to the "I-see-the-book-of-my-father-on-the-table-of-my-uncle" sort of thing which until quite recently represented the highest achievement of Western civilization in the art of language teaching. Even the Romance-speaking peoples of Frankland had to apply themselves to the study of Latin. They had to learn the complex case forms which the vulgar tongue had dropped, and the classic and late classic Latin vocabularies, in order to understand the Fathers of the Church. A good part of the woeful "decay of learning" over which Alcuin and his contemporaries lamented was a decline in the knowledge of Latin—the inevitable result of the widening gap between the common speech and the written language.

Alcuin was too much the professor even to consider the common languages, whether German or the *lingua romana rustica*, suitable subjects for study. Although a well-established tradition of vernacular literature already existed in England, Alcuin had no use for such studies. Writing to the Bishop of Lindisfarne, he warned against songs from *Beowulf*: "Let the words of God be read at table in your refectory. The reader should be heard there, not the flute player. What has Ingeld to do with Christ?"

In this respect his master Charles showed a more liberal and scientific bent. Charles took lessons in Latin grammar from Alcuin, and applied them by beginning to write a grammar of German. He also gave German names to the months and to the winds and, as we have mentioned, became the first German folklorist by making a collection of the traditional German lays. Though his successors did not think these works worth preserving, something of Charles's enlightened attitude toward his native speech lived on in his grandson, the talented historian Nithard, who wrote down the texts of the Strassburg oaths in their original languages.*

---

* In the spring of 842 two of the warring sons of Louis the Pious, Charles and Louis, formed an alliance against their brother Lothar. They took solemn oaths to observe this alliance faithfully; if they failed to do so, each of their subjects might consider himself released from his personal oath of allegiance to his king. Louis' men spoke German, Charles's men the *lingua romana*. In order for the oaths to be understood by the men of the other army, Louis swore in the Roman tongue and Charles in the *lingua teudisca* (*teudisca—teutsch, deutsch*). Nithard, who wrote the history of these troubled times at the request of his cousin Charles, was a product of Alcuin's schools and demonstrated the excellence of his early training by producing a thoroughly original work of history.

Around the Palace School as an institution in which the young people of the court were educated there grew up a kind of higher academy composed of the faculty proper of the school, the king and those among the officials of the court who had intellectual interests. This academy had no definite meeting place, no fixed composition, none of the appurtenances of the modern university. Much of the intercourse among the members was carried on by letter. Its sessions might be held after dinner, during or after a hunt, even—in later years—in the baths at Aachen. Informality was the rule.

Membership in the academy widened greatly in the later years of Charles's reign. But at the time Alcuin first arrived the chief intellectuals at the court were Peter of Pisa, who was considered strictly a grammarian; Paulinus, who became Alcuin's special friend and whom Charles later appointed Patriarch of Aquileia; and Paul Warnefried, who was called Paul the Deacon. Paul was by far the most interesting and talented of these older men.

A Lombard by birth, Paul had come to the court of Charles on a mission of mercy. Paul's brother had taken part in the ill-fated uprising of Hrodgaud of Friuli and had been brought to Frankland by Charles and cast into prison along with a number of other rebellious Lombards. There he remained for six years, until Paul wrote to Charles pleading for his brother's release. His petition was in the form of an elegy which Paul either delivered in person or followed up by a visit to the king's court. The poem spoke of "my brother, a captive going on seven years now, naked, in need and heartsore, while in her homeland his wife begs for food with trembling lips." By this ignoble trade, Paul goes on to say, she can barely keep her four children in rags.

Paul had evidently heard that well-turned verses were the surest way to move Charles. When he appeared at the court, around the same time that Alcuin arrived there, Charles received him amicably and respectfully but firmly refused to release Paul's brother or the other Lombard prisoners until he had extracted from Paul a reluctant promise to stay at the court as a teacher. Thus he exchanged one captive of the Warnefried family for another. Paul's captivity, however, was of the most pleasant and luxurious sort. He was offered land and money and was flattered by the king and his companions. Charles had Peter of Pisa write a poem to Paul praising him as the most learned of men, a Homer in Greek, a Vergil in Latin, a Philo in

Hebrew, a Horace in verse, and so on, and urging him to put aside his homesickness and strike roots in Frankland.

Homesickness was not the only reason for Paul's reluctance to stay with Charles. He was deeply attached to the family of the deposed Lombard king, Desiderius, and in particular to that king's daughter, Adalperga. In the "good old days" of Lombardy's independence Paul had been Adalperga's mentor. Because that highly intelligent lady found fault with the commonly used history of Rome by the fourth-century writer Eutropius, Paul undertook to write a "Roman History" for her which would be more comprehensive than that of Eutropius and would include Christian history as well.

Paul's loyalty to the old Lombard dynasty continued strong after Charles's conquest of Lombardy, and his national pride stood in the way of his serving Charles wholeheartedly. He had become a monk in middle life, probably after the collapse of the Lombard kingdom, and throughout his stay in Frankland he chafed to return to his beloved Monte Cassino. In one of his letters to his abbot at the famous monastery he wrote:

"I live among good Christians here, am well received by all . . . but compared to your cloister this court seems to me a prison; compared to the peace among you, life here is a tempest. Only my poor weak body clings to this country; with my whole soul, which is the only sound part of me, I am with you and imagine myself listening to the sweetness of your songs, or in the refectory with you refreshing myself more from the reading than the food, or watching each of your various occupations, seeing how the old and the sick are faring, or crossing the holy threshold which is as dear to me as paradise. Believe me, my master and father and all you devout flock, only the emotion of pity, only the commandment of love, only the demands of the soul are keeping me here for a while. These, and what is more than all of these, the silent might of our lord king."

When, after a few years, Paul was at last allowed to leave the Frankish court he returned to Monte Cassino and there spent the remaining years of his life writing his *History of the Lombards,* which has remained the best and virtually the only source for the history of that people whose independence Charles had destroyed. Unfortunately for historians, Paul did not bring the history down to his own day, either because he died before he could complete it or, more likely, because he was unwilling to recount the downfall of the dynasty with which he was linked by lasting ties of affection.

In spite of his loyalty to the family of Desiderius, however, and in spite of his grievance against a king who had kept his brother imprisoned for so many years, Paul formed equally strong ties of affection with Charles, who reciprocated his feeling. There was a fundamental similarity in the minds of the two men. Both had a wider range of emotion and a deeper interest in the real world than, say, those of which Alcuin was capable. Where Alcuin was a grammarian and teacher, Paul was a historian and—in the limited sense that it was possible for a medieval man to be—a natural scientist. His history of the Lombards opens with the curious speculation that northern climates are more healthful than southern climates and more favorable for the propagation of mankind, and on this ground he accounts for the numerous population of Germany. He comments on the greater length of the days in the northern summers. While staying with Charles at the royal villa of Thionville one Christmas he compares the declination of the sun with that of Italy in the same season by actually measuring his own shadow—an incredibly original act of experimentation for a man of his time.

It was in this practical, skeptical, essentially "modern" turn of mind that Paul resembled Charles. Where Alcuin turned automatically for information to a scriptural or patristic text, both Charles and Paul were inclined—again it must be stressed: within the limitations of the age—to look to the natural world for answers. Charles, indeed, sometimes embarrassed Alcuin with his persistent questioning and his fundamentally common-sense approach. He was capable of asking Alcuin wherein lay the essential difference between Christians and the pagan philosophers who also believed in dignity, nobility, virtue and pure morals. Alcuin lamely replied that the difference was "faith and baptism," which certainly did not satisfy the king. Or Charles wondered why the hymn which Jesus and his disciples must have sung before the Last Supper had not been recorded in any of the Gospels—a question which sounds like that of a schoolboy trying to trap the master. Charles also tried to extend the study of astronomy beyond its conventional function, which at that time was the calculation of the dates for Easter. He instituted a program of careful observation and recording of astronomical matters. In this he received the assistance of Irish scholars like Dungal of St. Denis or the Clement previously mentioned who afterward took over the Palace School when Alcuin retired. Charles was, in fact, passionately interested in astronomy and sought a deeper knowledge of it than any of his contemporaries were capable of giving him.

These practical studies, in which Paul and Charles shared a common interest, Alcuin could never fully understand. Alcuin was always content to study what had already been done, to compile from the writings of the Church Fathers, rather than to make any original contributions of his own. "What better purpose shall we ordinary men be able to devise," he once wrote, "in these loveless days of the world's last age, than that we should follow . . . the doctrine of the apostles, not inventing new terms, not bringing forth anything unfamiliar."

For all the respect in which Alcuin was held, he must sometimes have found it hard to keep up with some of the younger, quicker and perhaps more cynical minds in the court circle. The composition of this circle changed, of course, with the passage of time, as new persons moved into and out of official positions, were rewarded for their services by being appointed abbots of monasteries (like Chancellor Itherius, who became Abbot of Tours around 775 and remained in charge of that huge and wealthy monastery until his death, whereupon Charles gave it to Alcuin), or were sent on missions by the king. But the circle itself remained, loosely organized as a kind of informal academy whose members met at intervals to listen to lectures, read poems to one another, discuss questions of theology or astronomy and, in lighter moments, to exchange riddles. Alcuin brought with him from England the Anglo-Saxon fondness for riddles and found it matched by the Germanic traditions of his hosts.

Alcuin, too, introduced among the members of the court circle the use of nicknames by which they addressed one another. In the intimate circle Charles was addressed as King David, Alcuin himself as Flaccus, Charles's sister Gisla as Lucia, Charles's daughter Rotrud as Columba. Theodulf of Orléans was known for his poetic gifts as Pindar. Another poet of distinction, Charles's chaplain and intimate adviser Angilbert, was called Homer. And the future biographer of Charles, Einhard, was dubbed Bezaleel after the architect of the tabernacle (Exodus, 31). Alcuin himself justified this nicknaming in a letter to Charles's cousin Gundrada, the sister of Adalhard and Wala. "Intimate friendship often calls for a change of name. Thus the Lord himself changed Simon to Peter and called the sons of Zebedee the 'sons of Thunder.'" This whimsy became a Carolingian custom that lasted well into the next two generations.

Among all the brilliant men around him Charles easily stood out as the leading spirit, if not always the best informed. He was humble, and freely acknowledged his indebtedness to Alcuin, Paul or Peter. But he was not easily fooled or put off and was quite capable of criticizing his teachers and companions. "You say it is not worth while repeating what is already known," Alcuin once wrote plaintively to Charles. "Well, then, I don't know what the countryman Flaccus can say to the wise David that he won't know."

Like the medieval man he was, Charles pondered the mysteries of the Trinity and subtle metaphysical questions; like Socrates he examined the nature of justice and the distinctions between justice and law; and like the universal men of the Renaissance he interested himself in architecture, canal building, music, liturgy, languages, textual criticism of the Bible, poetry, sculpture and a host of other matters. Since he was also a man of action, an administrator, general and diplomat as well as hunter, swimmer and fighter, the portrait of a man seven hundred years in advance of his times is complete. No man of comparable many-sidedness can be found in the Middle Ages, and it is no wonder that his contemporaries—even those famous wits, poets and scholars of the court and Palace Academy who saw him every day at close quarters—should have stood in awe of him. It is the more remarkable that they also loved him fervently. "I loved so much in you," Alcuin wrote, "what I saw you were seeking in me." The warmth of his personality, his generosity, his hospitality (Einhard remarks that he was so fond of foreigners and entertained them in such numbers that they were a burden on both palace and kingdom), his loyalty to his friends and readiness to reward them, his kindliness and his affection for his wives, concubines and children—all these traits enabled him to live among people rather than above them, and saved him from that painful isolation which is the ordinary lot of great rulers.

It is important for us to bear this in mind, for Charles was now entering on a dark period of his life when the acids of political action were beginning to corrode his genial liberality and leave permanent scars on his personality. Just after the arrival of Alcuin, when the gay and earnest sports of the mind were giving Charles the greatest pleasure and when the whole culture of the Roman world was being thrown open to him, he was forced to turn his attention once more to the grim struggle with barbarians. He marched to the contest resentful of the interruption to his studies but with a clearer consciousness of which side he was on, of what principle he represented. During the next few decisive years he was more Roman than the Romans, and he fought his German cousins with the fury of a convert to a higher and more glorious cause.

CHAPTER TEN

The Breeding of Violence

THE YEAR 782 began quietly enough. Charles lingered long through the winter and early spring in his palace at Carisiacum (Quierzy), enjoying the stimulating company of the new arrivals, Alcuin and Paul the Deacon. He seemed reluctant to leave his new friends, and it was the beginning of summer before he started for Saxony, where the annual assembly was to be held. However, there were also more practical reasons for this late start. The old March Field had become a May Field and now seemed well on its way to becoming a July or August Field. The first postponements, under King Pepin, had probably been prompted by the necessity to give foreign ambassadors time to arrive at the assembly. Now Charles's vastly larger dominions made a later date essential, if army contingents from the remoter parts of Frankland were to attend. This was especially the case when the meetings were held in Saxony, the northernmost and easternmost part of Charles's domain. And since the annual assembly and the marshaling of the army were one and the same, there also had to be adequate fodder for the horses, which meant waiting until the grass was sufficiently high. Far more of the Frankish soldiery were now mounted than had ever been the case under Charles's father and grandfather.

Ambassadors came to the assembly in Lippspringe, at the headwaters of the Lippe River in Saxony. There were envoys from the Mongol Avars, the "Huns" as contemporaries called them, remembering the hordes of Mongols, under Attila, who had scourged Europe more than three centuries earlier. What their business was we do not know, except that they came "on account of peace." But their presence signified that Charles was already, so soon after Tassilo's submission, tightening his hold over Bavaria, so that Tassilo's Avar neighbors now felt the need of dealing directly with Charles.

Another set of ambassadors came from Sigifrid, King of the Danes.

The annals are significantly silent about their business. Probably they came to protest Frankish persecution of their Saxon fellow pagans. Probably Charles in turn protested against Danish support of Sigifrid's brother-in-law, the "war criminal" Widukind, that unrepentant agitator who continued to arouse the Saxons against their rightful overlords. Widukind had conspicuously stayed away from the Diet, although other Saxons came in great numbers to renew their allegiance. If Charles attempted to persuade or bribe the Danes to surrender him, he failed. Nor would the Danes admit Christian missionaries into their country. In a jesting poem addressed to Paul the Deacon and written about this time, Charles cheerfully alluded to Paul's efforts to win his brother's freedom and asked whether Paul would prefer to be chained in a dungeon or to court martyrdom by being asked to baptize the Danish king.

The Danes were still unrepentant heathens, but as yet they were not the menace they were to become in the next century when all the Continent lay at their mercy and every navigable river was a roadway for the terrible prowed ships that would suddenly disgorge fairhaired Viking warriors who mercilessly plundered the churches and monasteries of France and England. Five years were still to pass before "the army," as the helpless English later called the Danes, launched their first raid on English shores. Charles's successors, too, were to have many mournful dealings with the Northmen. But as long as Charles himself lived, the Danes were held in check; and after Charles ultimately completed his conquest of Saxony, they themselves built a solid wall of defense fortifications across the whole base of their peninsula, with only a single gate in it for the passage of traffic between Saxony and Denmark.

The conquest of Saxony was, in Charles's mind, already complete, and he therefore considered it his obligation to defend the Saxons against aggression. When word came to him that the Slavic tribes east of the Elbe River had begun raiding Saxony, he sent a detachment of troops against them. For the first time in many years he himself did not lead the army. With the annual assembly over, he was already hastening back to Gaul to resume his studies with Alcuin and Paul. This new flowering of intellectual life at his court filled him with such excitement that he begrudged time wasted on petty military operations. Nevertheless, he did not underestimate the raiders, for he placed three of his important officials at the head of the punitive expedition: Chamberlain Adalgis, Count of the Palace Worad, and Marshal Geilo. Saxon as well as Frankish soldiers were among their troops.

Meanwhile the indomitable Widukind had re-entered Saxony and was going about the country crying freedom and revenge, agitating against the cowardice or venality of the Saxon upper classes who had submitted to the Franks. Himself one of the wealthiest landowners in Saxony, Widukind enlisted the hordes of Saxon common men in a class war against their own nobles and a national uprising against the Frankish oppressors. As always his eloquence and his immense personal popularity won him a tremendous following. Revolt flared over all of Saxony.

What follows is a complex tale of military blundering, of which the details are somewhat obscure because the language of the annalists, like that of most war communiqués and official histories, aimed to cover up a disastrous Frankish defeat. But the main outlines are clear, and the horrible sequel is unfortunately all too clear.

By the time Charles's three officials had entered Saxony with their East Frankish troops, the Saxons were up in arms. The Saxon levy which they had counted on as auxiliary troops was now a part of the hostile force facing them. Recognizing the greater danger, they marched to meet the Saxons. Charles, meanwhile, had heard of the uprising; the Saxons had already started to burn churches and to send the missionaries fleeing for their lives. He immediately dispatched a relative of his, Count Theoderic, with reinforcements. Theoderic ordered Adalgis, Worad and Geilo to effect a junction with his troops.

The two armies met near the Weser River and marched together to the foot of Süntel Mountain, where the Saxons had taken up strong positions on the northern slopes. Theoderic proposed an enveloping movement to which the three court officials agreed. And then Chamberlain Adalgis, Count Worad and Marshal Geilo committed a fatal error: they scrapped the prearranged plans and disobeyed orders. Fearing that Theoderic, as Charles's kinsman, would get all the credit for a victory if he fought beside them, perhaps resentful of what they considered to be nepotism on the part of the king, they resolved to attack without waiting for Theoderic's troops to complete their part of the maneuver. They rushed recklessly upon the Saxons "as if they were pursuing fugitives rather than facing an army drawn up in battle order."

They were wiped out almost to the last man. Chamberlain Adalgis and Marshal Geilo were killed. The members of their personal bodyguard—the *comitatus* or sworn following—obeyed the Germanic tradition and preferred to die rather than survive their lords. Only a few men of the Frankish army escaped the Saxon encirclement and made their way to Count Theoderic's camp.

The news of this unexpected and needless defeat was a tremendous blow to Charles. With bitter memories of Spain raging in his mind— Spain, where lack of discipline and the desire for personal glory had cost the lives of so many of his closest friends—he hastily gathered another relief army and marched at all possible speed into Saxony. The time had not yet come, it seemed, when he could rest from the conduct of war and entrust even the smallest campaign to his lieutenants. The Romans had managed that; from their capital at Rome the emperors had directed the conquests of their generals and enforced the Roman peace to the farthest reaches of their empire. But with his Franks—his *barbarian* Franks, he must have thought in his anger and under the influence of his recent converse with Alcuin, Paul and Paulinus—nothing could be safely delegated. He had to do everything himself.

But his anger with his own unreliable men was as nothing compared with his fury toward the Saxons when he at last came within striking distance of them and found that, like the Basques in Spain, the hostile army had evaporated. Caught by the speedy Frankish march in a pincers between Theoderic's intact forces on the south and Charles's fresh troops on the north, the Saxon guerrillas hid their arms and melted into the population. Widukind, the instigator of the uprising, once more made good his escape to his Danish protectors. There was no one on whom Charles could take the blood vengeance that his own feelings and his Germanic traditions demanded.

Roncesvalles four years ago, and now the Süntel debacle! The sting of the new defeat revived the anguish of the one four years before. And mingled with Charles's rage and grief was the coldly rational knowledge that his prestige had suffered another severe blow. First the Basques and now the Saxons! These treacherous, incalculable, murderous Saxons who submitted every year, only to rebel every other year. Some final solution must be found for this maddening problem.

In his present mood there was one solution that came to his mind—

the way that his pious uncle Carloman the Elder had taken in the days when, as mayor of the palace, he shared the Frankish realm with Charles's father. More and more, as Charles brooded on the twin defeats in Spain and Saxony and on the needless slaughter of his friends, his palace officials (the "paladins" of the later Charlemagne romances), the recollection of Carloman's punishment of the Aleman-nian rebels obtruded on his thoughts. There were times when one had to start with a clean slate, he reflected, times when only ruthless-ness would do. These Saxons, abysmal, pagan, oath-breaking Saxons, understood only violence in its crudest form. Uncle Carloman had been right: there was only one way to treat these heathen Germans.

His mind clouded by emotion, not so much reasoning as rationaliz-ing an overwhelming passion, an insatiable rage that demanded some outlet in action, Charles ordered all the Saxon nobles to come to him at Verden on the Aller River, near its confluence with the Weser. The nobles came; they had not joined Widukind's popular uprising. Charles demanded the names of the ringleaders, and all denounced one—Widukind, who was safely out of reach. Charles was not satis-fied. He insisted, and the nobles recognized that their own heads were at stake. The last shreds of their honor and fellow feeling for their own countrymen fell from them. The dreadful atmosphere of the purge developed; in an orgy of denunciation they betrayed one another and the Saxon commoners who had followed Widukind. All who were accused were brought to Verden. Forty-five hundred men were condemned; forty-five hundred men were beheaded in a single day. "After he had thus taken vengeance," the annals declare, "the king went into winter camp at Thionville and there celebrated Christ-mas and Easter *as usual.*"

It was important for Charles to behave outwardly as though noth-ing unusual had happened. He who prided himself on the mildness and benevolence of his rule, who was always prompted by his deep religious impulses to be as merciful as possible, had committed an act of surpassing frightfulness. Perhaps he dimly understood that in killing the Saxons he had revenged himself on the Basques for the deaths of Roland and his other friends. Indeed the executions at Verden would tell us, if the romances and songs did not, how deeply Charles had been wounded that day at Roncesvalles. But motives were not justifications, and immediately after the act Charles must have been overwhelmed by repentance, frightened by his own capacity for brutality. He would need the prayers of many devout intercessors to atone for this crime. Nevertheless, his was a strong and obstinate nature. He had made his bed and he would lie in it; he would abide by the road he had set out on and disregard all tempting forks and turnings. Not for Charles was the atonement his uncle Carloman had found in the religious life. He had no intention of becoming a monk. Deep though his religious feelings might be, they ultimately expressed themselves—as did all his feelings, all his thoughts—in action.

Therefore he did not betray his inner turmoil; therefore he showed himself unmoved and celebrated Christmas and Easter as usual. He answered his own conscience and the opposition his act aroused among others by a hardening of his entire personality, by further harshness, more brutality.

For his act did arouse opposition. In our age of Hiroshimas, death camps and Katyn Forest massacres, the slaughter in a single day of four thousand five hundred human beings may seem no great cause for shock or surprise. We have lost that capacity for moral indignation which impelled Mombert, a nineteenth-century biographer of Charles, to say: "There are many horrors recorded in history, but hardly one more horrid than that butchery at Verden, which is, and must ever remain, the indelible stain on the name of Charles, and the foulest blot on his life." Charles's contemporaries, however, in spite of slavery and of some barbarous and brutal attitudes toward individuals, and especially toward criminals, had on the whole a greater moral sensitiveness than we of the twentieth century.

Charles's action shocked his contemporaries, and the several plots against his life which marked the next decade were partly the outcome of the executions at Verden. It is significant that the first conspiracy originated in Thuringia, a province immediately adjacent to Saxony, into which a number of Christian Saxons had emigrated. But not only Saxons sympathized with their fellows and condemned Charles's cruelty. During the next several years his cruelty was much talked about, and Charles's own Frankish nobles, who had accepted him for so many years, suddenly began fearing for their freedom and perhaps for their salvation. For certainly a man was endangering his immortal soul when he acted as executioner for a despot.

Those who considered the butchery at Verden the act of a cruel tyrant must have seen the hand of God in the punishment that was

meted out to Charles so soon after the Easter which he had celebrated as usual. Easter fell early that year—on March 23—but Charles
lingered at Thionville, for Hildigard was awaiting her ninth confinement in the less than thirteen years of their marriage. It was to be
her last; on April 30, 783, she died in childbirth. The infant girl,
who was named Hildigard after the mother, survived her little more
than a month.

Hildigard had been a favorite at court for her beauty and generosity
and perhaps also because, as queen, she rarely interfered with the
conduct of affairs. Through all the years of her marriage she had
been too young and too much occupied with her children to share
with Charles the burdens of administration in anything like the manner of Queen Mother Bertrada, who had exerted so powerful an influence on public affairs during the early years of Charles's reign.
Hildigard, the child bride, remained figuratively and literally in the
nursery all her life. In the sparse accounts of contemporaries her virtues appear as all sweetness and light, and her friendship with the
sainted abbess of Bischofsheim, Leobgytha, or Leoba, suggests that
an untroubled innocence was the key to her nature.

Leoba, Anglo-Saxon and a relative of St. Boniface, was dedicated
to the Church from birth. She grew up in a convent, knowing nothing but devotion to sacred studies and the religious life, one of those
pure, serene, devoted souls such as the cloistral life of the Middle
Ages could produce—a beautiful nun, perfectly content to be the
bride of Christ, always busy with her hands when she was not busy
with her books. Charles was fond of her and invited her frequently
to his court. Hildigard revered her, "loved her like her second self
and wanted her to stay always about her." But the saintly abbess, says
her biographer, "hated the noise of the court like a cup of poison" and
could not be prevailed on to remain long.

Hildigard seems to have had something of the same lovely innocence that she adored in her friend Leoba. There was a virginal quality about this woman who bore nine children. She had been married
so young and died so young that she never had the chance to know
the world. And but for Charles's cruel slaughter of the Saxons at
Verden, her death might have seemed quite natural, for she had already fulfilled her part in the world and in Charles's life. She had
graced the throne, had provided the state with male heirs and had
shared with Charles the period of his rise to great power. In the brief

span of twenty-six years she seems to have lived a complete life. But Charles's nature could not partake of her sweetness and light.

In the epitaph which Paul the Deacon, at Charles's request, wrote for Hildigard, there is an implication that contemporaries, too, thought she had lived out her destiny. In verses imitating the Vergilian device of interlocked order of nouns and modifiers:

> *Hic regina iacet regi praecelsa potenti*
> *Hildigard Karolo quae bene nupta fuit . . .**

Paul praises her beauty and spiritual virtues, but concludes that her highest praise is that so great a man chose her for his wife.

If Charles saw the loss of his wife as a just punishment for the crime of Verden, his feeling—and that of others—could only be confirmed by a second death in his family. Ten weeks after Hildigard, his mother, Queen Bertrada, was buried with great pomp beside his father in the Abbey of St. Denis.

Charles must have wept for Hildigard and his mother, for he had "the gift of tears," as his contemporaries would say; the ability in a man to weep easily was considered in the Middle Ages a divine blessing. Yet, far from being humbled, he determined to fly in the face of fate and public opinion. The period of mourning was cut short and that same year he married again. His new bride, Fastrada, was the young daughter of an East Frankish count named Radolf.

In addition to Charles's undisguised fondness for having a young woman to share his bed there were sound reasons of another sort for this hasty new marriage. He needed a mother to care for his numerous children by Hildigard and Himiltrude, and a queen to take charge of the many functions which had been fulfilled primarily by Bertrada. The royal court was an extension, on a vast scale, of the traditional Germanic household. The queen, as mistress of the house, supervised supplies of food and clothing, was responsible for honesty and good morals among the household servants, and in general saw to the smooth running of the whole complicated apparatus of court life. She directed the work of the chamberlain and treasurer so that, for example, it was she who decided what gifts were to be given to members of the household and to foreign ambassadors. Charles relied on

---

* Here lies the most excellent Queen Hildigard, who was wedded to Charles, the powerful king.

his queens to relieve him of all concern with domestic affairs in the court, so that he might devote his entire attention to the business of state. He liked also to assign to his wives greater responsibility for the administration of the royal estates than had been the case under the previous (Merovingian) dynasty.

Fastrada, the new queen, swiftly acquired a bad reputation. She was a strong-minded woman who, as Queen Bertrada had done, made the most of her prerogatives—which meant that in the eyes of the court officials, who with Hildigard had had things pretty much their own way, the queen now interfered far too much in household affairs and was charged with having too great an influence on Charles's conduct of the public business. Einhard, who came to the court during the last years of Fastrada's life and was therefore well aware of the court gossip about her, speaks of her cruelty with a bluntness unusual for him. It was believed, he says, that "under the persuasion of his cruel wife Charles deviated widely from his usual kindness and gentleness." Einhard was clearly in a position to know; the cautious manner in which he stresses that this was the general belief suggests that he himself did not entirely share it. Evidently Fastrada was not too likable, but it is preposterous to believe that Charles was so susceptible to feminine influence as the court gossip implied. Poor Fastrada was an unfortunate scapegoat who was blamed for the apparently sudden disappearance of Charles's natural amiability after the blood bath of Verden. Throughout his middle years harshness and ruthless determination were the dominant motifs of Charles's behavior. He was to experience a whole decade of frustrations and setbacks. His ambition was soaring; he longed to create a new *pax romana* in the West; but everything he built up seemed to fall apart again as soon as he turned his back. This period, when he met the malices of fate with a stubborn defiance, happened to coincide with the years of his marriage to Fastrada, and the queen was conveniently charged with the faults of the king.

In spite of a summer so searing that many people died of the heat, Charles found it necessary to call up the army once more and to march against the Saxons as soon as the funeral of Queen Hildigard was over. Violence had bred violence; after the stunning blow at Verden all Saxony rose against the Franks. For the first time the entire country was united against Charles. Westphalians, Eastphalians and

Angrians made common cause under the leadership of Widukind, and even the neighboring Frisians—apparently long since pacified and converted to Christianity—drove out their missionaries, sacrificed to the old gods and joined in the rebellion. Verden had been not only an act of surpassing cruelty but a political error of the first magnitude. The Saxon nobles who had hitherto yielded readily to Charles now threw in their lot with Widukind.

In the previous years, during which Charles thought he had been consolidating the conquest of Saxony, he had fought only campaigns. Now for the next three years he found himself engaged in a real war. According to the annalists, all the battles were Frankish victories. The duration of the fighting, the retreats after an alleged victory, or the Frankish failure to follow the enemy after what had been, according to the annals, an overwhelming slaughter of the Saxons, is sufficient indication that the war was replete with partial victories and partial defeats.

In the course of this prolonged struggle Charles's oldest son, young Charles, received his first training in actual warfare. At the age of thirteen he was placed in nominal charge of a sizable detachment which encountered the Saxons in battle and won another of those victories which was promptly followed by a retreat. The country was far from pacified, and Charles saw the necessity of keeping an army in Saxony throughout the winter. Significantly enough, he had to maintain his winter camp at the Eresburg, the strong fortress he had built during the first invasion of Saxony more than ten years before. Deeper into Saxony he dared not venture. But throughout the winter and the spring the Franks gave the Saxons no rest. The peasants who were the backbone of Widukind's forces suffered most. Farms were burned, cattle confiscated or killed by roving detachments of Frankish soldiers—the while Charles at the Eresburg directed the strengthening of the fortifications there and sent for new levies of troops from Francia. Even the death of his good friend and trusted adviser, Archchaplain Fulrad, did not weaken his determination. He was used to such blows by now. If they were a sign that God was incomprehensibly against his purpose of subduing and converting the Saxons by force, then Charles was in a mood to defy his God.

Gradually, Frankish numbers and Frankish organization won the upper hand in ravaged Saxony. Wherever the Franks came upon a Saxon burg they smashed the fortifications and burned the buildings to the ground. Resistance dwindled, only to flare sporadically here and there. But Widukind, the great noble who had committed class treason by becoming a peasant leader, could not help seeing that his followers were undergoing frightful sufferings. As their crops and homes were destroyed, as their women and children were led away into captivity, the spirit of his men flagged. Betrayed by their own nobles, who by now had recovered from the shock of Verden and had begun to fear their serfs more than they feared the Franks, the embattled farmers of Saxony had little chance. Widukind himself was beginning to wonder whether freedom and the old gods were worth the endless slaughter, the depopulation of Saxony, the blackened ruins that were left behind wherever the Frankish horde had passed. His allies had failed him; the Frisians had been quickly subdued, and his Danish brother-in-law was afraid to come to his aid. The situation could not have been more hopeless.

Yet for Charles also the situation was desperate, although his enemy could not judge how desperate it was. The prolonged war was straining the resources of the Frankish kingdom as well, and especially of the Thuringians, Alemannians and Eastern Franks, who bore the brunt of the fighting. For except in rare cases like the invasion of Spain, when a general levy was raised from among all the nationalities of the kingdom, Charles had found it practicable to call up only those who lived fairly near the theater of hostilities. Long campaigns meant the impoverishment of the small landowners who could not tend to their work at home. Driven into debt, they were forced to sell their land to the *seniores* (seigneurs) or the Church, give up their status as freemen and become "the men" of some great lord, lay or ecclesiastical. If possible, men attempted to become the vassals of lords who for one reason or another possessed immunity from the king's "ban"—who, that is, were not obligated to answer the call to arms. Thus the process of feudalization was speeded up and Charles's wars were ruining that class of freemen on whom the strength of the nation depended.

As the war continued, even the greater nobles felt the terrible drain, and Charles became aware of the growing resentment among the Thuringians and even the Austrasians, who had been fighting now for three years without letup. They could hope for no profit out of this costly war, since no booty was left in Saxony. As always happens in a long war, the original causes and aims were forgotten. Charles was blamed for his cruelty at Verden, and among the Franks there was widespread sympathy for the Saxons, expressed in the universal admiration for Widukind's heroic stand and in the many legends that sprang up around his seemingly miraculous escapes—such as the tale that he had fooled his pursuers by reversing the shoes on his horse.

In these circumstances Charles was at least as eager as Widukind to find a solution, and it was he who opened the negotiations with the Saxon leader. He did not sue for peace, but he offered terms, promising withdrawal of his army if the Saxons would accept Christianity, and Saxon autonomy under Frankish overlordship. Saxons, not Franks, carried his message to Widukind, as if to impress on the rebel leader that his own people were far from wholeheartedly behind him—a fact he knew only too well. Only Nordalbingia, the lands north of the Elbe River and immediately adjacent to Denmark, had been spared by the Frankish army; the territory under Widukind's control had shrunk to a small fraction of Saxony. Nordalbingia might serve as the focus of another rebellion, but not for years; there was little fight left in the Westphalians, Eastphalians and Angrians.

The Saxon envoys could appeal to Widukind to spare the people further suffering. And Widukind, whose successes had been due to his ability to measure the temper of the common folk, accepted the inevitable. He agreed to a personal meeting with Charles. But, remembering Verden, he demanded guarantees of his safety. Charles would have to give hostages to him. Charles consented, as he had previously consented to give hostages to Tassilo; the giving of hostages was not necessarily a mark of inferiority but simply the surest form of safe-conduct. It was agreed that Widukind would come to him at his palace in Attigny and make his submission there. Charles would withdraw his forces from Saxony. Perhaps this condition, vaguely recalled in the songs and legends that sprang up around Charlemagne, was the origin of the stipulation in the *Song of Roland* that King Marsile must travel to Aix, the capital of *Charles li reis*, there to receive the "law of the Christians" and become "his man."

Charles was generous with his old antagonist. When Widukind received *la lei de chrestiens*, Charles stood sponsor at the baptism. Kneeling to Christ rather than to the King of the Franks, Widukind repeated the baptismal formula that had been devised for the Saxons. The priest asked:

"Do you renounce the devil?"

"I renounce the devil."

"And all the devil's ilk?"

"And I renounce all the devil's ilk."

"And all the devil's works?"

"And I renounce all the devil's works and words, Thunar and Woden and Saxnot and all the demons who are their companions."

"Do you believe in God, the Almighty Father?"

"I believe in God, the Almighty Father."

"Do you believe in Christ, the Son of God?"

"I believe in Christ, the Son of God."

"Do you believe in the Holy Spirit?"

"I believe in the Holy Spirit."

So the indomitable Saxon leader accepted the "sweet yoke of Christ." The dramatic end to the long struggle made so deep an impression on the people of the Middle Ages that some prominent person seemed needed to immerse the Saxon chief in the waters of baptism, and later medieval legend pictured St. Boniface performing the rite, though Boniface had died thirty years before.

Overjoyed by this conversion, Charles heaped gifts on his former enemy and confirmed him in his possessions in Saxony. The surrender of Widukind and the conversion, along with the chief, of thousands of his followers meant that the Saxon war was over. There was a great sense of relief and a burst of rejoicing in all the lands under Charles's rule. At Charles's request Pope Hadrian ordered a three-day festival of thanksgiving to be held among all Christians throughout the world, even those beyond the seas. There was a slightly sour note, however, in his letter informing Charles of this action. For in addition to warm congratulations and a sincere pleasure in the great triumph for the Church, he took occasion to remind Charles of his own expectations. "You may count on this: if you fulfill the promises made to us and Saint Peter with a pure heart and a willing mind, God will place even mightier peoples under your sway."

With the military part of the struggle over, Charles proceeded to consolidate his great victory. His "capitulary on Saxony" emphasized that it had been enacted "with the consent of all," but its content was bound to confirm his growing reputation as a tyrannical oppressor. It was a law proclaiming a reign of terror in Saxony. Saxon autonomy was forgotten; the stress was on Frankish overlordship, and the Saxons were given the choice between Christianity and death. Under the law of the Franks the death penalty was a rarity; even homicide was not a capital crime. But the capitulary on Saxony, with unprecedented savagery, set down no less than fifteen crimes for which the death penalty must be imposed. Only one of these—the crime of perjury—carried the death penalty under traditional Saxon law. The other capital crimes were almost entirely crimes against Christianity. Forcible entry into a church and theft of church property, the burning of a church, killing any member of the clergy, hiding from baptism, conspiring with pagans against the Christians—all were punishable by death. So were cremating the dead according to pagan custom, and even eating meat at Lent! The two provisions making a capital crime of cannibalism and human sacrifice have been referred to earlier (see page 102). These crimes, too, were associated with the forms of pagan worship, which Charles was determined to stamp out at all costs.

Finally in the list of capital crimes were included the killing of one's lord or lady, or the ravishing of the lord's daughter. These provisions were Charles's repayment to the Saxon nobles who had supported him. In effect he was throwing the weight of the Frankish administration on the side of the Saxon upper class and against the freemen and serfs who had rebelled against their masters.

The Saxons were denied freedom of assembly as well as freedom of worship. Gatherings of Saxons were permitted only by order of the counts or the royal commissioner, except for judicial assemblies. And these were placed in the hands of the priests.

The priests, in fact, were given the power of life and death over the Saxons. The laws seem to have been calculatedly harsh in order to enhance the prestige of the priests by giving them alone the power to mitigate the harshness. For after the long list of capital crimes the most significant provision of the entire capitulary read: "If for these mortal crimes secretly committed any one shall have fled of his own accord to a priest, and after confession shall have wished to do penance, let him be freed from death by the testimony of the priest." Moreover, the churches were made inviolable places of refuge. "If anyone shall have fled to a church for refuge," the capitulary stated, "let no one presume to expel him from the church by violence, but he shall be left in peace until he shall be brought to court, and on account of the honor due to God and the saints, and the reverence due to the church itself, let his life and all his limbs be granted to him."

These two clauses were strokes of genius. By them the churches and the priests became the most significant factors in the lives of the terrorized Saxons. All Saxons now had an interest in building churches as quickly as possible, rather than in destroying them, and in having as many priests as possible in the country. Churches were the sole hope, priests the sole dispensers of mercy in a land in the grip of terror. In the hands of the priests was salvation not only in the next world but in this one. Theirs was the privilege of judging whether a man who had eaten meat during Lent should receive the death sentence or should be forgiven because he had done so "from necessity." They could decide whether a Saxon was truly penitent and should therefore escape death. At their pleasure they could relieve the Saxons from the heavy fines imposed for failure to bring infants to baptism within a year of the child's birth.

Unfortunately these ingenious measures, designed to speed the establishment of Christianity in Saxony by making the Church as much a necessity to the Saxons as their daily bread, were vitiated by one clause in the new capitulary so odious that the Saxons could never become resigned to it. The clause read:

"Likewise, in accordance with the mandate of God, we command that all shall give a tithe of their property and labor to the churches and priests; let the nobles as well as the freemen and likewise the liti, according to that which God shall have given each Christian, return a part to God."

This tax was supremely ill-advised. Like the Franks, the Saxons hated taxation on principle and hated it now all the more because it was imposed at a time when they were already impoverished by war. Without the imposition of the tithe the true and lasting conversion of the Saxons to Christianity and the integration of the country into the Frankish kingdom would undoubtedly have gone much more speedily.

There were men at Charles's court who understood this and who insistently argued against the attempt to tax the Saxons for the benefit of a church they hated and must still learn to love. Chief among these was Alcuin, who in any case felt strong ties of blood kinship with the "Old Saxons." In later years he wrote many letters to Charles urging a more lenient policy in Saxony, and while he was still at the court he must often have broached the matter to Charles directly. "If the light yoke of Christ were to be preached to the stubborn Saxons as insistently as the duty to render tithes," he argued, "perhaps they would not reject the sacrament of baptism." Even born Catholics were reluctant to pay their tithes, he pointed out; how much more unwilling must be those whose faith was still new.

But Charles, faced with the obduracy of the Saxons, was determined to be as stiff-necked as they. Death had removed the tempering influences of his mother and Archchaplain Fulrad, whose counsel had hitherto curbed Charles's autocratic impulses. Neither Alcuin nor Paul the Deacon could take the place of these two, and the literary, philosophical, musical and astronomical studies in which these two men guided Charles did not exert a humanizing influence on him. At this time they seem only to have nourished his arrogance. Charles was aware of the underground rumblings of unrest that were always present in his realm. A great fault cut across the kingdom of the Franks and Lombards from the North Sea to the Alps, following the linguistic frontier that divided the *lingua romana* from the *lingua teudisca*, or, as we would say today, the French tongue from the German. At any time the earth might slip and the frontier buckle along that fault, and sooner or later a deep quake was bound to occur. But meanwhile much could be done to lessen the havoc of frequent tremors, if Charles were willing to do it. Unfortunately the menace hardened his arrogance into inflexibility; he met the natural force with his own unbending will. For the time being that sufficed. Later he would have to make the concessions he now rejected, but by then much harm had been done to the suffering people and to his own character.

CHAPTER ELEVEN

Treason

THE NATURE of treason is equivocal; individual and state seldom agree on a single definition. In spite of some modern attempts to interpret "the meaning of treason" solely in the interests of the state, Patrick Henry's classic outcry remains the nobler statement of treason's duality. From the point of view of George III, the activity of the American Revolutionaries *was* treason; but under conditions of oppression there comes a time when men are prepared to refuse obedience to the state even at the risk of being damned as traitors. Treason can sometimes mean betrayal of what is good, true and just; but it can often mean a gallant though hopeless fight for freedom. Under an oppressive regime it is likely to mean the latter.

The Kingdom of the Franks and Lombards was at all times a more or less oppressive state—let us not deceive ourselves about that. From the common people, freemen as well as serfs, a good three days out of every week's work was exacted for labor on the lord's land. Taxation was heavy; in addition to the normal poll and property taxes which in the lands west of the Rhine had been paid since Roman days, there were sales taxes, pasturage taxes, taxes in kind on holders of manses, traditional holiday gifts to stewards and lords which had in fact become additional mandatory taxes. Harbor fees, bridge tolls and market tolls laid a burden on commerce and were such a nuisance to ordinary peasants as well as to traders that there were many attempts to evade them, in spite of the heavy fines imposed on evaders who were caught.

On top of the ordinary burden of taxations and tolls, fines and fees, dishonest officials lined their own pockets. There was little redress for the victims, since to economic injustice was added the political oppression inherent in the rapidly developing feudal system. Separation of the executive and the judiciary—the one principle indispensable for justice—did not exist. On the contrary, the same count who demanded more than his due from the peasants heard their appeals in his own court. The only check on his rapacity was the king himself, and the king could not be everywhere at once, although he later tried to be—by developing into a regular system the practice of sending out *missi* or royal commissioners on inspection tours.

When in addition to their normal burdens the common people of the Frankish realm had to provide fodder, food and gear as well as men for incessant military campaigns, the normal oppressiveness of the regime became unbearable. In later years Charles issued innumerable decrees aimed at easing the lot of the poorer freemen; but during most of the fifth decade of his life, when he was engaged on constant expansion of his power, he gave scant consideration to the spread of poverty and famine which was the direct result of his policies. Instead, he ruled with an iron hand, endeavoring to suppress discontent rather than to strike at its causes.

As always, the oppressed common people needed a leader drawn from the ranks of the oppressors, and they found him in Count Hardrad, a Thuringian nobleman, about whose personality nothing is known. The burdens of the Saxon war had rested most heavily on the peoples west of the Rhine, as we have seen, and Hardrad succeeded in raising the standard of revolt throughout Thuringia and parts of Austrasia. Franks as well as Thuringians were involved in a rebellion aimed at "diminishing the kingdom." A plot was also formed for assassinating Charles.

By now, however, Charles had apparently established a secret police—that indispensable adjunct to all autocratic rule. He was informed of the conspiracy in plenty of time, lulled the leaders into a sense of security, and then struck suddenly. An army entered Thuringia and treated it like conquered territory, devastating the land as had been done in Saxony. The conspirators were seized and brought before Charles and the national assembly at Worms. According to Einhard, only three of them were killed—resisting arrest—and there was much talk of Charles's clemency in condemning the rest only to exile or to blinding!

That there was a nationalistic impulse behind this uprising, a resistance to Charles's Romanized rule on the part of the Germans dwelling east of the Rhine, is suggested by the reply one of the conspirators gave to his accusers. Instead of denying the charge, he courageously threw back into Charles's face: "If my fellows had followed my advice, you would never have *crossed the Rhine* alive!"

The earth beneath the linguistic fault was beginning to groan.

At the opposite end of the Frankish kingdom, where the peninsula of Brittany jutted out into the Western Ocean, there was a smaller linguistic and national fault which was to send minor tremors through the body of France for a thousand years to come. This peninsula had been settled by refugees from the British Isles who had fled, three hundred and fifty years before, from the invading Angles, Saxons and Jutes. In their native isles the Bretons had become so debased that in Old English their name became synonymous with "slave." But among the fens and forests of Brittany they themselves were conquerors. They subjugated the native inhabitants and, in spite of the smallness of their numbers, long resisted conquest by the Franks. Roland, it will be remembered, had been warden of the Breton March. Marches were narrow strips of territory carved out of hostile country to guard the borders of the Frankish kingdom.

Though the wild interior of Brittany had never been conquered, the Frankish kings had succeeded in exacting tribute from the Breton chiefs. Perhaps this tribute—always paid reluctantly, of course—had recently been increased so that Charles might meet the expenses of the Saxon war. Or perhaps the Bretons thought to take advantage of Charles's engagement in Saxony. News traveled slowly and they might not yet have heard of Widukind's baptism and the end of the war. At any rate, they refused to pay tribute and prepared for defense, for which their terrain was ideally suited.

The few roads that led through the treacherous swamps were guarded by castles and fortifications, and the Franks whom Charles sent into the rebellious province under the command of his seneschal Audulf were put to hard fighting. They did not attempt to penetrate too deeply into Brittany and were content when they succeeded in capturing some of the rebel chiefs, who were then brought to the same assembly at Worms where the Thuringian conspirators were tried. Since their obligations to the Frankish crown were relatively vague, the Bretons were not treated as traitors. They were required only to pay homage to Charles: to kiss his feet, salute him honorifically and promise to pay the withheld tribute with interest. Charles made no attempt to push the conquest of Brittany any further—because of the difficulties and because the land was not worth the trouble.

In spite of these two campaigns in Thuringia and Brittany the chroniclers noted with astonishment that 786 was a year of peace. *"Hic annus fuit sine hoste"*—that is to say, there was no general levy of the army, nothing like the warfare on a grand scale which had stretched the resources of Frankland during the past three years. But the army marched nevertheless, or at least a part of it, for Charles was in no mood to take his ease. He was driven by a sense of restless urgency, by the feeling that he was getting older and had yet left many things undone, many areas of insecurity within and on the frontiers of his kingdom. The Thuringian and Breton revolts had been a moral shock to him and intensified his growing suspiciousness. He saw treason everywhere, and possibly with a good deal of justification. Rumors reached him, fed assiduously by the pope, who had his own interests in mind, that Arichis of Benevento, Tassilo of Bavaria and the Emperor Constantine were planning a great coalition to smash the power of the overweening Franks. Adalperga and Liutperga, the two daughters of the deposed Desiderius, were urging their husbands to unite against Charles. Perhaps they hoped still to free their father, who lived yet in his cloister in Frankland. And with Adelchis in Constantinople, representatives of the former Lombard dynasty were located at the three centers of Christian power in Europe outside Frankland itself. The Greek emperor was demanding the delivery of Charles's daughter Rotrud, to whom he had been betrothed five years before, and Charles was unwilling to surrender her. He did not see the marriage as an opportunity to make his daughter an empress; rather, he felt he would be giving his daughter as a hostage to a potential enemy.

Cousin Tassilo, meanwhile, had all these years been trying to fortify his position. He had been strengthening his army, had continued making donations to the Church with a generosity that far surpassed that of Charles, and had cultivated good relations with the pope. The Saxon war had given him the chance to shake off whatever obligations he had undertaken toward Charles in his submission of 781, and during that war he had even ventured to promote, as a test of strength, a border clash between Bavarians and Franks. It had been little more than a skirmish, but the Bavarians had won the field, and Charles had been too busy in Saxony to react. On his southeastern border also

Tassilo prepared for the inevitable struggle by making peace at last with the Avars, against whom he had been for years conducting a war of colonization and Christianization. He went so far as to enter negotiations with the khan of the Avars with a view to forming an alliance and encircling Charles's Lombard kingdom.

In the south of Italy Tassilo's brother-in-law Arichis also had been gathering strength. Arichis regarded himself as the legitimate heir of the kingdom of Desiderius. He had been attempting to enlarge his territory at the expense of the Duke of Naples, perhaps with the sanction of the Empress Irene, for the attachment of the Duchy of Naples to the Byzantine Empire was nominal. At any rate, he also maintained good relations with Irene, and simultaneously busied himself building very strong fortifications around the seaport of Salerno so that he would have a safe refuge in case his duchy was invaded.

Pope Hadrian, too, was busily plotting, although Charles in his present mood of suspicion may have exaggerated the extent of the pope's "treason." There can be no doubt, however, that Hadrian was dallying with the Greeks, attempting to play the Empire off against Charles and thereby gain concessions from Charles. In spite of the powerful opposition at home from the iconoclasts, Irene had remained steadfastly a defender of image worship. The prospect that all of eastern Christendom might soon be included within the orbit of the Roman Church was highly tempting to Hadrian, and when Irene called a synod at historic Nicaea to confirm the new era of revived image worship in Byzantium the pope agreed to send apostolic delegates—although he did not dare defy Charles to the extent of accepting Irene's invitation to attend the synod in person.

With such a whirlwind of intrigues and conspiracies rising, Charles could not remain idle. Fortunately his opponents had waited too long. Had they struck while his hands were still tied by the war in Saxony they might have shaken the foundations of his power. His adroit maneuver of five years before—the alliance with the Empire achieved at the price of Rotrud's betrothal—had given him time to defeat the Saxons. Meanwhile, his agents had been busy undermining the rule of his cousin in Bavaria. By bribes, persuasion and threats he had been winning over the Bavarian nobles. The great Germanic empire that Charles was building exerted a powerful pull on the Bavarians, similar to the attraction that the Reich was to exercise on Austria twelve centuries later. By his conquests of Saxony and Lombardy, Charles had united all the German states under his sway; he had in effect created a German Reich, and he now used every means in his power to foster the growing pro-Frankish sentiment among the Bavarian *optimates*. One of his strongest points, of course, was his legal position. Duke Tassilo had, after all, taken the oath of loyalty to him and to his sons, and powerful churchmen like Arno, Bishop of Salzburg since the death of Bishop Vergil two years before, considered the breach of an oath an unpardonable sin.

Nevertheless, the incorporation of the Duchy of Bavaria into the Frankish kingdom, which was Charles's ultimate aim, was not going to be easy. More than a military problem was involved. The recent revolt in Thuringia had shown Charles that he must consider public opinion more than he had hitherto been willing to do. The Bavarians, fellow Christians and fellow Germans, represented to all outward appearance no menace to the Frankish state. Tassilo was, after all, a close kinsman of Charles and had formally become his vassal. Charles knew that he had to convict his cousin openly and publicly of disloyalty before he could persuade his own nobles to take up arms against Bavaria. He had to put himself completely in the right, and to do so he would need the backing of the pope.

Another visit to Rome was obviously in order, and Charles again chose the winter—otherwise a time of idleness—to lead an army into Italy. He took with him a sizable striking force, but by no means the whole might of the Frankish kingdom, and crossed the Alps in midwinter. While he was on the march a variety of signs and portents at home announced that events of historic significance were impending. The annalists report that in December signs of the cross appeared on people's clothing. A week before Christmas tremendous thunderstorms, marked by terrifying displays of lightning, raged over the entire kingdom. Dead birds fell from the sky; many persons were killed by the lightning; and a fearful epidemic, that took many lives, followed.

Meanwhile, Charles proceeded south with his host and by Christmas had reached the city of Florence, then a tiny town still enclosed within its old Roman walls. Legend has it that he caused the statue of Mars, with which the fortunes of the city were linked, to be fished up out of the Arno—into which it had been hurled by barbarian invaders two hundred and fifty years before—and restored to honor near the Ponte Vecchio (that is, near a bridge dating from remote antiquity which was the predecessor of the present fourteenth-century Ponte Vecchio). The basis of the legend is that the fortunes of the city began to flourish again in Carolingian times, after a long period of decline. It is unlikely that the pious Charles would have gone to the trouble of recovering the statue of a pagan deity, and his recorded activities while in Florence were of a nature more befitting His Most Christian Majesty. He rode up the hill known as the Florentine Mount to the Church of San Miniato and set foot on the second-century pavement where the tourist still treads today. Sad memories of his last visit to Italy, with his beloved Hildigard, came to mind, and for her soul's salvation he made gifts of a number of houses to the Church of San Miniato. Perhaps he recalled, to the disadvantage of his present queen, how the robust Hildigard had always accompanied him on his journeys. For Fastrada seemed to be always ailing; she suffered severely from toothache and other unspecified afflictions and disliked the rigors of travel, preferring to remain comfortably at home in one of the palaces.

From Florence Charles went on to Rome, where a grand reception by Pope Hadrian awaited him—all the warmer since by now the news had spread that the Franks intended to invade Benevento. Arichis was thrown into a panic. Tassilo, for all his imposing military force, showed no sign of being ready to attack Charles's rear, and it was clear that no immediate help was to be forthcoming from Byzantium. The Beneventan duke saw himself soon joining his father-in-law in a monastery, and he resolved on a desperate appeal for mercy. Accordingly, he sent his elder son Romuald to Rome to plead with Charles and, virtually, to offer himself as a hostage.

Romuald was a handsome young man whose whole demeanor bespoke the high level of culture at the Beneventan court and whose courage in coming to the enemy camp was appreciated by Charles. Always susceptible to evidence of learning and high ideals, particularly in the young, Charles was almost won over by the young man's diplomacy and by the offer he brought: that his father would accept Charles as his overlord. But Pope Hadrian was indignant. How could Charles trust the unspeakable, perfidious, leprous, etc., Lombards who notoriously violated every law of man and God and were always seeking to harm the Holy See? Moreover, if peace were made now, how was he, the pope, ever to secure those cities in Beneventan territory which indisputably belonged to the patrimony of St. Peter?

The council of high-ranking Frankish nobles who had accompanied Charles into Italy sided with the pope. It is a commentary on the change in the political situation that the nobles who twelve short years before had been so reluctant to invade Italy at all were now urging military operations all the way down to the toe of the Italian boot. But the reason was not far to seek. They were thinking not in terms of policy but of the booty which they hoped to pick up in the cities of central and southern Italy. And since the prospective enemy showed himself so terrified of invasion, they assumed that the campaign itself would be easy. They expected to encounter little resistance and to come away rich.

Reluctantly Charles bowed to the persuasions of the pope and the recommendations of his council and continued the southward march through Italy. He passed through Monte Cassino, knelt on a slab of red marble before the grave of St. Benedict and undoubtedly inspected the piously preserved original copy of the Rule of St. Benedict, which he wished all the monasteries in Frankland to obey. Here too he probably bade good-by to his good friend Paul the Deacon, who in his longing to return to his native land and the peace of his monastic cell at Monte Cassino had withstood all the king's most tempting offers. Charles left Paul with an assignment—"to go through the writings of the Catholic Fathers and out of those flowery meadows to pick the loveliest blossoms and weave them all, as it were, into a wreath"—or, in less flowery words, to put together a collection of homilies which could be read on all occasions throughout the year. When Paul's collection was complete, some time afterward, Charles distributed copies among all the churches of the kingdom.

Before they parted Paul certainly urged on Charles that policy of leniency toward Benevento to which Charles was already inclined. Throughout his stay in Frankland Paul had maintained his old warm relations with the Beneventan duke and duchess. Ardent Lombard patriot that he was, he hoped by his influence to save at least one part of the ancient Lombard kingdom (whose history he was now engaged in writing) from utter extinction.

Consequently, Charles's mood had softened toward the Lombards by the time he arrived in the city of Capua—then still flourishing, though fifty years afterward it was to be utterly destroyed by the Saracens. Unlike the pope and his own nobles, Charles recognized that Bavaria was his foremost present problem and he was reluctant to go to war in the south while Tassilo's behavior was still open to question. When ambassadors from Constantinople came to Capua to demand delivery of the Byzantine emperor's promised bride, Charles's reluctance was redoubled. For he felt obliged to refuse their request, and it was obvious to him that this direct affront would soon be answered by military action on the part of the Empire.

When, therefore, Arichis abandoned his capital at Benevento, fled to fortified Salerno and from there sent another peace mission, Charles hesitated. Arichis was in any case offering total submission; he promised in advance to accept all the Frankish demands, whatever they might be; to give Charles, who already held Romuald, his younger son Grimoald as an additional hostage; and in fact to make all possible concessions, except that he would not appear before Charles for a personal interview. His wisdom in making this one condition was demonstrated by the fate of Tassilo the following year.

In the face of so complete a capitulation, Charles was able to resist the persuasions of Pope Hadrian and of his own nobles. To the immense disappointment of both parties he decided not to press the conquest. Instead, not only Arichis but all his people were ordered to take an oath of personal loyalty to Charles, and for this purpose Frankish *missi* were sent throughout Benevento. In addition, Arichis was to pay a large annual tribute. Charles accepted the younger son, Grimoald, as a hostage, along with a dozen other Beneventans "from among the people." He generously allowed Romuald to return home; he had evidently become too fond of the young man to wish to keep him in capitivity. Publicly it was announced that Charles's decision to refrain from invading Benevento was due to his laudable desire to spare the country the devastation of war.

In all the diplomacy, the pope had come away with the shorter end of the stick, and he was rather bitter about it. Charles had made peace with the enemy of the Holy See, Arichis, and had virtually broken diplomatic relations with the Empire, with which Hadrian had been flirting and in which he had hoped to find a counterpoise to the Franks so that the Church would not always have to remain the spiritual arm of the Frankish state. But although Charles apparently had the warmest personal feelings toward Hadrian, the outcome of his policies seemed always to be a slap in the face for the pope.

It is anticipating later events to imagine that Charles was fully aware of the potential conflict between State and Church and was bent on principle on keeping all power firmly in the hands of the state. He could not foresee the great "investiture controversy" in which the later Holy Roman Emperors would be involved; he could not even foresee the existence of the Holy Roman Empire, although some faint glimmering of his chances to become supreme arbiter of the West must by now already have been present in his mind. To Charles his title of "Patrician of the Romans" was no empty phrase. He considered himself the lord of Rome, and the pope his more or less faithful vassal. He was used to powerful vassals who tugged at the reins and would have made themselves independent if they had dared; was not this, in fact, his difficulty with Cousin Tassilo at the moment? And he had developed a technique for dealing with such wavering subordinates—a technique which consisted in alternate leniency and severity, in successive or sometimes simultaneous displays of the velvet glove and the mailed fist. This was the essential theme behind his treatment of the pope, although here he acted instinctively and only half consciously. For the relationship was complicated by his genuine reverence for the pope as spiritual guide and the direct successor to St. Peter.

He was, of course, aware of the pope's resentment, and on his return from Capua to Rome, where he wished to celebrate Easter once more and make the purifying pilgrim's round of the great basilicas, Charles resolved to conciliate Hadrian by another "donation" to the patrimony of St. Peter—the last of the Carolingian donations. He promised—once more without immediately fulfilling the promise, since again fulfillment depended on the pope's proving his claims—that the pope should have Capua and a number of other cities in Benevento and Tuscany. But even this latest donation was not a pure gift to placate Hadrian. In return for his promise Charles demanded a compensating service of far greater significance—namely, that the full weight of the apostolic condemnation be let loose on poor Tassilo.

The matter came up for immediate discussion because Tassilo, following the example of his Beneventan brother-in-law, also tried to win peace by sending ambassadors. In choosing Bishop Arno of Salzburg as one of his envoys Tassilo deliberately sent a person who not only enjoyed the respect of the pope but who was also known to be well liked by Charles. But the Bavarian duke had perhaps overreached himself. There is no clear evidence that the pro-Frankish bishop betrayed

his master, but the presumption is strong; certainly it is noteworthy
that Arno remained high in Charles's favor for the rest of his life. At
the very least, Arno provided Charles with a welcome pretext to insist
on Tassilo's obeying his oath to the letter, and the pope with an ex-
cuse for threatening the duke with anathema.

The negotiations were intricate. Bishop Arno and his fellow envoy,
Abbot Hunrich of Mondsee, first requested the pope's intervention in
the interests of peace between Charles and Tassilo. The pope declared that he was always ready to intervene in the interests of peace.
He was in fact quite unwilling to witness the total ruin of Tassilo
and urged Charles to be as merciful toward his cousin as he had recently been toward the Lombard duke.

Charles replied that peace between himself and Tassilo was his
dearest wish and that he was prepared to make an agreement at once.
But when he and the pope met with Arno and Hunrich, these envoys
stated that they had been sent only to transmit the replies of the king
and the pope and had no power to make any commitments in Tassilo's name. The ambassadors could not have behaved more undiplo-
matically if they had wished, and perhaps that is precisely what they
did wish. The pope took the opportunity to put matters right with
Charles; he flared up, threatened Tassilo and all his followers with
the apostolic curse if Tassilo failed to observe the oaths he had sworn
to Charles and—a significant addition—to Charles's father Pepin more
than twenty years before. Pressed by Charles, the pope went still
further. He informed the ambassadors that if Tassilo refused obedience to Charles, to Charles's sons and to the Frankish people, he alone
would be responsible for the bloodshed and the devastation of his
land that were sure to follow.

With this ultimatum of "be it on your own head" the ambassadors
returned to Bavaria, and Charles set out for his northern domains.
Fastrada and his family were awaiting him at Worms, and here he
decided to stay to call the national assembly and to gather together
the full military power of his kingdom, which he felt would be needed
for the invasion of Bavaria.

At the national assembly Charles made a speech; the express mention of it in the annals indicates that he felt he was swimming against
the stream of popular sentiment in Frankland. He described to the
assembled notables of the kingdom the course of events in Italy, explained the reasons for his decision not to invade Benevento, and

then went on to justify what must have seemed to them his peculiar desire to invade Bavaria now. He pictured the behavior of Tassilo's ambassadors in Rome as wanton insolence and an outright challenge to Frankish supremacy in Europe. Liutperga, Tassilo's wife, was the villainess of the piece; she it was who kept inciting her husband to defiance of the Franks. Tassilo was plainly plotting treason or he would have appeared here at Worms to attend the assembly, as it was his duty to do.

For all Charles's eloquence, the Frankish assembly was only partly convinced. The nobles were willing to let the military preparations go forward, but they felt that Charles could not in all honor treat his own cousin with less charity than the Duke of Benevento. Accordingly they insisted that Tassilo be given another chance, and envoys were dispatched inviting him to keep his oath to Charles and his sons, as the pope had ordered, and to present himself at Worms like any other vassal.

Like Arichis, Tassilo did not dare to come before Charles personally. When he refused, Charles had his pretext for war. The march of the armies began at once. Bavaria, nominally a subject province of the Frankish kingdom, was to be invaded as if it were inhabited by pagan barbarians.

The military preparations were impressive—in fact excessive. Charles must have had a fairly good idea of what was about to take place, but he took advantage of the opportunity to conduct a grand military maneuver to see how well the combined forces of his new and old subjects could work together. Lombard troops were ordered to advance from Bavaria's southern border. Austrasian, Thuringian and newly levied Saxon contingents moved down on Bavaria from the north. Charles himself led the main force, consisting primarily of the Romanized peoples from west of the Rhine, against the western border of Bavaria. Germany, said a contemporary, shook under the tread of the innumerable host.

The most powerful force of all, however, was the pro-Frankish "fifth" column which Charles had long had operating in Bavaria. Bishop Arno and his confederates among the Bavarian clergy spread word of Pope Hadrian's threat of anathema. The hopelessness of the coming struggle convinced those Bavarians who did not fear the peril to their souls, or who were not already persuaded by years of Frankish underground propaganda. In his time of need Duke Tassilo, who had ruled ably for thirty years, found himself deserted by his greatest nobles and prelates, unable to raise an army, urged by all his advisers to bow to the superior force.

Charles gave him time to consider. He and his armies waited by the river Lech on the border of Bavaria until the seditious elements had completed their work. And at last, seeing himself surrounded by treachery on all sides, urged on to continue his defiance only by his wife Liutperga, knowing that his only choices were to yield or to flee into exile as Adelchis had done, Tassilo capitulated. On October 3, 787, he presented himself to the king, solemnly placed his hands in Charles's as a sign that he recognized him as his lord, kissed Charles's knee and once more swore allegiance to him.

On this occasion he went further than he had six years before. He formally surrendered his dukedom to Charles by ceremoniously placing in Charles's hands a staff adorned with a male figure, signifying the power of rule. Charles graciously returned the staff to him to show that Tassilo was now receiving the dukedom from his hands, as many years ago he had received it from the hands of Charles's father Pepin. Whereupon Tassilo forced himself to utter the hateful words: "O King, the world is given to you for the good of all, and I shall pay my due service to you forever!"

Then, to demonstrate that the past was forgiven—and to suggest to the Bavarian nobles who were present and watching with eager personal interest that service to the Frankish king could be highly profitable—Charles loaded his cousin with bejeweled bracelets and gave him a horse whose blanket was made of cloth of gold. Accompanied by Frankish *missi* who were instructed to receive a loyalty oath to Charles from each and every Bavarian, and to keep an eye on Tassilo, the Bavarian vassal was permitted to return home, and the Frankish armies disbanded. Tassilo left his son behind as a hostage.

Why was Charles so forbearing when he already had Bavaria in his hands and had determined on the deposing of Tassilo? The official annals, of course, attribute his leniency to his "uncommon mildness"—an epithet which must have evoked from contemporaries a wry, if not bitter, amusement. Some later historians have seen his behavior as the acme of Machiavellian cunning: Charles, they argued, was in fact seizing complete control of Bavaria, but chose to leave Tassilo in office as bait for his enemies, the Greeks and the Avars, who would then launch a premature attack because they expected a simultaneous attack on the Franks by the Bavarians.

There were in fact such attacks in the course of the next year, but there is no evidence that Charles invited or welcomed them. In fact, such farfetched explanations are unnecessary. Subsequent events show that what concerned Charles at this time was public opinion in Frankland, which was not yet prepared for harsh treatment of his cousin. By his moderation toward Duke Arichis of Benevento he had already committed himself; he did not dare act with greater harshness toward Tassilo than he had toward Arichis. And, in fact, the terms of the agreement with Tassilo were essentially the same as those which had been given to Arichis earlier in the year, with the one highly important exception that Tassilo was required to appear personally before Charles.

The final act (but there was to be a weird epilogue) in the drama of the Rival Cousins took place the following year at Ingelheim, near Mainz, the site of one of Charles's greatest palaces and a favorite residence of his. Here in midsummer he convoked an all-national annual assembly which the principal men of all the provinces were required to attend—Saxons, Lombards, Alemannians, Franks—and, of course, Bavarians also.

Tassilo could not avoid coming this time. As soon as he arrived he was stripped of his arms and placed under arrest. A Frankish detachment was already on the way to Bavaria to seize Liutperga, their children and the household followers, and to secure the ducal treasury.

As soon as Tassilo's family had been brought to Ingelheim, there began one of the most carefully staged show trials in history. While the doomed man stood listening in helpless shame, his accusers rose one by one and brought forward their charges against him. Charles had seen to it that all the witnesses were fellow Bavarians, Tassilo's own subjects, who now claimed that they were only obeying their solemn oath of allegiance to the Franks in testifying against their duke. Their indictment contained all the elements that have become only too familiar to us in the political trials of contemporary history:

"He plotted to kill our noble and most excellent king's emissaries."

"He said to us that when we took our oath of allegiance to our lord king we should bear in mind that we did not mean it and that we were swearing falsely."

"He said in our presence that if he had ten sons as hostages, he would rather that all of them die than that he keep the terms of his pact, and he said that it was better for us all to die than to live like this, in servitude."

"He conspired with the foreign enemy, the bloodthirsty pagan Huns, inviting them to invade our country and promising that he would join forces with them to drive out the Franks."

Without benefit of secret drugs and physical or psychological tortures, but simply recognizing his helplessness and the fact that his wife and children were now in the hands of his enemies, Tassilo confessed. He made no attempt to deny the charges. He admitted everything, incriminated himself even more deeply, and threw himself on the mercy of Charles.

Besides these other accusations the ancient crime of *herisliz* was raked up to prove that the defendant's perfidy reached far back into the past. Twenty-five years before, Tassilo had deserted the army of Charles's father in time of war (see page 47). There was no statute of limitations on *herisliz*, but the matter had gone unmentioned and presumably forgotten during negotiations over the two agreements that Charles had made with Tassilo in the past seven years. Now it suddenly became the keystone of the prosecution's case, and since it was a charge that carried a mandatory death sentence, the assembled notables could see which way the wind was blowing. With one voice they demanded what Charles seemed obviously to want: death for Tassilo, though with what degree of inner conviction or dissatisfaction it is impossible to say.

At this point, having secured Tassilo's conviction, Charles placated whatever public discontent there was with the verdict and took occasion to play the part of a gracious ruler by tempering justice with mercy. In a manner reminiscent of the classic Greek tradition of permitting the defendant to suggest an alternative sentence to the court, he asked Tassilo what he wished to be done with him. Whereupon Tassilo, who knew what was expected of him, declared that he wished to atone for his many sins by becoming a monk. He asked only—a curiously contradictory note which betrayed his true feelings about his impending fate—that he not be shamed before everyone assembled here at Ingelheim by being tonsured on the spot. Perhaps he hoped still for some last-minute rescue, but none was forthcoming. Charles granted both requests; Tassilo was sent to the near-by mon-

astery of St. Goar and there shaved. His wife, his daughters and his
two sons suffered the same fate—confinement to convent and monastery for life.

With Tassilo out of the way, Charles proceeded speedily and de-
cisively to incorporate the Duchy of Bavaria into the Frankish state.
Bavaria was divided into counties administered by Frankish counts or
trustworthy Bavarians. Large numbers of Bavarian nobles suspected
of continued loyalty to Tassilo were sent into exile. The ducal estates were taken over by the Frankish fisc, the obligations of military
service extended to Bavarian freemen. In all these confiscatory acts
Charles was behaving with the strictest legality: Bavaria was a fief
which had reverted to Charles as its lord, and Charles disposed over
it exactly as if it were one of his own villas.

Charles's acquisition of Bavaria in effect created the German nation. No longer was there any large body of Germans outside the
Frankish state. The process begun three centuries before by the tribal
chieftain Clovis, when he began gathering together the petty Germanic kingdoms all around him, had now been completed. Germany
was united at last, and although the union was only temporary, although the centrifugal forces of feudalism were soon to pull her apart
again, there was time enough for a national consciousness, a sense of
Deutschtum, to sink in. Oddly enough, that national consciousness
had first been fostered by St. Boniface and the group of Anglo-Saxon
missionaries around him. Going about from tribe to tribe as preachers, they had recognized and stressed unity amid diversity and had
popularized the word and the concept *diutisk—deutsch*. Now the son
of the king whom Boniface had crowned and anointed was converting the linguistic, social and psychological unity into a political actuality. Is it pursuing speculation too far to see in this development of
a pan-German policy once again the influence of Boniface on the
impressionable mind of the boy Charles?

Only the Anglo-Saxons themselves, who had propagated the idea,
now remained outside the Germanic state that Charles had forged,
and for a while he entertained the thought of conquering them also,
now that Bavaria was his. He seized the first opportunity to pick a
quarrel with King Offa of Mercia, the most powerful king in England,
with whom Charles had up to now been on the best of terms. Young
Charles, his son, had asked for the hand of one of King Offa's daugh-

ters. Offa consented on condition that Charles marry his daughter
Bertha to his own Egfrith, whom Offa had recently made co-king.
Charles chose to take this friendly proposal for a doubly cemented
alliance as an insulting refusal; he reacted with an indignation which
puzzled his contemporaries, who did not guess what plans he was toy-
ing with. Alcuin, who was probably one of the few who could guess,
chose to ignore his knowledge. To a friend he wrote: "I don't know
what is going to happen. Some quarrel, fomented by the devil, has
come up between King Charles and King Offa. Trade between the
two countries has been stopped. Some say I am going to be sent to
make peace."

Apparently Alcuin was in fact later sent to patch things up, for
Charles soon realized that he was too deeply embroiled on the Continent to attempt an invasion of England. He had no fleet to cross
the Channel, and if he could build a navy, he would need it to fend
off the impending Byzantine invasion of Italy and to defend the ports
of Southern Gaul against the Saracens. The acquisition of Bavaria
had increased his land might, but it had not given him one additional
ship. It had, moreover, shifted the whole center of gravity of the
Frankish state toward the east and brought the Franks into direct
contact with the Avars. As soon as Charles fully realized where he
now stood, he abandoned any thought of attacking England. The
rumors of war died down; Alcuin was soon writing to Offa that Charles
considered him a faithful friend, and an amicable and profitable intercourse between the two kingdoms was resumed. Shortly before Offa's
death, a few years later, Charles sent him an Avar sword and silk
mantles, and indicated that he would be pleased to receive cloaks of
English wool in return. Cross-Channel trade was at this time perhaps
more vigorous than any other sea-borne commerce in Western Europe, for it alone was not menaced by Saracen pirates.

As a consolation prize for young Charles, who had missed out on
his English princess, Charles appointed him ruler over the Duchy of
Maine in Neustria. It might appear that Charles's eldest son was being given a more meager portion than either Louis of Aquitaine or
Pepin of Italy, but this was not the case at all. While Pepin and Louis
had been sent to "foreign" portions of the kingdom since earliest
childhood, young Charles had been constantly with his father, learning the business of government at his side. He was clearly the destined
heir to the Frankish "heartland"—to all those portions of the king-

dom settled by the Frankish people themselves. Perhaps Charles now gave him a token kingdom because the boy felt at a disadvantage vis-à-vis his younger brothers; perhaps also Charles felt that some time spent in the Romanized and Romance-speaking portion of the realm would be profitable to young Charles, who had spent most of his youth in German-speaking parts of the kingdom. Not that he disapproved of young Charles, who at seventeen was a son after his father's heart. Charles intended only to broaden this son's education; he did not worry about him as he worried about eleven-year-old Louis. He had Louis brought from Aquitaine often during these years and kept him by his side at Worms and at Regensburg, hoping to remove by example and by training the effeteness and excessive piety that he saw developing in the boy. Charles was much concerned, says the contemporary biographer of Louis, "that the king should not be without knowledge of the honorable occupations"—in other words, warfare—"or that he should be brought to shame by any traces of foreignness."

In this differing treatment of his two sons is contained the answer to the perennial question that has raged for centuries among French and German historians. Both French and Germans have claimed Charles for their own national hero. The Germans have stressed his conscious design to unite all the German tribes, his preference for living in the German-speaking parts of his kingdom, his interest in the German language and German folk songs, his suspicion of "Roman" influences as foreign—all quite true. The French have pointed out that he spent the better part of his life battling Germans in Saxony, massacring, oppressing and deporting them; that he considered himself the continuer of the highly Romanized Merovingian kings; that he ruled over almost the whole of what is now France; that he was equally energetic in adding Romanized lands to his domains; that his parents and grandparents preferred to reside in the valleys of the Aisne and the Oise and were buried at St. Denis; that the language of his court was Latin as much as German, and the language of his chancery entirely Latin; that his genealogists made a point of stressing his Gallo-Roman ancestry—also quite true.

Charles, however, thought of himself as Frankish and European— that is to say, neither French nor German, but both and neither. That he was keenly aware of the separate strains of Romanism and Germanism in his kingdom is clear. For this reason he wished his two sons to unite both elements in themselves, as they were already united in himself. His son Charles needed more of Roman culture; Louis, on the other hand, had not imbibed enough of the Germanic tradition. The third son, the young King of Italy, was receiving the most important elements of both traditions in equal measure from the Romanized Lombards, who, like the Franks just west of the Rhine (and Charles himself was one of these), represented the amalgam. Charles had no desire to build a German confederation; rather, he was slowly reconstituting at least the western half of the old Roman Empire. But he would not make the mistake that had been made by the Romans, who had built a barrier against the Germans to keep them out. Rather, Germans and Romans—and in the eighth century the people of Gaul were still being called Romans—would be united under the banner of Christ and the personal rule of the Carolingian *rex Dei gratia*. There were no French or Germans in Charles's City of God; there were only fellow members in the Mystical Body of Christ and the practical corpus of Frankish Western Europe.

CHAPTER TWELVE

Frontier Conquests

CHARLES had received one of Pope Hadrian's character-istic letters. The pope wrote:

"Your envoys, Chaplain Roro and Betto, came to us and asked whether the accursed Adelchis, the son of King Desiderius, has in truth come to Italy. As we have now learned from Bishop Campu-lus of Cayeta and by way of letters from the Pentapolis, Adelchis is now staying with the Emperor's ambassadors in Calabria, on the border of the Duchy of Benevento, and is planning to make trouble for you and for us.

"In consideration of these things, it seems to us altogether in-advisable to let Grimoald, the son of Arichis, go to Benevento. How-ever, do as Your Wisdom thinks best; but in case the Beneventans do not obey your orders, as they have promised, send an army against them at once—later it would not be advisable on account of the heat of summer. On the other hand, waiting from May until September would undoubtedly mean difficulties with Adelchis and the Greeks, for Greek envoys are staying with him, and there are others in Naples.

"We earnestly ask you to believe no one more than us in regard to Grimoald. You can depend on this—that Italy will not be peaceful if you permit Grimoald to go to Benevento. As we have learned secretly from Bishop Leo, Adalperga, the widow of Arichis, intends, as soon as her son Grimoald arrives in Benevento, to pretend to make a pil-grimage with her two daughters to the holy Archangel Michael on Mount Garganus. From there she will, however, travel to the city of Tarento, only eighty miles away, where her treasure is hidden. You must not think we are telling you these things because we are greedy for possession of the cities you have given to Saint Peter; rather, we are doing so solely out of concern for the security of the Holy Roman Church."

Charles knew quite well that Hadrian's true motive was expressed in this denial. Having received letters in a similar vein for some sixteen years, Charles understood his correspondent. He had no need to consult his shrewd chancellor, Rado—the successor and disciple of Itherius, who delighted as Itherius had done in putting spokes in the papal wheel—to unravel the deeper meanings of Hadrian's letter. Here were all the familiar combinations of gossip mongering, wheedling, striving for advantages for the Church, insecurity, pride and a singular penchant for seeing or fabricating intricate plots. The allusion to Adalperga was a not particularly artful attempt to arouse cupidity on the part of Charles and his Franks. Here was, the pope hinted, the vast treasure of the Beneventan state about to be carried away by the perfidious daughter of Desiderius; if the Franks hurried, they could capture it.

Nevertheless, there was always some real basis for Hadrian's warnings, though he might exaggerate the dangers or pervert the situation to his own purposes. For so shortly after Charles had arranged the affairs of Benevento, and while he was busy settling his score with Tassilo, an unexpected turn of events had thrown the whole of southern Italy into confusion. Within a month of each other Duke Arichis and his heir, Romuald, had suddenly died. Arichis was only fifty-three, Romuald twenty-five; poisoning by agents of the Empire, or by patriotic Beneventans outraged over their duke's submission to the Franks, has been suggested, but there is no evidence. Perhaps both the duke and his son were struck down by the plague which was sweeping through Frankland and may also have reached Italy.

After the deaths of their rulers, the Beneventans sent to Charles to request the release of Grimoald, the younger son of Arichis, whom Charles still held as a hostage. For nearly a year Charles hesitated to grant their petition. He would have liked best to incorporate Benevento into his Lombard kingdom, abolish the dukedom altogether and, as he was doing in Bavaria, divide the duchy up into counties under the command of Franks or reliable Lombards. But his conquest of the country was too new, and he could not spare the troops for a full-fledged occupation of southern Italy. With each expansion of his domains he was coming into contact with new enemies along the borders. The Frankish state was suffering from the difficulties that any growing imperial power encounters.

The most dangerous threat was the impending Greek invasion of

Italy. The Empire's territories in Calabria and Naples would serve as jumping-off points for the Empress Irene's armies, and the first attack would therefore come in Benevento—provided that Benevento did not voluntarily go over to the Empire, which was a possibility to be reckoned with. Yet, even though he could hardly trust the Beneventans, and even though Pope Hadrian insisted that they were preparing treachery, Charles wished to have them defend themselves, or at least to provide the bulk of their defense.

He had already made up his mind, for this reason, to send Grimoald back to Benevento. He had delayed so long not so much because of Hadrian's opposition as because he wished to attach the young man more strongly to himself. The archenemy was still Adelchis, who is pictured in later legendary accounts as a heroic figure of a man, so that even after twelve years the Lombards still admired him and considered him their legitimate ruler. Certainly he was an adroit diplomat. A prince without a kingdom, he had maintained himself at Constantinople during those twelve years amid all the intrigues of the Byzantine court. Now at least he had received military aid from his hosts and had landed with an army in Italy. Charles might well fear the influence of Adelchis on his young nephew, Grimoald.

Nevertheless, Charles had to take a chance on Grimoald. Pope Hadrian's letter only hardened his decision, for in and between the lines of it he read an attitude that he did not like. Hadrian seemed to think himself Charles's appointed deputy ruler in Italy. He was making agreements with Charles's envoys on the disposition of Frankish troops—and consulting Charles after the agreements, not before. Obviously Hadrian hoped to see the Duchy of Benevento broken up so that he could take possession of his cities. For Charles, however, dismemberment of Benevento was out of the question in the face of an immediate Greek threat.

Accordingly, after receiving the pope's letter, Charles decided to rebuff Hadrian once more. He sent Grimoald back to Benevento. He was gambling on the personal authority he felt he had acquired over Grimoald during the young man's stay with him as guest-hostage. Grimoald would owe a debt of gratitude to Charles for giving him back his heritage and installing him as duke. And in spite of family ties, the young man should not take kindly to his uncle's invading Italy at the head of a foreign army.

For the time being, the gamble succeeded. If Charles was trading future troubles for present advantages, that was, after all, in the very nature of statecraft. At present the integrity of Benevento was at stake, and for the purposes of Frankish policy Benevento could be handled far more easily if she were independent than if she were an imperial province. By nourishing the national aspirations of the Bene-ventans Charles was able to husband his own resources and avoid overextending his power.

Grimoald was received by the Beneventans with great rejoicing, and immediately took action in a vigorous, pro-Frankish sense. With two Frankish envoys in constant attendance on him he set about smash-ing Greek influence, which had increased enormously since his father's death. The wearing of beards in the Greek fashion was forbidden. Grimoald dutifully issued coins bearing the name of Charles, and dated his official documents by the regnal years of his Frankish over-lord. More important than these gestures, he gathered an army of Beneventan patriots, joined forces with Duke Hildebrand of Spoleto, and marched to meet the Greek army which actually landed in Ca-labria. Stiffened by a small contingent of Franks under Winigis (who was later to succeed Hildebrand as Duke of Spoleto), the Lombards administered an overwhelming defeat to the imperial forces. The Greeks fled back to their ships after losing some five thousand men. Adelchis, who was probably present at the battle, escaped and appar-ently retired from politics thereafter. He lived to a ripe old age enjoy-ing the title of patrician in Constantinople.

The Greek threat receded, not so much because of this single defeat as because a struggle for power was in progress in the Eastern Roman Empire. Young Constantine, eighteen years old and tired of being treated like a child by his mother Irene, conspired to arrest his mother and banish the eunuch Stauracius, who controlled the government under Irene. Irene's success at the Council of Nicaea in re-establish-ing image worship had won her powerful enemies in high places who gladly took the occasion to set up her easily influenced son as emperor in fact as well as name. Backed by the army, Constantine forced his mother to resign. Stauracius, the prime minister, was banished, and the image smashers were once more in power in Constantinople. But during the years of the regency Constantine had become too de-pendent on his mother to do without her for long. The ministers he chose lacked the financial genius of Stauracius, who had managed to lower taxes and yet to provide good pay and equipment for the army and to keep a large reserve in the treasury. After a year the in-decisive boy called his mother back from her splendid retirement in the Eleutherion palace; he embraced her and imagined that all would be well again. But Irene promptly began undermining his popularity by fostering her son's vices, and within five years after her return she had so far recovered the imperial power that she was in a position to commit the dreadful act that has made her name a byword for cruelty and unnatural motherhood.

Charles, meanwhile, was left free to devote himself to the multi-tude of projects that fired his mind as the expansion of his kingdom brought with it a wider variety of internal and external problems, as the conception of his ultimate aim grew clearer in his mind and as he himself approached ever closer to his fiftieth year. He had com-menced several building projects—a palace at Ingelheim, a palace at Salz, a palace at Aachen—and he had profited by the years of good relations with the Empire to hire Byzantine artisans and architects to help with the work, for Germans were still unskilled at building in stone.

He engaged also on an extensive project of monetary reform, which involved gradually replacing the old denarius, or silver penny, by a heavier penny of exact weight. To facilitate trade he struck an obolus, or halfpenny—an innovation. Around this time also he established new standards of weights and measures, introducing a heavier pound than the old Roman pound and a heavier *modius*, or bushel measure. These reforms were long overdue, for during the past century the en-tire monetary system had fallen into confusion, the amount of money in circulation had diminished greatly, and payment in kind had in many places replaced payment in coin. Counterfeiting and debasing of the coinage were widespread; so also was the giving of false weight and false measure. Charles recognized that a sound currency was es-sential to prevent the complete stagnation of economic life. To over-come suspicion of the new coinage, and to deal with the long-standing lack of confidence in the currency, he issued a decree providing that the new money "must be accepted by everyone, in every place, every city, every market." The heavy fine of fifteen solidi was imposed for violation of this order. He was more successful in reforming the cur-rency than in standardizing measures, and different traditional meas-ures continued to be used in the various provinces.

Charles began also at this time a sweeping reform of the Church.

This was a project that was never-ending, throughout his reign and long afterward, for the wealth and privileges of the Church attracted to it unscrupulous men as wolves are attracted to a sheepfold— to use an image characteristic of the times. Charles was in deadly earnest about these reforms; he considered himself as "defender of the Church" under the special protection of Christ and therefore under an inescapable obligation "to show thankfulness not only in heart and words, but in the constant doing of good works."

"You pastors of the Church of Christ are the leaders of His flock," he addressed his bishops and priests, "and you must be shining lights of the world, ready by your example and advice to lead the flock to the pastures of eternal life."

With this preamble he lashed out at the innumerable abuses and above all at the secularization of the clergy. There was no need for him to invent new laws; almost all the reforms he advocated had already been set down in the canons of the Church, but these canons were rarely enforced. He ordered again that bishops, abbots and abbesses must not go hunting or keep hounds and falcons. Churchmen must not carry arms. Pretended monks must be exposed. Bishops must not engage in usury or trade, or store grain in churches. The clergy were to be responsible for strict observance of Sundays:

"Men must not engage in agricultural work; they must not plow, reap, cut grass or set fences, dig for roots or fell trees; they must not work in quarries, build houses, garden, hold meetings or go hunting. ... Women must not weave, cut garments, sew, embroider, spin wool, beat flax, wash clothes in public, or clean sheep. The honor and repose of the Lord's Day must be observed in every way."

In his efforts to reform the monasteries and nunneries Charles was something less than successful. He might order monks to stay in their cloisters and cease wandering about the countryside; he might insist that abbesses must not write or transmit love letters; but the very necessity for such rules indicates that he was hopelessly opposing human nature. He was equally unsuccessful in his constant battle against superstition. He did his best, however, to stop soothsaying by the use of the Psalter and the Gospel, to prevent the priests (who were just as superstitious as the people) from baptizing bells and attaching slips of paper to them in order to prevent hail, to put an end to magic and weather-making, to persuade the clergy to destroy sacred trees, groves and springs, and to curb belief in such scandalous travesties of the Faith as "that forged letter said to have fallen from heaven."

Charles prescribed in detail the kind of shoes and dress the clergy were to wear, the manner in which they were to chant the psalms (after the Roman, not the Frankish, usage). He reminded the churchmen that one of their most important functions was the giving of alms and the protection of the poor and of widows and orphans. He urged them again to be diligent in establishing schools and in making copies of the necessary books. He spoke in the tones of a preacher and prophet against hatred, envy, avarice, violation of the marriage bond. In general it is clear that Charles took for granted the ecclesiastical nature of his position. He and not the pope was the head of the Frankish Church. He considered himself a "bishop of bishops," as the Monk of St. Gall put it. Nevertheless, he was not aiming at an independent Frankish Church; he desired and maintained an intimate connection between his Church and Rome. In his capitularies and admonitions he quoted frequently from the collection of canons that Pope Hadrian had given him during his visit to Rome.

Military activities were still occupying a great deal of Charles's time. But it was no longer necessary—or, for that matter, possible—for him to conduct all military operations in person. Under the command of able men to whom Charles had entrusted the government of King Louis' Aquitanian kingdom, steady progress was being made in the building of a Spanish March, a strip of buffer territory against the Saracens on the Spanish side of the Pyrenees. Alcuin wrote with joyous exaggeration that the Frankish troops had seized some three hundred miles of coast line from the Saracens.

These same able Aquitanian high officials had things pretty much their own way with a boy king reigning over them and with Charles's attention frequently diverted elsewhere. The revenues of King Louis' royal estates often never reached him, but Charles did not discover this until Louis was nearly seventeen. One day, when Louis was visiting him, he reproached the boy for stinginess in never bringing his father a present unless it were specially commanded. The boy told him that "since all the nobles thought only of their own interest, they neglected the public good and made public property into private property, so that he was master in name only and in fact suffered from want of almost everything."

The situation was a sad exposure of that feebleness of character which Louis was to manifest in all his later life. Charles took prompt action; a body of royal commissioners went back to Aquitaine with Louis and firmly but tactfully—for they did not want to make the young king unpopular in his own domains—saw to it that "the estates which had formerly served to supply the royal needs were restored to the public service."

Charles was grateful that he could entrust the conduct of the war in Spain to the redoubtable Count William of Toulouse, the warrior who was to live on in legend as one of the most famous of Charles's "paladins." For Charles himself did not ever again want to go near Spain; the memory of Roncesvalles was too strong and too bitter still, even after the lapse of more than ten years. He could rejoice that William firmly suppressed the recurrent rebellions among the Basques; he could certainly feel, when news reached him of the death of his old enemy, Abdur Rahman, that he would have no need henceforth to worry about his southwestern border. But that feeling was illusory; he always had to worry about all his borders.

After twenty years of rule Charles had at last succeeded in gathering around himself a corps of efficient generals, those men who were later to be immortalized in legend as his paladins—a word derived from the "counts of the palace" or "counts palatine." William and Theoderic were both kinsmen of his, as it happened. Count Gerold of Bavaria was the brother of his late wife Hildigard. Eric of Friuli was shortly to distinguish himself in the war against the Avars. His eldest son Charles could now be entrusted with the command of an army. But Charles himself did not intend, as yet, to retire from the direct conduct of his important campaigns, and while Winigis, Hildebrand and Grimoald were fighting for him in Italy, he himself set out on an expedition with a double purpose.

East of the Elbe River stretched the vast and unknown lands inhabited by numerous Slavic tribes—Sorbs, Abodrites, Bohemians, Welatabians, and others. The chief of these were the Welatabians, or Wiltzi, as the Franks called them, who lived along the southern shore of the Baltic Sea—then known as "a gulf stretching from the Western Ocean towards the East, of unknown length, but nowhere

more than a hundred miles wide and often much narrower." The
Wiltzi made war on the Saxons and on their other Slavic neighbors,
with whom Charles had some time since made a loose treaty of
alliance.

Charles had no desire to extend his conquests indefinitely eastward,
but he saw the need for creating here in the east another "march"
to protect his frontiers. Also he needed assurance that his northern
flank would be secure for the operations he was already planning in
the Danubian plain. Therefore, when the Abodrites appealed to him
for help against their neighbors, he promptly declared war on the
Wiltzi. Having raised a considerable army, which included Franks,
Saxons and Frisians, he marched across Saxony to the Elbe River, where
he effected a junction with his allies, the Abodrites and Sorbs. At the
Elbe he built two bridges of boats in the usual Frankish fashion,
threw up fortifications at both ends of one of the bridges to protect
his line of retreat before he moved into unknown hostile country, and
then advanced against the Wiltzi. His army ravaged as they went,
and apparently met with little resistance. By now his reputation had
grown so enormously that the mere news that Charles, the mighty
Frankish king, had appeared in person was enough to win the surrender of his enemies. A complete capitulation of the Wiltzi followed. Its terms included permission for Frankish missionaries to
preach in Welatabian territory, and the work of converting the Slavs
to Christianity began at once. It does not seem to have been pushed
with great vigor, however, perhaps because of language difficulties.

This campaign against the Wiltzi was only a prelude to an undertak-
ing which was considered by Charles's contemporaries "the greatest
of all his wars next to the Saxon war," and one which "he prosecuted
with more vigor than the others and with far more military preparation."

The Avars, a Mongoloid people, small, broad-shouldered, with long
hair that hung in tresses down their backs and was bound with rib-
bons, were always confounded by the Franks with the Huns, whose
name could still spread terror. They had first appeared in Europe in
the sixth century, they themselves fleeing from the growing power
of the Turks; they had conquered the Slavonian and Bulgarian tribes
of the Danube and the Elbe, bargained with the Emperor Justinian
and lent aid to the Lombards in the latter's conquest of Italy. Ultimately they settled in the Roman province of Pannonia—present-day

Hungary and Yugoslavia—and their empire at one time extended from
the mouth of the Danube to the mouth of the Oder. They received
enormous tributes from the emperors at Constantinople—as much as
120,000 gold solidi annually, as well as innumerable gifts of silks, spices
and even a golden bed which the proud khakhan of the Avars rejected
as unsuitable. The vast treasures of two centuries and a half were
accumulated in the palace of the khakhan within the city or encamp-
ment known as the Ring, because it was protected by circular walls—
nine concentric circles of walls, according to the Monk of St. Gall,
whose informant had fought in the Avar war.

After their abortive attempt to invade Bavaria and Italy as part of
their agreement with Tassilo, the Avars sent ambassadors to Charles,
offering to fix the borders between the two peoples. But the negotiations came to nothing, for Charles had already determined on war
and had issued orders for the first general levy of troops from all parts
of his kingdom since the Spanish expedition thirteen years before.
Even his recently acquired Slavic satellites were called on to supply
men for the Avar war.

Charles did not formally declare war until after he received word
from Italy that the initial attack by his son Pepin, leading Lombard
troops, had been an unqualified victory. From his camp on the borders of the Avar country Charles wrote to Queen Fastrada—the one
purely personal letter of his which has been preserved.

"Charles, by God's grace King of the Franks and Lombards and
Patrician of the Romans, sends his greetings to you, his dearly beloved
wife, Queen Fastrada.

"By this letter we wish to send you our love in the Lord, and
through you our greetings to our beloved daughters and all our lieges
who are with you. By God's grace we are in sound health and good
spirits.

"A messenger from our beloved son [Pepin] has reported to us the
glad news that he and the lord pope are in good health, and that all
is well in that part of our dominions. Moreover, he informs us that
the Italian troops which we ordered to occupy the borders facing the
Avars have penetrated into Avar territory. They engaged in a battle
with them. Almighty God in His mercy gave the victory to them and
they killed many Avars; never before, even in protracted battles, have
so great a number of the enemy fallen. Our men stormed their camp,
which was protected by a wall, and remained in it all night and the

next day until the third hour. They were then able to return laden
with spoils and without having to give battle again. They took one
hundred and fifty Avar prisoners and let them live, awaiting further
orders from us.

"We have ordered solemn prayers from Monday, the fifth of September, to Wednesday, the seventh, imploring God's mercy that He
may give us peace, health, victory and a favorable march, and that in
His mercy and goodness He will be our helper, guide and defender in
all our trials. Our priests have ordered that all who are not hindered
by sickness or too great age or youth shall refrain from wine and meat
during these days. Those who must drink wine during these three
days may purchase permission to do so—nobles by paying one solidus
per day, those in humbler circumstances by giving at least a denarius.
Everyone has given alms according to his means and good will. Every
priest, unless prevented by illness, has been required to say a special
Mass, and the clerics who know their psalms have chanted fifty psalms.
During these days all the clergy have walked barefoot. Such were the
decisions of our clergy, and we all joined with them and did as they
bade with the help of the Lord.

"Now we should like you to consult the clergy at home for the same
ritual there. Only please do not, yourself, do more than your weakened health permits. We leave this to your judgment.

"We have been much surprised that we have received no letter from
you since we left Regensburg. Write more often about your health
and anything else you wish to tell. Once more, greetings in the Lord."

Charles's rather pompous use of the regal "we," even when writing
to his queen, suggests that after more than twenty years of rule the
man and the king had become one. But through all the formality
the strength of Charles's affection for his fourth wife comes through.
The court might not like her, but Charles himself was clearly devoted
to her. And obviously she had the energy and ability to fill the place
of associate in the government which had formerly been the function
of Charles's mother. In spite of her delicate health it is Fastrada,
rather than the archchaplain, who is asked to order the ritual of
thanksgiving for victory. Perhaps the fact that she was a "strong"
queen was one reason why she was charged with cruelty. There is
also, it is true, a suggestion in the letter that Fastrada was in the habit
of acting on her own rather frequently and was slow to make an accounting to her husband, so that Charles had to ask her to write more
often.

The preponderant note of joy and excitement in this letter of Charles's is not sufficiently explained by a victory which appears to have been little more than a successful raid—only a hundred and fifty prisoners taken and the captured camp quickly abandoned. The likeliest reason for Charles's pleasure was that the raid had been conducted by young King Pepin in person and that his fourteen-year-old son had borne himself very well. The pride Charles took in this adventure of Pepin's was all the keener because he had just experienced a disappointment with Pepin's younger brother, Louis. Louis, just past thirteen, had been ordered to accompany his father on the Avar campaign and had been formally invested with his sword—the traditional Frankish ceremony marking the transition from boyhood to young manhood. But in the course of the march along the Danube to the Vienna Woods Charles realized that this son was not yet ready for war and perhaps never would be. Saddened, he had sent the boy back to Regensburg to spend the rest of the campaign with Queen Fastrada. Now, however, Pepin's exploit reassured him. He need not feel ashamed of at least two of his sons.

In their accounts of the Avar war the annals report nothing but victories. Of this first campaign, for example, they say that Charles and the armies of his two generals, Theoderic and Meginfrid, marched through and devastated with fire and sword a large part of Pannonia, and then returned without loss to Bavaria—except that the mounted warriors walked back home. For a terrible plague broke out among the horses of the army—"scarcely a tenth of so many thousands of horses survived."

It is difficult to reconcile this version with Einhard's statement: "How many battles were fought there and how much blood shed can still be seen by the deserted condition of Pannonia. The place where the palace of the khakhan stood is so desolate that there is not so much as a trace of human habitation." There can be little question, in view of the length of the Avar war, that Einhard's is the truer story. For although Charles himself led only one expedition into Avar territory, his generals fought there year after year and evidently pursued a policy of blood and iron.

In the fourth year of the war, which had been waged desultorily because it was interrupted by other concerns, Charles's policy of infiltration and propaganda bore fruit. "Fifth-column" tactics had long

After recommending that tithes not be imposed on the new converts, Alcuin continued:

"Above all, preaching and baptism must proceed in orderly fashion, so that the washing of the body in the holy waters of baptism will not have been in vain because the rational soul has as yet made no progress in the understanding of the Catholic religion. . . ."

These recommendations now appealed to Charles; he could not help seeing how mistaken his Saxon policy had been. The Saxons, in fact, were right now so troublesome that he had to devote his whole time to them, and he put his son Pepin in sole charge of the Avar war. On Charles's orders Pepin held a council with a number of bishops at his Danube camp. It was decided that such an ignorant, rude and unlettered people as the Avars would necessarily find it hard to understand the sacred mysteries. Baptism would therefore be administered only after instruction and whenever the convert was ready for it. Forcible baptism was banned; henceforth the Avars would be baptized as individuals, not by whole tribes, and those who had been previously baptized without having made a confession of faith were to be considered pagans who had merely had a good bath.

These humane principles established, Pepin promptly advanced into the Avar country again and set about rapidly reducing the numbers of the enemy who would have to be converted. The Lombards he led had forgotten their ancient debt to the Avars, and the war was prosecuted with great efficiency, which is to say with great cruelty. With Danube shipping to supply them, Pepin's armies were not dependent on the country for their supplies. Pepin duplicated Eric's feat of penetrating the Ring and found even more of the Avar treasure. He then razed the capital of the Avars to the ground and triumphantly carried the new spoils and a large number of prisoners (for whose liberty Alcuin successfully interceded) to his father at Aachen. This second influx of silver and gold into Frankland created, on top of the earlier one, a galloping inflation.

After the destruction of the Ring the Avars continued to put up sporadic resistance, and a number of minor but hard-fought campaigns were necessary before Pannonia was entirely pacified. But the worst of the war was over; the power of the Avars was thoroughly

broken and that ancient, if hardly peaceable, people soon disappeared
from history as a separate nation. Charles had extended the frontiers
of the Frankish state far down the Danube River. He now ruled over
all of non-Slavic and non-Byzantine Europe with the exception of
Spain, southern Italy and the marshy heart of that unconquered,
never-to-be-conquered peninsula of Brittany. He had pushed eastward
and westward, absorbing smaller political units in the course of conquest, until now his realm was in direct contact with the Byzantine
Empire in the east and southeast and with the Arab Empire in the
southwest. The three great powers of the Mediterranean world were
now confronting one another.

CHAPTER THIRTEEN

The Church

CHARLES had no minister of finance, no brain trust of advisers on economic questions, and apparently he could not himself foresee the economic dislocations which invariably resulted from his call-up of a general levy. The great military effort of invading Spain in 778 had been followed by the famine of 779. The levy of troops from all his dominions in 791, for the opening blows of the war against the Avars, again stripped the countryside of harvest hands. The armies, too, consumed vast quantities of provisions. In addition, the loss from disease in Pannonia of nine tenths of the Frankish horses was catastrophic to the whole economy. Actual farm work was not hindered, since oxen rather than horses were the principal source of animal power on the farm. But horses were used to transport men and their baggage, and their loss meant a breakdown in civilian transport.

Poor transportation and poor crops brought famine again in the year after the opening of the Avar war. So terrible was the situation, the annals relate, that people were actually forced to eat meat during Lent. This comment is both an indication of the tremendous force of the Lenten prohibitions and a revelation of what was actually happening. Lacking bread and grain, the people were slaughtering their cows, oxen, goats and surviving horses—which meant the future impoverishment of the peasants even though they might succeed in bringing themselves and their families alive through the year of dearth. Moreover, to a people dependent on grain, a diet of meat alone is a starvation diet.

Empty bellies stimulate discontented minds, and dissatisfaction throughout Charles's realm naturally followed. It was expressed first of all in an attempt on the part of the Beneventans to escape from what they now considered Frankish oppression—since Charles's war (no doubt in conjunction with unfavorable weather) had produced this famine.

Grimoald, who only a few years before had so co-operatively ruled Benevento as Charles's vassal, now led his people in rebellion. As a sign of intransigeance he married a Greek princess, stopped dating documents by the regnal years of the Frankish king, ceased issuing coins bearing Charles's name and gave every indication of planning to link Benevento with the Byzantine Empire. Charles considered the situation in Benevento sufficiently urgent to warrant his withdrawing forces from the Avar war, and he directed his two sons, Pepin and Louis, to lead Italian and Aquitanian troops into Benevento. But the famine itself, which was one of the contributing causes of the rebellion, defeated their efforts. The invading armies—evidently not nearly so well provisioned under the leadership of Charles's sons as they would have been under Charles himself—found that they could not live at all off the enemy country and were forced to abandon the expedition. Grimoald made the concession of divorcing his Greek wife, but he continued for years afterward to oppose Charles whenever he thought it safe.

The famine; the cost of war in the east and war in the south and war on the Spanish border; the shock of a devastating Saracen raid into Septimania; the absence of any results visible to many of Charles's greater vassals (for this was at the beginning of the Avar war, before the capture of the Ring and its treasure)—all this fed the growing discontent. With each successive year of war it became more difficult for the great nobles to round up the contingents they must—under penalty of heavy fines—bring to the national assembly. Men had to attend to their work at home some time, they complained, and Charles did not take this into account. Instead he scolded his counts for permitting resistance to military service. And he incurred their hatred when he attempted to check their rapacity by ordering that only the royal commissioners, the *missi*, could collect the "king's ban"—the fine imposed on every man who did not obey the call to arms.

The counts made a lucrative business out of the ban. This fine was so large that the ordinary freeman could not afford to pay it, and his land would fall forfeit to the collector (unless he could find a church or monastery willing to advance him the cash on condition that he keep his land until his death, or for a fixed term of years, when it would become the property of the lender). By ordering that only the state treasury could collect the ban Charles deprived the nobles of one of their principal means for enlarging their holdings.

The nobles had other causes for dissatisfaction. In decree after decree during these and the following years Charles attempted to check exploitation. His capitularies read like a list of charges against his officials. The counts often accepted bribes from those who could pay for release from military service, and drafted only the poorer men. The counts imposed forced labor on freemen; they seized the horses of freemen for their own use; they collected gifts from the people for the king and presented these gifts as their own; they demanded contributions in money and in kind not sanctioned by custom; they consorted with criminals whom they were supposed to punish; they (and the bishops) practiced usury. They had an especially refined and legal method for forcing freemen to sell their land or to "commend themselves" to the protection of the lord: a recalcitrant freeman would be ordered to attend the count's court so frequently that he would have to neglect his own farm. They pastured their own animals on the land of poor men. On their journeys to and from the king's court the nobles demanded provisions without paying for them. Sometimes they simply seized land, claiming it had been sold to them, so that Charles had to decree that all sales of land must be made in public, before several witnesses.

Charles had the deepest conviction that he would one day be called to account before the judgment seat of God for his governance of the kingdom. Bad officials, he literally believed, endangered his immortal soul, and for this reason if for no other he fought against abuses by the very men whom he had appointed to administer his kingdoms and to dispense justice. Again and again he threatened his corrupt officials with every punishment from "loss of the king's favor" to confiscation of their property and the death penalty. He also devised an amusing but quite effective penalty: a negligent official might find a royal commissioner and large entourage settling down on him and living at his expense until he obeyed orders and corrected his faults.

But Charles's chief weapon against the unreliability of his counts was these very royal commissioners, or *missi dominici*, as they were called. The missi—literally "those who are sent"—became one of the distinguishing features of Charles's administration. Although he borrowed the idea from the church practice of the bishop's *visitation* (a bishop was required at least once a year to make the rounds of his see and inspect parishes and abbeys), the institution of the missi was essentially Charles's creation. The name missi is encountered before Charles; even the Merovingian kings sent out representatives to act for them on special occasions. But at some time during the first ten years of his reign Charles established a regular series of inspection tours. The men who were sent out were given great prestige and power—their word was the king's word—and traveled a circuit around a definite territory which was known as the *missaticum*. The missaticum of a missus was changed frequently. For Charles wanted to avoid the association of the official with a territory. Unlike the count, the missus had no regular seat of power, therefore could not become a danger to the crown and was less susceptible to corruption. He remained what Charles intended him to be: the personal representative of the king.

The missi usually traveled in pairs: a bishop or abbot, and a count or other secular official. Thus they not only kept an eye on each other but could attend to church as well as government business. Four times a year, in the months of January, April, July and October, they set out on their missions. With what anxiety careless or corrupt officials awaited these visits can easily be imagined. If the missi were dissatisfied with the work of a lower official, they could discharge him; higher officials they sent to the king's court for judgment. They read out at public meetings the king's latest decrees, translating these from the Latin into the vulgar tongue so that no one could plead ignorance of the law. They investigated the conduct of priests and monks, especially in regard to sexual matters; they checked on the mode of life of bishops and abbots, on their administration of church property and on the discipline they maintained in their monasteries. They examined the judgments and financial records of the counts, vicars and hundredmen. They held court, hearing appeals from the decisions of the counts, bishops or lesser officials, seeing to it that widows, orphans and ordinary freemen were not being refused justice, checking the encroachments of the nobles on church and private property, ordering the return of excessive or unjust fines, freeing men whom the nobles had wrongfully enslaved.

The institution of the missi was an inspired remedy for the evils of corruption and oppression. It made it possible for Charles to be everywhere at once in his kingdoms. Although the system could

be no better than the men who were sent out, and these were sometimes as dishonest or rapacious as the officials they were supposed to
correct, the missi were the best answer that could be devised to the
growing feudal power of local lords. And the lords did not like it at
all.

Limiting the counts' freedom of action in their own territories, and
centralizing administration in the hands of the less corrupt missi,
benefited chiefly the *pauperes* of Charles's dominions. That had a
military as well as a humanitarian aspect. It was necessary, after all,
"to keep the people able to perform their service next time," as one
of Charles's decrees naïvely put it. Charles realized that the ordinary
freeman with a small amount of property was after all the backbone
of his army. But the nobles, of course, bitterly resented the state's
poaching on their private preserve. When to this interference with
their privileges was added the pressure of hard times, they began mut-
tering darkly about the influence of Queen Fastrada, who had changed
their hitherto noble, mild and generous king into a cruel tyrant. When
Charles, after the first campaign against the Avars, stayed in Bavaria
and indicated that he intended to continue the war, their dissatisfaction culminated in conspiracy—the second major conspiracy against
Charles within six years.

The rebellious counts found a suitable figurehead in Charles's unfortunate eldest son, the hunchbacked Pepin, who by now could
clearly see that he was being passed over in the succession. For although he still ranked technically first in court by reason of his age,
and although his name in the litanies of prayer for the royal family
still preceded the names of Charles's other sons, he had been given
no lands to rule, no territory of his own, no military or administrative
post. He had seen his mother degraded, his name conferred on one
of his brothers, and had grown up under the tutelage of three successive stepmothers. It is scarcely surprising, in the circumstances, that
the boy hated his half brothers and could be persuaded to hate his
father.

The discontented counts found it easy to "seduce Pepin with vain
promises of royal authority." Charles and his three sons by Hildigard
would be killed, and Pepin the Hunchback would then be set on the
throne. Unlike the regional revolt in Thuringia in 786, this plot was
strictly an attempt at palace revolution; the state was to be left intact,
but with a new head, and presumably with the nobles' having far

more say in the government than they had under Charles. The conspiring noblemen felt that they could easily handle young Pepin, who would never enjoy Charles's popularity among the Franks.

The plot came very close to success. Pepin feigned illness, in order to get away from the court and confer with the conspirators. What then happened must be read between the lines of the annals, unless we wish to accept the dramatic and highly romanticized story of the Monk of St. Gall.

According to the Monk's account, Pepin had gone to the Church of St. Peter in Regensburg to meet his fellow conspirators. After their conference, in which all the details of the plot were discussed, they suddenly became suspicious of eavesdroppers and began to search the church. Sure enough, they found a Lombard deacon named Fardulf hidden under the altar. Instead of killing him, as might be expected, they made him swear not to expose their secret. Trembling for his life, Fardulf took the oath; but as soon as he was released he rushed straight to the palace. In spite of all difficulties he passed through the seven bolted gates and knocked on the door of the king's private apartments. Charles, amazed that anyone should dare to disturb him at this time of night, ordered the women "who stayed by him to wait upon the queen and princesses" (our chronicler is, after all, a monk) to go to the door and see what was wanted. When they saw the wretched deacon they shut the door in his face and, "bursting with laughter and stuffing their dresses into their mouths, they tried to hide in the corners of the apartment." The king demanded to know what it was all about, and they said that a half-dressed, raving fool was asking an immediate audience. Charles at once ordered them to admit the man. Fardulf fell at the king's feet and told all he knew. The unsuspecting conspirators were then all seized early in the morning.

Fardulf was in fact the person who exposed the conspiracy. A Lombard who had remained faithful to King Desiderius, he was exiled into Frankland when Charles took over the Lombard kingdom. Later, however, he rose in Charles's favor, for Charles respected a man who did not immediately jump on the band wagon of his new regime. Fardulf was a distinguished poet and a close friend of the greatest poet of the age, Bishop Theodulf of Orléans, and Charles was quick to forgive him for political opposition, as he had forgiven Paul the Deacon. The conspirators evidently did not realize that the surest way to win a poet's affection was to listen to his poems. They probably assumed that Fardulf still nursed a grudge against Charles, and took him into their confidence, thinking that he would gladly join in the plot. But by now, eighteen years after the fall of the Lombard monarchy, Fardulf had transferred his loyalty for good and all, and he promptly betrayed the conspiracy.

That is probably the kernel of truth behind the Monk of St. Gall's fantastic story.

There are no records of Charles's feelings; we can only imagine how deeply he must have suffered to learn that his own son had plotted to kill him. As if he could not bear to handle the unsavory business alone, he called an assembly at Regensburg to judge the conspirators. All were, of course, judged guilty of high treason and sentenced to death. But Charles could not bring himself to punish poor Pepin with the others. Instead, the sentence was commuted and the young prince was sent to the monastery of Prüm. There he lived out the remainder of his life in obscurity.

Charles realized that for the first time in his long reign he had been in serious peril, and he set in motion a vigorous purge in the attempt to discover any other conspirators. When the investigations were over, he called another assembly at which he rewarded those who had stood loyally by him with gifts of gold, silver and silks. Fardulf came in for the most splendid reward of all: he was made abbot of the fabulously wealthy monastery of St. Denis. So wealthy was it that Fardulf was able to build at St. Denis a guesthouse for the king and his retinue.

While Charles was meeting a direct political attack on his life he was simultaneously busy fighting heresies which threatened the deep foundations on which his power rested. There is no obvious connection between the conspiracy and these religious questions. Yet it is probable that Charles would have been more alert to political undercurrents had he not been so preoccupied with theological problems and subtle disputes over points of doctrine. The principal matters under discussion were the adoptianist heresy and the controversy over images.

The account given by the Frankish annals of the origin of the adoptianist heresy can scarcely be excelled for clarity, although it errs—as the annals always do—on the side of brevity. "Urgel," the annalist tells us, "is a city in the Pyrenees Mountains. Bishop Felix of that city, a Spaniard by birth, was asked in a letter by Bishop Elipand of Toledo what we should believe regarding the manhood of our Lord and Saviour Jesus Christ: whether in His nature as a man He is to be considered a true Son or merely an adopted Son of God. Bishop Felix, without due reflection and against the old dogma of the Catholic Church, declared Him an adopted Son; moreover, in a treatise addressed to the aforesaid bishop he attempted stubbornly to defend his wrongful opinion."

Heresies flourished on the fringes of the Catholic world, where Christian theologians came into contact with the cool rationality and the enlightened skepticism of Moslems. Toledo was under Saracen rule, and although the Saracens tolerated the Christians, they were also ever ready to dispute with them. Bishop Elipand, an old man of nearly eighty, had Moorish friends with whom he engaged in amicable theological debate, and his conceptions of orthodox Catholic doctrine had unconsciously been colored by his environment. He was, moreover, hot-tempered and stubborn, not inclined to take back anything he had once said. It was perhaps by chance, and in the heat of argument, that he first made his fateful statement asserting that Christ was a Son of God by adoption, for he was replying to a different heresy by another Spaniard. But once he had declared his opinion he abided by it, and, since he was proud of his reputation for sanctity, he was both amazed and mortally offended to find himself attacked for unorthodoxy. He began gathering around himself a party, and in a short time the Spanish Church was virtually split in two.

Looking around for allies, Elipand appealed to one of the finest theologians and most devout clerics in Spain, Bishop Felix of Urgel. Felix took up the cause, defying Pope Hadrian's condemnation of the doctrine of adoption as blasphemy and "serpent's venom," and made it his own—so much his own that it came to be known also as the Felician heresy; so much so that the ecclesiastics of the time were constantly punning on his name which, since it meant "happy" in Latin, gave them the opportunity to refer to him constantly as "*in-felix*"—"unhappy" or "unfortunate." But it took more than papal warnings and puns to silence a man who was not only eloquent and learned but whose reputation for purity and saintliness in behavior was so great that it reached Alcuin. Several years after Felix had already become involved with Elipand's heretical doctrine Alcuin, ignorant of this, wrote to the Bishop of Urgel asking to be remembered in his prayers because "I have heard so much about your piety."

Felix' episcopal seat in Urgel was part of Charles's Spanish March, and the adoptianist doctrine spread rapidly north and south through Spain and Aquitaine. Before long Charles had to take notice of a controversy which was dividing the Church to such an extent that it could almost be said there were "two churches quarreling with each other over the One Christ." The hierarchic principle on which his state power was founded was threatened by schism in the Church. So intertwined were Frankish State and Church that the weakening of the one followed automatically from the weakening of the other. The Felician heresy was as dangerous to official Frankland as, say, the Titoist heresy today is dangerous to Soviet communism. In attacking the structure of Catholic dogma Felix and Elipand were committing political acts.

But it would be wholly mistaking the quality of Charles's mind to imagine that he intervened solely from political motives. On the contrary, he was fascinated by the theological question itself—his religious conservatism shocked and his riddle-loving temperament attracted by the intricacies of the argument. In spite of the busyness of his life and the thousand distractions of administration and warfare he found time to study the matter, and he proved to be as well equipped to deal with it as any of the professional ecclesiastics of his day, including his faithful adviser and teacher, Alcuin. He did not let himself be deterred by the temporary absence of Alcuin, who was visiting England, or by his involvement in the Avar war, or by the threatening famine, but called a synod of bishops from Frankland and Italy to meet in his palace at Regensburg to deal with the new doctrine. Felix was ordered to be present to state his case.

The synod was a curious medley of democratic and autocratic procedure—with autocracy triumphing in the end. Charles himself presided and made it quite clear that he wanted the heresy condemned. Felix, facing virtual martyrdom or recantation, chose the opportunity to fight for his opinions at some later date. When the synod declared his beliefs "condemned to eternal anathema" and ordered book-burnings of his and Elipand's writings, Felix accepted the verdict and stated that he was convinced of his error. He would go back to his diocese a changed man and undo the harm he had already wrought.

Charles remained suspicious of him, however, and packed him off to Rome under guard of the poet Angilbert, Charles's friend, privy councilor and unofficial son-in-law. In Rome Pope Hadrian set Felix the penitential task of composing a treatise *against* adoptianism. In the pope's presence the "unhappy" bishop laid this tract on the body of St. Peter (on top of Charles's and Pepin's donations? one wonders) and fervently swore that he would henceforth hold to the belief that Jesus Christ was the true and not the adopted Son of God. He was then released from what amounted to imprisonment "and returned to his city"—that is, to Urgel, though apparently not to his powers and prerogatives as bishop.

If he had actually been convinced by the learned Frankish doctors, the rationalistic atmosphere of Spain soon unconvinced him again. Safely out of Charles's reach, Felix recanted his recantation and proceeded to disseminate adoptianism more vigorously than ever, concentrating his propaganda on the Frankish province of Septimania.

Bishop Elipand, meanwhile, was pushing his fight vigorously. He held a countersynod of Spanish bishops who then sent their decisions in favor of adoptianism to the Frankish clergy, and also transmitted a letter to King Charles himself, asking him to declare in their favor. Charles was infuriated by the tone of the letter; it sounded, he said indignantly, as though they were trying to teach him instead of learn from him. (A measure of his self-confidence in theological matters!) And they had the effrontery to remind him of the fate of Constantine, who after his conversion by St. Sylvester had been seduced into Arianism by his serpent of a sister and had subsequently gone *ad infernum*.

He was perhaps even more annoyed with his own clergy for their inability to reply conclusively to the arguments of the heretics. For, as was the custom, the Spaniards had liberally peppered their document with quotations from the Fathers of the Church but had omitted to indicate chapter and verse, so that it was difficult to tell whether these quotations were corrupted and taken out of context— as the Frankish theologians thought they must be—as Elipand and his colleagues had made out an astonishingly good case for themselves.

It would be impossible for the modern reader to follow with any interest whatsoever the tedious quotations and the hairsplitting distinctions which for ten years engaged the passions of King Charles and his contemporaries. But the essence of the adoptianist heresy we can easily understand: it was an attempt, paralleled by many more recent trends in religious thought, to rationalize the irrational. In asserting that Christ in his human form was the Son of God in name only, Bishops Elipand and Felix came close to denying the divinity of Christ. They never went that far, but the logic of their position carried them to the point of rejecting one of the fundamental mysteries of their religion: the virgin birth. Ultimately they objected reasonably that it was "against nature" to assume that "a virgin could bear a son without having had connection with a man." All very true, but in being unable to believe "that which is absurd" they were abandoning Catholicism. And Charles saw this with great clarity.

It was time, Charles felt, to bring the siege engines to bear, and he wrote to Alcuin to come back from England and lead the struggle. Alcuin, with his characteristic warmheartedness and good nature, and with his feeble grasp of philosophical problems, could not see that the "one little word" *adopted* made so much difference. He wrote a friendly appeal to Felix—like the admonishments to the good life which he was constantly showering on his pupils—to mend his ways and come back to the fold. "Revered father and dear brother," he wrote, "with humility I dare to beg you, if your foot has slipped and you have stumbled in the way, regain your standing, come back bravely to fight the battles of the Lord. Do not follow new inventions, contrary to the Faith. . . ."

Probably nobody but Alcuin thought this appeal would take effect, and Charles went ahead with preparations for a great Church synod which was to have a dual purpose: to condemn the adoptianist heresy and to reassert Frankish supremacy in ecclesiastical matters. For that supremacy had been threatened by the Empress Irene's Council of Nicaea, seven years before, which had laid claim to being an ecumenical council of the Church and which, to Charles's mind, had propagated heresies as dangerous as those of Felix and Elipand. More dangerous, in fact, since they were backed by the imposing state power of the Empire.

Charles's great palace at Worms had burned down in a single night in 790, and his new palace at Aachen, though rapidly nearing completion, was still swarming with workmen under the direction of his future biographer, the architect Einhard. As meeting place for his synod, therefore, Charles chose a town—probably it was then little more than a settlement, although a Roman town had been situated on the spot—which significantly bore in its name the name of his nation: Frankonovurt or Frankfurt, the ford of the Franks. (Here, legend has it, a hart pursued by the Franks showed them the way to cross the River Main.) His intention was to symbolize the role of the Franks at a synod which he insisted was a true universal council of the Church, in contrast to the Greek Council of Nicaea. More strongly than ever before, Charles was bent on stressing his function as *rector ecclesiae*.

The Council of Frankfurt opened on June 1, 794, and from the start the records of its discussions and decisions were kept with extraordinary care. An archives room was set up in the palace at Frankfurt for the purpose.

On the opening day Charles himself sat on his high seat in the hall of the Frankfurt palace. The archbishops and bishops of the realm, along with the papal legates, Bishops Theophylactus and Stephanus, and Patriarch Paulinus of Aquileia, also sat. Around them stood the priests, deacons and other members of the lower clergy. At Charles's request Alcuin, who was not a priest, was admitted to the fellowship and prayers of the council because he was "a man of great learning in the doctrines of the Church." Charles's chancellor, Abbot Rado, then read aloud sentence by sentence the entire epistle from Elipand and the other Spanish bishops.

After the reading Charles rose and, standing on the step to his throne, spoke at great length, with that easy fluency which was his even when dealing with so complex and insubstantial a subject as this: that "the Son of God became the Son of Man and by virtue of his divine nature was born the Son of God, by virtue of his human nature the Son of Man," and that he is "both true God and true Man."

"What is your opinion?" he concluded. "I hold that now, since this insane pestilence has been growing ever more flagrant and penetrating ever more deeply into the borderlands of our realm, it is necessary to exterminate it by the use of every means."

This forceful demand for immediate action embarrassed all the clergy present. The heretical treatise of the Spanish bishops contained some strikingly orthodox truths, and their errors, as Alcuin admitted to Charles, had crept into the minds of some of the most faithful teachers among the Franks. Only after several days of deliberation was the council able to arrive at its predictable conclusion:

the Felician doctrine was unaminously condemned as heretical and Felix was threatened with anathema "if he persisted in his error." Three volumes of anti-Felician writings, containing the findings of the Frankfurt synod, a tract by the Patriarch of Aquileia, and another tract by the pope, were dispatched to Elipand and the Spanish bishops for their edification and correction. These were accompanied by a letter from Charles in which he pointed out the political consequences of attempting to split the Church. He wrote:

"We had long ago resolved to help you in your secular troubles [with the Saracens]. But this will remain impossible as long as you tolerate heresy. Instead, we must break off all communion with you. Return to the arms of your tender mother, the Church, lest the anathema be put upon you. Do not withdraw from her maternal love, who calls all to the kingdom of her Beloved Son."

Neither the decisions of the synod nor Charles's open threat had the desired effect, and the heretical doctrines continued, as we shall see later, to spread through Spain and the adjacent portions of the Frankish kingdom. But for the present nothing more could be done, and the Frankfurt Council turned its attention to the other doctrinal dispute which was, perhaps, of greater personal concern to Charles than adoptianism and to which he had devoted a great deal of attention and thought during the past five years. It was only natural that Charles should take a stand on image worship, which had been the burning question of the age—though especially in eastern Europe— for more than fifty years. And it was only natural that his position should have been one eminently distinguished by a clearheaded and common-sense approach to a question that aroused theological and political passions as could no other.

The stark symbol of the cross had sufficed for the adornment of primitive Christian churches. By degrees, however, for the instruction of the people and "to recall to them the past," pictures of scriptural stories, of Christ, the Virgin and the saints, had been introduced into the churches of both East and West. There also grew up the custom of placing statuary at crossroads and other public places, icons in houses, and religious paintings on the walls and ceilings of secular buildings. Everywhere, but more particularly in Italy and in the East, candles were lighted before these images, miracles attributed to them

and "adoration" accorded them. By the superstitious they were literally worshiped as the pagan idols had once been worshiped. Image
worship signified, to the minds of the eighth-century iconoclasts, a
reversion to outright paganism on the part of a population in some
cases not too far removed from its heathen past.

In the West the similar superstitious impulse took the form of a
craze for relics, for the bone or fingernail of a martyr or a nail of the
true cross. A man like Einhard, in his dignified old age, was not
above rejoicing naïvely over his successful theft of some relics. In the
East men devoted toward the visible representations of human beings
all the fervor which they were unable to feel toward a sternly invisible,
unknowable and inconceivable God. The production of images was,
in the East, on a far greater scale than in the West. Every Eastern
church had its iconostasis—a tall, painted wooden screen separating
the sanctuary from the main body of the church. And it might also
be said that in the East the artists were so much more gifted than
those of the West that their mosaics, paintings and statues invited
those excesses of adoration which bordered on idolatry. For it must
not be forgotten that out of this corruption of primitive Christianity,
out of this passion for the substantial image, there arose that great
religious art which was the glory of the Middle Ages in both East and
West.

As in the case of adoptianism, the austerity of near-by Moslems
(who when they ultimately conquered Constantinople covered the
wonderful Byzantine paintings and mosaics in Hagia Sophia and the
other churches with coats of plaster) influenced the early reformers
in the Eastern Church. The Greek emperor Leo the Isaurian, in his
attacks on image worship early in the eighth century, contented himself at first with eliminating only images which were within reach of
the people and could be touched, kissed and otherwise adored. Those
high enough only to be seen were allowed to remain. But so strong
was the feeling on both sides, among image smashers and image worshipers, that it was impossible for any of the Greek emperors to
maintain a compromise position. A long and bloody history of riot
and revolution, of barbarous torture and mutilations on both sides,
marked the struggle between the religious reformers and the con-
servatively superstitious populace of the Byzantine Empire.

With the coming to power in Constantinople of Irene and her son
Constantine, the image worshipers, as we have seen, gained the as-

cendancy for the time being. Irene's Council of Nicaea in 787 declared that he who adored images adored the substance depicted within them, and pronounced violent anathemas on all who called images idols. Papal delegates, we will remember, participated in this council and accepted its claim to be a universal council of the Church.

The Nicaean decrees were transmitted to Charles by Hadrian in a Latin translation, and Charles was horrified by what he read. Some historians, who are inclined to see the ponderous weights of history easily tilted by the flick of a tiny lever, have suggested that the whole quarrel stemmed from a mistranslation. The Greek word *proskynesis*, it is pointed out, was translated into Latin as *adoration* rather than *veneration*, and the Council of Nicaea was therefore made to say that images must be adored—that is, accorded the worship due to God. But this explanation can hardly be supported in the face of the evidence that the Latin *adoratio* was susceptible to a variety of meanings in the eighth century. (Einhard's essay on "The Adoration of the Cross" is one of the most striking examples of this.) Charles was angered by the whole spirit of the Nicaean decrees which, for all the distinction which they made between worship and veneration (or, as Einhard put it, *oratio* and *adoratio*), were saturated with an Oriental tendency toward idolatry which was supremely distasteful to him.

Charles and the entire circle belonging to the Palace Academy turned their attention to a study of the theological problem involved in the question of image worship. The fruit of their work was a list of eighty-five criticisms of the Council of Nicaea, which Angilbert took to Rome and delivered to Pope Hadrian. Angilbert, in the name of Charles and the court theologians, held long conferences with Hadrian in which he went over the Frankish criticisms point by point, explaining and enlarging on them. It was obviously a delicate situation, since the pope had already accepted the Nicaean decisions in their Latin translation. Never before had Charles openly opposed the pope in a matter of doctrine. Such opposition, after all, ill accorded with his position as Defender of the Faith. To ease the affront he was simultaneously careful to indicate his respect for Hadrian's authority by submitting to him the adoptianist thesis drawn up by the Spanish bishops—"because the Holy See has more experience than we in the interpretation of the apostolic tradition."

Hadrian also was in a difficult position. He certainly did not want to offend Charles. At the same time he was reluctant to jeopardize his *rapprochement* with the Eastern Church by attacking the work of Irene's council. Church practice in Italy, moreover, leaned toward profound veneration for images, if not exactly worship of them. The popes, from Gregory the Great on, had concentrated their efforts on combatting iconoclasm rather than the excessive cultivation of images. For reasons of tradition, of personal inclination and of practical politics, therefore, Hadrian felt that he had to reject Charles's criticisms.

In his reply to Charles the pope wound himself into knots trying to put his direct affront in the least offensive way. He assured Charles that he had received Angilbert "with love" and listened to him as if he were the king himself, that he had considered carefully the "mellifluous" royal arguments, that he was interested solely in defending the tradition of the Holy Catholic and Apostolic Roman Church and was not acting out of any personal pique. He then proceeded to answer each *reprehensio* of Charles with a *refutatio* of his own. There was only one point in the entire set of eighty-five which Hadrian was willing to agree to. Charles had written: "We desire our apostolic lord and father, as well as the whole of the Roman Church, to know that . . . we permit anyone who wishes, for the love of God and his saints, to set up images inside or outside the churches, but that we shall never force anyone to worship them, nor allow any others to destroy them." With relief and all too obvious flattery Hadrian made much of this point, declaring that it plainly represented the ideas of Charles himself as against the mistaken views of his advisers.

The pope concluded his letter by appealing to Charles's sense of practical politics as well as his religious fervor. If he did not accept the Nicaean decrees, he said, the Greeks would slip back into iconoclasm and he, the pope, would be responsible for the loss of their souls. And then, lest Charles harbor any suspicion that he was busy intriguing with Constantinople, Hadrian hastened to indicate that he was making demands on the emperor:

"We have until now refrained from addressing the emperor in regard to the Council of Nicaea and have only suggested that if they have restored the images, they ought to restore to the jurisdiction of Saint Peter the dioceses and patrimonies illegally taken from us at the time of the destruction of the images. No answer to this has as yet been received. . . . We therefore propose, if you think well of it, to thank the emperor for restoring the images, but at the same time to urge him forcefully to restore the aforesaid dioceses and patrimonies. In the event that he refuses to make restitution, we would declare him stubbornly persistent in error and a heretic."

Charles was hardly pleased by Hadrian's rejection of his cherished ideas and by the pope's covert attempt at blackmail. For that last clause in Hadrian's letter amounted to saying: You, too, have not restored to St. Peter the patrimonies you promised, and now you are propounding to me doctrines that are not in the apostolic tradition. Prove that you are not a heretic by making restitution of the lands the Lombards took from the papal patrimony. Then, perhaps, I will be more accommodating on points of doctrine.

This effrontery was more than Charles's hot temper could bear. For all his respect for papal authority he felt that he himself was the true head of the Church, *rector ecclesiae*, and he was determined to prove it. The outcome of his resolve to put the pope in his place was a long tract discussing the whole question of image worship—the *Libri Carolini*, or Caroline Books.

By a curious misunderstanding of the nature of a great man, historians and biographers have long taken it for granted that Charles could not possibly have written the books which bear his name. Although all his contemporaries testified sincerely that he was the peer of the best thinkers of his day, there has lurked in the back of the minds of most of his biographers the unconscious image of Charles as a rude, unlettered barbarian, mighty in the realm of practical affairs, to be sure, but wholly incapable of literary productions of any kind. It has therefore been assumed that someone else—Bishop Theodulf of Orléans, possibly, or else Alcuin—was the author of the Caroline Books.

The probability is that Charles himself was the author, just as he claimed to be. The opening words of the Caroline Books distinctly state that the work is his: "Here begins the tract of the most illustrious, excellent and honorable Carolus, by divine command King of the Franks and ruler of Gaul, Germany and Italy, together with their adjoining provinces, against the synod which stupidly and arrogantly has recently been held in the Greek lands in favor of the adoration of images." The whole angry tone of the treatise, its immoderate name-calling, its constant political allusions, its harping on favorite subjects of Charles, are clear evidence of his personal authorship. He hurls words like "inept and infamous" at the Greek council; he accuses Irene and her son of ignorance and pride. He is particularly disgusted by the idea of a woman's trying to play the part of a learned theologian. This, he says, is contrary to all divine and natural laws. (One is tempted to see in this charge a reflection of Charles's irritation with his wife, Fastrada, whose interference with the affairs of state was becoming scandalous.) He takes up his perennial complaint against some of his own ecclesiastics and accuses Irene's patriarch of Constantinople, Tarasio, of violating all the canonical rules by going from the military camp to the altar, from the clash of arms to the celebration of the mysteries. He rails at the princes and priests of the Orient for their "arrogant ambition and insolent appetite for vain glory."

The reflectiveness, the vigor and even the prolixity of the Caroline Books mark them as the work of Charles. The mild-mannered and courteous Alcuin could never have brought himself to use such forceful language; Theodulf of Orléans, had he been the author, would have framed his insults more subtly. Neither would have gone to such pains to deny the claim of the Council of Nicaea to universality. Certainly these two men, and many of the other theologians in and about Charles's court, discussed the points of doctrine with the king and suggested scriptural and patristic quotations to him. Certainly Charles employed a research staff as any modern statesman would. But it is equally certain that he was not so dependent on staff work as are some modern heads of state. The actual work of composition was almost certainly his. He was as capable of writing a book on image worship as he was of delivering a lengthy address on adoptianism to the assembled clergy of the realm at the Frankfurt Council. The man whose favorite book was Augustine's distinctly difficult *City of God* and who devoted a great part of his time to legislating for the Church was a theologian in his own right.

He was fearfully busy, of course. In the years between the Council of Nicaea and the Council of Frankfurt Charles was occupied with wars in Pannonia, Benevento, Spain and Saxony, was engaged on a canal-building project and the construction of his palace at Aachen, was coping with conspiracy and integrating Bavaria into his kingdom. But he was accustomed to thinking on his feet, to speaking fluently, to making use of scribes, and he must have solved the problem of

limited time as so many modern statesmen have done—by dictating.
That is almost certainly how the Caroline Books were composed.
Charles had no need of ghost writers.

These books were laid before the Frankfurt synod, and the synod
unanimously accepted them. The second Council of Nicaea was,
in accordance with Charles's wishes, denied the title of Seventh
Ecumenical Council of the Church, and its doctrines were condemned. Pope Hadrian's only alternatives were to swallow the offense to his authority or to break with Charles, and he was in no
position to make a break. The papal legates cast their vote also for
the rejection of Irene's council, and Charles's highhanded revision of
dogma was put on record with the tacit consent of Hadrian, if hardly
with his good will.

Charles, for his part, was not personally vindictive. Having won
his point, he did all he could to restore the pope's self-esteem and the
public's awareness of his respect for the Holy See. For proceedings of
the synod carefully set forth that he had asked and obtained the
pope's permission to release Archbishop Hildibald of Cologne from
the canonical requirement that a bishop reside at his episcopal seat,
so that Hildibald might serve at court as archchaplain.

A great many other matters were taken up by this busy Council of
Frankfurt. An attempt was made to regulate the profiteering in grain
that had resulted from the famine by fixing prices for grain sold by
the bushel and for the bread made from various grains. The ordinance, incidentally, throws light on the esteem in which various grains
were held, for a bushel of oats was to be sold for one silver penny, or
denarius, a bushel of barley for two, rye for three and wheat for four.
New weights for the amount of silver in the denarius were established.
Stricter application of the Benedictine rule in monasteries was ordered. The synod sensibly admonished: "Let no one think that God
may be worshiped in only three languages, for man can pray to God
in every language, and if he asks righteously will be heard."

But the two most dramatic events of the synod were an ordeal and
an abjuration.

The ordeal arose out of the investigation into the conspiracy of
Pepin the Hunchback, of two years earlier. Among the suspects was
Bishop Peter of Verdun, who for reasons unknown to us was appar-
ently often accused of disloyalty. Unwilling to appear tyrannical in

the case of so high a church dignitary, Charles submitted the question to the decision of the synod. The synod resolved that Bishop Peter must testify under oath along with two or three "compurgators" or oath helpers that he had not engaged in any conspiracy against the life of the king. The bishop was unable to find anyone who would back his unsupported testimony, and therefore decided of his own accord to appeal to the judgment of God by having one of his men undertake an ordeal, while he himself swore to his innocence before God alone—without the use of relics or the Gospels—praying God to aid his man in the ordeal. As if again to assert the independence of the Church, the proceedings of the synod stressed that Bishop Peter suggested the ordeal of his own accord, without being ordered to do so by the king or the synod. His man was successful, and the king accepted the verdict and restored the bishop to his "pristine honors"— that is, reinstalled him in his office from which he had, presumably, been temporarily suspended.

The other dramatic scene was provided by a figure who must have seemed to those present at the synod to have risen from the grave. In our day we have seen many a great figure of the Russian Revolution suddenly reappear out of utter obscurity, take his place on the witness stand in a sensational show trial and with the mechanical submissiveness of a marionette disavow a long list of previous crimes. So it was at the Council of Frankfurt. Suddenly, in the midst of the assembly, Cousin Tassilo emerged from the wings and begged forgiveness "for the crimes which he had committed during the days of the Lord King Pepin against him and the Kingdom of the Franks, and for his disloyalty toward our most pious Lord King Charles. He humbly asked forgiveness and declared that for his part he had, in all sincerity, abandoned all rage and vexation over what had been done to him. He renounced all claims to any legitimate property rights in the Duchy of Bavaria held by himself, his sons or his daughters, and to avoid any future quarrel declared without reserve his forgiveness. Prompted by sympathy, our lord freely forgave Tassilo his faults and restored him fully to his grace. . . ." Three copies of this testimonial to Charles's graciousness were solemnly drawn up. One was deposited in the archives, one in the palace chapel; and the third was given to Tassilo so that he might have it beside him in the monastery of Lorsch as a precious memento.

The motivations for this singular display of humility, penance and

clemency are not far to seek. Tassilo had after all been a great ruler
of a rich duchy, and after six years he still had a considerable following. In all his dealings with this cousin of his Charles had been
scrupulous about establishing the legality of his position, and he felt
that the semblance of voluntary renunciation on the part of Tassilo
was needed to stifle any whispers that he had acted tyrannically. After
the conspiracy of two years before, Charles was taking great pains to
make concessions to public opinion.

There is even a remote possibility that Tassilo meant what he said.
In an age when rulers voluntarily withdrew from the world, six years
in a monastery might have stripped from so religious a man the last
shreds of worldly ambition. But whether he meant it or not, his appearance at the synod was obviously at Charles's instance, not his own.
Thereafter, holding the document which set forth his abandonment
of all hope, Duke Tassilo of Bavaria returned to his cell at Lorsch, and
was henceforth ignored by the annalists. Not even the date of his
death is known.

CHAPTER FOURTEEN

Charles at Home

CHARLES remained at Frankfurt for some time after the synod finished its work, and there, on August 10, 794, his fourth wife died. Fastrada had been blamed for Charles's own faults. But there must have been something to the rumors, some real ground for her unpopularity, since even so intimate a member of the court circle as Theodulf could find little good to say of her. As unofficial poet laureate of the realm the gifted Bishop of Orléans was requested to write Fastrada's epitaph. To judge by the result the task was distasteful to him. He contented himself with the cliché that cold death had snatched her away in the flower of her life and that she had left behind the better part of her soul, King Charles himself, "whom God grant long life."

Charles soon consoled himself with a beautiful young Alemannian girl named Liutgard, and his court was by now so hardened to scandal that when he got around to marrying her formally no one bothered to record even the year of the ceremony. Liutgard herself, moreover, had so winning a personality, was so openhanded, deeply religious, charming, beautiful, cultured and eager to learn (the epithets are those of contemporary poets), that even so prim a man as Alcuin did not mind her initially unorthodox status. She lived only six years at Charles's side and missed participating in his greatest triumph. But they were good years, perhaps the most domestic in Charles's life, so that Liutgard may have spent more actual time with her husband than any of Charles's previous queens. She was also Charles's first intellectual wife, as interested in the liberal arts as he was himself. Theodulf in one of his poems pictures her at the school: "Generous of hand, gentle of soul and mild of speech, doing good to all and working harm to none, she studiously pursues the liberal arts, storing her studies in the retentive hold of her mind."

Unlike Charles's other wives, who had followed him about in his restless progresses from one battlefield to the next, or from one palace to the next, up and down the whole of his far-flung realm, Liutgard had a real home which she could beautify and govern. It was the most magnificent of his dwellings—the brand-new and rapidly growing palace at Aachen which became, after the end of the Frankfurt synod, his permanent residence. Here at Aachen Charles remained almost constantly for twenty years. Here there unfolded that brilliant, tumultuous, exciting life of a court and capital city which so stimulated the imagination of his contemporaries.

There were several reasons for Charles's choice of Aachen as the site of his new capital. Aachen lay in that well-watered country of low, rolling hills between the Rhine and the Meuse which had long been the heart of the Carolingian family's power. Liége, Heristal and Düren, favorite residences of Charles in the early days of his reign, were situated near by. So also was Cologne, and both Liége and Cologne were important cities, the residences of archbishops. The region was close to the ever-troublesome Saxon country, yet guarded from incursions of the Saxons by the Rhine, which was a more formidable barrier to the Saxons than to the Franks, who possessed shipping, and small boats enough to build bridges of boats. Moreover, Charles had built (or was building about this time) a great wooden bridge across the Rhine at Mainz, only forty miles as the crow flies upstream from Cologne. A few miles to the north of Aachen ran one of the principal military and commercial arteries, the old Roman road between Cologne on the Rhine and Maestricht on the Meuse. Smaller roads existed connecting Aachen with this highway and with Cologne, Maestricht and Liége; these were no doubt vastly improved by Charles in the course of his road-building program.

In addition to this strategic importance Aachen recommended itself to Charles for its warm medicinal springs with their mildly sulphurous waters. He loved swimming, constantly practiced it and was "so expert that no one could be fairly regarded as his superior." The great marble swimming pool which he had constructed at Aachen could hold as many as a hundred bathers at one time, and Charles used to invite to the bath "not only his sons, but also his nobles and friends, and at times even a great number of his followers and bodyguards."

Perhaps a third reason that prompted Charles to establish his capital at Aachen was that it was a place of no importance. A small royal villa existed there, and Charles's father is mentioned as having stayed there once in 765; before that date the name of the town is nowhere recorded. Like so many great rulers, Charles also was ambitious to create a city out of nothing, to build in stone a lasting monument to his name. Perhaps Pope Hadrian had done him no disservice in reminding him of Constantine the Great. Like Constantine, Charles (who was already beginning to be referred to as Karolus Magnus, Charles the Great) would build a New Rome to surpass the grandeur of the old. At the back of his mind was also a memory of another great Germanic king, Theodoric the Goth, whose beautiful and impressive edifices at Ravenna Charles had admired and whose equestrian statue he carried off to adorn the new capital at Aachen.

It fell in beautifully with Charles's plans that shortly after his palace at Worms burned down, and the need for a new palace at Aachen therefore became acute, a young man with singular gifts as an architect should have come to his court. The young man had been raised at the monastery of Fulda, which had grown so rapidly under Abbot Sturm and his successor, Baugulf, that the sounds of hammers, saws and the mason's trowel virtually never ceased there. Baugulf had replaced Sturm's small and primitive church by a huge basilica to enclose the tomb of St. Boniface, so that the students who attended his monastic school had ample opportunity to learn the craft of building at first hand. The young man in question, whose name was Einhard, profited much from these practical lessons.

Charles's policy of gathering the best minds of the kingdom around himself was well known. Since Einhard was one of the most brilliant students the Fulda school had produced, Abbot Baugulf quite naturally sent the young man to complete his education at the Palace School. There Einhard, "whose remarkable gifts and intelligence gave much promise of the wisdom for which he was later to be famous," became a devoted student of Alcuin's and acquired a Latin style far superior to that of most of his contemporaries. He also very quickly became a member of the intimate court circle, for nothing delighted Charles more than a bright young man. There was no one, we are told, to whom Charles more familiarly confided his secrets.

Einhard was a small man, and his friends at court used to joke about his size; but they evidently held him in the highest respect. When he built himself a house at Aachen, Alcuin provided an in-

scription for the entrance in which he punned on the last half of
Einhard's name, pretending that it meant *nard*—that is, perfume.
The inscription read:

> The door is small, small also he who dwells within.
> But, reader, do not despise the small nard contained in this body.
> For nard, though a spiny plant, exudes a sweet perfume:
> In her little frame the bee bears delicious honey for you.
>
> Remember, the pupil of the eye is small indeed,
> And yet it directs the acts of the body it animates.
> It is thus that Nardulus directs all of this house.
> Passing reader, say this: Hail to you, little Nardulus.

Not only Alcuin but Charles was fond of the young man. Einhard
himself, in the preface to his *Life of Charles*, gives as one of his principal motives for writing his little book "the unbroken friendship that
I enjoyed with the King himself and his children from the time I first
began to live at his court. . . . He has made me his debtor both in life
and death, so that I should be justly condemned for ingratitude were
I to forget all the benefits he conferred upon me." But it was not so
much the scholarly Einhard, running about with books, busy as an
ant (as Theodulf described him), and exuding the sweet perfume of
learning, whom Charles favored so highly. Rather, it was Einhard
under his other nickname of Bezaleel—"filled with the spirit of God,
in wisdom, and in understanding, and in knowledge, and in all manner
of workmanship, to devise cunning works, to work in gold, and in
silver, and in brass, and in the cutting of stones . . . and in carving of
timber." It seems very likely that Einhard directed the building of the
palace at Aachen and perhaps aided the work of Odo of Mainz, the
architect of the chapel.

Palace and chapel were planned as an ensemble and with an unconscious symbolic indication of the relationship of church and state in
Charles's mind. For the palace was situated on top of a hill, and the
chapel—though it attained the size of a cathedral—at the bottom.
Connecting the two was a long covered gallery, so that Charles and
his court could attend services in any weather without discomfort.
The whole area between the two great edifices was landscaped with
plantings, pavilions and porticoes.

The chapel at Aachen was a work that seemed to contemporaries "half human, half divine." Workmen were recruited from all parts of the kingdom and from abroad for the building of it. Pope Hadrian gave Charles mosaics and marbles from Rome and Ravenna to beautify it. Octagonal in shape, like San Vitale at Ravenna after which it was modeled, the chapel's central space was surrounded by a gallery and topped by a cupola roofed with sheets of lead. A golden apple adorned this cupola, and Charles lavished gold and silver on the decoration of the interior, provided doors of solid brass and supplied the church with so many ecclesiastical vestments "that not even the doorkeepers, who form the lowest order in the church, needed to appear in their ordinary dress when they performed their duties."

As long as his health allowed—and he was hardly ever ill—Charles attended this church three and four times a day. He insisted on dignity in the services, Einhard says, and "constantly warned the sextons not to bring anything dirty or improper into the building or to permit anything of the sort to remain there." The necessity of such warnings suggests that the problems of upkeep in public buildings have remained the same through the ages.

From afar the visitor to Aachen would see the huge bronze eagle with outstretched wings that perched on the palace roof. The palace itself was built to be half parliament building, half private residence. The rectangular reception hall on the first floor—a hundred and fifty feet long by some sixty-five feet wide—had three large semicircular bays on each of three sides. Below this hall, on the ground floor, were probably the servants' and service quarters. Various attached buildings contained the private apartments for Charles and his family, the treasury where gold, silver and precious stones were kept, a sizable library, baths, a wardrobe, a room for the archives, and a weapons room. Italian marble was used lavishly; the stairs leading down to the swimming pool, for example, were of marble. Among the luxurious furnishings are mentioned three tables of silver and one of gold "of remarkable size and weight." One of the silver tables contained a map of Constantinople, another a map of Rome, the third a map of the whole world.

Around the palace were grouped the houses of Charles's more important officials, and outside the complex formed by palace and chapel there sprang up a sizable town and a market place to care for the needs of the court and courtiers. Aachen swarmed with thousands of people, most of them in one way or another serving the court. The officials were numerous, and care was taken that they came from all parts of the country, so that petitioners or those seeking justice would be sure to find someone at court who spoke their own language and would represent them. The chaplain was responsible for the clergy and for all ecclesiastical affairs. He was in charge of the archives and of the secretariat, and served in general as one of the king's principal advisers. The chancellor, whose official functions seem sometimes to have overlapped with the chaplain's, was perhaps chiefly responsible for foreign affairs.

The count of the palace was a combination of chief magistrate and minister of the interior. Almost all aspects of secular administration fell within his province, as did nonecclesiastical lawsuits. Where the count of the palace was confronted with decisions for which legal precedents were lacking, "or which came under the cruel terms of the old pagan customary law to which Christian views or the canons of the Church were opposed," these were submitted directly to Charles. And Charles was guided by the principle that "secular law must yield to the justice of God."

In addition to these three most important officials there were also the chamberlain (in charge of the treasury), the seneschal (in charge of the household servants), the constable (in the original sense of the word, *comes stabuli,* count of the stables), the cupbearer, the chief doorkeeper (*ostiarius*—a very important officer, since he controlled access to the king), four masters of the hunt, the master falconer, cellarer, and others. Each of these officials was in charge of a large staff, and each required a corps of servants to wait upon him. Each had families and children who required tutors, nurses and attendants.

The population of the palace was further swelled by the numerous visitors from abroad to whom Charles gave hospitality: pilgrims, foreign scholars, envoys from other countries, exiles such as King Eardwulf of Northumbria. Many nobles, lay and ecclesiastical, came to the court for longer or shorter stays either because they had business to transact or because they could not resist the attraction of the bustling life there. In addition there were many young men being "nourished" at the court—that is, receiving their finishing education there. We have seen that Einhard was originally one of these. Prisoners, too, were brought to Aachen to be exhibited at the court as warrants of military victory and often to be kept in servitude for many years or for their lifetimes.

To feed all these people wagon trains of provisions were brought to

Aachen from the other royal domains and from private estates. High officials were provided for at the expense of the state; others had to shift for themselves, which meant that a busy market sprang up in the new town. Peddlers and merchants, attracted by the wealth concentrated at the capital, brought their silks and spices to the luxury-loving nobles and the even more luxury-loving bishops. Cripples and beggars swarmed around the palace, drawn by Charles's reputation for charity. Nor were the common vices of a capital lacking, for one decree provides for the whipping of prostitutes. "Their procurers must carry them on their backs to the market place to receive their punishment; if the procurers cannot or will not do this, they themselves are to be lashed." Thieves and robbers also fled to the capital for safety, because there they could lose themselves among the crowds.

All the hurly-burly of town and palace revolved around a single person: Charles. Einhard, Theodulf and Angilbert have pictured for us Charles's personal habits and the gay, busy, colorful life of the court, where the most was made of every minute. Even while he was dressing Charles admitted his friends and officials to his antechamber, listened to lawsuits and pronounced judgments, gave orders to his servants and transacted other business. (From this time-saving custom of his arose the French ceremony of the levee.) He kept an eye on everything that went on in his palace—according to the Monk of St. Gall a gallery was built around his apartment so that "he could see all who came out or went in, and what they were doing"—and carefully shut his eyes to the scandals surrounding his daughters, which he did not want to acknowledge. Or so Einhard puts it. Perhaps it would be more accurate to say that Charles took a far more lenient view of sexual license than some of his contemporaries and that he granted to his daughters the same freedoms he permitted himself. At least one of Charles's sons, the priggish Louis, strongly objected to his sisters' conduct and put an end to it as soon as he was in a position to do so.

The scandals were in a sense inevitable. For in spite of his daughters' beauty and desirability, Charles refused to give them in marriage to any man. "He said he could not part with their company," Einhard declares. Certainly he was very fond of them, and they of him. Theodulf pictures them waiting on their father tenderly, bringing him flowers, fruits and wine, and says: "What he found charming in one was the sweetness of her voice, in another the freshness of her smile, in this one the grace of her bearing, in that one *her rebelliousness*." But there were probably political motives also in his refusal to allow any formal alliances; these might upset his arrangements for the succession by giving sons-in-law some tenuous claim to the throne. If we read the biography of Louis the Pious aright, Charles seems to have explained his treatment of the girls by reminding Louis of past dark incidents in the family—in particular of Hiltrud and Odilo, the mother and father of Tassilo. For Charles's aunt, Hiltrud, had married Duke Odilo without the consent of her brothers, Pepin and Carloman the Elder, and a great deal of trouble for the Frankish kingdom had flowed out of that defiant act of female emancipation. Informal liaisons with men not so powerful as the erstwhile Duke of Bavaria were another matter. Charles had no objection to these, and several of his daughters availed themselves of his indulgence. Princess Rotrud, for example, whose betrothal to the Emperor Constantine had been broken off, consoled herself with a Count Roriko of Maine. The couple had at least one son, who ultimately became abbot of St. Denis.

That Charles was well aware of what was going on is indicated by an amusing bit of court gossip which survived some three hundred years in oral tradition before it was finally set down by a monk at the monastery of Lorsch. The story as it is told concerns Einhard and his wife Imma, but the persons involved were undoubtedly Angilbert and Charles's daughter Bertha.

Angilbert, it seems, "was loved by all at the royal court, but even more ardently loved by the king's daughter Bertha. Some time passed; from day to day their mutual love grew. But fear of the king's wrath prevented them from risking a rendezvous. Nevertheless, fervent love conquered all. For this excellent man, afire with incurable love and not daring to approach the maiden through a messenger, at last gathered up his courage and in the dark of night secretly crept to the maiden's chamber. He knocked very softly, saying he had a message from the king, and was admitted. But as soon as he was alone with her they exchanged intimate talk and kissed and followed the urge of their love."

Before dawn Angilbert rises from his couch intending to return by the way he had come. But to his terror he sees that a heavy snow has fallen, and is afraid to leave. The footsteps of a man in the snow beneath Bertha's window will surely betray him. At last Bertha hits on the idea of carrying her lover on her back to his own house and then returning in her footsteps.

Charles, however, was in the habit of rising four and five times during the night. (This is historical, not legendary.) He had slept little that night, and rose at the break of dawn in time to see his daughter "staggering along under her burden, scarcely able to walk, and then going back swiftly." The king watches the whole affair with mingled astonishment and sorrow. He consults with his courtiers, and they propose various harsh punishments for the man who has dishonored the king's daughter. Charles decides, however, that he "will not impose any punishment upon my scribe for this distressing act, since that would increase rather than diminish the disgrace of my daughter. Rather, it is more dignified and suitable to the glory of our kingdom to forgive them, since they are so young, and to unite them in legitimate marriage."

Legitimate or not, the relationship of Angilbert and Bertha amounted to a marriage. Angilbert has warmly described his beloved, wearing a golden diadem, with golden filaments sparkling in her gleaming hair, her snowy shoulders covered by an ermine wrap, her dress adorned with pearls and gems, her belt shining in many colors. And he praises her voice, her virile mind, her flashing eyes, her shapely mouth, her beauty of face and carriage, declaring that in all these attributes she is the very image of her royal father. Angilbert and Bertha had a house of their own near the palace, and in one of his poems, an "Eclogue to King Charles," Angilbert (referring to himself as Homer) asks his poem:

> To the lovely garden speed
>   Where amid the grass and flowers
> Homer with his sons would play,
>   Spending there delightful hours.
> Spy upon them: Are they well?
>   Growing safe from sickness, fire,
> Firmly sheltered by the walls
>   That no thief gain his desire?
> May both house and boys be strong!
> See to this, my little song!

Angilbert, though Charles had appointed him abbot of St. Riquier, was distinctly a secular person in spirit. His semiofficial title of *auricu-*

lus, literally the king's "ear," suggests what confidence Charles placed in him. He was also a great favorite of Alcuin's, although the difference in the two men's temperaments was very marked. Alcuin, in the words of Theodulf, was a man of porridge and cheese; Angilbert loved the wine and savory meat that enabled him to sing. Yet Alcuin, with all his simplicity, piety and frugality, was as susceptible as everyone else at court to the winning personality of worldly Angilbert. The two men might quarrel, but then Alcuin would send a poem to Angilbert asking that harmony be restored between "Flaccus" and "Homer."

Angilbert had an eye for feminine beauty and has described, though in rather conventional poetic terms, the other women of the king's household. The occasion is a royal hunt. After Charles, whose "richly caparisoned steed is decked out with gold and precious metals and is prancing with pride at having been singled out to be the great king's mount," come the serfs, bringing "long boar-hunting spears tipped with sharp steel, and folded linen nets. They lead up the leashed hunting dogs, boarhounds with savage teeth, wild to spring upon their prey."

Apparently the hunt starts immediately after a religious service, for the party is pictured as leaving "the sacred porch of the lofty basilica." Then, late of course—which is not surprising, considering how elaborately she is dressed—"the queen whom all await emerges from her royal apartments, the beauteous Liutgard whom the king has taken to wife. Her gleaming throat has stolen the tender tints of the rose. The scarlet with which her hair is laced seems less dazzling than her locks. Bands of purple girdle her white temples. Gold threads band the edges of her cloak. Her shoulders are hung with jeweled collars flashing in multicolored fires."

Still later "the bright band of royal daughters appears." The order is governed by strict protocol. First comes Rotrud, "her pale blonde hair intertwined with ribands of violet and strings of pearls. A coronet of gold studded with precious stones circles her heard. A brooch fastens her rich raiment." Then comes Bertha, described above, then "lily-white Gisla, appareled in a purple gown shot through with tints of mauve, her face, her hair gleaming with many lights." Angilbert praises "the rosy glow of her marble throat, her silvery-white hands, her forehead bright as gold, the brilliance of her glance before which Phoebus' rays seem dull." Next is Rothaid. "On her breast, on her throat, among her hair flash jewels of various sorts. A silk mantle drapes her white shoulders. Above her radiant forehead a coronet of pearls gleams. A gold pin mounted with a pearl crowns her coiffure." Then Theotrade, an adolescent girl at this time, but "no less lovely than her older sisters. About her mild face her hair is of a brightness greater than gold. Rare emeralds adorn her lovely neck." Her greatest pleasure is to wear "Sophoclean buskins"; is this a fashion note on her hunting costume, or does it imply that the royal family engaged in parlor dramatics? There are references to a theater at Aachen!

Not mentioned as part of the crowd were the king's mistresses, those ladies of obscure official standing whom Louis, when he succeeded to the throne, found it necessary to drive from the palace. The names of some of these "concubines" are recorded—Maltegard, Gerswinda, Adalhaid, Regina—but Einhard discreetly evades saying whether they were successive or consecutive. Let us imitate his discretion, since we cannot know for sure.

Much of the hunting was done in a great park attached to Aachen and completely surrounded by walls. With perhaps some exaggeration contemporaries asserted that every kind of savage beast was contained within this vast natural-habitat zoo, including panthers, tigers, rhinoceroses and even dragons. We have no accounts of a dragon's being brought to bay, but we do have a description of Charles dispatching a wild boar while the whole court looks on:

"A wild boar dashes across the valley, the hounds in hot pursuit. The noise of the dogs guides the hunters through the depths of the forest. One of the hounds flies with unerring instinct over the wild boar's track, without uttering a sound; others, thirsting for blood, howl loudly. . . . The forest rings with the loud echoes of the wild din. The notes of the horn rouse and quicken the most savage instincts of the savage brutes and lead them to where the infuriated boar shows its terrible tusks.

"The rustling leaves drop from the shaken boughs; the boar escapes, bounds away from its pursuers up the steepest places. Grunting fiercely, it climbs the most inaccessible points of the rocky crest. At last, exhausted by its efforts and unable to run any longer, it sits panting on its haunches. The dogs have tasted its blood and felt its tusk. Some are driven back; others, fiercer than the rest, are tossed bleeding into the air.

"At that supreme moment the king arrives on the scene. Fleeter than the bird in its flight, he breaks through the crowd, strikes the beast's breast with his sword and drives the cold blade home to the hilt. The wild boar falls, blood streaming from the deadly wound, and dies. . . . The whole royal family, girls and all, have witnessed the feat from a commanding point."

On returning from a morning hunt in the crisp, cold air of a northern winter, Charles and his family would sit down together to the main meal of the day, the principal course being a roast which the hunters brought in on spits. He rarely gave large banquets; he preferred the quiet of a domestic dinner at which there would be either singing or readings from St. Augustine and from histories. Perhaps Alcuin, but more likely Theodulf or Angilbert, would rise during the meal to read aloud one of their poems. Some of the stouthearted warriors at table were not up to these intellectual doings. Theodulf describes one Wibod who claps his hand to his thick head in despair and glares at the poet until the king reproves him with a glance. The Wibods were probably more at ease with the Frankish songs and ballads that the minstrels sang. On festive occasions, when a larger company was present, the king was not above having the company entertained by jugglers and acrobats. But what he loved above all were the intellectual sports of the Palace Academy, which have been described earlier. The company at dinner was unusually sober for a great noble's household in those times, for Charles "despised drunkenness in everyone, and especially in himself and his friends." But it imbibed deeply and with a gay good humor of, in Alcuin's phrase, "the wine of learning."

CHAPTER FIFTEEN

"Like a Dog to its Vomit"

THE completion of the palace and chapel at Aachen and the establishment of the court there were the outward symbols of a profound change that was taking place within the Frankish kingdom and within the heart of its ruler. Duke Eric's capture of the hoarded treasure of the Avars, which brought so much new wealth all at once into Frankland, was another such symbol. Long-cherished dreams would soon be fulfilled; of this everyone was convinced, although everyone also hesitated to say what these dreams were. A new tone could be sensed in the quickening tempo of events, in the embassies from distant parts of Europe and even Asia, in the numerous wars that Charles was henceforth able to conduct simultaneously at the farthest extremes of his kingdom. For all the ease and intimacy with which the court circle associated with Charles, even these closest friends began to confer fawning flatteries on him. He was still their good David who loved poets, but he was also "the glory of poets"—"*David amat vates, vatorum est gloria David*"—even to one so near and dear to him as Angilbert. It was as if everyone were suddenly struck by the consciousness of what this man in the prime of life meant to him, to his country, to the world. The new tone was engendered by the aura of *greatness*. Carolus had become Carolus Magnus; Charles had become Charle-magne, Charles the Great.

A mythology sprang up at court around this new greatness. So glorious a king could have descended only from the noblest stock. Not only he but the entire people of the Franks must be of heroic lineage. With Celtic imagination the Irishman Dungal declared that the "Master of the world had led the royal people of the Franks from Troy to these coasts, had given these fields to them and subjected all nations to the just rule of the Franks." In other words, the Franks were being equated with the Romans, who also had reputedly descended from the Trojans and who had subjected all nations. A sense of manifest destiny was taking possession of the intellectuals around Charles. These men, many of them not Franks, identified themselves with the Franks and were more imperialistic than the Franks themselves. Had they not, under their great king, extended their sway to the mouth of the Elbe and the little-known forests of Bohemia? Had they not penetrated deep into the plains of Pannonia? Their king reigned from Denmark to the borders of Calabria. Where in Europe was there any greater—and the fateful word was spoken—any greater *imperium*?

Besides material conquests they could pride themselves on the possession of the things of the spirit. Their king was not only the most powerful, but "most Christian" and "most pious"—and these epithets were not empty phrases; they expressed his consistent solicitude for the spiritual welfare of the people, so that a violation of the Ten Commandments was interpreted as an act of disloyalty toward the king. As Defender of the Church and Patrician of the Romans he received homage from the pope himself. God stood at his side and aided him in the conversion of pagan peoples, Saxons, Slavs and "Huns." The Lord had given him "wisdom and strength to lead many souls to the love of Christ." He was "master of the vineyard," sending many workers to labor among the vines. He carried two swords; with the one he defended the Church from without against the attacks of the heathen; with the other he struck within the Church against false doctrines. He would challenge even the pope on questions of dogma, and his followers were convinced of his rightness. His wisdom, Theodulf said, knew no bounds; it was "broader than the Nile, mightier than the ice-covered Danube, not less than the Ganges." He possessed the penetration, said Alcuin, to see through "all that is mystery and darkness, down to the very bottom of all things." These tributes were not mere flattery; none remotely resembling them was ever paid to his powerful predecessors. The testimony of Alcuin alone, whose integrity is beyond question, is sufficient to banish forever the fantastic myth of Charles as an ignorant barbarian.

No one seemed to think that Charles's incessant wars were inconsistent with his being a prince of peace. The order, equity and charity which he established within the borders of his realm justified in men's minds the epithet "pacific" which was regularly applied to him. In the reign of Charles men were beginning to sense again what the

state of Europe had been under the *pax romana*. Peace always seems
more peaceful to the victor than to the vanquished. And the Franks
were winning almost everywhere now.

There remained one flaw in the long tale of triumphs, one banner
missing from the parade of trophies that Charles's son Pepin, or his
generals Duke Eric, Count Gerold and Count William of Toulouse,
brought home again and again to Aachen. Charles and his namesake
son, young Charles, also were bringing home trophies, but these were
of another sort: wretched human beings, men, women and children,
forcibly uprooted from their homes. The worst of it was that there
seemed to be an endless supply of them, and annual expeditions were
required to round them up. It was an unpleasant business, and yet
Charles felt that he was saving the souls of these people. For the
monster Frankish state seemed to have swallowed an indigestible mor-
sel in Saxony.

For seven years after the dramatic conversion of Widukind there
had been quiet in Saxony. The Saxons had busied themselves repair-
ing the ravages of the war years, reluctantly building churches, sullenly
paying their tithes and contributing their levies to Charles's military
expeditions. Exhausted by war, they had submitted to the reign of
terror initiated by the Capitulary on Saxony of 785. But there remained a fragment of Saxony still unconquered, to spread the in-
fection of freedom throughout the rest of the country. This was
Nordalbingia, the Saxon lands north of the Elbe River, which bordered directly on the Danish kingdom. Protected by the great width
of the Elbe at its mouth, by the marshy character of the land and
by the proximity of their Danish allies, the Nordliudi (northern people) had been able to preserve their independence. Charles had, in
fact, recognized the difficulties of attempting their conquest and had
left them pretty much to themselves, depending on his Slavic allies
to the east, the Abodrites, to keep them in check. Meanwhile Bishop
Willehad's missionaries in the adjacent province of Wigmodia (on
the left bank of the Elbe) did what they could to wean the Nordalbingians away from the worship of Woden.

To the oppressed Saxons of the conquered provinces the independence of their northern neighbors was a constant reminder of their
own lost freedom. The executions at Verden, the capitulation of
Widukind, were gradually being forgotten in Saxony. The injustice
of Frankish exactions of tithes and men's lives seemed all the more

galling when contrasted with the exemption of the Nordliudi. Only a demonstration that the Franks were not omnipotent was needed to set off a rebellion. In the middle of the summer of 792 that demonstration was provided by the Nordalbingians. They seized a favorable opportunity to wipe out almost to the man a Frankish detachment entering the mouth of the Elbe.

This was only an incident such as could happen at any time in those wild regions. As he had done before in the case of a skirmish between Bavarians and Franks, Charles chose to ignore it, refusing to be diverted from his plan to push the war against the Avars. Nordalbingia, like Brittany, did not seem to him worth the effort of total conquest. He could foresee a long, hard campaign among marshes and tidal flatlands for a prize not worth the having. A little loss of prestige was not important; he would not permit a few savage tribesmen to affect the great movements of his civilized state.

This broad view proved, however, to be a miscalculation. The southern Saxons were encouraged by the semblance of Frankish weakness. Their hatred of Frankish rule, of tithes, conscription and Christianity, exploded all at once. And the first victim was Count Theoderic, the survivor of the Süntel debacle of ten years before, who now as then was in charge of gathering Saxon levies. Theoderic had commanded Saxon and Frisian contingents in the first invasion of Avar Pannonia. When he now appeared again to collect fresh troops for service there, the would-be conscripts rose up against him. Theoderic and his men were massacred, and a fever of rebellion swept the entire country. Churches were burned, bishops and priests driven out, killed, or captured and held for ransom. The Lorsch annals mirrored the indignation of Charles and the Franks: "What had been concealed in the Saxons' hearts was made manifest: like a dog that returns to its vomit they returned to the paganism they had once thrown up, again abandoning Christianity, deceiving both God and the Lord King who had heaped such benefits upon them [!]."

Charles's fury at this new "perfidy" is understandable. He made light of it, however; he was unwilling to admit the magnitude of this setback. But he knew that what was at stake in Saxony was the whole slowly growing structure of the new Western Roman Empire he was attempting to build. By now he was quite conscious of his goal, and each successive stroke of policy drove toward it. The most important lesson he had learned from history, which he studied with avidity, was the peril of a numerous people of warlike barbarians on the borders of a great empire. If the Franks could not assimilate the Saxons, they themselves would ultimately be destroyed.

He had accomplished with comparative ease his goal of integrating civilized, Christianized countries like Aquitaine, Lombardy and Bavaria into the Frankish state. There it had been a matter of taking over and adapting existing governmental organizations. But in Saxony, with its largely tribal structure, the organs of government had first to be created; then the people had to be taught or forced to obey them. The Church, with its hierarchical setup patterned after the old Roman state, had been his chosen instrument for imposing on the Saxons the principles of monarchism and a firm secular government. That program had seemed well on its way to success. Now Charles was forced to realize that within a few months the work of years had been undone.

In addition, he had to abandon the campaign against the Avars; without Theoderic's contingents he preferred not to risk it. Also he did not want to invade Saxony without a large force, and the bulk of his army was encamped along the Danube, or in Italy on the borders of Pannonia. The men could be moved fairly quickly, but how, in the space of a summer, could he transport all their supplies to Saxony? Portage overland from the Danube to the Rhine was a slow and laborious business. If only there were a water route between the two great rivers!

At Regensburg in Bavaria, where the news of the Saxon uprising had reached him, he discussed the problem with some of the experts with whom he always surrounded himself. Some "who claimed to understand these matters" assured him that a navigable canal could be dug between two small rivers which were tributaries of the Main (which flows into the Rhine) and the Danube. Then whole armies could easily be transported by boat from Danube to Rhine and back again from the Rhine to the Danube when the Saxon emergency was over.

With characteristic energy Charles took his whole court up the Danube to the Altmühl River to supervise the work in person. Thousands upon thousands of men were brought in and a great ditch, more than a mile long and three hundred feet wide, was dug—entirely by hand, of course! While the monks of the vicinity complained that it was blasphemy to change the face of nature, and while the people, the serfs, slaves and soldiers who did the digging no doubt called the business "Charles's folly," the weather entered into a conspiracy against the project. It rained and rained; the site of the canal, marshy enough by nature, became a sea of mud which flowed back into the ditch as fast as it was taken out. Before the end of the year Charles recognized that his efforts were wasted, and he ordered the canal abandoned. Traces of it still remain, however, after almost twelve centuries, and a German village named Graben (ditch) marks the scene of so much frustrating labor.

The failure of the canal removed the last hope Charles had of restoring order in Saxony immediately. He could not bring in any Aquitanian soldiers; they were needed for defense against the Saracens, who had simultaneously launched a successful hit-and-run raid in Septimania. It is testimony to the flexibility of his mind that, worried though he was about the military situation on many fronts, he could nevertheless turn his attention to the questions of religious doctrine which were to be discussed at the Frankfurt synod the following year. Meanwhile, he went ahead with large-scale preparations for the punishment of the Saxons, and just after the synod and the death of Fastrada he entered Saxony.

His deliberation made possible a bloodless victory. He had by this time gathered enough men to divide his force into two armies, one commanded by himself, the other by young Charles. The Saxons, massing south of Paderborn, found themselves caught between a Frankish army approaching from the southeast and another from the west. As they had done many times in the past, the Saxons surrendered without a fight. Charles took hostages, and both armies went home.

Such, at any rate, is the peculiar account of this campaign given by the annals. Had Charles returned to a policy of excessive confidence in the Saxons' word? It does not seem likely, since the annals also tell us that the very next year Charles, "remembering the Saxons' perfidy," again entered Saxony with an army and ravaged the country. More likely there was some compelling motive for his mildness, but we do not know what it was. The actual events and the true motivations of both his and the Saxons' behavior during this and the following years are obscured by the brevity of the contemporary annals and by the partisan Frankish coloring all of them give to the story. Obviously each year's operations could not have been so successful as they are painted by the annalists, for in spite of the seemingly more important war against the Avars Charles took personal command in Saxony and returned to the struggle year after year. His pertinacity was outdone only by that of the Saxons themselves. For six years, from 794 through 799, he appeared in Saxony every summer, each time pushing farther toward the north, toward the marshlands of Wigmodia and Nordalbingia to which the die-hards among the Saxons retreated.

Meanwhile, he had conceived of a new method for dealing with the Saxons. He was older, wiser, more forbearing than he had been during the last wars in Saxony. The black years had passed; Carolus Magnus wished to forget the horrors that had been committed by a younger Charles. The prosecution of the war was still cruel, for devastation always marked the passage of a Frankish army anywhere. And his new treatment of men who refused to abandon their hope of independence and their love for their own religion was still savage. But the surpassing cruelty of the executions at Verden was never repeated, although the provocation was greater now.

The desperate remedy Charles applied to the cancer of freedom in Saxony was the massive removal of malignant matter. Previously he had always taken hostages in considerable numbers. Now he tried mass deportation. Frankish troops rounded up thousands of Saxons in vast man hunts and forcibly removed them to Frankland. The bad and the good—that is to say, the Saxon patriots and the pro-Frankish converts—were gathered together indiscriminately. Many who had remained Christians and loyal to Charles over the years, enduring the hatred of their secretly pagan neighbors, were treated as harshly as those who had always joined every uprising against the Franks. To be Saxon was to be condemned.

The suffering of these displaced persons, who lost all they had, and the bitterness of a war in which Saxon was ranged against Saxon as well as Frank, in which sudden assassination was the only Saxon defense against overwhelming superiority in numbers and equipment—the whole pattern of the war is laid bare in a petition presented twenty years later to Louis the Pious:

"Our father's name was Richard, our uncle's Richolf; both were Saxons and had their inheritance in the Saxon land. While they were in the service of your father, the Lord Charles of blessed memory, their kinsfolk and neighbors, hating them for their Christianity, plundered all their goods. For they saw that my father and uncle held fast to the Christian faith and would not deny it. Then it happened that the Lord King sent my uncle Richolf across the Elbe as a missus, along with Count Rorich, Count Gottschalk, Count Had, and Garich, all of whom were killed there while trying to establish Christianity. At the news of this, my father Richard hurried to report to the Lord King. While he was on the way, my mother was captured and held for ransom. All our goods and valuables were taken by the robbers as booty. My father at once stole back secretly and freed my mother, secretly as a thief, and fled with her to the district called Marsham, where she had property. Here he remained until, at the command of the Lord King, the Saxons were removed from the country. At that time my parents were taken away along with the others. Torn from their own soil, they had to live in exile for many years, until my father died. There remained only my mother, my sister and myself. We three are still alive by God's mercy. But we have not received our father's inheritance. Therefore, most pious emperor, let help come to us also, and at least have your faithful servants determine whether that inheritance rightly belongs to us or not. There are still many witnesses living in those districts who can be questioned, so that the truth may be brought to light, O mildest and most illustrious emperor!"

What action the emperor took is not recorded.

As the war dragged on, as campaign followed campaign and no victory seemed to put an end to the fighting, Charles began to listen more attentively to those at his court who had long argued for more lenient treatment of the Saxons—foremost among them Alcuin. At home, among his Franks, Charles had always sought the consent of the people, had been sensitive to the course of public opinion and more than once acted contrary to his own wishes rather than ignore the opinions of his notables. Perhaps the time had come in Saxony to dispense with repressive measures and seek to govern with the consent of the governed. He had tried terror in the past, was still employing terror when he took every third man as hostage in certain districts. But terror produced only fresh rebellions. What would happen if he abolished the sanguinary special laws governing Saxony?

No revision in the laws was practicable until Charles had completed the reconquest of all Saxony south and east of the Elbe River. The marshy province of Wigmodia, between the Weser and the Elbe, held out the longest. Protected by the rivers, by the sea, by canals, marshes and fortifications, it was a district of poor or no roads and a widely scattered population. Charles made immense preparations. Large boats were taken along; they were constructed in four sections which could be drawn overland by horse or mule teams. Nails and tools for putting them together, wax and pitch for calking the joints, were carried along so that the boats could be quickly assembled and used for water crossings.

In fierce fighting the Franks broke through the fortifications, crossed pathless heaths and perilous swamps, burning and destroying all dwellings as they went. They swept on all the way to the North Sea, and at last the harried populace gave up. "From all ends and corners" of the district they came to Charles to surrender, and this time he took so many "hostages" that it later became necessary for him to settle Franks in Wigmodia to repopulate the land. Every third Saxon, *with his wife and children*, was forcibly deported to distant parts of Gaul.

That, Charles now felt, was the ultimate limit of terror. All the Saxons who had participated in the rebellions, and many who had not, had been deported. The three main divisions of Saxony—Westphalia, Angria and Eastphalia—no longer had the means or the will to resist his authority. Nordalbingia had not yet been conquered, but perhaps the Nordalbingians could be won over peacefully if they saw that Charles was offering the other Saxons a policy of moderation. He himself was as weary of the cruelty and destruction as the victims.

In October of that year, after the summer's campaign in Wigmodia had been fought to its successful conclusion, Charles convoked an assembly of notables at Aachen. Representatives from the three Saxon provinces were invited. The outcome of their deliberations was a new decree, the *Capitulare Saxonicum*, which tacitly repealed the harsh special laws of 785. Second-class citizenship was abolished. The Saxons were at last placed on a plane of equality with the other members of the Frankish kingdom. The long list of capital crimes, which had made the earlier Saxon Capitulary an instrument of repression, was quietly omitted. Instead, Saxons were to pay the same fines as the Franks (sixty solidi, the "king's ban," as this fine was called) for violation of the "king's peace," for crimes against widows and orphans, rape, incendiarism, failure to report for military duty. Instead of death penalties for offenses against priests, fines even lower than those required from Franks were imposed. The king was even given the power to commute to banishment the sentences of criminals who would be punished by death under traditional Saxon law. Charles was here following his fundamental policy of not infringing on the existing laws of a nation or country. The Germanic tradition that each man should be judged by his local law was still stronger than any principle of centralization. But in cases where men's lives were at stake, Charles now mitigated the harshness of local law by providing for clemency at his personal discretion. This clause also gave him the opportunity to intervene in favor of Saxons who had run afoul of Saxon law or Saxon prejudice in remaining loyal to their Frankish masters.

The *Capitulare Saxonicum* is conclusive evidence that the new Charles had fully emerged, the "merciful and clement Charles," to speak in the adjectives of his contemporaries. This mercifulness was not really new; rather, Charles had partly returned to his natural self, to the kindhearted and friendly self and the benevolent ruler he had been before the massacre at Verden and the deaths of Hildigard and his mother. His friends associated the change with the disappearance of Fastrada from the scene and with the gentleness of Liutgard. But the new queen seems to have been rather a sign of the change than a cause of it. One important factor must certainly have been the inevitable mellowing of age: Charles was now fifty-five, growing stout, and already had a mane of fine white hair.

Another factor was the lifting of the burdens of administration. His three sons were now old enough to rule in their own right, relieving Charles of much petty detail. At Aachen Charles was assisted by young Charles, who seems to have been with his father constantly. In Italy and Aquitaine Pepin and Louis acted as virtually independent sovereigns in the internal government of their kingdoms. Charles still retained the over-all direction of policy, especially in foreign affairs, and both Pepin and Louis attended him frequently at Aachen, to receive his orders or simply to be with him, sharing in the family pleasures and coming once more under his full influence, which absence might have weakened. Never, it seems, did they fail to respect his least wish, to carry out all his instructions. Charles no longer had to exhaust himself being everywhere at once, seeing to everything in person. He could afford to spend year after year patiently retaking Saxony because Italy was being well governed by Pepin, Aquitaine by Louis, Neustria and Austrasia by young Charles, Bavaria by his brother-in-law Gerold. He could also conduct campaigns on several different fronts because of these capable sons and the fine crop of professional generals his endless wars had produced. The year that Charles pushed to the North Sea in Saxony, for example, Duke Eric was again fighting the Avars, and Pepin, with a force of Lombards and Bavarians, had advanced into the lands of the Slavic tribes of eastern Pannonia and Dalmatia (present-day Yugoslavia). At the same time Louis was sent into Spain with an army—although he, unlike Charles's other sons, was notably inept and the real power of command was wielded by William of Toulouse.

After the conference at which the new decrees for Saxony were laid down, Charles returned to Saxony with his army and court to spend the winter there. He was bent on consolidating what he had won by such hard fighting. On the banks of the Weser he built barracks and large buildings to house troops and court, creating a new town which he named Herstelle, after the Carolingian family seat of Heristal on the Meuse. Both Pepin and Louis came to visit him here, and here also he received a gift in the form of a magnificent tent (which would come in handy in the circumstances) from Alonzo, King of Galicia and Asturia in Spain. The bulk of the army was distributed throughout Saxony, as had been done twelve years before when he first wintered in Saxony, at the end of the first phase of the war. Meanwhile emissaries, among them several Saxon Christians, were sent to the Nordalbingians to sound out their temper and to bring them tidings of the new, more tolerant Frankish regime. But if Charles had hoped to win over the Nordliudi, he was disappointed. The missi were those mentioned in the petition of Count Richard's son, quoted above; they were killed or held for ransom. Charles could do nothing about this immediately, except pay the ransoms. It was early in the year and the grass was still too short to provide fodder for the mounted Frankish army. And worse news followed. The Wigmodians, once more inspired by the example of their neighbors, again rebelled. In the summer, when Charles was at last able to march, he had to ravage the district of Wigmodia for the second time.

In these difficult circumstances he made skillful use of his Slavic allies, the Abodrites. Advised by Frankish missi and with the aid of some Frankish troops, these Slavs invaded Nordalbingia and inflicted a bloody defeat on the Saxons. One of the Frankish commanders claimed that four thousand Saxons fell at the first encounter and many more during the rout that followed. But there may well have been exaggeration here, for the Saxons asked for peace terms and were apparently granted fairly liberal ones. Charles still did not attempt to incorporate Nordalbingia into the Frankish state. He merely took hostages from the Nordliudi and received their promise of submission, and possibly some tribute. Thrasko, Duke of the Abodrites, came to him to deliver into his hands more Saxon hostages, and Charles cemented relations between himself and his pagan allies by praising Thrasko to the skies and lavishing gifts on him. Perhaps at this time he also hinted that he would grant Thrasko the territory of the Nordalbingians—when it was ultimately conquered. The Slavs would form a useful buffer between Frankland and the Danes.

For the present, however, Nordalbingia remained unfinished business. Great events had taken place in Italy and in the Eastern Roman Empire. Southern and eastern Europe were in ferment, and Charles felt that he had lingered long enough on these northern affairs. He hurried back to Aachen to receive ambassadors from the Empress Irene.

CHAPTER SIXTEEN

The Road to Rome

THE TWO envoys from Constantinople were Michael Gan-glianos, former patrician of Phrygia, and a priest named Theophilus. They came, they said, in the interests of con-tinued peaceful relations between Frankland and the Em-pire, and they presented credentials signed in the name of Irene, *Emperor* and Autocrat of all the Romans. But what of Constantine, Rotrud's onetime betrothed? Was he no longer the emperor? Smooth-ly the emissaries explained that Constantine had made himself so hated by the people that at last his own men had seized him and blinded him. Although forbidden by the Patriarch of Constantinople to commit bigamy, he had put his wife into a convent and married his mother's lady-in-waiting, Theodota. Clergy and people were outraged. Theodore, abbot of the monastery of Studion at Constantinople and the great reformer of Byzantine monasticism, spoke for all when he declared: "Woe to the land that has a child for king." Whereupon Constantine shut down the monastery and had the monks whipped. No doubt he would have returned to the devil-inspired persecution of images if the people had not risen in their wrath. Now, grief-stricken though she was by the fate of her unfortunate son, whose vices she had been unable to check, his mother Irene had graciously bowed to the will of the people and consented to bear the burdens of the state alone.

Such was the tale the ambassadors told, and in the absence of other evidence they were believed. At their request Charles released a Byzantine prisoner he was holding (the brother of Bishop Tarasius of Constantinople, captured probably during the abortive Greek in-vasion of Benevento ten years before) and sent the envoys back with the usual gifts.

But the truth soon leaked through to Frankland, and Charles

learned that he had been deceived. Irene, the shrewd and ruthless empress, the unnatural mother, had spent the years since her reconciliation with her son deliberately corrupting Constantine. She had catered to his vices, persuaded him to excesses, encouraged him in all actions that would contribute to unpopularity. After five years of this she capped his bad reputation by engineering a military disaster. The patrician Stauracius and army officers in her pay deliberately sabotaged Constantine's preparations for a campaign against the Arabs. The young emperor returned from the unsuccessful campaign to find a conspiracy in full bloom against him. As he left the Hippodrome, soldiers of the Imperial Guard surrounded him. He escaped them and crossed to the Asiatic shore of the Bosporus, where he thought he would find protection among loyal Anatolian troops.

Irene and her fellow conspirators were terrified. But the iron-willed mother drove the others on, threatening to reveal their part in the plot unless they captured the emperor. Their lives at stake, the conspirators took the further risk, and this time they succeeded. Constantine was seized and taken to the Purple Room in the palace at Constantinople, the very room where Irene had brought him into the world. The day of his capture Irene's henchmen entered the room and here, where he had first opened his eyes, they blinded him, nearly killing him in the process.

So well had Irene succeeded in her plan to make her son unpopular that in Constantinople high and low applauded the punishment of the emperor. Although Theophanes, the chronicler, asserts that after this act of cruelty the sun was darkened for seventeen days, so that ships at sea went astray, such notables as Abbot Theodore, now restored to favor, had only praise for Irene. When she rode forth in a golden chariot drawn by four white horses and driven by four of her highest dignitaries, she scattered gold among the crowd, and the people hailed her with wild enthusiasm as if she were a living image of the Virgin Mary.

If this news from Constantinople was shocking, the stories that soon reached Charles's ears from Rome were equally so. To understand what was happening there it is necessary for us to go back a couple of years to the treasure of the Avars, which Charles had distributed so lavishly.

We will remember that Charles had set aside a large part of the

Avar spoils as a gift to Pope Hadrian—another of the many consolation prizes with which he was in the habit of placating the pope for the always withheld territories that he had once promised Hadrian and that Hadrian so insistently reminded him of. But before the coins and swords, the silks and precious stones, the golden bowls and delicate glass goblets could be dispatched across the Alps, word reached Charles that his old friend and antagonist had died on Christmas Day, 795.

Charles wept. More than ever a prey to guilty conscience, given with advancing age to searching his heart for sins of omission and commission, particularly in regard to his religious duties, he felt that he had missed a last chance to convey to Hadrian that his policies had been well meant, that if with one hand he had to deprive the Church of its due because political interests forced him to continue the program of the Lombard kings, with the other hand he nevertheless gave unstintingly to the Holy Mother out of his new-found wealth. Now Charles could no longer make amends. Awareness of this irrevocability wiped out whatever bitterness toward Hadrian still lingered as a result of their recent disputes over dogma. He ordered prayers for the pope's salvation throughout his kingdom. He sent letters to English churches requesting similar prayers and providing valuable gifts to pay for them. He also had a marble tombstone prepared in Frankland for the adornment of Hadrian's tomb. The poets at the court competed in the writing of the epitaph, and Alcuin's was (rather unfairly) chosen over Theodulf's to be inscribed on the stone in letters of gold.

This epitaph was, incidentally, one of Alcuin's last services to Charles at court in Aachen. Past sixty, with his thoughts turning more and more toward making his peace with God (although he had been at peace with Him all his life), Alcuin had been longing to escape from the bustle of court life and the burdens of being all at once Charles's private tutor, his minister of education, his link with the kings of England, his adviser on the conversion of pagan peoples and his specialist on the adoptianist heresy, to name only the more important of his many functions. Though never a monk or priest, he had always been a churchman at heart, and for a time he thought of retiring to the monastery of Fulda. But Charles was too fond of him to let him depart from the court unrewarded, too aware of Alcuin's gifts to permit him to waste them on a simple life as an unassuming monk. He kept Alcuin about him until he could find a fitting place for the great scholar's retirement.

The opportunity came shortly after the death of Hadrian when Itherius—the former chancellor who had so often thwarted Hadrian's plans—died at Tours, where he had been abbot for some twenty years. Charles promptly appointed Alcuin, who was seeking the quiet life, as the new abbot of Tours—a monastery with possessions so vast that its lands were worked by twenty thousand slaves. Here Alcuin was to spend the last years of his life, busier than ever, still in charge of a school, engaged in a multitude of literary projects, conducting a theological controversy, creating a model scriptorium for the copying of books, watching over the spiritual and physical well-being of the many monks in his charge, directing, admonishing and advising his former pupils all over Europe, and in constant correspondence with Charles's sister Gisla, with Charles's cousin Adalhard, with Charles's sons and daughters and with the other members of the court circle. Above all his letters poured out to Charles himself, to his "beloved David," for although he himself had so ardently desired to withdraw from the court, he missed the stimulus of Charles's presence and sometimes felt, with a touch of bitterness quite alien to his character, that he was rusticating at Tours.

Alcuin's epitaph for Hadrian spoke of the pope's zeal in beautifying the churches of Rome, of his generosity toward the poor, his pious care for his flock, his goodness and his assurance of salvation. It was written as if Charles himself were the author; Charles, speaking, says that he is bowed with sorrow and takes pride in linking his name with Hadrian's.

The distress at Charles's court over the death of Hadrian changed to consternation when it was learned who his successor was. The election of a new pope, Leo III, on the day of Hadrian's burial seemed to some, because of its speed and unanimity, a miracle. To Charles it must have looked more like a *coup d'état*. Although the biographer of Leo III testifies to the purity of his life, the alarm at the Frankish court suggests that he bore a much less savory reputation in Aachen.

Leo, conscious of his dependence on the good will of the Frankish king, and probably aware that he had enemies in Charles's court as well as in Rome, hastened to make an ostentatious display of his allegiance. In his letter to Charles announcing his election he sent the symbolic keys to the grave of St. Peter, the standard of the City of Rome and a promise of obedience and loyalty. Also he asked Charles to send an emissary to administer the oath of fidelity to the people of Rome.

Hadrian had never gone so far, and probably Charles preferred the former pope's obstinate insistence on his rights to Leo's obsequiousness. But good or bad, the office made the man, and Charles resolved to send to Leo the Avar spoils which had been set aside for Hadrian. Angilbert, who had been preparing to leave with the gifts, was well acquainted with the politics and personalities of Rome, which he had visited frequently as Charles's envoy. He could fulfill Leo's request and administer the oath of allegiance to the Roman people. But above all he had the personal authority to impress on the pope in conversation certain warnings which Charles felt were necessary.

Angilbert carried with him a letter of congratulations on the unanimity of Leo's election and on the pope's promise of humble obedience. This letter contained that definition of Charles's and the pope's respective tasks which has been referred to earlier: that Charles will defend the Church against heretics and pagans, while the pope must lift up his hands like Moses and pray for the success of the king's arms. The letter then continued in a vein that was, to say the least, strange considering that it was addressed to the supreme head of the Church:

"In your wisdom you will surely adhere everywhere to the canonical decrees and always follow the statutes of the Holy Fathers. May you be a shining example of perfect holiness. . . . May your light so shine before all men that they will see your good works and praise your Father Who is in Heaven."

As if this reminder to the pope were not blunt enough, Charles provided Angilbert with secret written rather than oral instructions (so that they could be produced, if necessary, in case the pope doubted that Angilbert was saying no more than what Charles had ordered him to say) which went a good deal further. The mere existence in writing of such sentiments must have been an unspeakable humiliation to Leo, for Angilbert was ordered:

"As far as the course of your conversation permits, and he prove amenable, zealously admonish our apostolic lord to be honorable in all his conduct, and especially to regard the holy canons. Remind him to govern the holy Church of God well. Repeat to him frequently how brief is the honor he now holds and how infinite shall be the duration of his reward if in such high office he does well. Ad-

vise him most urgently to put a stop to the heretical sale of offices
and the other abuses which, as you well know, we have frequently
complained of."

Simony had evidently existed under Hadrian; but the reference to
it here perhaps suggests that Charles thought the new pope himself
may have purchased his office. It is at any rate clear from these instructions to Angilbert that Charles had no great confidence in Leo.
It is also clear from subsequent events that the unanimity of the
pope's election was more apparent than real. Nevertheless, there is
no hint that Charles thought of deposing the pope and ordering a
new election. Charles was too good a son of the Church for that.
Moreover, Alcuin used his influence to the utmost in Leo's favor, for
Alcuin had—as he put it in a letter to Leo—always had the highest
regard for the "princes and pastors of the See of Rome." Underlying
Alcuin's attitude toward the pope was the seed of the doctrine of
papal infallibility, which was unofficially held in the Church through
much of the Middle Ages, although not to be made dogma for nearly
a thousand years. Although that doctrine refers specifically to the
pope's dogmatic pronouncements and not to his personal conduct,
the very phrase has always tended to confuse these two aspects.

Leo, for his part, did all in his power to reassure Charles and to
prove his reliability. The heresy of adoptianism was still flourishing
in Spain, Septimania and Aquitaine, in spite of its condemnation by
the Frankfurt synod. Felix had produced a new treatise which so
shocked Alcuin that he rushed off a letter to Charles before he had
even read it through. "Out of curiosity I ran through a few pages of
it," Alcuin wrote, "and found worse heresies and greater blasphemies
than anything I had read before in his writings." The arguments of
Felix were again so impressive that Alcuin felt it necessary to ask for
help. "I alone will not suffice to answer it," he wrote Charles, and
asked the king to send copies of the adoptianist treatise to the foremost theologians of the day—Patriarch Paulinus of Aquileia, Archbishop Richbod of Trier and Bishop Theodulf of Orléans—and to
Pope Leo.

Leo leaped at the chance to perform a service for Charles. He called
a synod at Rome to thrash out the problem of adoptianism. No less
than fifty-seven bishops, as well as a large number of priests and deacons, attended the sessions in St. Peter's—and, of course, produced a

vigorous excoriation of the heresy. Once more anathema was pronounced on Felix of Urgel if he refused to renounce his heretical
dogma; he was declared "condemned before the tribunal of God, excluded from the holy and apostolic Church of God, and alienated
from our fellowship."

But Felix was no more impressed by the decisions of this synod
than he had been by the deliberations at Frankfurt four years before.
He continued to win adherents at an alarming rate, and Charles became convinced that it was necessary to lay hands on the man and
make him repeat his recantation of 792. Bishop Laidrad of Lyons was
accordingly ordered to go to Spain and bring Felix back by hook or
crook. Laidrad was a Bavarian whose appointment as Bishop of Lyons
points up Charles's supranational and supraracial policies. The previous year Laidrad had accompanied Theodulf on a tour of inspection
through Provence and Septimania, visiting Vienne, Valence, Avignon,
Nimes, Narbonne and numerous other cities. He was, accordingly,
familiar with the area in which the adoptianist heresy was spreading,
and since at this time Theodulf was studying the new treatise by
Felix, the two men no doubt spent some time during their travels
discussing the entire question. Perhaps they also talked over the personality of Felix and decided that he must be approached with an
offer of safe-conduct and the assurance of an opportunity to present
his case in full before an assemblage of churchmen.

Laidrad succeeded in his delicate mission. He based his appeal to
Felix on the heretic's known love of disputation. In Charles's name
he promised that Felix would be guaranteed personal safety if he
came to Aachen, would be listened to respectfully and would be allowed to bring with him as many of his disciples as he cared to have
for support. On these conditions Felix took an oath to attend the
forthcoming council. Bravely, for he could not fail to remember
how he had been overborne by his opponents seven years before, Felix
kept his promise. And Charles kept his, which he had made through
Laidrad.

The synod, attended not only by bishops, priests and deacons but
also by the secular notables of the realm, met at Aachen in June 799
(possibly June 800, but this seems less likely). A great deal was at
stake; everyone sensed that the unity of the kingdom was bound up
in the unity of the Church. And although the Franks did not share
the passion of the Greeks and Spaniards for theological disputes, they

were men of their age, as concerned with religion as modern man is with politics.

In respectful silence, King Charles in their midst, they sat and listened while the Spanish ex-bishop set forth his views. Inevitably these were bolstered by scriptural and patristic quotations, but they culminated in an appeal to reason: Which was nobler, obedience to God or to a serf, a mere man, for that was what Christ had been, though a son of man illumined by the spirit of God?

Alcuin, who had been laboring diligently in the interval, with the aid of a whole secretariat of his pupils, now rose up to answer Felix. What novelties was this man introducing, bringing forth strange doctrines and sweetening them with citations from the Fathers like a sword smeared with honey? Where was his humility, where his obedience to the commandments of Christ? What impudence—to defy all the rest of Christianity and cling to his heretical doctrines in his little corner of the world! Did he claim divine revelation? Had God on some solitary mountain whispered the word "adoption" into his ear?

For six days the two men hurled arguments at each other. Alcuin had amassed new quotations from the Church Fathers, from Bishop Cyril and Pope Gregory, and even from questionably orthodox Origen. Some of these pronouncements were unfamiliar to Felix. By himself, in his remote Spanish province, surrounded by those whom he had converted, universally admired for the goodness of his life, Felix had been able to withstand all the epistolary blasts that came down on him from Tours, Aquileia and Orléans. But it is hard for any man to stand against the unanimous public opinion of his time and against its foremost spokesman. Face to face with Charles, whom he respected as his king and as a great benefactor of the Church, confronted by an audience whose hostility grew as the king showed his approval of Alcuin's and Paulinus of Aquileia's speeches, Felix must have realized—as he could not so long as he remained in Spain—that there was no hope of converting these men. By persisting in his belief he was only cutting himself and his followers off from the One Body of the Church. As a bishop who had obeyed the canons all his life, who did not hunt, hawk, fight or fornicate and who therefore had acquired a reputation almost of saintliness, the organizational and hierarchic spirit of the Church was strong in him. He could convince the simple priests and peasants of the Spanish and Aquitanian countryside, but he could make no headway with these heads of church and state. And if he did not yield, there was always the possibility that the secular power of the state might be used to suppress his heresy by force. There it sat, that secular power, embodied in the person of Charles, immovably opposed to his doctrines. Felix might court martyrdom for himself, but had he the right to involve his followers in the consequences of his convictions?

In the end he gave in, as he had done once before, as Charles had known he must. Beaten, he composed or signed a statement twice stressing the voluntary nature of his submission: he had come to the synod of his own free will, not compelled by violence, and had been convinced by argument, not by force. Now "by the grace of God and wholeheartedly I have returned to the universal Church," he declared. He confessed his regret for having stirred up dissension within the Church. To Alcuin he said that he had no hard feelings and was sincerely grateful for having been corrected in his error. Alcuin, never prone to examine motives and always ready, in his simpleness and goodness of heart, to accept the word of a penitent, wrote joyously to his friend Arno, now Archbishop of Salzburg: "He loves me very much, and all the hatred which he had against me has turned into sweet affection."

Charles was not so trusting. He ordered Bishop Laidrad to keep Felix under strict supervision at Lyons for the rest of his life. At the same time a group of preachers, headed by Laidrad, Abbot Benedict of Aniane and Bishop Nefridus of Narbonne, was sent into Aquitaine and the Spanish March. Armed with Alcuin's pamphlets against adoptianism, and above all with Felix's letter of recantation, they made reconverts by the thousands among bishops, priests, monks and laymen. Although Bishop Elipand at Toledo remained obdurate, he was too old to counter with missionary work of his own. Felix had been the soul of the adoptianist movement, and after his surrender the heresy swiftly declined. Spain had been saved for an orthodoxy that in future years was to outdo the rest of the Western world by its narrowness.

The question of religious orthodoxy was so important to Charles that he went through with this synod in spite of the disturbing news that had reached him from Rome just before it opened. In Rome the simmering hatred for Pope Leo III had boiled into open revolt. His conduct in office was so notorious that the pious Alcuin, on receiving a letter from Arno detailing some aspects of the pope's mis-behavior, hastened to burn the letter lest it fall into the wrong hands and provide fresh food for gossip.

Leo's meekness toward Charles and his exaggeratedly pro-Frankish policy also seem to have outraged the pride of the Romans. Com-parisons between Leo and the late Hadrian were inevitable, and it would be remembered that Hadrian had always held the interests of Rome herself foremost. In fact, the revolt against Leo came from a party of Roman nobles who had gathered around a nephew and a former notary of Hadrian, either one of whom might well have been considered a logical successor to the papacy. These men held high office in the Church; their names were Paschalis and Campulus. Mem-bers of the old aristocracy of Rome, they were the natural enemies of the low-born Leo. And the populace, apparently, were in sympathy with the aristocrats rather than with the pope who had emerged from their own class.

On April 25, 799, as Leo was proceeding on horseback to the church of that St. Lawrence who had been martyred by being roasted on a gridiron, Paschalis and Campulus joined the procession and rode with him. Concealing their intentions, they chatted amiably with him un-til, near the church, a band of their fellow conspirators burst out of ambush and fell upon the pope. The unarmed people in the pro-cession scattered in terror. Caught between Paschalis in front and Campulus behind, both of whom now turned on him, the pope had no chance to escape. To guard against any chance of mistaken identity, Campulus and Paschalis had not worn their chasubles, ex-plaining to the pope that they felt ill. The pope, in full ecclesiastical vestments between the two more plainly dressed men, was therefore instantly spotted. He was pulled from his horse, stripped of his robes and beaten so badly that he was left lying half dead. According to his own story, the plotters attempted to put out his eyes and cut out his tongue. Rumor, abetted by the partisans of the pope, swiftly transformed the attempt into actuality and declared that his sight and speech had been restored by a miracle. The story is confused, the details are obscure. Apparently the conspirators left the pope lying in the street, but afterward returned, took him to the monastery of St. Erasmus and held him prisoner there.

In the dead of night his chamberlain, Albinus, came with a rope and lowered the pope down the walls of the monastery. Leo fled outside the walls of the city, to the protection of St. Peter's. Rioting and civil war broke out in Rome. The opposition party pillaged the chamberlain's house. Charles's faithful Frankish Duke of Spoleto, Winigis, rushed to Rome with troops and carried Leo away to the safety of Spoleto.

Charles, when the news reached him, must have recalled the disorders in Rome during the first year of his reign, when the antipope Constantine, who had been installed in office by force, was removed by force to make way for the election of Pope Stephen III. At that time Charles had taken no action beyond sending Frankish ecclesiastics to attend the Roman synod which tried the antipope. At that time Charles, in office for only six months, the ruler of a small, truncated kingdom, had had no vital interests in Rome and no real power to intervene in Roman affairs, in spite of his title of Patrician of the Romans.

How utterly different was the situation now, thirty years later! Now he was the ruler of a vast empire. The people of Rome had taken an oath of loyalty to him, like all the rest of his subjects. His title of patrician was no longer meaningless; he could, if he wished, sit in judgment on the pope himself. Religious awe might make him reluctant to depose a pope, and yet he had never been one to evade responsibilities. With a clear consciousness of what his decision meant, with the understanding that he would never have done this to Hadrian, Charles ordered that the pope be brought before him. Leo was still pope, and Charles specified that as such he was to be "conducted honorably" and treated with respect. At the same time, he neatly balanced what might seem a prejudgment of the case by carrying out his intention to campaign in Saxony. The pope would be brought to him at his camp in Paderborn. Meanwhile, Charles consulted with his friends and advisers.

Alcuin's orthodox, conservative soul was stunned by the news of the rebellion against Leo and the attempt to mutilate him. "Men blind in their hearts have blinded their own Head," he wrote indignantly. Not for a moment did he consider that Charles had any course but to support the pope and punish the conspirators in Rome, so that the pope might be able to "serve God without fear."

His opinion, as always, weighed heavily with Charles, who was also inclined to back Leo out of another sort of orthodoxy. As king and head of state, as a ruler who had suppressed conspiracies against himself, Charles naturally had little sympathy for rebels. Although their cause might be just, their undermining of established authority was repugnant to him. Almost three years to the day before the attack on Pope Leo in Rome, King Ethelred of the Anglo-Saxon kingdom of Northumbria had been killed by his own people. When Charles heard of this he burst into a fury against the Northumbrians, calling them "treacherous, wicked people, murderers of their kings, worse than the heathen." The uprising against the pope struck him, similarly, as that basest of crimes: betrayal of a lord.

But in addition to sentiment there were practical reasons prompting him to throw the weight of his authority on the side of the pope. Leo had been compliant to his wishes before; now he would be completely at Charles's mercy, a puppet pope who would have no choice but to do Charles's bidding. If Charles sustained him in office, he could serve as the instrument for bringing about the fulfillment of Charles's own dreams, of the unvoiced needs of the peoples of his realm and of the ardently expressed hopes of the intellectuals in the court circle. These last sensed that a new era was about to begin, and longed for a dramatic act to crown that beginning. What else was Alcuin saying when he wrote to Charles:

"Hitherto there have been three persons in the highest position in the world. The first was that Apostolic Sublimity who rules as Vicar in the Chair of Saint Peter, and you have informed me of what has been done to him. The second is the imperial dignity and secular power of the Second Rome [i.e. Constantinople], and everyone is talking about how impiously its governor has been deposed, not by foreigners, but by his own fellow citizens. The third is the royal dignity in which you have been placed by the dispensation of our Lord Jesus Christ, so that you are ruler of the Christian people. Your power is more excellent than theirs, your wisdom more shining, your royal dignity more sublime. Behold, upon you alone rests the salvation of the churches of Christ."

What else was Theodulf saying when he called Charles "head of the world"? And Angilbert when he applied to Charles such terms as "august" and "pacific"—the very words which shortly afterward were to be incorporated into his new title? When these men reminded Charles that he already ruled over the "Christian empire" and the "Christian people" they were thinking hopefully of that union of a Christian with a Roman empire which had been the underlying conception of Augustine's *City of God*.

The practical steps that must be taken to achieve that union were on the minds of Charles and his advisers when Pope Leo arrived at the raw new town of Paderborn in Saxony, where perhaps the only amenities were the church Charles had built and rebuilt (after Saxons burned it) and the "palace" in which he was staying.

What memories of his childhood must have stirred in Charles as the pope drew near to Paderborn! Forty-five years ago Charles's father had sent him forth to meet Pope Stephen on that memorable occasion of the first visit of a pope to Frankland. Charles rounded the circle and completed the pattern by sending his own son, King Pepin of Italy—now a young man of twenty-two—at the head of a large military force to greet Pope Leo. A poetic fragment ascribed to Angilbert pictures the pope lifting his hands to heaven and praying fervently for the well-being of the Frankish people. Then he took Pepin into his arms and embraced him tenderly. They walked side by side to meet Charles, who had meanwhile ordered his army: "Come, you nobles, let us greet the pope as we are wont to go into battle!" Spears, helmets and javelins waved; shields clashed on shields like thunder. "The cavalry advances as to a charge; the trumpets blast out their brilliant fanfares; the ground trembles; the banners wave brightly above the host. The warriors are transported by the desire to hear the pope's voice; a fiery ardor enters the very marrow of their bones."

After the display and the charge, the army is lined up in a great circle, within which is a smaller circle of the clergy arranged in three choirs under the sacred banner of the cross. In the center of these two circles, towering above all, stands Charles, awaiting the pope. He is dressed in gleaming armor and wears a golden helmet on his head.

The pope is suitably impressed by "the glorious spectacle of that vast host of so many nationalities, so different in speech, dress and arms"—for Louis is there also, with Aquitanian troops, as well as Pepin with his Lombards. Young Charles, with his Neustrian Franks, has more serious business to attend to; he is away in the north receiving Saxon hostages from the Abodrites.

Charles comes forward, kneels respectfully before the pope, then rises to embrace him warmly. Hand in hand the two walk past the kneeling soldiers, and the pope blesses them. Clergy and pope chant,

"Glory to God in the highest." Then Charles and the pope together enter the church, where the pope celebrates a solemn pontifical Mass. After Mass Charles invites the pope to a banquet in his wooden palace. The great hall is adorned with embroidered tapestries (which Charles would have brought with him; these were not permanent appointments of a residence of minor importance). The chairs are ornamented with purple and gold. At the meal the king and pope sit side by side, drinking strong Falernian wine out of golden goblets.

Quite aside from Charles's fondness for a good show, all this pageantry had a purpose. Leo had just come from the "golden citadels of Rome" (Charles's own phrase), a city with a history of fifteen and a half centuries behind it, a city still of great monuments and luxurious civilized living. Paderborn, in the heart of the Saxon wilderness, had not existed a quarter of a century before and was still more of a great camp than a town. It was all the more important, therefore, for Charles to impress Leo with the power, wealth and luxury at his disposal. Leo must understand that even on the fringes of the Frankish domains, even in the midst of a military campaign, Charles the king lived in *imperial* splendor. Even though Leo came as a suppliant, as a pope who was not safe in his own city, he still represented a tremendous moral force. He possessed, in fact, the only power in the West comparable to that of Charles. Although Charles could if he wished issue orders to the pope, he preferred to enlist Leo's cooperation. The spectacular reception of Leo at Paderborn is good evidence that by now Charles had already made up his mind, or been convinced by Alcuin's arguments, that the pope must be supported. Besides, what were the charges against Leo? Alcuin mentions "adultery and perjury." Certainly Charles was no one to judge harshly any sort of sexual misdemeanors, and he was enough of a statesman to understand that a ruler could not always be bound by the truth. He rarely sought to impose on others disciplines he himself could not accept: his treatment of his daughters is a case in point.

The pope stayed in Paderborn for more than three months. Meanwhile Charles sent for Arno, who at the moment was engaged in missionary work among the Slavs of Dalmatia. Arno had been in Rome the previous year to receive his archbishop's pallium and had become aware of the seething discontent among the populace. He had, in fact, been in some danger personally and on his return had disobeyed Charles's orders to go directly to Dalmatia because he considered his

information on the Roman situation of such importance that he had
best report to Charles first. Now, with the most vital problem of his
career facing him, Charles wanted Arno's advice. He also needed
the Bavarian to conduct the pope back to Rome. Arno had the knowledge and the prestige to accomplish such a delicate mission successfully.

Arno, who was one of Alcuin's closest friends, had garnered some
damaging evidence against Leo. Nevertheless he was wholly of Alcuin's mind: orthodoxy must prevail and the pope must be defended
against all his enemies. Alcuin was at this time bombarding both
Arno and Charles with letters urging this course. These letters constituted replies to a strong party at Charles's court which argued that
the pope must be deposed. There were others at court who wanted
Leo to take an oath to clear himself. We do not know who these
anti-Leo partisans were; perhaps among them were those Irish intellectuals like Clement, Dungal and Dicuil who had lately come into
favor with Charles. Along with their own peculiar method of calculating the date of Easter they might also have brought the traditional
antipapal sentiments of the Irish Church. Alcuin, at any rate, was
horrified by these suggestions. The pope was appointed "to judge, not
to be judged," he insisted, and he urged Arno to "labor for the authority of the Holy See."

At the same time Alcuin was writing repeatedly to Charles suggest-
ing that he abandon the war against the "unspeakable Saxons," point-
ing out that it was keeping him from more important tasks: "to travel,
govern, do justice, renew churches, defend the oppressed, make laws."
In pursuing the lesser gain Charles might lose the greater, Alcuin
said—a double-edged phrase having reference both to the salvation
of Saxon souls and to Alcuin's hopes that God might "multiply"
Charles's crowns.

These letters of Alcuin's provide some hint of what was discussed
between king and pope during that long summer in Saxony, for no
word of their conversations is recorded by the incurious or discreet
annalists of the time. Certainly they talked about the "vacancy" in
the throne of the Roman Empire—for was not Irene's assertion that
she, a woman, was Roman emperor on the face of it preposterous?
So Charles and his contemporaries thought, and Pope Leo, who was
eager to clarify remaining ambiguities in his legal status with regard
to Constantinople, agreed heartily. For Leo's predecessor, Hadrian,

had engaged in such a bewildering series of breaks and *rapprochements* with the Empire that Leo could not be sure to what extent the papacy had renounced its original allegiance to Constantinople.

It must therefore have been very welcome to Leo when, toward the end of his visit, an ambassador arrived from Michael, the Patrician of Sicily, which was then imperial territory. Michael was evidently ready to switch Sicily from the Byzantine to the Frankish camp if Charles could send troops to drive out the imperial garrison there. For Leo such a weakening of the Empire's power in Italy would strengthen his hand against his own enemies within Rome, who would naturally be turning to the Byzantines for aid against the pro-Frankish pope. An invasion of Sicily also appealed to Charles; the difficulty was that he had no navy and that at this juncture he preferred not to become involved in open war with the Empire. If he were to take the great step that all his friends were urging on him, and to which his own ambitions inclined him, he would need at least the passive acquiescence of the "Emperor" Irene.

He had an additional reason for a temperate policy toward Constantinople. His entire eastern front had just been seriously weakened by the tragic loss of two of his finest generals. Gerold, his commander in Bavaria, had been assassinated in strange circumstances while marshaling his army for battle against the Avars. "Killed by persons unknown as he rode along the line inspiring his men," wrote Einhard. And Eric, the famous Duke of Friuli, the general who had first breached the Ring of the Avars and brought the "Hunnish store" back to Aachen, had fallen victim to an ambush set by Dalmatian Croats near Fiume. Like Roland at Roncesvalles, Eric had died fighting, hitting back at the enemy until his shield was shattered, his lance splintered and his body pierced by arrows.

The entire court mourned the death of these men. Paulinus of Aquileia, whose territory Eric had defended and extended, composed an elegy in Eric's honor in which he cursed the place where the hero fell: No more must the refreshing dew or the fructifying rain fall upon this coast; henceforth let no purple flower bloom, no grain spring from the soil, no grapevine wind around the elm; let the fig tree wither, the pomegranate fail to grow. . . . Alcuin gloomily saw the tidings as a sign of more evils to come. And Charles himself must have shared the sorrow of these others, for Gerold had been his beloved Hildigard's brother, and Eric in many respects a spiritual brother of his—a warrior "of subtle mind" with a bent for the contemplative and religious life. That these men should have fallen just now, when his relations with the Byzantine Empire were certain to become increasingly complex and dangerous, was indeed a bad sign. But where Alcuin was characteristically intimidated, Charles resolved to go forward with his plans.

These plans involved restoring Leo to the full powers of his office, seeing to it that the pope was safe in Rome and then receiving from Leo a *quid pro quo*. Most of the details of the program that was carried out with such dispatch within one short month during the winter of the following year must have been decided between Charles and Leo during this summer at Paderborn. The Saxon land, which two hundred years hence was to be the cradle of Holy Roman Emperors, unwittingly and unwillingly fostered the creation of the first of them.

When all the arrangements for the future had been settled, as far as it was possible to do so a year in advance, and when the summer's campaign in Saxony was over so that troops were available in case they should be needed in Italy, Charles dismissed the pope. Escorted by Archbishops Arno of Salzburg and Hildibald of Cologne, and no doubt by a sizable body of Frankish soldiery, Leo returned to Rome. He arrived there at the end of November 799. Whether the rejoicing in the city was as widespread as the official accounts would have us believe is certainly open to question; at any rate the people of Rome continued hostile to Leo for many years afterward. However, he and his Frankish bodyguards were in firm control of the situation now. Shortly after his return a commission of Frankish envoys, bishops and counts both, heard the charges against him. Since the trial took more than a week, it is strange to read that Paschalis, Campulus and the other conspirators "had nothing to say." Evidently they thought they had a good case, or they would have fled from Rome, not stayed to face the Frankish court. But the decision of the court reflected the judgment that had already been passed at Paderborn by Charles himself. The pope was declared not guilty, and his accusers were arrested and sent to Frankland for Charles himself to deal with.

Charles, meanwhile, had returned to Aachen to prepare for the tremendous year before him. He was no sooner settled in the capital when a monk arrived from Jerusalem bringing the blessings of the

Patriarch of the Holy City and various relics from the sepulcher of the Lord. Here was convincing evidence indeed of how far the fame of the Frankish king had spread. Stimulated and delighted by the tales the monk told of the holy places, which so few of his generation had seen, and of the wonders of the great Moslem cities of Bagdad and Damascus, Charles resolved to keep up this fortunate contact. He was also "moved to compassion" by the monk's stories of the poverty and sufferings of the Christians of the Near East, and promised to send money to them. Actually the lot of these Christians was probably not too bad under the tolerant Moslem regime of Harun al-Rashid.

When, after Christmas, the Palestinian monk asked leave to go home, Charles sent along with him a priest of the court named Zacharias, who was entrusted also with gifts for the Patriarch of Jerusalem and for the various holy places.

Around the middle of March Charles left Aachen to begin a tour of inspection of his realm—the first in many years. He visited the Channel coast, which was beginning to suffer from raids by the Northmen, for the great period of Viking expansion was just starting. Whether these Northmen came from Norway, or whether they were Danes serving King Göttrik (the successor to Sigifrid) and pursuing a deliberate policy of harrying the Frankish kingdom, it is impossible to say. Einhard classifies them all as Danes. Probably sheer adventurers and members of Göttrik's navy were both involved. They were raiding not only the North Sea and Channel coasts but places as far south as Aquitaine. Charles set up a system of watchtowers and armed guards along the coasts and commenced the building of a fleet. His interests were expanding into the seas, which he had neglected during the greater part of his reign. Now, as a Continental conqueror must, he was discovering the importance of the North Sea, the Atlantic and above all the Mediterranean. He also sent Frankish troops to occupy the islands of Minorca and Majorca, both in order to save the inhabitants who had appealed for help against Moorish pirates and in order to protect the coasts of Gaul and the Spanish March. Charles was beginning what would become a prolonged effort on the part of the Christian nations to wrest control of the Mediterranean from the Saracens. That effort did not end until a thousand years later when, at the beginning of the nineteenth century, the fledgling United States Navy broke the power of the Barbary pirates.

While on the coast Charles relaxed for a while and tried his hand at ocean fishing, a sport new to him. Then he turned toward Abbeville to celebrate Easter at the Monastery of St. Riquier, as the guest of Angilbert, whom he had appointed lay abbot there ten years earlier. He prayed before Angilbert's large collection of relics, viewed the new church his son-in-law had built and the fine library to which Angilbert alone had added some two hundred volumes. Alcuin came here, too, in spite of his arthritis and his hitherto cool relations with Angilbert. The occasion was not purely social, we may imagine. Certainly one of the chief topics of conversation must have been Charles's forthcoming visit to Rome.

From St. Riquier Charles traveled again along the coast to Rouen. Here a messenger from Louis met him, bearing a request that he visit Louis in Aquitaine and see for himself how his son was handling the subkingdom. But Charles could not overcome his aversion to entering Aquitaine, with its still-painful memories of the Spanish disaster and Roncesvalles. Instead he asked Louis to meet him at Tours, where he was going to continue his talks with Alcuin and to pray at the grave of Frankland's most important saint. Both his elder sons, young Charles and Pepin, were already with him. Liutgard had come also, and probably his daughters, so that the entire family was reunited at Tours.

These conferences with his sons, and with his chief advisers and closest friends, suggest the pressure of impending events, the epoch-making decisions that were being taken. The visits to the shrines of saints, the prayers before relics, indicate the mood that Charles was in at this time—a mood of dedication, of determination and confidence, but also of humility and a desire for divine help. At a time when he might well have been filled with pride and self-assurance, he consulted longest with the man who, of all his friends, was in character and in conduct the soul of humility. That man, of course, was Alcuin.

He lingered longer at Tours than he had expected, for here the beautiful Liutgard fell ill and suddenly died. What was it about him that no woman could survive long at his side? The burning energy that had sent him prowling through the years up and down his whole realm, and beyond its borders, that had carried his power across the whole of western Europe, seemed to consume wives as though they were fuel to stoke the fires of empire. He seems to have fallen into a deep depression from which Alcuin attempted to lift him by quoting the words of the philosopher Anaxagoras on being informed of the death of his son: "I knew I had begotten a mortal."

But even sorrow could not deter Charles now. After the funeral of Liutgard he continued the royal progress and paid a visit to the third among his closest friends, Bishop Theodulf of Orléans.

The consultations were then over. Charles had obtained what advice the best minds among his circle could give him, and he had seen that his lands were at peace. At the national assembly, held that August in Mainz, he could announce that he was departing for Rome to settle the case of the pope and the conspirators who had attacked him, to look to the affairs of the rest of Italy and to punish Duke Grimoald of Benevento for his defection from Frankish overlordship. This last gave Charles a pretext to take a sizable army with him to Italy. Nothing was said at Mainz about the real purpose of the expedition. It would not do for Charles to forget that for his subjects in Frankland he was King of the Franks, no less and no more.

Now at last Charles was ready to set out on the road to Rome. This was to be his fourth and his last visit to the city that was, Alcuin had recently reminded him, "the onetime mistress of the world."

CHAPTER SEVENTEEN

Carolus Augustus a Deo Coronatus

ON THE way to Rome Charles stopped off at Ravenna for a week. Here, in the old capital of the Exarchate, he could receive reports on the state of his eastern borders. Here, too, he could gather courage for what he was about to do by reflecting on another great German who had ruled all Italy from this city: Theoderic. He gazed on the equestrian statue of Theoderic and exclaimed that he had never seen its like. Then, with Pepin in charge of the army, he continued south along the coast to Ancona. Here Charles and Pepin parted. Pepin went south with the troops to lead a punitive raid against Grimoald. Charles crossed the Apennines to Rome. A sizable body of troops went with him. The oxcarts that followed in his train were heavily laden with silver and gold.

The humility, this time, was all on the side of the pope. When Charles, after riding down lanes of singing and cheering pilgrims and citizens, reached the steps of St. Peter's he swung from his horse and strode up to greet the pope. No falling on his knees and kissing each step this time. Charles was coming to this city as master. And the pope, although restored to office, was still under a cloud. The investigation held the year before by the Frankish envoys had scarcely satisfied the Roman nobles.

The rehabilitation of the pope proved to be far more difficult than Charles had expected. He called a full-scale synod to examine the charges against Leo, and the Roman people witnessed the tremendous scandal of a pope on trial. For the public also was admitted to watch the throng of archbishops, bishops, abbots and counts, both Frankish and Roman, deliberate the pope's case.

Campulus, Paschalis and the other conspirators had been brought back from Frankland to present their charges. Their sympathizers in

Rome must also have testified against the pope, for the trial lasted a full three weeks. The evidence seems to have been so incriminating that Charles could not persuade the synod to pronounce a clear-cut verdict in the pope's favor, although they also did not condemn him. The Frankish annals are undoubtedly covering up when they assert that no one wanted to give evidence against the pope.

This "hung jury" was an unforeseen embarrassment. While Arno (in spite of his secret information on Leo's conduct), Theodulf, Riculf and the other Franks vigorously defended the pope, members of the Roman clergy argued that he had already compromised himself too gravely. Charles found the affair slipping out of his hands. In desperation he resorted to the compromise that had been suggested the year before at Aachen. The pope would have to clear himself by taking an oath—this procedure being quite in accord with the legal concepts of the age. It was all very well for Alcuin, far away in Tours (he had been too ill to risk the long journey to Rome), to denounce such a proposal as an insult to the dignity of the papal office. But some dramatic act was needed to restore confidence in the spiritual head of Christendom.

On the twenty-third of December, in the presence of Charles, the assembled synod, and as many people as could crowd into St. Peter's, Pope Leo mounted the pulpit and swore to his innocence. He said:

"It is well known, dearest brethren, that wicked men have risen against me and *attempted* to mutilate me, and that they have raised grave charges against me. The most gracious and illustrious King Charles has come to this city with his bishops and notables to investigate this matter. Therefore, not acting out of compulsion but of my own free will, I, Leo, Pope of the Holy Roman Church, declare myself before God, who knows my conscience, and before Saint Peter, Prince of the Apostles, in whose basilica we are gathered, that I have not committed or caused to be committed the heinous crimes of which I have been accused. I take this step of my own free will, in order to remove all suspicion—although there is no such requirement in the canons of the Church and although I do not wish to make a precedent of this or to impose upon my successors or upon our brothers and fellow bishops any such rule."

Whereupon Charles and all the clergy loudly sang the ancient "*Te Deum laudamus*" and praised God, the Virgin Mary, St. Peter and all the saints of God for having preserved their pope sound in body and soul. And then, to add to the pageantry of a day which for all its ambiguities lifted a burden from the conscience of Christendom, the priest Zacharias arrived in Rome. He had accomplished his mission to Jerusalem successfully and had with him two monks sent by the Patriarch of the Holy City. These monks had brought for Charles a banner and the keys to the Holy Sepulcher and to the city of Jerusalem. There is certainly the suggestion of skillful staging in this auspicious omen. Charles was now the acknowledged master of the two most important centers of the Christian faith.

Pepin, meanwhile, had been ordered to return from the Beneventan front so that he would be present in Rome on Christmas Day—ostensibly for the anointment of his elder brother Charles as king. Final preparations were made for the event at which the now "purified" pope would preside. There can be little doubt that Charles himself had a hand in organizing the ceremony which then unfolded with the smoothness of a well-rehearsed play.

On that Christmas Day, the first of the new century, the great nave and the four vast side aisles of St. Peter's basilica were filled with a motley throng of Romans, Franks, Bavarians, Lombards, Septimanian Goths, Pyrenean Basques and even Anglo-Saxons and Greeks. Close to the altar were Charles's daughters and sons (except Louis) and Charles himself—for the second time in his life wearing the long Roman tunic and cloak, bound with a golden belt, and Roman sandals studded with jewels. On the altar before him, glittering with the light from thousands of candles, reposed a magnificent golden crown. Silken hangings, golden censers and solid-silver candelabra reminded all of the wagonloads of treasure that Charles's men had brought back from the Ring of the Avars. And in that reminder was implicit the dignity he had attained to: that of greatest lord in the Western world, converter of the pagan, tamer of the barbarian.

The High Mass proceeded. Charles knelt in prayer. Was he weary, worried, elated, proud? We cannot know, and it would be impertinent to try to guess the thoughts of such a man at such a moment. He rose to his feet. Leo III stepped forward, lifted the golden crown from the altar and placed it on his head. The basilica rang as the Romans shouted: "*Carolo Augusto, a Deo coronato, magno et pacifico imperatori Romanorum, vita et victoria!*" ("Long life and victory to Charles Augustus, crowned by God the great and pacific Emperor of the Romans!")

Three times they roared the acclamation.

Pope Leo fell at Charles's feet and kissed the hem of his cloak, as was the custom at the Byzantine court.

After a lapse of three and a quarter centuries there was once more a Roman emperor of the West.

Then young Charles was crowned and anointed king of, so to speak, Old Frankland, this act sanctifying the appointment his father had made some ten years before.

There is no mention in our texts of the part, if any, played by the Franks, Lombards, Bavarians, Saxons and other "barbarians" who were present in St. Peter's that day. The Romans hailed Charles; the Romans chose an emperor of the Romans and did so in the prescribed legal form. For the acclamation was the essence of the ceremony; the coronation by the pope was no more than the cue. Roman senators participated in that acclamation! For the Roman Senate still existed, although its functions had been so reduced that it was really no more than the municipal government of Rome.

Nor was the idea of an emperor so strange to the Romans. Until recently they had been living under the rule of a Roman emperor, although his residence was Constantinople and his actual power in Rome was negligible. Now, according to the theory that had been zealously popularized by Frankish and papal propagandists, the throne at Constantinople was vacant (since the person nominally in possession of it was a mere woman). What was more logical, then, than for the Romans to reassert their ancient rights and make themselves an emperor? And how flattering this was to the Romans' pride! Accepting the crown of empire at their hands was by far the most inspired step Charles could have taken to reconcile the Romans to Frankish rule and to their pro-Frankish pope whom they had tried to depose.

Perhaps this—that the day was uniquely a Roman holiday—provides a clue to the mystery surrounding the coronation of Charles. For his biographer Einhard records that Charles "so disliked the title of Emperor and Augustus that he affirmed he would not have entered the church that day, even though it was so high a church festival, if he had known what the pope intended to do." This startling statement has been subjected to endless examination and interpretation. If Charles actually said it—and Einhard is not always trustworthy— what could he possibly have meant? Had he intended to crown himself, and did Leo forestall him and place the crown on his head in order to magnify the prestige of the papacy? The interpretation falls because it accepts one part of Einhard's statement and rejects the other—namely, that Charles "disliked the title." Moreover, the words of the acclamation, "crowned by God," imply the mediation of the pope.

Was Charles in fact unwilling to accept the imperial crown, and had the pope outwitted him, creating an emperor because only an emperor could legally judge the conspirators of the antipapal party? This "surprise theory," which is based directly on Einhard's words, has been accepted by many historians. It has been worked out in innumerable variations, with the most refined subtleties of reasoning, the most careful collation of sources. Yet it seems hardly tenable in the light of all the evidence that at least a year of planning went into the preparation of that Christmas Day ceremony. Was there, then, no meaning at all to the allusions to imperial dignity in the letters and poems of Alcuin, Theodulf and Angilbert? No meaning to Leo's long stay at Paderborn the year before? And if the coronation by Leo was unexpected, how is it that Alcuin in his letters showed no surprise?

A good many students of the question have considered Alcuin the moving spirit behind Charles's assumption of the imperial title, and a few have even held the preposterous theory that the pope plotted with Alcuin and other Frankish nobles behind Charles's back. Others have dismissed Einhard's statement on the ground that it was a mere phrase of modesty, akin to the convention that in the early Middle Ages required a bishop to run away from the people who elected him and to hide, protesting his unworthiness for the office. Or that, it might be added, requires a presidential candidate in the United States to disclaim any such aspirations.

The question can never be definitely settled. Possibly Einhard put those words into Charles's mouth because he was troubled by the "Roman holiday" aspect of the coronation. Einhard was one of the few native Franks among Charles's intellectual circle, and it is noteworthy that in his biography he consistently pictures Charles as a German *Volkskönig*—a king embodying the spirit of the Franks, close to his people, dressing in the Frankish national costume, concerned with the Frankish language and songs, taking a simple, direct, paternal interest in his people. Einhard does not like to think of his master as a remote, autocratic, awe-inspiring Roman emperor living hemmed in by ceremony, inaccessible to the common people. And it is possible that this feeling of his was shared by a good many Franks. For the King of the Franks to rule over a Frankish Empire was one thing; quite another for him suddenly to become Roman emperor. There was no love lost between Franks and Romans. What now if the new emperor decided to rule his old kingdom from Rome? From being the masters of Europe the Franks would become subject to absentee rule. And would not their king himself ultimately be corrupted by Roman "timidity, avarice, luxury, lying, viciousness"? Were they always to kiss the king's knee, or even his foot, instead of standing before him?

In fact Charles was quite aware that the Franks felt uneasy about his new title. He carefully continued to style himself "King of the Franks and Lombards," although these titles might well be considered as contained within the supreme office of emperor. He never again donned Roman dress. And after this visit he never again set foot in Rome.

Whatever the explanation for Einhard's amazing statement that Charles did not desire the imperial title, the surprise theory is certainly disposed of by Charles's actions immediately after the coronation. For he showed his pleasure by raining gifts on the churches of Rome: a silver table, golden vases, a golden chandelier weighing fifty pounds, set with precious stones, golden chalices, a cross set with sapphires, an altar, a paten of gold weighing twenty-two pounds, and so on; the list in the *Life of Leo III* takes up two pages. He distributed three thousand pounds of silver among the poor of Rome. It does not seem likely that he produced these gifts on the spur of the moment. They had been brought over the Alps from Frankland for an occasion of more importance than the anointment of his son Charles.

The significance of this anointment of young Charles, incidentally, has been overlooked by many commentators. Charles himself had already made this son a king. If he now sought confirmation of that appointment in the form of a ceremony performed by the pope, he obviously had no objection to the pope's taking so important a role. Papal anointment was entirely in accord with Charles's religious ideas and with the tradition that had been established by his father half a century before. How, then, can it be thought that Charles was unwilling to have the pope give him the imperial crown? He had nothing to fear from Leo, who was completely at his mercy.

Let us assume, then, that Einhard was either mistaken or deliberately falsifying the record and that Charles never said he did not want the imperial crown. It is a fair assumption, on the evidence, that he did want it, that it represented the culmination of his ambitions and that he willingly accepted the burdens and responsibilities of the title—although perhaps with misgivings and a humility which was increasing in him as he approached old age.

A few days after the coronation Charles, in his new capacity, tried Paschalis, Campulus and the other conspirators against Pope Leo. Under Roman law they were guilty of the crime of lese majesty, and Charles condemned them to death. Perhaps at Charles's secret instigation the pope interceded for them, asking mercy, which the emperor granted. They were sent into exile in Frankland. Fifteen years later, after the deaths of both Charles and Leo, the new pope, Stephen IV, strengthened his position among the Roman nobility by asking Louis the Pious to release them.

For the rest of the winter Charles busied himself establishing his authority in Rome. He implicitly washed his hands of Leo personally (though not politically) by making sure that no pope could ever again be installed by a twenty-four-hour election. Henceforth he as emperor would have the right to revise the election of the pope. Consecration of a new pope could take place only with the emperor's written consent and in the presence of imperial missi.

Charles also began sending his missi throughout the papal territory—a clear indication that he intended to exercise direct rule in the "patrimony of St. Peter." He compensated himself for his lavish expenditures by collecting taxes, so that the pope later complained that his own dukes were unable to gather their regular taxes. He displayed his sovereignty by issuing decrees, sitting in judgment, deposing and punishing papal judges, appointing others. He had the pope and all the people of Rome take a new oath of allegiance to him as emperor. He issued new imperial coins. He required that documents be dated by the years of his reign. Leo's misrule had left him much work to do, but there was probably another motive for his long stay in Rome. He would want to study the records stored in such abundance in the city, especially in the papal archives. He would want to read and discuss the history of Rome—to learn, in short, how an emperor was expected to behave. Although he personally continued to practice

Frankish simplicities, there was to be henceforth a marked increase in ceremoniousness at his court.

It was hard for him to break away from this city which he loved and which now had given him the ultimate honor in the Christian world. He waited also because he was anxious to learn the reaction of the Byzantines to his taking the imperial title. He seems, too, to have hesitated to return to Frankland, as if in doubt about the reception his Franks would give him.

But he dared not stay away too long. From Aachen he knew he could rule Rome; he did not think he could rule Frankland from Rome. And so, after Easter, he set out for home, moving slowly through Italy and continuing to make his personal presence felt in the papal possessions, in Spoleto, in Ravenna. While he traveled, as if nature wished to prove to the people of Italy that an earth-shaking event had taken place in Rome, a tremendous earthquake destroyed whole towns the length and breadth of the peninsula and caused the roof of St. Paul's basilica in Rome to cave in.

When Charles reached Ravenna he gazed again on the gilded bronze statue of Theoderic seated on a charger, bearing his buckler and brandishing a lance in his right hand. And suddenly Charles gave orders that the huge statute should be transported somehow across the Alps, to be set up in the middle of his courtyard at Aachen. He would carry back with him the most impressive symbol he had seen of imperial glory.

Perhaps it was on this return journey to Aachen that Charles, intoxicated with success, first conceived the project of uniting the entire Christian world under his scepter. The news that his Aquitanian armies had at last, after a prolonged siege, succeeded in taking Barcelona, and that ambassadors from Caliph Harun al-Rashid were bringing him messages of friendship and magnificent gifts, raised his self-confidence to the point where nothing seemed impossible. The woman who reigned in Constantinople called herself the Roman Emperor. He was now her equal, Emperor and Augustus. Eastern and Western Empire were twain and one like man and wife.

Charles sent an embassy to the Empress Irene requesting her hand in marriage!

He was free to do so. To Charles, who looked on himself as an instrument of God, the recent death of Liutgard must have seemed an act of Providence, part of a divine plan to unite once more after

five centuries the sundered halves of the Roman Empire. Since Liutgard's death Charles had given rein more than ever before in his life
to his weakness for women. He had taken the Maltegards, Gerswindas,
Reginas, Adalhaids, and the unnamed others, to his bed. But he had
refrained from marrying any of them. He could marry once more and
rule a greater empire than any Roman emperor before him, for he
had conquered *Germania*. And Irene, for all her fifty years, was reputedly still one of the most beautiful women in the world. At the
same time, marriage to her would establish without question the
legitimacy of his title—which the Byzantines would otherwise probably not recognize. It was hard for Charles, as for all his contemporaries, to overcome the tradition of centuries. Under that tradition
there was only one legitimate Roman emperor in the world: the one
who reigned at Constantinople. Charles longed to have his new title
ratified by that emperor.

Irene, for her part, was romantically tempted by the idea. In all
the years since the death of her husband Leo she had withheld herself
from any man. For all that she had the body of a courtesan, she was
espoused to power and had feared to share her rule with a man. Her
chief ministers were eunuchs. But now, her empire beset from without by Arabs and Slavs, her position assailed from within by the
eternal intriguers of the Byzantine court, she needed the support that
a man could give, and the might that Frankish armies would provide.
And as a woman she was attracted by all that she had heard of
Charles, by his physical strength, his intellectual attainments and his
genius as ruler and conqueror.

But for the very reasons that the plan of such a marriage appealed
to her, it was unwelcome to all who held power under her at the
Byzantine court. Her favorites, no less than her enemies, were not
minded to accept a foreign master. The plot against her, long brewing, now found general support, and a sudden palace revolution deposed Irene and elevated a general named Nicephorus to the throne.
With tears in his eyes, it is said, the new emperor appeared before the
empress the following morning, apologized to her and protested that
the uprising had taken place against his will. Irene, tired, perhaps,
of the unending battle for position, put up no resistance; she even
turned over the hidden treasure to Nicephorus and asked only that
she be permitted to live in the Eleutherion palace. But Constantinople
stirred restively; the empress was popular, and the people were ready

to move to defend her. Nicephorus dared not keep his promise, even if he wished to, and Irene was sent into exile on the lonely island of Prinkipos. Even there the new ruler felt that she was too near to Constantinople, and she was later sent to Lesbos, where she died. Her body returned from exile by the same route—first to Prinkipos, then to Constantinople—and the woman who had blinded her own son was ultimately hailed as a martyr and canonized. After all, she had restored the images!

The overthrow and death of Irene burst the bubble of Charles's grand, if somewhat fantastic, plan to unite the two empires. Fantastic because, given the conditions of the time, so large an empire could not have been viable. Communications were poor; a year was required for ambassadors to go and come between Constantinople and Aachen. The great Roman roads of antiquity had been crumbling for centuries, and many more years than Charles had at his disposal in the remainder of his life would have been needed to rebuild them. Empire means urban culture and flourishing commerce; Europe's great cities had shrunk to the size of small towns, and her economy was now largely agricultural and autarchic, although trade had by no means entirely died out. Above all, neither Rome nor Constantinople had unrestricted control of the Mediterranean, and without the Inland Sea true imperial power in Europe was unthinkable.

Nevertheless, Charles's "Restoration of the Empire," as he called it on his new coins, was far from meaningless. While the peoples in his Western Empire still did not have that sense of unity as Roman citizens which had been one of the most striking characteristics of the old Roman Empire, a beginning had at least been made in creating oneness out of diversity. Europe was closer to being united than it would ever be again. To the glamour and the grandeur of Rome had been added the universality of the Catholic Church. The new empire was in theory at least St. Augustine's Rome, the Christian Empire, which for the sake of the very catholicity of the Church required a temporal as well as a spiritual head.

As a Christian empire it differed fundamentally from the Byzantine absolutism of Constantinople. Its emperor recognized that he was bound by unalterable laws not of his or any man's making. He considered that he had been "crowned by God" for the sake of the people's welfare, that he was responsible to God for their peace, prosperity and salvation. In Charles's day, that is, the phrase "by the grace of God" was an expression of humility, not of arrogance. His was therefore a monarchy limited by a respect for divine and human law. Such a monarchy had all the faults and evil potentialities of any benevolent despotism, but under Charles himself benevolence predominated over despotism. At this time the chief danger to the lives and liberties of the people was the power of the great nobles, not of the king. Charles's accession to empire temporarily checked the growth of that power. Feudalism was set back, though not for long; the psychological and economic forces that were fostering it could not in the long run be withstood.

The conception of a limited Christian monarchy coincided with the Germanic theory of a king or tribal leader bound by the law of the tribe. While the Franks had put by the democratic traditions that survived among the Saxons, they had by no means accepted unlimited absolutism. Now that he had become emperor, Charles hastened to reassure his people that he did not intend to impose an alien despotism on them. One of his first acts as emperor was that of a purely Frankish king: he ordered the codification of the two basic laws of the Franks, the Salic and the Ripuarian.

He also continued his efforts to win formal recognition of his new title from Nicephorus. His envoys, Bishop Jesse of Amiens and Count Helmgaud, had been waiting in Constantinople when the palace revolution that overthrew Irene took place. Nicephorus sent ambassadors of his own back to Frankland with them, and a peace pact was drawn up at Aachen. In return for peace Charles demanded acceptance by Nicephorus as "brother emperor." Negotiations dragged on, but Nicephorus hesitated for a long time to recognize the existence of a Western Roman Empire. In the interval Charles did what he could to apply pressure—a moderate pressure so that Nicephorus would not be driven into implacable hostility. Charles saw to it that Pepin kept making stabs into Beneventan territory. But he did not push the war there because he feared that total conquest of Benevento would be too great a blow to the Byzantines. The threat of such conquest was more important to him. And at the same time he cultivated the friendship of Harun al-Rashid—again posing a threat: the possibility of an alliance that would crush Byzantium between the Arabs on the east and the Franks on the west. Not that Charles had any intention of joining Saracens in a war against Christians, but he was quite content that this should appear to be his aim.

CHAPTER EIGHTEEN

Reforms

CALIPH HARUN AL-RASHID, who was to be immortalized in the *Arabian Nights* as was Charles in the Charlemagne Romances, ruled over an empire so civilized and so brilliant that by comparison all of Europe seemed a primitive agricultural community. Its capital city of Bagdad, only forty years old, already numbered a population of hundreds of thousands. Built on the broad Tigris River, it satisfied the desert dweller's love of water with splendid fountains and public parks. Palaces and mosques, lavishly ornamented with marble, tile and beautiful geometrical mosaics, provided the setting for a life of luxury unknown to Western Europe (except for Umayyad Spain). The nobility dressed in silks and brocades, perfumed their beards, amused themselves with polo and horse racing. At royal weddings the bride would be showered with pearls instead of rice.

To Charles there came from this wonder of the world, this city of paved, policed and lighted streets, this empire where private scholars required four hundred camels to transport their books, an embassy in answer to the envoys he had sent to Bagdad four years earlier. Charles's active diplomatic relations with Harun al-Rashid were a by-product of two persistent themes of Frankish foreign policy: pressure on the Byzantine Empire and a virtually perpetual war against the Umayyad Saracens of Spain. Bagdad and Aachen could meet in hostility toward Cordova and Constantinople.

While Charles paused at Pavia, on his way back to Aachen, word reached him that an ambassador from Harun had arrived in Pisa. This ambassador brought the news that Isaac the Jew alone had survived of the three emissaries Charles had sent to Harun. Two Franks named Lantfrid and Sigimund had died en route, but the much traveled Isaac was returning with numerous presents from the caliph. One of these presents was so bulky that Isaac was unable to transport it across the Alps during the winter. The awed annalists carefully noted the exact date of its arrival in Aachen: July 20, 802.

Harun, in response to a request from Charles, had sent an elephant! Its name was Abul Abbas (after the founder of the Abbaside dynasty).

Medieval bestiaries tell us what Charles had hitherto known about elephants. They are mountainous in bulk—"for indeed elephant in Greek is called *mons* in Latin"—and when seeking for pasture they move in flocks like sheep. "Back to back they unite," but they can bear young only once in their long lifetimes of three centuries. If the hair of an elephant is burned in a house, snakes and all poisonous things will promptly leave it—surely a useful property if one has an adequate supply of elephant hair. When the mother is bearing young, she is very much afraid of falling, since the form of her legs makes rising again difficult. Therefore she rests by leaning against a large tree; cunning hunters will observe the tree that the female elephant habitually uses, then cut it half through, so that it falls next time she leans against it, and she with it. But if the hunter is not there to capture her at once, she will groan long and at last will trumpet. Then the whole herd will come to her rescue and try to raise her. Unable to do so, they will join in trumpeting loudly, until at last the smallest of all will come to her aid and by strange instinct will contrive to lift the fallen female.

Thus it is, Charles would be reminded by the natural philosophers of his time, that Christ comes to men's aid in answer to the prayers of men and, though humble and small himself, can lift men up whom even Moses was unable to raise out of the mire of original sin.

Since Charles had been given only one elephant, and that a male, he was unable to observe the wrinkle-skinned beast's habits of copulation or parturition. But he was grateful to Harun for having satisfied his curiosity to see an elephant, and he and all the Franks took tremendous delight in the huge beast with the dexterous nose. Abul Abbas accompanied Charles on all his royal progresses, causing a great stir everywhere. Unfortunately it did not live out the three centuries allotted to it by the bestiaries. Evidently the rigors of a northern climate were too much for it, and after eight years it suddenly died.

By contrast with the incessant activity during the year preceding the coronation, Charles seemed to be taking life easy during the next few years. Small wars went on against Benevento and the Spanish

Saracens, but Charles left the conduct of them to his sons and generals, and they were not pushed very energetically. He himself was busy with less spectacular but more important work: reorganizing and reforming the administration of his realm, and defining the relation between his kingship and his emperorship. The new laws, the stream of capitularies which were the outcome of his deliberations, reveal a Charles whose sense of civic and religious responsibility toward his people—always a dominant motif in his life—had become almost obsessional. He admonishes, he exhorts, he preaches like a Biblical prophet-king. And he is intensely dissatisfied with the state of affairs. There remains so much to be done before that state of perfect goodness and equity which he now envisages can be made a reality within his empire.

More than ever before he now made use of the missi to carry his personal influence throughout the land. Since Theodulf had recently impressed on him, in a long and witty poem describing his personal experiences as a missus, how frequently the missi accepted bribes and dispensed justice with something less than an even hand, Charles now revised his criteria for the selection of missi. Previously he had sent out men from among his poorer officials. Henceforth, he decided, only those who were so powerful and wealthy that they were above corruption would be employed for this vital duty. This meant, of course, imposing still more burdens on his comparatively few high officials. But there seemed no other way to make sure that his orders were obeyed and that the dishonest practices of entrenched local officials were curbed.

Along with the missi he sent the most detailed written instructions. One of these contained the text of the revised loyalty oath which was now to be sworn to him as emperor. The new oath read:

"I once more take oath to the Lord Charles, the most pious emperor, son of King Pepin and Queen Bertrada, that I am faithful as of right a man ought to be to his lord, to his reign and to his law. And this oath which I have sworn I shall keep and wish to keep to the extent of my knowledge and understanding from this day henceforth. May God who created heaven and earth aid me, as well as the patronage of these saints." [The oath, that is, was sworn on the relics of saints.]

Charles ordered that all should be informed of the many things which he considered to be comprehended by the oath: "not only, as many have heretofore thought, fidelity to the emperor in regard to his life, or not introducing an enemy into his kingdom, or not consenting to or keeping silence about the disloyalty of others." On the contrary, the oath involved the whole conduct of men's personal life, set forth in forty chapters of considerable length. First and foremost of them all, and most revealing of the theocratic nature of Charles's regime and of the increasingly religious turn of his mind, was the provision that "the oath comprises the following meaning: that everyone should voluntarily strive according to his intelligence and strength to keep himself entirely in the holy service of God. For the emperor cannot exercise the needful care and discipline upon each individual."

After this general injunction—surely to our twentieth-century way of thinking a most amazing paragraph in a state paper—came a list of orders designed to protect the property and the rights of the emperor. No one may conceal a slave of the emperor, or take possession of a fief of his, or neglect his summons to military service, or interfere with his taxes, or oppose his enterprises. Also: "No one shall dare to plunder or harm the holy churches of God, or widows, orphans or foreigners; for the emperor himself—after God and his saints—has been appointed their protector and defender."

Again and again Charles returned to the theme that the poor, the widows and the orphans deserved protection and charity. "Nor shall anyone be kept back from the right path of justice by . . . fear of the powerful." For the hundredth time, also, Charles repeated his admonitions to the clergy, now stressing that the obligation to live in accordance with the canons of the Church was implicit in their oath of allegiance to him. Bishops, abbots and abbesses must not oppress those under them by severe or despotic rule, but must guard their flock with love, mercy and charity, and by the example of their own good works. Abbots should conform in all respects to the Benedictine rule; they should live with their monks, be obedient to their bishops, not sell the property of the Church. Monks must not wander around, must not even go outside the monastery unless compelled by great necessity. If they have to travel, the bishop shall provide them with a certificate of good character. Monks "shall avoid all pursuit of gain or desire of worldly things. For avarice and concupiscence are to be avoided by all Christians in this world, but chiefly by those who have renounced the world and its desires. . . . The pernicious rumor has come to our ears that many in the monasteries have been taken in fornication, abomination and uncleanness. . . . Most of all it saddens and disturbs us that some of the monks are found to be sodomites."

Nonmonastic priests, the "secular clergy," must be "not fornicators, not thieves, not homicides, not rapers, not quarrelsome, not wrathful, not proud, not drunken; but chaste in heart and body, humble, modest, sober, merciful, peaceful."

The above instructions, and others that Charles issued at this time, can be read in reverse as a catalogue of all the evils of the day. "Judges must judge justly, according to the written law, not by their own judgment. . . . Our judges, counts or missi must not extort payment of a fine from those poor persons to whom the emperor has in his mercy forgiven what they ought to pay. . . ."

The sincerity and the hortatory tone in the paragraph against murder fully justify the epithet "bishop of bishops" which was applied to Charles in another sense. It is also a further chapter in the long struggle of the state to regulate the custom of private vendetta. By making the payment of wergeld compulsory, Charles was taking a long step forward toward the conception of murder as a crime against the community rather than against the clan. His argument was not in terms of polity, but of religion. The paragraph merits quotation at length:

"With every kind of protestation we command that men leave off and shun murders, through which many of the Christian people perish. If God forbids hatred and enmity to his followers, how much more does he forbid murders. For how can anyone hope to be pleasing to God who has slain His son Who is nearest to Him? Or how can anyone believe that Christ will be gracious to him who has slain his brother? It is a great and inevitable risk to arouse the hatred of men, besides incurring that of God the Father and of Christ the ruler of Heaven. By hiding, one can escape them for a time; but nevertheless one falls by some chance into the hands of his enemies. And where can one flee God to whom all secrets are known? By what rashness can anyone hope to evade His wrath? Therefore we have taken care to avoid by every possible regulation that the people committed to us to be ruled over perish by this evil. For he who has not feared that God will be angry with him will by no means find us gentle and merciful. We rather mean to punish with the greatest severity him who dares to commit the crime of murder. . . . Wherever, under the devil's influence, a murder has occurred, the guilty one must straightway hasten to make his amends and shall immediately pay the wergeld to the kinsfolk of the dead man. And this we firmly decree under our ban, that the relatives of the dead man shall by no means dare to carry further their enmity on account of the evil inflicted, nor refuse to make peace with him who seeks it. Rather, they shall pledge their faith to make a lasting peace, and the guilty man shall make no delay in paying the wergeld. When, moreover, through the influence of sin, anyone shall have slain his brothers or his relative, he shall straightway submit to the penance imposed by his bishop, and without any circumvention. By the help of God he shall strive to work out his atonement; and he shall pay the fine for the slain man according to the law, and shall be fully reconciled with his relatives. And having pledged their faith, let no one thenceforth dare to start hostilities. And whoever shall scorn to make proper amends shall be deprived of his inheritance until we have rendered our judgment."*

Here, as in all the legislation of his reign, but more especially of this period, the boundaries between church and state, between the penalties ordained by God and those imposed by Charles, have been almost entirely rubbed out. The intensity of Charles's religious feeling at this time is fully expressed in the sentence: "The poor, widows, orphans and pilgrims shall have consolation and protection, *so that we, through their good will,* may merit the rewards of eternal life rather than punishment." And in this: "No one shall refuse shelter and fire and water to pilgrims going through the land in God's service, or to anyone traveling for the love of God and the safety of his soul. If anyone shall wish to do a further kindness to them, he shall know that his best reward will be from God, who said Himself: 'And whoso shall receive one such little child in my name, receiveth me.' And again: 'I was a stranger and ye took me in.'"

Military reforms also were long overdue. Charles had earlier refused to lighten the burdens of army service, but now it was becoming increasingly clear that he must act. Since the coronation men had been flocking to the monasteries or giving their lands to the Church in order to enjoy ecclesiastical immunity. While sternly forbidding this practice and ordering that no one might be consecrated to the priesthood without his approval, Charles also attacked the problem at the root. He directed that only the owners of at least three *manses* would be required to perform military service. An owner of

* Translation (slightly amended) by Ernest F. Henderson.

two manses would combine with another possessing a similar amount of property, and only one of the two would be sent to the army. Out of every six proprietors of half a manse, only one need go; the others paid a tax to support the costs of his military service. For those whose wealth was reckoned in money rather than land, similar arrangements were made.

Compensatory privileges were granted to the counts. These were now permitted to have four men stay at home to guard their families and take care of necessary work. Bishops were allowed two men. Such reforms were now possible because Charles had at his disposal, in his extended empire, a much larger population to draw on for soldiers than he had had in the earlier part of his reign. And reforms were temperamentally possible for him now because he was no longer the harsh and inflexible person he had been in the decade following his failure in Spain and the debacle at Roncesvalles.

The same man who in all sincerity sought to protect the *pauperes* of his empire, who provided a sliding scale of fines based on ability to pay and who urged all his officials to practice justice and mercy, was at the same time crushing out the last embers of resistance in Saxony. Aging though he was, he could still endure the hardships of a campaign, and he personally led a large Frankish army against the people whom he had been fighting on and off for thirty-two of his sixty-two years. What prompted this campaign must have been the same sort of guerrilla warfare and obstinate refusal to accept Christianity that had kept Saxony in turmoil for a whole generation.

This time Charles again enlisted the services of Thrasko, prince of the Slavic Abodrites. He sent also detachments of Frankish troops into that ever-turbulent region of moors and swamps between Weser and Elbe where so many revolts against Frankish rule had started. There was little fighting. Another mass man hunt took place. The province of Wigmodia was swept nearly clean of Saxons. Men, women and children were deported by the thousands.

But the main object of the campaign was the conquest of Nordalbingia. Caught between Slavs and Franks, the Nordalbingians were unable to resist effectively. Saxons poured across the border at Schleswig to the safety of Denmark. And Göttrik, King of the Danes, suddenly appeared on this border with his entire fleet and all his mounted men. His posture was half afraid, half threatening; he wanted to attack the Franks, but did not quite dare. Charles peaceably invited him to a conference, and for a while it seemed that the Danish king would accept. But his men persuaded him that a personal interview with Charles on Frankish territory would be too dangerous, and he finally contented himself with sending envoys who demanded an end of the persecution of their Saxon brethren. Charles retorted with an equally sharp demand that Göttrik surrender the Saxon fugitives. Vowing revenge, Göttrik withdrew, and Charles calmly proceeded to settle the affairs of Nordalbingia. As a reward for the Abodrites' faithful allegiance, he turned the entire province over to Thrasko. Then, with thousands of wretched Saxons in his train, who were to be distributed throughout Frankland, he returned to Aachen.

The long war was over at last. From now on there was to be no more resistance among the Saxons. Their conversion to the Christian faith and their integration into the Frankish empire—"so that Saxons and Franks united and formed one people"—proceeded without interruption. A generation later there would arise among the Saxon people the author of that remarkable Christian poem *Heliand* which has been described earlier in this book. A century later the center of power had shifted to the former frontier area, as Toynbee would say, and a Saxon dynasty began to rule the Frankish empire. The qualities that had inspired the Saxons to stave off conquest for a third of a century enabled them soon to turn the tables on their conquerors. But it was a new and different Saxony that again came to the fore in the tenth century. It was a Saxony that Charles had created, a Saxony that had accepted the religion and the governmental institutions of the Franks.

Charles knew that this time his task was done. As a gesture of satisfaction he spent the fall hunting in the Forest of Ardennes. During this vacation he had time to reflect on the death of Alcuin. Alcuin had died in May, and it may be that Charles took the field personally that summer in order to forget, amid the familiar sights and smells of camp life, his grief over the passing of his old teacher. His relations with Alcuin had been somewhat edgy during the last two or three years of Alcuin's life, and this must now have caused him regret. After all the years of harmony, culminating in Alcuin's great service to him during the debates on adoptianism, Charles had taken an angry tone toward his old friend.

Shortly after the coronation, trouble had arisen between Bishop

Theodulf and Alcuin. A clerk of Orléans imprisoned for some crime had escaped to the sanctuary of St. Martin's Church in Tours. Alcuin had granted him protection and was prepared to have him dispatched to Charles for judgment, as the man requested. But Theodulf sent officials to fetch him back. A struggle ensued between Theodulf's officials and Alcuin's followers, who were trying to protect the right of sanctuary. A rumor went through the town that the shrine of St. Martin was being desecrated by the men from Orléans; rioting followed; and Theodulf's men were nearly killed by a mob before they could be rescued by Alcuin's monks.

Theodulf and Alcuin promptly wrote to Charles letters of explanation. But Theodulf's arrived the day before Alcuin's letter, and Charles's response was to reprimand Alcuin:

"Your letter seemed to us far more angry even than Theodulf's, one not written in charity, but in defense of the guilty man and in accusation of his bishop. . . . We are exceedingly surprised, however, that it has seemed good to you all to oppose our authority and ordering. It is perfectly evident that such decrees of ours have their origin in ancient usage and in constitutional law and that no one has the right to hold them in contempt. We are the more exceedingly astonished that you preferred to yield to this criminal's prayers rather than to obey our will."*

Charles attempted to soothe Alcuin's feelings by flattering him a little and placing all the blame on the monks of St. Martin's. He referred to rumors about the loose living of the monks which, if they were current about so great a monastery as St. Martin's under the direction of an Alcuin, certainly describe conditions in many more of the monasteries of Frankland. Charles wrote:

"Well do you know, you who are called the congregation of this monastery, and the servants of God—may the description be a true one!—how many charges and how often are brought against your manner of life, and not without cause. . . . It was I who, for your sakes and for the abolishing of the community's bad reputation, chose for you a fitting master and ruler and called him from a great distance, that by his counsels and rebukes he might teach you to live aright

---

* This and the following quotations relating to this incident translated by Eleanor Duckett, *op. cit.*

and, as one devoted to religion, might train you by the example of his own goodly conduct. But unhappily, everything has turned out otherwise, and the Devil has found in you his ministers, so to speak, for the sowing of discord where least of all it should be sown, between two wise men, doctors of the Church. The very men who ought to correct and punish sinners, those men you force toward the sin of envy and anger. In God's mercy they will not listen to your evil promptings."

Alcuin, always unwilling to see evil in anyone, defended his monks, declaring: "I have never known them such as I hear they are said to be by those more ready to accuse than to save. . . . They serve God worthily in the churches, and, I speak with all sincerity, I have never seen men anywhere working more perfectly in daily life for your health and for the firm standing of your Christian rule."

Charles had declined to accept Alcuin's excuses and had sent a personal representative to clean up what he must have privately thought of as "the mess in Tours." Had he acted rightly to turn on the old man who had defied his displeasure in defense of a principle Charles himself recognized as sacred: the right of sanctuary? Now that anger had evaporated with the passage of time, Charles could not fail to appreciate the extent of his loss.

The aged scholar, who had died in the spring when his beloved "cuckoo" was returning to Tours, had brought a springtide of learning from England to Frankland. His work at court, in the Palace Academy, and as minister of education, had left its lasting mark in the flourishing schools that now were attached to the cathedrals and monasteries at Orléans, Corbie, St. Denis, St. Wandrille, Fulda, St. Gall, Reichenau and Lorsch, to name only the most important. In Tours his scriptorium was turning out numerous copies of books— not only scriptural and patristic texts but the Roman classics also. (More than ninety per cent of the Latin writings have been passed on to us in Carolingian copies, or in manuscripts based on Carolingian copies. Alcuin can be considered directly responsible for the tremendous revival in the production of books.) Above all, Alcuin had trained so many young men to replace himself that it did not seem possible for the light of learning ever again to be extinguished so thoroughly as it had been during the early part of the eighth century.

It was a curious kind of learning, to be sure, with great gaps in knowledge of the natural world, with a serene ignorance of the achievements of, for example, ancient Greek science, and with an obsessive interest in allegorical interpretation of all phenomena. But still it was far more than brutish ignorance. There was a bit of chemistry and mineralogy, for example, in the fanciful categories set forth by Hrabanus Maurus, Alcuin's pupil, who wrote an encyclopedia. (Hrabanus classified "common stones" such as: rock, cliffs, flint, gypsum, sand and lime; "excellent stones" such as: jet, asbestos and moonstone; and included ivory and pearls among his minerals.) What was important was the impulse to classify, to satisfy curiosity, to probe nature a little. Although Alcuin himself took a rather narrow view of the liberal arts, his insistence that his pupils study the classics and the Fathers of the Church put them in touch with greater minds than theirs or his. He himself did no original thinking, but in preserving a tradition which otherwise might well have been lost he provided a base from which others could go on to ask questions. Only a single generation separates Alcuin from one of the really original thinkers of the Middle Ages, John Scotus Erigena.

As a poet Alcuin was inferior to his friend-enemy Theodulf, whose *"Gloria Laus et Honor"* is still sung on Palm Sunday, or to Hrabanus, the probable author of the great hymn *"Veni Creator Spiritus."* His poems are usually florid and artificial, poor imitations of Roman models. Yet he could hit off lines of exemplary directness and simplicity, as in his verses for a departed pupil, the "Cuckoo." After bewailing his absence, Alcuin says in the last lines:

> *Sis semper felix utinam, quocunque recedas,*
> *Sis memor et nostri. . . .*
> (Be happy always wherever you may go,
> And spare a thought for us. . . .)

And Alcuin caught the timbre of imperial splendor in the lines on St. Michael which he wrote for Charles, implicitly comparing Charles to the warrior archangel and identifying Charles's empire with the City of God:

> *Te namque profitemur esse*
> *supernorum principem civium . . .*

Semper te sancti honorant angeli.
(We profess you the prince of the citizens
Of the regions above . . .
Forever the holy angels honor you.)

Yet Alcuin's aspirations had always been humble, his conception of himself modest. With precision he summed up in one line of the epitaph he had written for himself what he most wished himself to be remembered for:

Alchuine nomen erat sophiam mihi semper amanti.
(Alcuin was my name; wisdom I always loved.)

While Charles himself, of course, had no perspective on the work Alcuin had done for him and for civilization, he could easily measure its immediate results. Bright young men like Sigulf, Candidus, Fredugis and Amalar went on missions for him and taught his children and grandchildren. His library was full of books, and in his chancery the scribes used the fine, clear handwriting known as Carolingian miniscule, which Alcuin had fostered in the scriptorium at Tours. His own mind was stocked with the lessons in grammar, rhetoric and astronomy that Alcuin had given him. Above all, he had memories of a warm friendship, of Alcuin's long and sincere attachment to him, of happy hours spent in high converse and simple gossip, in exchanging riddles, reading and writing poetry. And he alone knew what part Alcuin had played in the events leading to his coronation as august and pacific emperor of the Romans.

Charles's hunting vacation in the Ardennes woods was interrupted by the news that Pope Leo wanted to celebrate Christmas with him wherever he cared to receive him. The annals are quite frank in their statement that the pope had seized a welcome opportunity to get away from Rome: evidently he was in trouble again. A pretext had been supplied by the extraordinary news that some of the blood of Christ had been found in the city of Mantua. Charles, ever on the alert to track down relics or to suppress superstitions, had requested the pope to look into the matter, and Leo had left Rome with significant alacrity. Apparently there was some doubt as to the genuineness of the find, for the results of the investigation are passed over in silence.

Leo, unpopular as ever in Rome, clung desperately to Charles as his sole support against the hostility of the people he ruled. Charles could not have been altogether pleased by this evidence of continued turbulence in Rome and of Leo's inability to cope with it alone; but he put a good face on the matter, celebrated Christmas and Epiphany in high style, with the pope's presence gracing the religious side of these festivals, and then sent Leo home laden with gifts as an ostentatious sign of his good will. In the course of this visit Charles probably discussed with the pope a matter much on his mind since the death of his friend Alcuin. He must reckon with "the inevitable tendency of all earthly things to fall into decay," as he put it, and by that phrase he was thinking not so much of his own aging body as of the empire he had built up. He was concerned with "the perpetuity of this government," and he therefore decided to undertake now, while he was still in good health, the division of the realm among his sons. A written testament was all the more necessary since he now had three more sons by his concubines, Regina and Adalhaid. To avoid future discord it had to be made clear that these infants, Drogo, Hugo and Theoderic, were to have no share of his empire. Only his three sons by Hildigard—Charles, Pepin and Louis—were to be considered his legitimate heirs. To lend his testament greater moral authority than a father's wish, he would have Leo witness and ratify the document.

At Christmas the following year all three of his sons assembled at Aachen—young Charles having just returned from leading a large-scale invasion of Bohemia in which he had demonstrated once again, to Charles's satisfaction, that he was the most capable of the three. The annals tell us that Charles celebrated Christmas together with them "with joy and exultation." We shall not go far wrong if we assume that his gladness sprang from his having found his sons content with the portions he had allotted them and in agreement with the principles he laid down for their conduct after his death. Nevertheless, he took the precaution of repeating in the written text of his testament the injunctions he had given them orally.

Most historians and biographers have failed to recognize that in attempting to fix the continuity of his government Charles was a prisoner of arrangements he had made twenty-five years earlier, long before his full power had unfolded and before he possessed a clear conception of what he wished to do. When he had established subkingdoms for his sons in 781 he had tied his hands. That division of the realm could now no longer be undone. Although he now understood how essential it was for the empire to remain integral, he could make it so only by disinheriting two of his sons in favor of a third—and both sentiment and policy were opposed to such a course. He had clearly favored his eldest, young Charles, all along, but he did not dare to place Charles above the other two by giving him the title of emperor. Since no tradition of primogeniture existed in Frankland, such a step would almost certainly lead to bitter quarrels and possibly warfare among his sons.

Within the limitations imposed by the faulty Frankish rules of succession and by his own past mistake, Charles sought the next-best solution. He divided the empire formally into the three existing sub-kingdoms, adding to them the newly conquered lands adjacent to them. To Louis went the whole of Aquitaine, Vasconia and the Spanish March, the southern part of Burgundy, the Provence and Septimania. To Pepin he assigned Lombardy and Bavaria "as Tassilo had it" and Alemannia south of the Danube. Charles received the lion's share—everything else.

Careful provision was made in the testament for further division of the kingdoms among the surviving brothers on the death of one or the other. But "if to any of these brothers should be born a son whom the people wish to choose as his father's successor to the throne, we desire that the uncles of the boy give their consent and allow their brother's son to rule in that part of the kingdom which his father, their brother, possessed." This clause may well have been an expression of belated remorse on the part of Charles for his seizure of his brother Carloman's kingdom. Yet the emphasis in the testament is on the probability that the brothers will take over a deceased brother's kingdom. Later, as we shall see, Charles changed his mind about this.

The heart of the testament, however, was not the careful ordering of boundaries but the effort to preserve the idea of a unified realm. Pepin, Louis and young Charles were strictly enjoined to live at peace with one another, never to invade a brother's frontiers or attempt to diminish his territory. On the contrary, each was to aid the other against domestic and foreign enemies. None of the brothers was to receive a subject of his brother "who for whatever cause or crime shall flee to him for refuge." Any freeman after the death of his lord could become a vassal of another lord in any one of the three kingdoms. Although none of the brothers could acquire land in a brother's kingdom, any ordinary citizen could do so—as if the three kingdoms were one. Marriages across the borders of the kingdoms were to be encouraged—"since by such affinities the several nations may be more closely bound together."

Above all, the policy of a united kingdom in firm alliance with the Roman Church was to be maintained. "We command and ordain that the three brothers join in the care and protection of the Church of Saint Peter, as was done by our grandfather Charles, by our father Pepin, of blessed memory, and by ourselves; that with God's help they will shield her from her enemies." The theocracy was to survive Charles's death. If the three brothers continued to strive, as he had done, for the City of God, there was hope that the divided realm would remain one in spirit. If it did not, his work would fall to pieces. He could not govern after his death; he could only appeal to his sons to follow in his footsteps. Certainly he remembered that his father Pepin, on his deathbed, had made a similar attempt to preserve the unity of Frankland in spite of partition; that he and his brother Carloman had in theory both been kings of Frankland, even though each was assigned his particular portion.

Recollecting the bitterness of those early years, Charles could not help feeling doubt that his plan would work. At the end of the long testament he expressed his concern—based perhaps on a knowledge of his son Louis' character—in these astonishing words: "As to our grandsons, the sons of our aforesaid sons, born or to be born, we command that none of our sons, for any cause whatsoever, shall have any of our grandsons, who may be accused of crime, put to death, mutilated, blinded or forcibly tonsured without a just trial and investigation. On the contrary, we wish them to be held in honor by their fathers and uncles."

His fears in this case proved prophetic, for not long after his death Louis caused Bernhard, the son of Pepin of Italy, to be blinded.

The text of Charles's testament was carried to Rome by Einhard, who at this time was coming more and more into prominence as an adviser and privy councilor to Charles, a young man whom everybody considered to have the emperor's ear. In Rome Pope Leo put his signature to the document. And Charles, as if the troubles of his younger years were beginning all over again, turned his attention to simmering conflicts in east, west, north and south. His three sons were now his executive arms, but as always before his was the guiding intellect. As he had pointedly stated in the final paragraph of his testament:

"All these things, moreover, are here in order set forth and established on the condition that so long as it may please God to preserve our life, our power over this government and empire shall remain unaltered and unimpaired . . . and that we may have the full obedience of our beloved sons, with all the submission due a father from his sons, and an emperor and king from his subjects."

CHAPTER NINETEEN

The Last Years

I N THE earlier years of Charles's reign the Mediterranean was
scarcely ever mentioned in the annals. Now, in the imperial
period, the Inland Sea became a prime area for the deploy-
ment of Frankish forces and the expansion of Frankish interests. That alone is proof that Charles was taking his title of emperor
seriously and was attempting to win back the control of the Mediterranean which had once enabled Rome to rule the world. Unfortunately for the ultimate unity of Europe, he started from scratch and
started too late. The Franks never achieved true naval power. As
G. M. Trevelyan has remarked, "The Franks were landlubbers."

Charles recognized and attempted to remedy the situation. He ordered the building of ships at all ports; he issued legislation providing
for the drafting of men into the navy as well as the army. The new
navy operated principally in the western Mediterranean against Saracen raiders, for the war which was being fought on land in Spain had
been extended to the sea; the Spanish Umayyads repeatedly attacked
Sardinia and Corsica, were driven off either by the inhabitants or by
the Frankish fleet, and returned to the assault. The tough Sardinians
frequently sent them flying back to their ships, but the Corsicans,
either less hardy or more unlucky, were carried off by the hundreds to
slavery in Spain.

Charles directed Louis to capture the Spanish bases from which
these Saracen expeditions operated. But Louis was incapable of the
kind of military leadership that was called for. His Aquitanian armies
could penetrate the Spanish countryside, could even undertake hit-
and-run raids across the Ebro, burning crops and farmhouses and
making the lives of the inhabitants miserable. But they were rarely
able to hold territory or to take any fortified place. Years of cam-

paigning were required before the single city of Tortosa, at the mouth
of the Ebro, fell to the Franks.

In the east, meanwhile, Charles engaged in a ticklish cold war—
which occasionally blew hot—with the Byzantine Empire. In 805,
profiting by internal rivalries among the Byzantine administrators,
Charles had obtained formal control of Venetia and Dalmatia. Venice, founded three centuries before by refugees from the Huns, was
just beginning its rise to greatness; shortly after this time the first
piles would be driven into the muck to support the vast basilica of
San Marco. Already there were doges conspiring to win independence for their city by playing off against each other the two great
powers of the Western and the Eastern Empires.

The Venetians, aware of Nicephorus' troubles with Harun al-Rashid, evidently hoped to take advantage of the Byzantine weakness.
When Constantinople proved strong enough to send a fleet that
blockaded the Venetian coast, the lagoon dwellers performed a swift
about-face. They renounced their allegiance to Charles and submitted
once more to the Eastern Emperor.

For Charles, Venice was important not as the key to the Adriatic
but as Byzantine territory, as a pawn with which to bargain. He at
once ordered Pepin to take the city by force of arms. Now the ship-
building program of the past few years proved its worth, for Pepin
was able to conduct amphibious warfare. The campaign was tedious,
and most of the details that have come down to us appear highly
questionable. At any rate, after a long siege by sea and land Pepin became the master of Venice. Soon afterward Greek and Frankish naval
forces clashed off the Dalmatian coast. The Franks were worsted.

Meanwhile, Charles continued to put indirect pressure on Nicephorus by assiduously and ostentatiously cultivating his friendly relations with Harun al-Rashid. His emissaries, returning with Arab
ambassadors from Harun's court, ran the Byzantine blockade of the
North Italian coast and put into the port of Treviso. They brought
with them fabulous gifts from the workshops of the Orient. Frankish
courtiers gaped at silks, brass candelabra, vials of perfume, jars of
salves and balsam and a tent even more beautiful than that given
Charles ten years before by the King of Asturias. The curtains were
of "byssus dyed in many colors"; the tent had so many apartments
that it resembled a palace; it was, says a poet, so high that no archer
could shoot an arrow to its roof. The magnificent gift came, alas,

too late, for Charles's camping days were nearly over. Still, he would have one more opportunity to use it.

More appropriate for an aging man who must count the hours remaining to him was an intricate brass water clock with a mechanism which dropped bronze balls on a bowl beneath to strike out the hours. There were also twelve knights who emerged from an equal number of windows with the passage of the hours and who by their motion caused the windows to shut behind them. The chronicler adds that there were other devices in this clock too numerous to be mentioned. From the detailed descriptions by annalists who generally confined themselves to a single line to report a battle or a diplomatic event, it is clear that the Arab gifts made a great hit.

Charles took pleasure in these gifts and welcomed Harun's assurances that Christian pilgrims to the Holy Land would be well treated. But even more important to him was the effect that his intercourse with Harun must be having on Nicephorus. For Harun had become Nicephorus' most dangerous enemy since, in a moment of recklessness after his accession to the throne, the Byzantine emperor had challenged the caliph. Refusing to pay to Bagdad the tribute which Irene had consented to, Nicephorus sent to Harun a message of defiance— containing, incidentally, one of the oldest-known allusions to the game of chess: "The queen [Irene] considered you as a rook and herself as a pawn. That pusillanimous female submitted to pay a tribute the double of which she should have exacted from you barbarians. Restore, therefore, the fruits of your injustice. . . ." And the Greek ambassadors cast a bundle of swords at the foot of the throne.

As Gibbon continues the tale in his rolling periods:

"The caliph smiled at the menace, and, drawing his scimitar, sam-samah, a weapon of historic or fabulous renown, he cut asunder the feeble arms of the Greeks without turning the edge or endangering the temper of his blade. He then dictated an epistle of tremendous brevity: 'In the name of the most merciful God, Harun al-Rashid, commander of the faithful, to Nicephorus, the Roman dog. I have read thy letter, O thou son of an unbelieving mother. Thou shalt not hear, thou shalt behold my reply.' It was written in characters of blood and fire on the plains of Phrygia."

Harun kept his word; the Arab armies scoured the lands of the Empire, and Nicephorus was compelled to buy an uneasy peace at a price greater than Irene had paid. In the circumstances, the news that Charles was in constant diplomatic correspondence with Harun was extremely disquieting to Nicephorus. Since at the same time he was also at war with the Bulgarians, the Frankish capture of Venice and threat to the Dalmatian coast added to his worries. He grew more attentive to the hints from Frankish quarters that a settlement could still be had in exchange for recognition of Charles as Emperor of the West.

The ambassadors of Nicephorus set out from Constantinople to discuss terms with the conqueror of Venice.

In the north also the years after the division of the realm were turbulent.

The sudden rise to power and violent outward expansion of the Northmen in the ninth century is one of the many mysteries of the historical process. A change in climate, producing famines at home; the pressure of increased population; a sudden improvement in the techniques of seafaring; imitation by others of successful raiders— these are among the many explanations that have been suggested.

Whatever the cause, the policy of the Northmen now changed. The Danes had remained cool but unaggressive neighbors throughout the greater part of Charles's reign. During his long struggle with the Saxons they had done no more than receive Saxon fugitives and lend moral but little material support to their brother pagans. Had they struck earlier, while Charles was still building his empire, they might seriously have checked the growth of Frankish power. But they waited—perhaps in more recent years they had waited in the hope that the aging Frankish emperor would soon die. Now they suddenly decided to challenge the mightiest state Western Europe had known since the decline of Rome.

The war opened with Danish infiltration of Charles's Slavic confederates. Repulsed, King Göttrik went on the defensive for a time and constructed a wall along the northern bank of the Eider River running all the way from the Baltic to the North Sea, with only a single gate in it to admit merchant traffic between Saxony and Denmark. But after engineering the assassination of Charles's foremost Slavic ally, Duke Thrasko of the Abodrites, Göttrik launched a huge raid from two hundred ships on the islands and coastal towns of Frisia. In three pitched battles the Danes defeated the Frisians and imposed a tribute on them.

The Northmen with their ring mail and red cloaks seem from the first to have inspired terror among the Franks. In later years the very sight of their striped sails, the high dragon prows and the long lines of yellow and black round shields hung over the sides of their ships, would paralyze resistance. And now even Charles, who a few years before had calmly gone hunting while his sons did the fighting for him, became alarmed. He sent his missi throughout the country to levy the full man power of Frankland. And he himself left Aachen at once with what troops he had at hand.

But for the first time in his life he moved indecisively. Should he march against the Danish fleet in Friesland? Or would the main Danish attack come in Saxony? Göttrik himself, Charles learned, had not accompanied his fleet to Friesland. He was still at home, gathering more forces for the main attack and boasting that all Germany was already a Danish province, that soon he would appear at Aachen with his army.

Charles hesitantly crossed the Rhine and waited at Lippeham in Saxony for the bulk of his army to assemble. There, in no-longer-rebellious Saxony, one of the visible symbols of his glory faded away. He had brought with him into Saxony the most prized of the gifts he had received from Harun, Abul Abbas, the elephant. Perhaps he hoped that the sight of the gray monster would strike terror into the hearts of the Danish soldiers. But to the sorrow of Charles and the consternation of the Franks, who were sensitive to omens, the elephant died suddenly. The annalists recorded its loss as if it were a member of the royal family.

When the main body of his army joined him, Charles advanced north to fateful Verden on the Aller, where nearly thirty years before he had taken frightful vengeance on the Saxons. As if the place were accursed, word was brought to him here that Rotrud had died—Rotrud, his favorite daughter, the fair-haired eldest, whom he had once betrothed to the Emperor Constantine. This news, when only a few months before he had lost his beloved sister Gisla, the abbess of Chelles, "whom he had always treated with the same affection and respect as his mother," had a devastating effect on him. Ten years before, when his wife Liutgard had died, Charles had been resilient enough to go on with his plans without faltering, to carry through the trying and delicate maneuvers that led to the coronation. But now, faced with simple military decisions such as he had been making all his life, he was incapable of action. While the army chafed, a heart-sick Charles marked time.

However, his waning luck still held. Although he had surrendered the initiative entirely to the Danes, they did not attack. Soon he learned of what was going on in Denmark. The Danish nobility had split over the question of war with the Frankish Empire. A strong party opposed Göttrik, arguing that the old lion of Aachen could still claw and that even the "Dane Wall" would not save Denmark from an aroused Charles. Perhaps Frankish secret diplomacy had something to do with the dissension among the Danes, but we are entering the realm of pure guesswork here; there is no evidence for or against this possibility. At any rate, the opposition party succeeded in assassinating Göttrik. A nephew of Göttrik seized the throne and called off the war with Charles. Göttrik's sons retired to Sweden and prepared for civil war.

But if this was lucky for Charles, it was the only good fortune he had that year. A plague had been sweeping Frankland, possibly carried back from Benevento, where Frankish armies were being decimated by epidemics. So deadly had the plague been two years earlier that Charles and his court had fled from Aachen in the early spring. Probably Gisla and Rotrud had been victims of this unnamed disease. Now, with a sister and daughter but recently buried, word was brought to Charles at Verden that his son Pepin was dead. Dead at thirty-three; Charles had been that age when he conquered the Lombardy which Pepin afterward ruled for him. The young king left behind him a numerous family—a son named Bernhard, and five daughters, whom Charles ordered brought to Aachen to be raised with and by his own daughters. Bernhard was sent to Fulda to study under Alcuin's pupil, Hrabanus Maurus, and be groomed for the kingdom his father had held.

Even the news that a peace mission from the Emperor Nicephorus was on the way was only another reminder of the tragedy. The mission had come originally to deal with Pepin as conqueror of Venice. Charles now had the sad duty of ordering that the ambassadors from Constantinople be sent on to Aachen where he himself would negotiate with them.

The death of Pepin was the greatest but not the only calamity. Blows were falling on the people as well as the people's chief. The oxen that drew the wagons of the army, and the cattle that had been brought along to supply meat were mysteriously perishing. The murrain, following so close on the human epidemic, traveled through all of Europe. It produced enormous hardship and aroused superstitious terror among the populace. A wave of hysteria surged through the Frankish Empire, and particularly Lombardy and Bavaria, where the cattle plague raged most fiercely. Remembering all the deaths by disease that had resulted from the campaigns against Grimoald of Benevento, the people attributed this new disaster to the same ill-omened ruler. They ignored the fact that Grimoald had died in 806 and had been succeeded by his treasurer, whose name happened also to be Grimoald. Agents of Grimoald, it was alleged, were sprinkling a poisonous powder on fields and meadows and into wells and springs to kill the cattle. Scenting seditious activity everywhere, frenzied mobs seized totally innocent persons, bound them to boards and flung them into rivers. "The astonishing part of it was," remarks a contemporary, "that these persons gave testimony against themselves and confessed to possessing and distributing the powder." It would have been impossible, he adds sensibly, for the poison to have been scattered over such immense stretches of country even if every man, woman and child in Benevento had set out with three cartloads of powder each. "Yet this thing was believed by all Christians, though pagans would scarcely have been taken in by any tale so utterly absurd." The hunt for supposed foreign agents continued, in spite of Charles's efforts to check it by decree, until the cattle plague passed of its own accord.

In a mood of despair so bleak that for a time he considered casting away the scepter of sovereignty and taking up the staff of the pilgrim or the lowly monk, Charles set out for Aachen. In haste to leave the curse of Verden behind him, he started the march before dawn. Suddenly "a meteor flashed across the heavens with a great blaze, passing from right to left through the clear sky." His horse shied, and he who had spent a large part of his life in the saddle was thrown. He was hurled to the ground so violently, Einhard tells us, "that the girdle of his cloak snapped, and his sword belt slipped from it. When his attendants ran up to assist him, they found him disarmed and disrobed." His javelin, too, which he was holding in his hand when he fell, was flung "twenty paces and more away from him."

"Disarmed and disrobed"—Einhard reckoned it as a portent. Horses must have shied under Charles many times before in his life, but always before he had mastered the unruly animals as he had mastered the half-tamed subjects of his domains by his unique combination of forcefulness and patience. This time he lost his grip. Age, grief, the bane of Verden and approaching evil times might be suggested as explanations by his followers. Charles would have none of this nonsense. Yet from this time on he dwelt more than ever before on his religious responsibilities, and secretly he took to wearing a hair shirt under his robes.

Back at Aachen, the Emperor Nicephorus' ambassador was waiting for him. Charles received him with cordiality; he was the *Spatharius* or Sword-bearer Arsafius. A tentative treaty of peace was signed, in which Charles agreed to surrender Venice and several maritime cities on the Dalmatian coast in return for recognition of his imperial title.

After the Greek ambassador departed, Charles sent three envoys of his own back to Constantinople. They were Bishop Heito, Count Hugo of Tours, and Ajo of Friuli—the latter a Lombard like Fardulf who had once resisted Charles's rule in Lombardy and later been forgiven by Charles and risen high in the Frankish diplomatic and administrative service. These envoys carried a signed copy of the treaty of peace and a long letter from Charles to Nicephorus that was singularly humble in tone—the tone of an old man scarcely daring to hope that he would win one last triumph before the end.

More and more often now the slow wasting of his physical powers would be reminding him that this end could not be far off. He who had always enjoyed the best of health was now hampered by various ailments. What their cause was, the medicine of his time was incompetent to say. Indeed, a cause hardly needed to be sought, now that he had reached his seventieth year. It was clearly time for him to be making his final arrangements for departure from this life or— he still indulged the thought—for departure from the world and retirement to the peace of a monastic cell.

The division of 806 had been a political document, a disposition of the territory of the empire he had forged. Now, five years later, he made an equally conscientious division of his personal property. He intended later to make bequests to his daughters and to his three "illegitimate" sons, but, as Einhard observes, he began on this too late and did not live to carry out his design. It is indicative of his frame of mind that the assignment of his treasure (that is, the *hoard* which, like every Germanic ruler, he too had accumulated), made largely for the salvation of his soul, was carried out first. The text of this document has been preserved by Einhard; its primary aim was the distribution of alms "such as Christians usually make from their possessions" and also so that his heirs "shall clearly know what belongs to them and may therefore divide his goods without disputes."

The total property found on a given day in the treasury was accordingly divided into three lots; two of these were further divided into twenty-one parts, one for each metropolitan city (the seats of archbishops) in his domains. Twenty-one boxes were made, filled with gold, silver, jewelry and royal garments, and these were to be further distributed by the twenty-one archbishops. In other words, Charles was giving two thirds of his movable property to the Church!

But even that was not the total of his gifts for the sake of his soul. The third lot was to be kept for his personal use so long as he lived. But on his death *or voluntary withdrawal from the affairs of the world* it would be divided into four parts, one of which would be added to the share of the twenty-one cities, one distributed as alms, the third given to the servants of the palace, and the fourth reserved for his children and grandchildren.

He further ordered that "the books of which he collected a great many in his library" were to be sold at just prices and the money given to the poor.

"It is well known that among his other property and treasures there are three silver tables and one very large and massive one of gold. He directs and commands that the square silver table, upon which appears a representation of the city of Constantinople, together with the other gifts set apart for the purpose, shall be sent to the Basilica of Saint Peter the Apostle at Rome. The second table, of circular shape, and ornamented with a picture of the city of Rome, shall be given to the Bishop's Church at Ravenna. The third, which in beauty of workmanship and weight surpasses the other two, and is made in three circles displaying the plan of the whole universe skillfully and delicately drawn, together with the golden table already named as the fourth, shall be applied to increase the third part which is to be divided among his heirs and used for alms."*

So great was Charles's authority even after his death that the provisions of this extraordinary will—which reserved for his children and

* Translation, slightly amended, by Jacob Mombert.

grandchildren only a twelfth part of his treasure—were faithfully carried out.

Among the thirty signers of this document as witnesses were Charles's old friends Arno, Theodulf and Laidrad, his archchaplain Hildibald, his son-in-law Angilbert and his cousin Wala, the brother of Adalhard and the son of that uncle Bernhard who had accompanied Charles across the Alps long ago when he conquered the kingdom of Lombardy. Wala had risen high in Charles's favor in recent years; shortly after the drawing up of this will he was sent to Italy to assist his brother Adalhard in directing the affairs of that kingdom.

Sister, daughter and son Charles had lost in the previous year. Now, his grief still fresh, he heard that Pepin the Hunchback had died at his monastery of Prüm. If we may credit the Monk of St. Gall, Charles had long since forgiven his deformed son for plotting against his father's life and had even on one occasion asked his advice. Certainly after twenty years the news of this son's death could bring only sorrow.

But worse was to follow. Now that only two heirs were left, Charles was perhaps considering at this time altering his plans for the succession and conferring the imperial title after all on his able namesake, Charles. Louis, the incompetent King of Aquitaine, had time and again expressed his preference for the religious life. Perhaps he would voluntarily become a monk (although in the past Charles had sternly forbidden him to consider any such step) and leave the field clear for a united Frankish empire under young Charles. Young Charles, in so many ways the image of his father, seemed destined to be emperor, to hold together what Charles had built and possibly to extend it. He was generally viewed as the true successor to his father, who would have taken over the realm "had not the Lord pleased otherwise."

But that same year, at the beginning of dreary December, young Charles also died. The cause of his death is not stated, except that his last illness began with a headache. With him died, though none knew it at the time, the last hope that the Carolingian Empire might endure. Three strong rulers—Charles the Hammer, Pepin the Short and Charlemagne—had built a dissension-racked petty kingdom into a great empire within a single century. A fourth could have smoothed out the newly welded joints, strengthened the raw new junctions, and so consolidated the power of that empire that the Northmen would

have battered in vain against its outlying defenses. Had the Carolingian Empire been given a respite of forty or fifty years, France and
Germany might never have reached a parting of the ways, the Scan-
dinavian colony of Normandy might never have existed, and there
would have been no William to conquer England. The cultural im-
petus that Charles had given to all of Central Europe would not
have been choked off by the Northmen. Instead of burned libraries,
wrecked monasteries and feudal castles dotting an anarchic and autarchic countryside, a prosperous civilized life might have continued
to burgeon within the shelter provided by a strong centralized government.

These ifs of history are, of course, the idlest speculation, but they
do suggest how great a tragedy had befallen Charles, and the state
he had created, when young Charles died. For individuals are as significant to history as social factors. And Charles himself was wise
enough to understand the implications of his loss. Instead of the
young hero whom he had reared by his side, the feeble Louis would
now have to succeed him. Louis, with whom he had been perennially
discontented, who had too quickly acquired the "foreign" ways of his
Aquitanian kingdom, for whom Charles had always had to provide
governors and generals to administer his affairs, who sent his armies
into battle ahead of himself and arrived only after the victory to parade through the streets of a captured city; Louis who was laggard,
ungenerous, too amiable, easily swayed by whatever counselor had his
ear at the moment.

After young Charles's death the only consolation for Charles was
his religion. His thoughts turned more and more away from the
things of the world. He conducted a lengthy correspondence with
his archbishops on religious matters, reproved so eminent an ecclesiastic as Laidrad of Lyons for his failure to understand fully the meaning
of baptism and ordered the dignified bishop to bone up on the subject
like a schoolboy. He made preparations for the holding of great ecclesiastical synods throughout the realm, and he set to work with
the help of Syrians and Greeks correcting the Vulgate text of the four
Gospels.

For as long as possible he put off taking any action on the succession. He ignored the buzz of gossip at court, the pressure from all
sides urging him to disinherit Louis, to give at least the inheritance

of young Charles to Pepin's son Bernhard, with Wala as Bernhard's temporary guardian.

Ill, lame, despondent, indifferent, convinced that the deaths of so many loved ones must be punishment for sins of omission, he devoted himself to the writing of long sermons to the people and clergy of the realm, admonishing them in the articles of faith, spelling out the Creed, reminding his people of the duties of a Christian man. It must have seemed strange to the people to hear the heralds read aloud in the public squares such preachments as: "Be humble and kind to one another. . . . Envy, hatred and violence keep men from the Kingdom of God. . . . Remember that the Apostle says we must all appear before the Judgment Seat of Christ. . . . Life is short and the hour of death uncertain; it is wise to be prepared. Remember that it is a fearful thing to fall into the hands of God. Confess your sins, show penitence, give alms and the Lord will be merciful. . . ." Yet these were the public documents that the old king composed, while the pressing business of state was left to underlings.

The affairs of the realm did not interest him. News that Harun al-Rashid had died, that Adalhard had succeeded by skillful diplomacy in restoring Benevento to vassal status, that the Danes were embroiled in civil war—this news left him cold. But he roused himself out of his abstraction when word was brought that Byzantine ambassadors had come with the long-awaited peace treaty, the long-desired recognition.

Perhaps the tale of the Monk of St. Gall is true—that Charles at this time permitted himself a senile practical joke to punish the Byzantines for having made him wait so long and anxiously. As the Monk relates it, the envoys were led first before the count of the stables, seated on a high throne in the midst of his subordinates. The Greeks therefore were about to fall on the ground in Byzantine fashion, to adore the emperor. But they were prevented from doing so and urged on. Then they came to the count of the palace, with a group of his nobles, and again mistook him for the emperor and abased themselves before him. But they were driven on with blows and told, "That is not the emperor." Next they came to the master of the royal table, surrounded by his servants. Again the same performance took place, and they were scornfully informed that this man was not the emperor. Among the chamberlains, dressed more sumptuously than all the preceding nobles, they felt sure that they had come into the presence of the emperor. The chief of the chamberlains corrected their error, but promised that he would use his influence so that possibly the ambassadors might be admitted to the royal presence. At last they were brought before the emperor himself, so decked out in gold and jewels that he glittered like the rising sun. Whereupon the envoys were so overwhelmed that they fell to the ground in a faint.

The story is more characteristic of the Monk than of Charles. In all probability the envoys—Bishop Michael and First Sword-bearers Arsafius and Theognostus—were welcomed with a respect consonant with the rich gifts and the friendly message they brought. They informed Charles that Nicephorus had died the previous year in battle against the Bulgarians. However, the new emperor, Michael, was willing to approve the peace treaty which had been discussed with Nicephorus.

Stricken by gout, plagued by fevers, still mourning the deaths of his children and also of the last of his unofficial wives, Adalhaid, Charles summoned up the strength to receive the ambassadors in a dignified ceremony in the basilica he had built at Aachen. He handed to them the peace treaty signed by himself and his dignitaries. Thereupon the ambassadors sang a litany in Greek, praising Charles and for the first time addressing him by the coveted title of *Basileus*. The recognition for which he had fought by patience and address, plus a little force, during more than a decade had come to him at last.

Nevertheless, Charles did not feel absolutely secure about it. No written confirmation of his title had been handed to him at this time. What he wanted from the Byzantine emperor was a formal instrument, written in Greek and likewise signed by the emperor and his nobles. To secure it he sent Archbishop Amalarius and Abbot Peter off to Constantinople. His anxiety, his timidity before the legally constituted Emperor of the Romans, the importance to him of the title and his willingness to humble himself in order to have the recognition down in black and white can be read in the letter which these envoys carried with them. Charles omitted the provocative phrase "of the Romans" in the list of his titles, and he stressed the identity of interest of the two *Christian* empires. The letter read in part:

"In the name of the Father and the Son and the Holy Ghost. Charles, by the grace of God Emperor and Augustus, King of the

Franks and Lombards, wishes his beloved and honorable brother Michael, the glorious Emperor and Augustus, eternal salvation in our Lord Jesus Christ. We thank the Lord Jesus Christ, our true God, for having conferred upon us so indescribably rich and great a gift— that while we still live He has established the long-sought and ever-desired peace between the Eastern and the Western Empires and has peacefully united His holy Catholic Church. . . .

"We have sent our ambassadors before your glorious countenance, beloved brother, with the request for the confirmation of this treaty. . . . It is right and proper and in accord with the agreement made with your envoys that our ambassadors should receive from you yourself, beloved brother, the document of the treaty, so that they may transmit it to us. Therefore we ask you, glorious and beloved brother, if you are in agreement with the treaty prepared by us, that you have a corresponding document written in the Greek language, counter-signed, and handed over to these our ambassadors. . . ."

As evidence of his good will, Charles surrendered possession of Venetia at once. He was destined to wait in vain for the counter-signed document; all the formalities between Constantinople and Aachen were not completed until after his death.

Recognition, however, could now be accepted as a fact. If Charles himself were still dissatisfied, his courtiers could point out that the three Byzantines had been plenipotentiary ambassadors. And with the evidences of his failing health growing plainer every day, they now pressed him to make his decision on the disposition of the imperial title. Otherwise, they warned, chaos and civil war might ensue after his death.

The situation is not wholly clear, but it seems that there were two principal parties at court, the one headed by Theodulf and the other by Einhard. Theodulf could rehearse all the well-known arguments against Louis, which Charles himself must often have put forward in their private conversations. He could point out that young Bernhard, Charles's grandson, promised to have the sterling qualities of his father Pepin. During Bernhard's minority, moreover, he would have the guidance of one of the most reliable older men in the empire, Charles's cousin Wala.

Einhard naturally favored Louis, a young man his own age, his former classmate at the Palace School. Raised in a monastery himself, a courtier all his life rather than an administrator like Bishop (now Archbishop) Theodulf, a diligent, pious and scholarly little man completely lacking in the humor, the intellectual brilliance and the cosmopolitanism of Theodulf, Einhard appreciated his own virtues and defects in Louis. And Einhard had a certain advantage; he was constantly at court, while Theodulf of necessity was usually away, busy with the affairs of his see of Orléans.

While both parties hammered away at him, Charles remained in an agony of indecision. He forestalled taking any definite action at the national assembly of 812, held at Aachen, although he formally appointed young Bernhard King of Italy to succeed his father. This might or might not be a step toward the imperial title. At any rate, Charles made it clear, by this grant, that he did not intend to have Louis inherit the whole empire and rule it alone.

The followers of Louis, and Louis himself, took alarm. How much of Louis' renowned piety and humility was hypocrisy is difficult to say, but it is definitely stated that he had set his hopes on securing the imperial title. He now sent a high official of his, his chief falconer Gerricus, to Aachen to sound out the temper of the court and if possible learn his father's intentions. Einhard's party welcomed Gerricus eagerly, informed him of Charles's failing health and urged him to advise Louis to come to Aachen at once. Perhaps the sight of his sole surviving son might sway the teetering balance in the emperor's mind.

Gerricus carried the message to the king. Louis conferred with his nobles, all of whom thought the suggestion sensible. If Louis wanted the power, he must be prepared to go after it. Louis, however, still hesitated, fearing "to arouse his father's suspicions." This peculiar phrase (it is used by the contemporary biographer of Louis) seems to mean that Louis thought his father would suspect him of planning a *coup d'état* to seize power without waiting for the father's decision. It may well be that Einhard's party, impatient with the old emperor's refusal to clarify the succession and fearing that he might not live to do so, proposed that Louis force the issue. But Louis did not dare.

It is hard to say how conscious Charles was of all the whisperings and intrigues. At any rate, he at last came round to the only possible solution. Contemptuous though he might be of his son, he had to recognize that his cousin Wala was nearly his own age and might not long outlive him. Bernhard, on the other hand, was still an adolescent. Louis, lacking though he was in all the qualities Charles most valued, was the inevitable inheritor. Moreover, the deaths of his two strong sons and the survival of the weak one must be in accord with the inscrutable counsels of God. Charles bowed, as always, to Providence. At a solemn conclave of his nobles he put the question of the succession to them. If we may believe a poetic account by a notorious sycophant, when Einhard stepped forward and urged the nomination of Louis, Charles gave his consent. He sent for his son.

During this last summer of his life Charles kept Louis by his side, doing his best to instruct a poor pupil in the daily practice and the underlying principles of statecraft. Louis had been King of Aquitaine since the age of three, was now a man of thirty-two, married and with children of his own. No doubt he thought he had been ruling his own kingdom for many years. But Charles knew that in fact he had been compelled to intervene repeatedly in the affairs of that kingdom, that his counts and missi had done much of the work of administration for Louis. Now he concentrated all his rapidly departing strength on conveying to Louis the wisdom and the practical knowledge he himself had acquired in forty-five years of rule. He instructed Louis "in how to reign and keep order in the realm." But above all he told him "how he ought to live"—that is to say, he strove to impart to his son (as he had tried to do often in years past) something of the firmness, the breadth, the understanding and even the readiness to be ruthless on occasion which had made him a great ruler. Mediocrity that he was, Louis learned only the ruthlessness, and this he practiced on the most unsuitable occasion against a person whom he had twice sworn to cherish.

In September the official ceremonies began. A great national assembly was held, attended by secular notables and bishops, abbots, priests and deacons from the whole empire. Charles formally proposed that Louis be made emperor. His word was still law; when he appeared before the assembly, lame from gout and leaning on his son's arm, the opposition was silenced. The assembly unanimously gave its approval to the transfer of the imperial title to Louis.

The following Sunday, September 11, 813, Charles donned the ornate imperial robes which he so seldom wore: a garment of cloth of gold, jeweled boots, a golden girdle and a diadem of gold and precious stones. Leaning on his son's arm, he went to his beloved basilica and up to the main altar. An attendant placed a golden crown—"different from the one he wore"—on the altar, which was higher than the other altars of the church. There it sparkled while father and son knelt in prayer for a long time.

Then Charles rose, and while a great crowd of bishops and nobles listened he turned to his son and poured out all at once the innumerable admonishments he had given Louis separately in recent weeks. He asked his son to love God—and to fear Him; to keep the Commandments; to *govern* the Church and to protect her from evil men. He commanded him again to be always kind to his sisters and his younger brothers, his nephews and all his other kinsfolk; to honor the priests as his fathers and to love the people as his sons; to compel the arrogant and the wicked to walk in the way of salvation; to cherish the abbeys and be a father to the poor; to employ only loyal and God-fearing men who would not accept bribes; to deprive no man of his honors or lands without sufficient cause, and to show himself at all times irreproachable before God and all the people.

The sermon rambled on and on, while Louis knelt and meekly listened. At last Charles wound to an end. He asked his son whether he would obey all these commands. Louis dutifully replied—and doubtless meant it at the moment—that with the help of God he would obey with gladness and faithfully observe all his father's instructions.

Thereupon—the accounts are conflicting at this point—Charles either placed the crown on Louis' head or ordered him to place it on his own head. In any case, the important fact was that no priest officiated. Much has been made of this omission; it has been interpreted as indicating Charles's regret that he himself had been crowned by the pope, as expressing Charles's determination not to give any further political advantage to the Church. But it is equally likely that Charles simply took for granted that he himself was the highest religious as well as secular authority in the western world. No archbishop, not even the pope, could confer the sanctification which was his to give because he was head of both State and Church.

It can scarcely be doubted that Charles's thoughts during this ceremony must have lingered on the two sons he had lost and that into his admonition to Louis he put all the fervor of his hope that this last son, by grace or necessity, might acquire the valor, the integrity and the firmness that those other two had possessed by nature.

As if to emphasize that he was granting Louis the title but not exclusive rule over the empire, Charles took this occasion to declare once more his appointment of Bernhard as King of Italy. Nevertheless, Louis would be Bernhard's superior.

That was Charles's last public act.

A few days afterward, laden with gifts from his father, Louis set out for Aquitaine. Before father and son parted "they embraced and kissed each other, and out of joy in their love began to weep."

Charles, seemingly invigorated by having at last thrown off the tremendous burden of indecision, went hunting. For an entire month this man of seventy-one camped in the woods near Aachen and rode in pursuit of stag and wild boar. Early in November he returned to the palace and spent the unusually harsh winter on the work he had long had in hand—correcting the text of the Gospels.

On the twenty-first of January, after his daily bath, he suffered a sudden attack of high fever. His custom had been to alleviate these now familiar fevers by fasting, and he accordingly abstained from food. The fever was complicated by "a pain in the side which the Greeks call pleurisy." Since he still refused (or was unable) to take nourishment, he weakened rapidly. A week after he had taken to his bed he sent for his archchaplain, Hildibald of Cologne, and received Holy Communion (not Extreme Unction, which was not then in use) from this old friend. For another day and night his body resisted death. At dawn the following morning, still quite conscious, he put out his right hand and feebly made the sign of the cross. Then, it is said, he closed his eyes and softly sang the verse of the psalm: "Into thy hand, O Lord, I commend my spirit."

Shortly afterward he died.

There was some doubt at first as to where he ought to be buried. Long ago, at the very beginning of his reign, he had declared his wish to be buried beside his grandfather, father and mother in the Cathedral of St. Denis. But after nearly half a century that request had been forgotten. But it was soon agreed that the only fitting place for his body was the church at Aachen which he himself had built. There he was laid to rest on the same day that he died. Over his sepulcher of white marble was erected a gilded arch bearing the following inscription:

"Beneath this tomb lies the body of Charles, the great and orthodox emperor, who nobly increased the kingdom of the Franks and reigned prosperously for forty-seven [actually forty-six] years. He died in his seventies in the year of the Lord 814, in the seventh indiction, on the fifth day before the Calends of February [January 28]."

Epilogue

AND SO the great reign had come to an end.

When Charlemagne's contemporaries recorded in his epitaph that he had nobly increased the kingdom of the Franks they were setting forth what to them was perhaps the most obvious testimony to his greatness. Here was an achievement that impressed alike the lowliest serf and the most powerful magnate: out of the small half kingdom that had been his original possession Charles had forged an empire. He had taught the Franks to think of themselves as a chosen people like the Jews of the Old Testament, destined to rule, obligated to carry the true religion to the benighted pagan world, and certain to be rewarded by God so long as they remained faithful to the Church and to their anointed overlord. The popular enthusiasm for "the most serene Augustus" was reflected in the biography of Einhard, who somewhat exaggerated the conquests of Charles in the telling, giving him credit for sovereignty over Slavs and Bretons whom he had never really subdued.

Yet some of the other accomplishments of Charles's reign survived far longer than that expansion of his dominions which was followed so soon afterward by rapid contraction. For he had changed the face of Europe inwardly as well as outwardly. In spite of his love for hunting and his jealous preservation of the royal forests, he did not, as was later said of William the Conqueror, "love the tall stags as if he were their father" to the point of ruining his peasants. On the contrary, in an age when the wealth of the nation depended on agriculture, he fostered the clearing of land, the breaking of new ground and the consolidation of conquest by colonization of the thinly populated forested tracts of central Europe. He pushed also the redemption of land that had been allowed to fall out of cultivation during the confusion and invasions of the early eighth century. This work of colonization continued after his death; from Aquitaine to Saxony the ravaged land of Europe was gradually put once more to the plow, and in Germany the frontier inexorably receded toward the east.

The extent to which Charlemagne consciously promoted a revival of trade and industry has been hotly debated—some German historians picturing him as responsible for a burgeoning of commercial and industrial activity, some French historians maintaining that he did little or nothing. Unless fresh evidence is discovered it seems unlikely that the controversy can ever be definitely resolved. But whatever his deliberate policy was, some stimulus to the general economic life of his realm was the inadvertent outcome of many aspects of his government: the improvement of roads, the repair and building of bridges, the establishment of hospices for pilgrims (which were used by merchants), the limitation on the imposition of new tolls, the extension of the frontiers, the increase in wealth resulting from war booty, and the internal peace and good order of his administration. His contacts with the East, with Constantinople, Bagdad and the Holy Land, extended the physical as well as the mental horizons of his subjects and undoubtedly increased East-West trade, which had never entirely ceased but which had been reduced to a trickle during the early part of the eighth century. His abortive naval enterprises checked to some extent the depredations of Saracen pirates and also had the effect of encouraging mutual exchanges between East and West.

The closer commercial contact between East and West was counterbalanced by the widening politico-religious split which was also the outcome of Charlemagne's policies. For hundreds of years there had been doctrinal and administrative tensions between the Churches of Constantinople and Rome. The rise of iconoclasm in the East strained the relationship still farther, and Charles, by enabling the pope to throw off the overlordship of the Eastern Emperor, destroyed the formal prerequisite which might yet have preserved the unity of the two Churches. When a *rapprochement* between patriarchate and papacy was being zealously backed by the Empress Irene, Charles had deliberately interfered. The position he took, and forced the papacy to take, on the questions of image worship and the procession of the Holy Spirit (the so-called *Filioque* controversy) offended the Byzantine theologians and materially contributed to the ultimate schism between the two Churches which finally occurred two and a half centuries after his death.

Within his own empire, however, Charles had been anything but a schismatic. His campaigns against heresy, his concern with canon law, his insistence on the application of the Benedictine Rule in monasteries, his introduction of Roman liturgy into Frankland (the Sacramentary prepared by Alcuin at Charles's direction later formed the basis of the Roman Missal still in use), his substitution of the Roman for the Frankish mode of chanting—these and other reforms furthered the uniformity of Catholic doctrine and practice and enormously strengthened the Church. His aid to pilgrims and to Christians overseas, his endowments of monasteries and churches, his regard for the morals of the clergy and the improvement of their education, fully justified his title of *"rector et defensor ecclesiae."* The numerous synods that were held during his reign, and his own personal interest in theological questions, stimulated a revival of theology that lasted long after his death.

Charlemagne's tradition of stable government and sound administration was swiftly abandoned by his successors, but both his son Louis and his grandson Charles the Bald imitated his patronage of learning. One of the major original thinkers of the Middle Ages, John Scotus Erigena, was attracted to the court of Charles the Bald. The schools at Fulda, Tours, St. Gall, Reichenau, Lorsch and many other monasteries continued to flourish in spite of the troubled times that followed Charlemagne's death. He himself remained the model for the enlightened ruler, whose example such kings as Alfred the Great of England and Otto I of Germany respectfully followed. At the end of the ninth century the reputation of Frankish learning was still so high that King Alfred sent to Frankland for scholars to help him reeducate England. And it has been said, perhaps without overmuch exaggeration, that the foundation of all modern education was laid by Charlemagne with the assistance of Alcuin.

The political consummation of Charlemagne's lifework, the *"renovatio"* of the Roman Empire of the West, was in the minds of his contemporaries and post-contemporaries a continuation of the ancient Roman Empire. The twelfth-century Bavarian *Kaiserchronik*, for example, treated Charlemagne as one of the greatest in the succession of Roman emperors from Augustus to Conrad III. Yet this same chronicle unwittingly bears witness to the fundamental difference between the new and the old empires when it identifies Charlemagne so closely with the Church that Pope Leo III is pictured as the emperor's brother. The legend-building that began immediately after the death of Charles often altered historical fact in this way in order to present a symbol of historical truth. Charlemagne had united Church and State into an organic theocracy such as had never been achieved by the Christian Roman emperors, whose subjects were always more than half pagan—clandestinely when not openly. By grafting Augustine on Augustus he produced a political entity different in kind from the classic Roman Empire whose heir he considered himself. The people of the Middle Ages signified their understanding of the difference when they spoke of the *Holy* Roman Empire.

In theory a political structure founded on two such solid rocks as the imperial idea and the Catholic Church should have had excellent prospects of survival. But even while it was being erected it was also being undermined. Throughout the latter part of Charlemagne's reign social changes were taking place which were ultimately to destroy his empire. Although he opposed these changes, they were partly of his own making.

One clause in the Division of the Realm of the year 806 bore witness to the transformation in Carolingian society which was going on under the eyes of the emperor. Eight years before his death Charlemagne seems to have resigned himself to accepting a new order that was being wrought by forces beyond his control. (This is not to say that the new social order was the sole cause for the breakup of the empire, but it was a very important factor.)

"A free vassal [*homo*]," the clause in Charles's testament read, "shall have the right, after the death of his lord, to commend himself to whomsoever he wishes within the three kingdoms; the same applies to a man who has not yet commended himself to anyone."

The terminology, in this early year of the ninth century, is already that of feudalism. By the end of the century society would be governed by the feudal principle that there should be no man without his lord. As yet the complex interrelationships of cross-vassalage and subinfeudation were inchoate, but the numbers of free men who had "not yet commended themselves to anyone" were rapidly diminishing. The many wars by which Charlemagne had built his empire accelerated the process, for the impoverishment brought about by military service, or the desire to escape such service altogether, forced freemen to accept dependency on great lords. The nobles, hungry for power and more land, were on their own account seeking to enrich themselves at the expense of their lesser neighbors or the crown estates. Charlemagne had continually fought their greed. He had employed his missi to limit the worst abuses on the part of the "magnates." We will remember that in Aquitaine especially he had intervened on behalf of Louis to recover royal revenues alienated under the feeble rule of his son.

Now that same son had inherited the empire. He had taken over dubiously, hesitating even to come to Aachen until after his chief rival, Wala, hastened to him and made submission. Louis' prestige was so low that the other nobles avoided paying their obligatory homage until Wala had made it clear that he would not oppose the succession. And even though Wala sacrificed himself in the interests of harmony and the preservation of the empire intact, a strong party continued to favor Bernhard of Italy as the successor to Charles. Among the supporters of Bernhard was Charles's influential old friend Theodulf, the Bishop of Orléans. Perhaps with the prescience of poets Theodulf foresaw the ruin that Louis' weakness and irresolution would bring down on the country. Within a few years after Louis' accession Bernhard, urged on by many men in high position, attempted an abortive revolt which Louis was able to crush. A number of the rebels were put to death and Louis, forgetting his father's injunction in that same testament of 806—that the uncles must exercise mercy toward their nephews—ordered Bernhard himself to be blinded. Because he would not submit "patiently enough" to the mutilation, the boy was killed in the process. Louis' later public penance for this cruelty did not add to his popularity.

From the first Louis lived in fear and trembling of his own nobles and tried to buy their support by reversing his father's policies. Charles had always maintained an equilibrium between the demands of local officials and the rights of the central government. He had ignored distinctions of birth and appointed even former slaves to hold high offices in the state; such men were not only often more capable but also more dependent on him than the nobles who possessed hereditary lands of their own. He had also shifted his bishops and counts around at will, placing Lombards in Neustria, Franks in Lombardy, Bavarians in Burgundy. Always he had jealously guarded the crown's prerogatives and had kept a firm grip on his inherited or acquired royal estates, which constituted the private property of the Carolingian house. For these were the chief source of royal revenues. Charlemagne's high officials were paid for their services by the assignment of crown land in the form of benefices. The officials attempted to convert this "loaned" land into hereditary, freehold property. Charles had firmly resisted this tendency.

The difference between the strength of the father and the weakness of the son is most clearly seen in their relationship to the nobles of the realm. Charles had been secure enough to defy the prejudices and ambitions of his officials. He won their loyalty and affection even when his decrees ran counter to their interests. But Louis' only means of controlling them was bribery, and in his vain attempt to curry favor with them he stripped himself more and more of the real sources of power. A revealing indication of his folly was a decree issued to protect the privileges of the counts against excessive interference by the missi—when the institution of the missi had been created by Charlemagne for the express purpose of curbing the counts. Worse still, in an age when private ownership of vast tracts of land, and control over numerous vassals, was becoming the key to power, Louis played fast and loose with his inheritance. "So generous was he," declares his contemporary biographer, "that he did something unheard of in ancient books and in modern times: he gave away to his followers to be their eternal possessions royal vills which his father, grandfather and great-grandfather had owned before him."

In this "dissolution of the Carolingian fisc" some historians see a principal cause for the breakup of the Carolingian Empire. The struggle among the sons of Louis, they argue, centered around possession of the crown estates in the Austrasian heartland where the Carolingian House had its beginnings. For Louis, whose reign had been a succession of intrigues, upheavals and internal conflicts, had no sooner died than his sons went to war against one another. Pious though Louis may have been, prudent he certainly was not. His susceptibility to the influence of his second wife, the redoubtable Judith, the favoritism he showed to her son (the later Charles the Bald), his frequent partitionings and repartitionings of the Empire, made inevitable the civil wars after his death.

The sons of Louis, during their wars with one another, were forced to continue their father's ill-advised policy: they won partisans by giving away the crown lands. Thus they helped to build up the great feudal fiefs whose holders soon became more powerful than the kings themselves.

Meanwhile, as Frank fought Frank and the empire was internally hacked into fragments, the Northmen came in their longboats. They sailed up the great rivers of France and Germany to kill, plunder and exact tribute from the helpless inhabitants of what had been, so short a time before, Charlemagne's impregnable dominion. While the monks prayed daily, "Deliver us from the fury of the Northmen," the nobles refined the art of fortification and learned to build stout castles of stone to which the people of the surrounding countryside could flee when the dragon prows appeared. Each fief became a petty kingdom in itself, and by the time the Northmen were placated by the cession of Normandy—a century after Charlemagne's death—the Carolingian Empire was virtually extinct.

But although the political structure that Charlemagne had created disintegrated so soon after his death, his personality, his aims and his accomplishment dominated the imaginations of men for centuries. Side by side, a real and a legendary Charlemagne marched across the ages, the two figures gradually merging until the founder of the Holy Roman Empire became one with a fabled hero who led his paladins into battle against the never-ending hosts of the infidel, and with a Christian saint before whom votive candles were lighted.

Preservation of the memory of the real Charlemagne was assured by the popularity of Einhard's biography. Written some fifteen years after the ruler's death, it was copied often, as the large number of extant manuscripts proves. Here was a portrait of a mighty emperor of simple tastes whose supremacy was recognized from Britain to far-off Bagdad; of a great defender of the Church who never failed to rush to the aid of the Roman pontiff; of a legislator; of a lover of arts and letters; of a general who fought many wars with unfailing success (except for that notable defeat in Spain which Einhard described in detail); of a militant evangelist of the Faith who converted Saxons, Slavs and Avars by force of arms. And since copies of the Royal Annals (also attributed to Einhard) were often included in manuscripts along with the biography, the medieval reader had a fair opportunity to ascertain a good many of the facts about Charlemagne.

But there were also elements in Einhard's biography that became food for legend. In following the example of Suetonius, from whom he borrowed his style, method and sometimes language, Einhard had listed the signs and portents that preceded the death of the emperor. He had mysteriously refused to say anything about his subject's birth or early life. He alluded discreetly to the loose conduct of Charlemagne's daughters. He spoke of Charles's friendship with "Aaron"— that is, Harun al-Rashid. The later legend-makers found much in Einhard that they could make use of.

A nonliterary, popular tradition, expressing nostalgic memories of past glory under the great emperor and incorporating many anecdotes that must have been common property, was written down in the latter part of the ninth century by the Monk of St. Gall. The Monk's *Gesta Karoli Magni* is replete with superlatives: Charlemagne is presented as supremely wise, merciful, just, pious, religious and terrible, a man of iron before whom no enemy can stand, ever ready to defend the humbler of his subjects, preferring the lowborn to the highborn; but also possessing a shrewd sense of practicality like the youngest son in fairy tales. Supernatural elements also enter into the Monk's picture of the "most holy emperor." Miracles abound: artisans of the basilica at Aachen who attempt to cheat Charles are punished by divine retribution. Charles is clairvoyant and prophesies, in the authentic saintly tradition, the evils that the Northmen will inflict on his land in future years. The *Feats of Charles the Great* show in how idealized a form Charlemagne had already, within seventy years after his death, entered into the psychic life of the common people.

The legend grew rapidly thereafter as the golden age of Charlemagne glowed more brightly in memory. In *chansons de geste*, saints' lives, chronicles, monks' tales, and in the local traditions of Aachen, Worms, Liége, Bremen, Hamburg, Mainz, St. Denis and a host of other places associated with his name, a new Charlemagne was created, noblest of the defenders of the Church, justest of judges, and endowed with all the virtues and the miraculous powers of a saint. When Christianity set out to rescue the Holy Sepulcher from the hands of the infidel, it seemed evident that so splendid a hero as Charlemagne must once have ruled over the Holy Land. Out of the few brief references in Einhard to his relations with Harun al-Rashid and the Patriarch of Jerusalem was fashioned the image of a crusading emperor who had himself visited the Holy City. By a confusion with his grandfather, Charles Martel, Charlemagne was also pictured as throwing back the hosts of Spanish Saracens and saving Christendom. Gradually, in the pages of the "Pseudo-Turpin" and the *Chanson de Roland* there formed the conception of Charlemagne as the greatest of all crusaders who ever took the Cross.

Parallel with the hero-emperor there developed the rather startling idea of the emperor-saint. Miracles aplenty were already attached to his name. The one major difficulty remained the record of his "licentiousness." Shortly after his death a monk had seen him in a vision, lodged in purgatory, the offending part of his body being perpetually gnawed by a vulture. By the twelfth century, however, it seemed clear that he had made due penance for this sin. The monk who pretended to be Turpin, Archbishop of Reims, gave wide currency to the story of Charlemagne's soul in the claws of demons, in grave danger of being carried off to the flames of hell. But the emperor is saved when St. James tosses into the eternal scales the stones and beams of all the churches Charles had built.

In the middle of the twelfth century, when Frederick Barbarossa suppressed the warring dukes of feudal Germany and in large measure restored the authority of the imperial title, the glorification of Charlemagne reached its culmination. Frederick fancied himself a second Charlemagne, and he drew heavily on the prestige of his great predecessor to bolster his own pretensions. As against his rival, Louis VII of France, he wished also to claim Charlemagne for Germany. Frederick was supporting the antipope, Pascal III, against Pope Alexander III and needed some dramatic act to attach Germany to the cause of the antipope. For reasons of political strategy, therefore, but motivated also by his genuine reverence, he resolved on the canonization of Charlemagne.

The formal act took place on December 2, 1165. At a resplendent ceremony in Aachen, in the presence of numerous bishops and magnates, the Translation essential to the making of a saint took place. That is, Charlemagne's body was removed from the "sarcophagus where it had reposed for three hundred and fifty-two years" and placed in a reliquary. Then the imperial manifesto was solemnly read. Of Charles, Frederick Barbarossa said:

"He yearned with all the power of his being toward the rewards of eternal life. His works and the numerous collections of his public acts display his efforts to disseminate the glory of the Christian name. . . . In extension of the Christian faith and conversion of the pagan peoples he was a mighty champion and a veritable apostle. . . . And although his body was not pierced by the sword, the trial of many sufferings, the perilous combats in which he engaged, his daily willingness to die for the conversion of the infidel, have made of him a martyr. Therefore we now proclaim and venerate him as one of the elect upon earth, and a holy confessor. . . . Encouraged by the urgent request of our dear friend Henry, King of England, with the consent and by the authority of the Lord Pope Pascal, and having taken counsel with all the princes lay and ecclesiastical, we have held this solemn court for the purpose of elevating, exalting and canonizing the most holy emperor. . . ."

Irregular though this canonization was, it seemed to stand, since in the years to come the legitimate pope neither encouraged nor prohibited the cult of the new saint. Charles willy-nilly was entered into the community of the blessed. In his lifetime he had brought his aims closer to fulfillment than almost any other ruler in history. In the days of wrath that closed in on Europe after his death much of his political order passed away, giving place to forms he would not have countenanced. Legend again made him an effective figure. Sainted and magnified by myth, he was rediscovered by each of the rare strong rulers who came after him as the supreme prototype of sovereignty.

Bibliography

Bibliography

Sources

Bibliotheca Rerum Germanicarum. Monumenta Carolina. Ed. P. Jaffé, 1867.
Böhmer, J. F., and Mühlbacher, E.: *Die Regesten des Kaiserreichs unter den Karolingern,* 1908.
Heliand. Ed. Moritz Heyne, 1883.
Monumenta Germaniae Historica:
  Scriptores.
  Scriptores rerum germanicarum in usum scholarum.
  Capitularia regum francorum. Ed. Boretius and Krause, 1883-1897.
  Concilia aevi Karolini. Ed. Werminghoff, 1906, 1908; Supp. ed. H. Bastgen, 1924.
  Diplomata Karolinorum. Ed. E. Mühlbacher, 1906.
  Epistolae Karolini aevi. Ed. Dümmler *et al.,* 1892-1928.
  Poetae Latini aevi Karolini. Ed. Dümmler et al., 1880-1928.
Patrologia Latina, v. 97-98, 1862. Ed. J. P. Migne.

Authorities

Abel, Sigurd, and Simson, Bernhard: *Jahrbücher des Fränkischen Reiches unter Karl dem Grossen,* 1883, 1888.
Allen, Philip S.: *The Romanesque Lyric,* 1928.
Anglo-Saxon Chronicle, The: Tr. James Ingram, 1928.
Artz, Frederick: *The Mind of the Middle Ages,* 1953.
Baker, G. P.: *Charlemagne and the United States of Europe,* 1932.
Barnes, Harry Elmer: *An Economic History of the Western World,* 1937.
Boissonade, P.: *Life and Work in Medieval Europe,* tr. Eileen Power, 1927.
Boos, Heinrich: *Geschichte der rheinischen Städtekultur,* 1897.
Brosien, Hermann: *Karl der Grosse,* 1885.
Buckler, F. W.: *Harunu'l-Rashid and Charles the Great,* 1931.

Buhler, Johannes: *Das Frankenreich*, 1923.

Calmette, Joseph: *Charlemagne, Sa Vie et Son Oeuvre*, 1945.

Clapham, J. H., and Power, Eileen: *The Agrarian Life of the Middle Ages*. The Cambridge Economic History, v. 1, 1941.

Curtius, Ernst Robert: *Europäische Literatur und Lateinisches Mittelalter*, 1948.

Cutts, Edward L.: *Augustine of Canterbury*, 1895.

Dahn, Felix: *Die Könige der Germanen*, v. VIII, 1899.

Dahn, Felix: *Urgeschichte der germanischen und romanischen Völker*, 1883.

Davis, H. W. C.: *Charlemagne, the Hero of Two Nations*, 1900.

Dopsch, Alfons: *Die Wirtschaftsentwicklung der Karolingerzeit, vornehmlich in Deutschland*, 1912-1913.

Duckett, Eleanor Shipley: *Alcuin, Friend of Charlemagne*, 1951.

Fauriel, M.: *Histoire de la Gaule Méridionale sous la Domination des Conquérants Germains*, 1836.

Fichtenau, Heinrich: *Das Karolingische Imperium*, 1949.

Folz, Robert: *Le Souvenir et la Légende de Charlemagne dans l'Empire germanique médiéval*, 1950.

Freeman, E. A.: *Western Europe in the Eighth Century and Onward*, 1904.

Fülöp-Miller, René: *The Saints that Moved the World*, 1945.

Galahad, Sir: *Byzanz*, 1937.

Gaskoin, C. J. B.: *Alcuin*, 1904.

Gibbon, Edward: *The Decline and Fall of the Roman Empire*, 1787.

Goette, Rudolf: *Der Kulturkreis um Karl dem Grossen*, 1925.

Grant, A. J.: *Early Lives of Charlemagne by Eginhard and the Monk of St. Gall*, 1922.

Gregory of Tours: *History of the Franks*. O. M. Dalton, tr., 1927.

Halbedel, Anton: *Fränkische Studien*, 1914.

Halphen, Louis: *Charlemagne et l'Empire Carolingien*, 1947.

Halphen, Louis: *Etudes critiques sur l'histoire de Charlemagne*, 1921.

Hamlin, Talbot: *Architecture through the Ages*, 1953.

Harnack, Otto: *Das Karolingische und das Byzantinische Reich*, 1880.

Hauck, Albert: *Kirchengeschichte Deutschlands*, 1904-1912.

Hinks, Roger: *Carolingian Art*, 1935.

Hodgkin, Thomas: *Charles the Great*, 1897.

Hochstetter, Mathilde: *Karl der Grosse, König, Patrizius und Kaiser als Rector Ecclesiae*, 1934.

Hollnsteiner, Johannes: *Das Abendland,* 1948.

Howell, Wilbur Samuel: *The Rhetoric of Alcuin and Charlemagne,* 1941.

Inama-Sternegg, Karl Theodor von: *Deutsche Wirtschaftsgeschichte bis zum Schluss der Karolingerperiode,* 1909.

Ker, W. P.: *The Dark Ages,* 1904.

Kleinclausz, A.: *Charlemagne,* 1934.

Kleinclausz, A.: *Eginhard,* 1942.

Lacroix, Paul: *Manners, Customs and Dress during the Middle Ages.*

Laistner, M. L. W.: *Thought and Letters in Western Europe A.D. 500 to 900,* 1931.

Lintzel, Martin: *Der sächsische Stammesstaat und seine Eroberung durch die Franken,* 1933.

Lintzel, Martin: *Karl der Grosse und die Sachsen,* 1934.

Mombert, J. I.: *A History of Charles the Great,* 1886.

Mullinger, J. B.: *The Schools of Charles the Great,* 1887.

Newton, A. P., ed: *Travel and Travellers of the Middle Ages,* 1930.

Nickel, Walther: *Untersuchungen über die Quellen, den Wert und den Verfasser der Vita Hludovici des Astronomus,* 1919.

Norris, Herbert: *Church Vestments, Their Origin and Development,* 1950.

Oelsner, L.: *Jahrbücher des Fränkischen Reiches unter König Pippin,* 1871.

Pirenne, Henri: *Mohammed and Charlemagne,* tr. B. Miall, 1939.

Power, Eileen: *Medieval People,* 1924.

Rendell, A. W.: *Physiologus,* by Bishop Theobald, 1928.

Rosenstock, Eugen, and Wittig, Josef: *Das Alter der Kirche,* 1937.

Rüngeler, Josef: *Das Bild Karls des Grossen in der Zeitgenössischen Annalistik und in der Gedichts- und Briefliteratur,* 1937.

Russell, Charles Edward: *Charlemagne, First of the Moderns,* 1930.

Saint Augustine: *The City of God.* Tr. Dod, 1950.

Sédillot, René: *An Outline of French History,* 1953.

Sergeant, Lewis: *The Franks,* 1898.

Taylor, Henry Osborn: *The Medieval Mind,* 1911.

Thompson, James Westfall: *The Dissolution of the Carolingian Fisc in the Ninth Century,* 1935.

Trevelyan, G. M.: *The History of England,* v. I, 1952.

Vétault, Alphonse: *Charlemagne,* 1888.

Waddell, Helen: *Medieval Latin Lyrics,* 1933.

Waddell, Helen: *The Wandering Scholars*, 1932.

Wahl, R.: *Karl der Grosse*, 1934.

Walch, J. L.: *Karolus Magnus*, 1947.

Wattenbach, W., ed.: *Die Geschichtsschreiber der deutschen Vorzeit. Achtes Jahrhundert, neuntes Jahrhundert*, 1888.

West, Andrew Fleming: *Alcuin and the Rise of Christian Schools*, 1892.

Index

INDEX